JUN 2 8 2006

St. Paul's

ARCHITECTURE

St. Paul's

ARCHITECTURE

A History

Jeffrey A. Hess and Paul Clifford Larson

Published in cooperation with the City of St. Paul Heritage Preservation Commission

University of Minnesota Press

MINNEAPOLIS • LONDON

The University of Minnesota Press gratefully acknowledges assistance provided for the publication of this book by the John K. and Elsie Lampert Fesler Fund.

Unless otherwise credited, all photographs were taken by Paul Clifford Larson.

Published by the University of Minnesota Press
111 Third Avenue South, Suite 290
Minneapolis, MN 55401-2520
http://www.upress.umn.edu

Library of Congress Cataloging-in-Publication Data

Hess, Jeffrey A.
   St. Paul's architecture : a history / Jeffrey A. Hess and Paul Clifford Larson.
      p. cm.
   "Published in cooperation with the City of St. Paul Heritage Preservation Commission."
   Includes bibliographical references and index.
   ISBN-13: 978-0-8166-3590-0 (hc/j : alk. paper)
   ISBN-10: 0-8166-3590-0 (hc/j : alk. paper)
   1. Architecture—Minnesota—Saint Paul—19th century.
2. Architecture—Minnesota—Saint Paul—20th century.
3. Saint Paul (Minn.)—Buildings, structures, etc. I. Larson, Paul Clifford. II. Title. III. Title: St. Paul's architecture.
   NA735.S24H47 2006
   720.9776´581—dc22

                              2006003049

Printed in the United States of America on acid-free paper

The University of Minnesota is an equal-opportunity educator and employer.

12 11 10 09 08 07 06   10 9 8 7 6 5 4 3 2 1

CONTENTS

ILLUSTRATIONS

PREFACE

St. Paul Heritage Preservation Commission

For fifty years, the St. Paul Heritage Preservation Commission has been the official guardian of the city's remarkable architectural legacy. Its starting point was a pilot study of eighty-nine buildings identified by its predecessor, the Historic Sites Committee of the City Planning Board. Now we oversee six extensive historic districts and more than sixty individually designated buildings.

We are gratified that the government and citizens of the city have grasped the many ways that the public interest is served by the preservation of so large a part of our architectural legacy. But identifying and helping to guide the preservation of particular historic buildings is only part of what we do. Like all citizens imbued with a preservation conscience, we do not protect old buildings as part of an outdoor museum; we protect them because they are part of ourselves, part of who we have become as a human community.

This study was commissioned to provide a basis for this larger preservation consciousness. It lingers only briefly over buildings that are gone and eschews lengthy consideration of established landmarks. We desired the focus throughout to be on the living legacy in toto, understood not as a parade of isolated monuments earmarked for celebration and preservation but as a fabric that runs through the city. The authors have indeed accomplished this goal.

We hope that the citizens of St. Paul will share our pride and pleasure in *St. Paul's Architecture* and the story it tells. Beyond that, we anticipate for the book a long-lasting life as a ready and useful tool for understanding each moment and each instance, past, present, and future, of the city's expanding architectural heritage.

ACKNOWLEDGMENTS

Like the architecture it chronicles, this book is the product of a particular time and place. Conceptually, it is rooted in the historic preservation movement, which came of age in St. Paul in the mid-1970s with the creation by city ordinance of the municipal Heritage Preservation Commission (HPC). The agency's mission was to protect cultural values as expressed in the built environment. In the early 1980s, in collaboration with the Ramsey County Historical Society, the HPC embarked on a three-year Historic Sites Survey that sent architectural historians to every city street, as well as to several neighboring suburban communities. All ensuing research into the architectural legacy of the city hinges in some way on the outcome of this pioneering survey.

Supported by federal, county, city, and private foundation funding, the Historic Sites Survey benefited from the work of dozens of people but owed a special debt to its three lead historians, Patricia A. Murphy, Susan W. Granger, and Gary Phelps. The survey yielded an immense amount of data, including thousands of descriptive inventory forms on individual sites and scores of research dossiers on architects and builders. It also produced a spiral-bound project summary, *Historic Sites Survey of Saint Paul and Ramsey County, 1980–1983: Final Report*, coauthored by Murphy and Granger. The basic text for historic preservation in St. Paul, this study traced the historical development of the city's neighborhoods,

analyzed the nature of historic building types, and identified specific sites that seemed worthy of preservation by virtue of their historical associations or architectural significance. Several of the structures highlighted by the report were nominated to the National Register of Historic Places as part of the larger project.

Once the Historic Sites Survey was completed, the HPC confronted the task of sharing the project's findings with a wider audience. Other American cities had gone through a similar process, and there were several models, most typically in the form of a published field guide showcasing notable structures with brief architectural and historical descriptions. The HPC rejected the traditional field-guide format in favor of an extended narrative that would treat the city's architecture as part of a broad historical continuum rather than as a collection of "frozen moments." The new undertaking would be made possible by financial assistance from the National Park Service through a series of Certified Local Government Grants administered by the Minnesota Historical Society.

The initial contract for this book was awarded to Jeffrey A. Hess, a public historian based in the Twin Cities who specializes in the study of the American built environment. With HPC approval, Hess subsequently arranged for a second author, Paul Clifford Larson, an architectural historian who contributed to the original

Historic Sites Survey and had been retained as photographer for a pilot publication initiative.

A work of this magnitude could not be accomplished without the cooperation of several institutions invested in the history of the state and the city. We are particularly grateful for the ready assistance of the Minnesota Historical Society in procuring images as well as information from their bottomless archives and large microfilm collection. The Northwest Architectural Archives of the University of Minnesota also provided considerable documentary support for our work. Much of the early building-permit work was done in the storage vaults of the City of St. Paul, always with the exceptional cooperation of Licensing, Inspection, and Environmental Protection, now the parent department of the HPC. We also relied heavily on the St. Paul Public Library, both for its St. Paul Collection and for its interlibrary loan service. Hard-to-find resources were also made available to us at the Magrath Library of the University of Minnesota and the DeWitt Wallace Library of Macalester College. Ramsey County Historical Society has been unstinting in its generosity, allowing us to copy a ream of St. Paul and Ramsey County Historic Sites Survey forms at low cost and providing access to building permits

that are now in its keeping. Finally, several Heritage Preservation Commission members have added valuable input during the long incubation and early draft stages of this project; we are particularly grateful for the support and commentary of former HPC chairman Bob Frame.

Much of the research for this book was undertaken by direct contact with the buildings, their owners, and their designers. We are especially thankful for the time given to us by Bruce Abrahamson, Ann Billeadeau, Valerie Card, W. Brooks Cavin, Elizabeth and Winston Close, Georgia Ray DeCoster, Foster Dunwiddie, Marjorie Edwards, Dick Faricy, Gar Hargens, Donald Hausler, Kara Hill, Donald and Elizabeth Lampland, Louis Lundgren, Peg Marrinen, Tom Minter, Charles Nelson, Ralph Rapson, William Scott, and William G. Shepherd.

The authors owe a final debt of gratitude to the University of Minnesota Press, in particular to editors Todd Orjala and Pieter Martin, for the unflinching faith and abundant skills required to shepherd this project through to its completion. They will surely be as relieved to see this book on their shelves as the many readers who have anticipated its arrival for a decade will be pleased to place it on theirs.

Jeffrey A. Hess
Paul Clifford Larson

FIGURE I.I. St. Paul skyline from the southwest, 2005

INTRODUCTION

St. Paul has long been known for its magnificent residential drive known as Summit Avenue, but the city's architectural heritage is much more than this single road through the past. Preservation districts now embrace the warehouses of Lower Town, the houses nestled around Irvine Park in Upper Town, the largely working-class neighborhoods of Dayton's Bluff on the East Side, and the extreme west end of the city's old transportation corridor on University Avenue. For all of these marks of recognition and preservation of its architectural heritage, there has been no connected effort to view St. Paul's landmarked areas and buildings as part of a continuous development. This book takes up that challenge.

We have chosen a somewhat unusual framework for an architectural history. The general progression is chronological, but the story unfolds in a succession of five quite different chapters. Each chapter offers its own approach, chosen for its power to shed light on a particular era's architectural legacy. Successive chapters present their stock of buildings within a framework that is illuminating for that period.

The focus of the book throughout is on buildings that have survived. Lost buildings receive notice only if they were an anchoring presence in the cityscape or represent a type with no living examples. Addresses and other locational clues are provided for each building mentioned in the text in the belief that direct observation can reveal

values and stir associations that a narrative can only hint at. By appreciating more deeply the buildings still with us, we build hope for a future that will have fewer occasions to mourn its architectural losses.

The opening chapter tells the story of St. Paul's architectural beginnings, from the establishment of the first permanent enclave at the Lower Landing in 1840 to the onset of the nationwide depression of the mid-1870s. Seeking a unifying theme or general trend would falsify the scattered character of the city's early development. This chapter therefore focuses largely on individual structures and their owners, beginning with the log chapel that gave the city its name and climaxing with the rugged stone Alexander Ramsey House. The buildings in this chapter have been selected for the degree to which they illuminate the founding of the city, then linked through their aesthetic character, method of construction, siting, and associated personalities.

St. Paul at this early stage is largely a vanished city, forcing the exposition to wander now and again from the book's focus on extant buildings. Yet the legacy of mid-nineteenth-century St. Paul still shapes the city's sense of place and identity. During its first two decades, St. Paul established itself as a state capital and cathedral city, a transportation and warehousing hub, and a flats-and-bluffs river town. It also acquired the picturesque, New England look that still inspires comment from eastern visitors. The city's first public monuments, concentrated neighborhoods, and commercial rows may have disappeared, but its small public squares, particularly Irvine, Rice, and Smith (now Mears) Parks, each retain considerable vitality, and the city's proliferation of narrow streets, skewed grids, and terminal vistas continue to madden as they charm.

The second chapter immerses the reader in the city's period of most rapid growth, when it attained its present boundaries and emerged as a regional metropolitan center. The building boom of the 1880s attracted and nurtured the city's first flock of professional architects, many of whom helped usher the city into the twentieth century. Cass Gilbert, the renowned architect of the State Capitol, was among these; so was Clarence Johnston, the official State Architect for thirty years. Because the collective work of this growing professional community defined so much of the city's emerging character, this second part of the story gravitates around the architects themselves as a creative and energizing force in the city. Unlike the master carpenters who had previously held sway, this new class of professionals tended toward a visionary view of their work, either as artistic creation of a high order or as a business upon which the city's—and America's—future would depend. They looked constantly to the east— sometimes no farther than Chicago—for inspiration and direction. Over the next forty years, spanning a second generation of the profession, St. Paul accumulated much of its most characteristic and enduring building stock.

The third chapter focuses on architectural fashions between the world wars. During that period an obsession with style and mood in the arts, both fine and practical, swept the nation. Like Hollywood movie sets, architectural styles looked to other countries and times for inspiration, dressing up the past and the foreign in equally exotic clothing. The Edward Brooks House on Mississippi River Boulevard, now the residence of the president of the University of Minnesota, captures the formalizing aspect of this period; at the other extreme are the sprawling quasi-medieval cottages that dot the streets just east of the river. Architectural fashion gave free rein to a dozen styles or substyles simultaneously. Rather than supplanting each other, they lived in uneasy harmony, each boasting its own advantages but none innocent of stealing pieces from the others.

By the end of World War II, the lion's share of the land within city limits had been developed. For the next forty years, from 1945 to 1985, the focus of both city officials and the architectural community was largely on rebuilding. As projects dramatically increased in cost and complexity, their design and construction became team efforts involving both private and public players within a conceptual framework generally known as city planning. Its climactic monument was the Capital Centre project of the 1970s, from which downtown is still progressing or recovering, depending on one's point of view. This institutional context, combining the Modernist zeal of the postwar architectural profession with the widespread public perception of a city in need of radical repair, informs the fourth chapter.

These four chapters take the history of the city as far forward as it was intended to go at the inception of the book. But as the timeline of research and assimilation stretched, a new period grew up, now nearly two decades in length. As these buildings are still relatively fresh in creation and use, they are the hardest to describe and assess within a sound historical context. In addition, they grow out of multiple and often conflicted impulses. Modernism and preservation consciousness no longer have the purity that marked their early clashes and accommodations of the 1970s. Both are equally informed by a respect for the living past and the urgency of present developmental needs and opportunities.

The final chapter makes no attempt to extend the panoramic efforts of the earlier chapters, nor does it make any judgments by selection or omission as to the best or most characteristic architecture of the past two decades. Considered purely on their architectural merits, the corporate headquarters of St. Paul Insurance Companies (now the St. Paul Travelers Insurance Company) and the Science Museum of Minnesota assuredly have their critics as well as their devotees. Our purpose is simply to lay bare the multiplicity of contexts, geographical and historical, within which architectural creation continues to happen in St. Paul, with examples of particularly clear contextual responses.

This book was many years in the research and writing, but the end result is faithful to the original thematic conception developed by Jeffrey Hess and approved by the Heritage Preservation Commission. Although the authors share responsibility for all of the text, each of the chapters fell most heavily on the shoulders of one or the other. Chapters 1 and 4 are largely Hess's work and reflect his voice, whereas the second, third, and fifth are for the most part the creation of Paul Larson. Hess, however, contributed most of the information about the city engineering office and its work to the second chapter, and Larson's research and writing helped to drive the fourth chapter to its completion.

Every historian, indeed every friend of old buildings, is bound to have a different slate of favorites. Well before the closing chapter many readers familiar with the city will find some of their personal favorites omitted. In reference to individual buildings we can only say that what makes this book worth writing is the fact that St. Paul's architectural heritage is rich enough to exceed the compass of any single-volume study. The best that can be hoped for is a *selection* that does justice to the chronological, stylistic, and typological scope of that heritage.

There is a larger issue here, however, one deserving of a less cryptic response. The chapter themes have been chosen in part for how wide a canopy they spread over the buildings of their respective periods. The most significant buildings of the late nineteenth century, for example, were all architect-designed, just as the leading architecture of the period between the wars conscientiously pursued one of the period's many popular stylistic options. This leaves out of consideration a good deal of the city's historic building stock. St. Paul's streets are lined with ordinary houses and business blocks that grew up without an architect and lack any clear earmarks of style. We have left these simple structures for another sort of history, not because they are unimportant but because their architectural values, even at the level of floor planning and material choices, are largely derivative from the kind of buildings that leave a more conspicuous architectural legacy.

Occasionally, ordinary buildings are shoved under a different sort of umbrella altogether, identified by the tag *vernacular*. But vernacular architecture properly speaking grows up within long-standing local or regional traditions and makes distinctive use of local materials. For a time, it looked as if the rugged limestone houses and business blocks of the 1850s and 1860s would initiate such a tradition. But St. Paul simply had too short a history as a roughly hewn river town for the vernacular impulse to survive more than a generation. By the time of the city's great building boom of the mid-1880s, it had already succumbed to the influence of eastern and European-trained architects and the domination of national architectural currents. The lion's share of standing local buildings that tempt the application of the term *vernacular* are in fact little more than either toned-down versions of styles and plans originally developed by architects or utilitarian structures responsive to needs and requirements that lack the impetus of a distinctive regional culture.

Historic fabric weaves through every area of the city, and we have tried to honor its ubiquity with a broad geographical sampling. If a disproportionate number of references are to buildings in the downtown area or along the broad westward axes formed by Summit Avenue and West Seventh Street, that is only because these areas happen to be especially clear and well-preserved carriers of pervasive architectural themes. Continued preservation activity in old residential areas such as the East and West Sides, or along commercial strips such as University and Payne Avenues, could raise many exemplars on a par with those illustrated here. It is our hope that this study will be taken not as an exhaustive guide but as a tool for viewing and valuing all of St. Paul's splendid architectural legacy.

CHAPTER I

St. Paul's Founding Years

1840 – 1875

Before the airplane, before the motor car, before the railroad, there was the river, and the grandest river of all was the Mississippi, a majestic glide of water 2,350 miles long, sweeping through the heartland of the young American nation, carrying all manner of traffic, trade, and tradition upstream and downstream, between Minnesota and the Gulf of Mexico.

In the mid-nineteenth century, the city of St. Paul prided itself on being at the head of navigation on the Mississippi, and its citizens viewed the river through proprietary eyes. Early efforts at civic promotion put ink on innumerable illustrations showing as much of the river as of the town (Figure 1.1). As the northernmost port for all but local cargo on the Mississippi, St. Paul was a crucial transshipment point, a place for unloading, warehousing, and reloading merchandise for overland trade. When early residents counted the steamboats crowding the shore, when they watched the long lines of oxcarts trundling off with goods for the hinterlands, they sometimes credited their city's origin to a purposeful selection of a strategic location that "must necessarily supply the trade of all the vast regions north of it to the rich plains of [Canada], and west to the Rocky Mountains, and east to the basin of the great lakes." But this was something of a fiction. In actual fact, St. Paul straggled into existence pretty much by accident.[1]

The great German geographer Johann Georg Kohl

puzzled over St. Paul's location when he visited the city in 1855. "To me, at first glance," he wrote, "St. Paul seemed misplaced." Having studied the relationship between river transportation and urban growth throughout Europe and North America, Kohl was certain that "somewhere around here, at a confluence of rivers of the Upper Mississippi Valley, a big city had to be born." But a far better choice seemed to be about eight miles upstream from St. Paul at the juncture of the Mississippi and Minnesota rivers, "where the countryside spreads into a still broader and more beautiful landscape, soil is more fertile, and management of transportation by land and water is easier." Indeed, this was the very site that the federal government had purchased in 1805 from the region's Dakotas for future use as a military outpost. Named **Fort Snelling** in honor of its first commandant, the new installation arose on the west bank of the Mississippi in the early 1820s (Figure 1.2). In addition to the land occupied by the fort itself, the army also laid claim to a strip of territory on both sides of the Mississippi extending about ten miles north to the Falls of St. Anthony—the future birthplace of the city of Minneapolis.[2]

The U.S. Army eventually proved to be a very jealous guardian of its Minnesota property. Like other frontier garrisons, Fort Snelling attracted a miscellaneous collection of squatters illegally occupying government or

FIGURE I.I. *St. Paul, Minnesota, in 1853,* engraving (anonymous), 1891. This view of St. Paul, based on a daguerreotype taken from Dayton's Bluff, remained a popular subject with local engravers for half a century. Courtesy of the Minnesota Historical Society.

American Indian land. Military authorities paid little attention to the local populace until the summer of 1837, when Major Joseph Plympton assumed command of Fort Snelling. Plympton was disturbed to find over 150 people living near the fort who "were in no way connected with the military." He was even more concerned that no one, including the War Department, seemed to know the exact boundaries of the Fort Snelling military reservation. With the permission of his superiors, he prepared a preliminary map and sent it off to Washington. In July 1838, Plympton informed the settlers on the river's west bank that they were trespassing on military land.[3]

Plympton's eviction notice coincided with the U.S. Senate's ratification of treaties with the Dakotas and Ojibwes opening the Mississippi's east bank to American settlement. Several of the Fort Snelling squatters promptly moved across the river outside of army jurisdiction, where they were soon joined by newcomers to the region. The largest settlement was a Swiss and French Canadian enclave at Fountain Cave, about four miles downstream from Fort Snelling. Although Plympton had succeeded in distancing the settlers from the fort, he believed they were still too close for the proper maintenance of military discipline. The post's surgeon, Dr. John Emerson, sent Washington the unpleasant particulars:

"We have been completely inundated with ardent spirits, and consequently the most beastly scenes of intoxication [have prevailed] among the soldiers of this garrison and the Indians in its vicinity. . . . The whiskey is brought here by citizens who are pouring in upon us and settling themselves on the opposite shore of the Mississippi River."[4]

In the fall of 1839, the War Department authorized Plympton to draw up a new map of the military reservation, and he responded by extending the boundary southward along the east bank until it stretched beyond the Fountain Cave settlement. When the settlers refused to leave their homes, the War Department dispatched a federal marshal, who in the spring of 1840 supervised the destruction of their cabins. Gathering up their livestock and household possessions, the small band of refugees trooped dispiritedly downstream in search of new farmland. They came to roost about eight miles below Fort Snelling, just beyond the new bounds of the military reservation. Here they found a few scattered cabins and the unforgettable face of one Pierre Parrant, an unabashed whiskey seller who had previously lived at Fountain Cave.[5]

Chroniclers have not treated Parrant kindly. According to his chief biographer, Parrant was "coarse," "intemperate," "licentious," with a face indicative of his

FIGURE 1.2. View of Fort Snelling from Mendota, lithograph (anonymous), 1830. The fort overlooked the confluence of the Minnesota and Mississippi rivers. The tree in the foreground invokes the fort's wilderness setting, but it was probably an artistic invention; by this date, soldiers had denuded the riverbanks to keep the garrison supplied with firewood during the frigid Minnesota winters. Courtesy of the Minnesota Historical Society.

character: "[He] had only one eye that was service-able. He had another, it is true, but such an eye! Blind, marble-hued, crooked, with a sinister white ring glaring around the pupil, giving a kind of piggish expression to his sodden, low features." Appropriately enough, Parrant was known throughout the region as "Pig's Eye," and by extension, so was the river-bluff area surrounding the hovel where he carried on his nefarious trade.[6]

Parrant sold his claim to one of the newcomers and moved on, but his nickname lingered behind. Curiously, no one seems to have minded living in a place called "Pig's Eye" until a visit by the Roman Catholic priest Father Lucien Galtier, who erected a church for the faithful on the edge of the river bluff between what later

became Cedar and Minnesota Streets. On November 1, 1841, Father Galtier blessed the new chapel and dedicated it to St. Paul. As he later explained, "I expressed the wish, at the same time, that the settlement would be known by the same name, and my desire was obtained."[7]

Throughout the 1840s, St. Paul remained primarily an agricultural community. Most of the early settlers, to quote geographer Paul Donald Hesterman, "looked for a place to farm, not to build a city." In the spring of 1849, when Minnesota Territory was officially organized with St. Paul as its capital, the entire settlement counted about two hundred people and thirty buildings. Except for an occasional framed structure, built from lumber hand-hewn on the spot or brought in from sawmills

FIGURE I.3.

Built of notched and pinned hand-hewn logs, the Chapel of St. Paul was barely fifteen years old yet soon to be razed at the time of this view, ca. 1855. A throng of shops constructed of mill-cut lumber were already crowding it out of its location at the foot of Jackson Street. From a daguerreotype by Joel Emmons Whitney; courtesy of the Minnesota Historical Society.

on the St. Croix River, log cabins were the rule. None of these early buildings has survived, but the best documented is the little **Chapel of St. Paul** of 1841, which gave the town its name (razed; Figure 1.3). The chapel would be engulfed by downtown growth before the end of the decade, surviving only long enough to pose for a daguerreotypist in 1855 or 1856.[8]

Constructed of round oak logs by French Canadian carpenters who were members of the congregation, the Chapel of St. Paul illustrates how the area's French-speaking community adapted American building techniques. Traditionally, French log construction in the Great Lakes region and upper Mississippi valley relied on vertical posts. Sometimes the posts stood closely together to form a palisade, and sometimes they stood at intervals, walled together by stacked horizontal members with cutaway knobbed ends set into grooves running the length of the vertical posts. The Chapel of St. Paul, however, employed neither of these techniques. Photographs show that the building was constructed of horizontal logs notched together at the corners—a standard American construction practice of the Appalachian frontier that moved westward with the course of settlement. When expertly done, corner notching was sufficient to lock the logs in place. But in communities where the technique was not well established, builders often lacked competence or confidence in the method, leading them to secure the horizontal logs with additional

fastening. Apparently such was the case with the Chapel of St. Paul. According to one of the workmen, Isaac Labissonniere, "The logs, rough and undressed, prepared merely by the ax, were made secure by wooden pins."[9]

In 1847, the citizens of St. Paul took their first self-conscious step toward making their scattering of buildings into a bona fide city. A group of landholders got together and platted about ninety acres into town lots. Bounded by St. Peter Street on the west and Wacouta Street on the east, the plat stretched along the river for one-half mile, running back from the water's edge to Seventh Street, about one-third mile. The surveyor was Ira B. Brunson of Prairie du Chien, Wisconsin, who in an indirect way had been one of the founding fathers of St. Paul. Six years earlier in his role as federal marshal, Brunson had rousted the Fountain Cave settlers from their homes, sending them downriver to join "Pig's Eye" Parrant.[10]

If Brunson had hoped to make amends for past behavior, he was disappointed. His plat was almost universally condemned "for the narrowness of the streets, irregularity of their courses and absence of alleys." The harshest criticism came from James M. Goodhue, the city's first newspaper editor, who arrived in St. Paul in 1849, the same year the plat was officially filed. "The projectors of this town," Goodhue declared, "appear to have had but the smallest possible idea of the growth and importance that awaited St. Paul":

FIGURE I.4. *Saint Paul, Capital of Minnesota,* color lithograph based on a drawing by topographical engineer Max Strobel, 1853. St. Paul is seen here as viewed from a popular vantage point in Mendota. Panoramic prints were often used to advertise cities to potential immigrants and investors. Courtesy of the Library of Congress.

The original plat was laid off in a very good imitation of the old French part of St. Louis, with crooked lanes for streets, irregular blocks, and little skewed-angular lots, about as large as a stingy piece of gingerbread broken in two diagonally; without a reservation fit to be called a public square; without a margin between the town and river; without preserving a tree for shade; without permanent evidences of boundaries made by the survey. In fact, it was a survey without measurement, a plan without method, a volunteer crop of buildings, a sort of militia muster of tenements. So much for the old plat.[11]

Neither Brunson nor the town site proprietors were truly to blame. The real culprit was the area's topography, which had enough highs and lows to frustrate the orderly intentions of any surveyor. Only a few yards back from the river, the land rose into a sheer ninety-foot bluff breached by a narrow ravine, which carried

Jackson Street down to a steamboat landing. Those nimble enough to scale Jackson Street came upon an open terrace, sloping up to Wabasha Street and fanning out like an amphitheater to still another bluff line paralleling the river (Figure 1.4).

On this terrace, Brunson attempted to impose a traditional gridiron plat, eliminating alleys and skimping on streets to reserve as much space as possible for building. Although Brunson's lines were straight, the terrain was ragged. Ten thousand years before, at the close of the last ice age, a retreating glacier had littered the town site with gravel and boulders, depositing a sixty-foot hill across the future paths of Third, Fourth, Fifth, Sixth, and Seventh Streets, between Jackson and Wacouta Streets. Crowned by the **First Baptist Church** (razed) in 1849, this lofty eminence became known as "Baptist Hill." Its difficult approaches may well have inspired generosity, for in 1849, two landowners donated part of the hill to the public for open space, eventually known as Mears Park. Elsewhere in the town site, the ground quickly gave way to expose shelves of limestone bedrock, a formidable obstacle to street excavation. It took almost a full decade of blasting and digging through river bluff, bedrock, and hillside before the actual streets approximated the lines of Brunson's plat. One advantage was that there was always plenty of fill to level off swampy areas and to expand the steamboat landing.[12]

On contemporary maps, Brunson's plat was listed as "St. Paul Proper." But everyone called the area "Lower Town" to distinguish it from the "Upper Town" community located just upstream. Platted in 1849 as "Rice and Irvine's Addition," Upper Town was about the same size as Lower Town, reaching back to the second bluff line and westward to Elm Street. At the foot of Chestnut and Eagle Streets, it had its own steamboat landing, separated from the "Lower Landing" by the steep river bluff crowding the shore. The merchants at each end of the city fully intended their own section to be the dominant business center, and they waged a bitter rivalry that prevented them from even agreeing about the time of day. As the local press noted with exasperation in 1856, "Great inconvenience has been experienced in St. Paul, owing to the want of standard time. Usually, upper and lower town time differs five, ten and even fifteen minutes, each section persisting in the correctness of its own regulator."[13]

Lower Town eventually triumphed over its rival, partly because its business community was more aggressive and partly because the Lower Landing was better situated to take advantage of future transportation developments.

About one-half mile east of the landing, the Trout Brook–Phalen Creek valley pierced the river bluff, offering a natural corridor for railroad construction through the city. When the first tracks were laid in the early 1860s, linking St. Paul with St. Anthony about eight miles to the west,[14] the Lower Landing became the river-rail transshipment point, firmly establishing Lower Town as the city's center of commerce. Since all future rail lines tied in to the Trout-Phalen corridor, Lower Town remained the hub of transportation after the decline of steamboating in the 1870s.

Although the contest between Upper Town and Lower Town was decided within a decade or two, it left a permanent mark on the appearance of St. Paul. In platting Upper Town, the proprietors made no attempt to coordinate their street grid with the earlier Brunson plat of Lower Town. Instead, they proclaimed their independence by skewing their grid at a forty-five-degree angle to St. Peter Street, the western boundary of Brunson's plat (Map 1.1). In the words of Goodhue, "the two plats appear to have taken a running jump at each other, like two rival steamboats."[15]

The several plats that eventually conjoined Upper and Lower Town were skewed at yet other angles, creating a curiously "Old World" setting of twisting thoroughfares with closed vistas. Confined by the two bluffs to a relatively narrow strip of land, St. Paul's business district, especially after the 1880s, could expand only by increasing the height of its buildings, which further accentuated the cramped bustle of its hilly streets. All

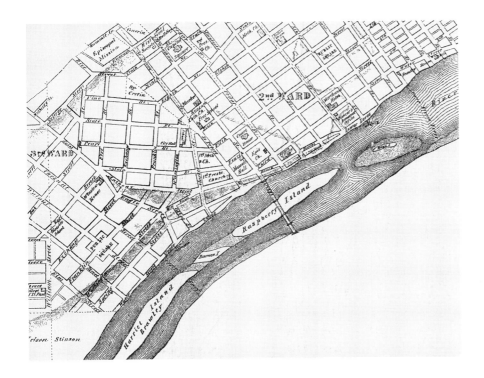

MAP I.I.

A detail of Goodrich and Somers's "Map of the City of St. Paul, Capital of Minnesota," 1857. This was one of the first printed maps to clearly indicate Upper and Lower Town, occupying the third and second wards respectively.

this was in sharp contrast to the open prairie, checkerboard plan of Minneapolis—the "twin" city still several miles distant that would always serve as St. Paul's comparative. Although St. Paul was only about a decade older than Minneapolis, its streetscape would for many decades evoke a fuller sense of habitation, a more cosmopolitan sense of complexity. "St. Paul," observed one visitor, "is not so extreme as Boston in its labyrinth of streets and disjointed connections, but . . . I have, myself, been some weeks finding my way here." "I have heard it said," wrote another, "that St. Paul was a metropolis when it had a population of but 5,000, as contradistinguished from other cities which remained villages when they had a population of 100,000." "The numerous curves, corners, angles and *cul de sacs* of this irregular street system," remarked still a third, "give fine opportunities for architectural effects." "Minneapolis," concluded a fourth, "is the beginning of the West, St. Paul the last outpost of [the] East."[16]

Despite its "eastern" look, St. Paul emerged as an urban center in a typically western way. The bucolic quiet of the 1840s ended abruptly with the organization of Minnesota Territory in the spring of 1849. As the territorial capital of a vast undeveloped region, St. Paul was suddenly the place to make one's fortune, and each

new steamboat—eighty-five by the end of the season— unloaded its horde of aspirants. "We advise settlers who are swarming into St. Paul in such multitudes," announced the local press, "to bring along tents and beddings . . . as *it is utterly impossible* to hire a building in any part of the village; although builders are at work in every direction." In the month of May alone, seventy wood buildings went up, more than doubling the housing stock of the previous decade. "It looks," said one observer, "as if the seed for a multitude of tenements had been scattered yesterday upon a bed of guano, and had sprouted up into cabins, and stores and sheds and warehouses, fresh from the saw mill."[17]

The new construction excited attention not only because it was tangible evidence of civic progress, but also because it showcased a new type of building technology, which had been developed in Chicago during the previous decade. Instead of the heavy, mortised-and-tenoned timber supports of traditional wood construction, the new technique utilized a lighter skeletal framework nailed together from milled lumber. Because of its seeming flimsiness, the new system initially was derided as "balloon framing," but the nailed lumber skeleton satisfactorily withstood the ravages of midwestern weather. As both a term and a technique, balloon framing soon became standard usage in American construction practice. Balloon framing was quick, it was comparatively cheap, and it helped provide shelter for the eight hundred citizens residing in St. Paul at the close of the 1840s.[18]

Compared to what was to come, 1849 was a relatively slow year. Fueled by unprecedented immigration from Europe and by rising wheat prices, the truly frantic boom occurred in the mid-1850s, when one hundred thousand settlers poured into southern Minnesota to buy land recently ceded by the Dakotas. As the immigrant's gateway to the prairie, St. Paul quickly became one of the busiest towns in the West. Its hotels accommodated the transient swarm, its banks financed the purchase of land, its shops provisioned the new farms and town sites, and its number of residents swelled beyond accurate reckoning. At the height of the boom in June 1857, one population estimate ranged between twelve thousand and seventeen thousand people. By that time, the city's limits, once confined to Upper Town and Lower Town, had expanded more than a mile in every direction except the river, extending beyond Dayton's Bluff on the east, to Minnehaha Avenue on the north, and to Dale Street on the west. Town lots purchased in 1849 for $35 were selling seven years later for $1,500.[19] The German geographer Kohl was dumbfounded by the dizzying pace of speculation and the spiraling price of property:

We were shown an ugly swamp, black with muck, a splendid buffalo wallow, which to us looked like something that, as people say, could not be given away.

But, we were told, this swamp had already had half a dozen owners, remaining in its natural dismal-swamp state all the while, and now is worth I don't know what exorbitant sum. And this swamp may very well remain swamp still more years, pass to new ownership another six times, double its price at each sale, always with the expectation that when it is drained and the city's houses approach very near, it can be parceled out at even higher prices.[20]

The bubble burst in August 1857, when a New York bank defaulted, setting off a chain reaction of business failures across the country. The entire economic system had been floating on inflated hopes and puffed-up collateral; it sank like a stone when punctured by the demand for hard cash. The ensuing depression was particularly severe in St. Paul and the rest of Minnesota Territory, which had not yet developed a significant agricultural or manufacturing base to offset its "import" of goods from the East. Although some capital had been accumulated through trade and lumbering, it had gone into real estate speculation. In St. Paul, people soon had nothing left to barter except their suddenly worthless town lots. According to one witness who experienced the hardship firsthand, "Ruin stared all classes in the face. . . . Everybody was struggling to save himself. All the mercantile firms suspended or made assignments. All works of improvement ceased, and general gloom and despondency settled down on the community." Nearly half the city's population decamped.[21]

St. Paul did not fully recover until the end of the Civil War, when a new round of prosperity pushed the city's population past thirty-three thousand people in 1875. During this period, St. Paul inaugurated a private, horse-drawn street railway system, primarily linking the Lower Town and Upper Town areas. The city also doubled its geographic area, most notably annexing the "West Side" of the Mississippi, previously the independent village of West St. Paul. The mid-1870s, however, witnessed another national financial collapse. Although less affected than in 1857, St. Paul once again felt the pressure of economic retrenchment, which slowed municipal enterprise for the remainder of the decade.[22]

In terms of St. Paul's architectural heritage, the period before 1875 is unified by one overriding fact: very little remains. In 1983, an architectural survey of the entire city, including several immediate suburbs, identified only forty-six buildings "where research points to a pre-1875 construction date." About one-third appeared to predate the Civil War.[23] The loss of the antebellum building stock was already well advanced by the last quarter of the nineteenth century. For example, in 1874 a St. Paul newspaper nostalgically called the public's attention to an 1857 photograph of Third Street (now Kellogg Boulevard), formerly the business center of Lower Town:

Now 1857 is not such a very great time ago, but the changes since then are wonderful. Third Street was then lined with balloon frames of every possible size and style. Almost every one of these have since burned down and are today supplanted by elegant blocks of stone and brick. It revives memories of the past to look at these old views. They are decidedly "historical."[24]

Although fire claimed its share of early St. Paul buildings, most were torn down to make way for more substantial structures. The first settlers had little inducement to build lasting architectural monuments. In fact, circumstances strongly encouraged them to build fast, small, and cheap. Building materials, when available at all, were extremely expensive. By 1851, St. Paul had its own brickyard and two steam-powered sawmills, but the local press frequently noted that "lumber and brick are scarce here." The demand for skilled labor also exceeded the supply: "Many of our master builders say that they could have done three times as much work this season . . . but for the scarcity of mechanics." In addition to the high cost of construction, the speculative mania of the times further discouraged anything except the most basic type of shelter. Why waste money on buildings when those same dollars could be loaned out at 3 percent per month?—not to mention the untold riches awaiting investors in raw land.[25]

In 1856, an informal census of the city counted 1,342 houses. Of this number, less than 1 percent was stone; 9 percent, brick; and the remainder, wood frame, two-thirds of which stood only one story in height. The following description seems to be typical for the period. It concerns a house erected for a tradesman's family

During the 1850s, small gabled wooden boxes were the norm in both Upper Town and Lower Town. The William and Catherine Dahl House, moved from 136 Thirteenth Street to 508 Jefferson Avenue, is the sole surviving representative of the type.

on St. Peter Street between College Avenue and Tenth Street in 1861:

> Our little home was a frame house; the builders were Richard Ireland (the father of the archbishop-to-come), Tom Grace (brother of the then Bishop of St. Paul), my father, and perhaps a plasterer. The "house" was about 12 feet long and 10 feet wide; . . . later an addition of the same dimensions was added, also a shed in which the kindling was kept and where Father did his home tasks in wagon making. There was no well or pump and Mother got her water from a sort of communal pump and well about fifty yards away. . . . Our house [had] two rooms—a front room or "parlor" and the living room in which cooking and all else was done.[26]

It is important to bear in mind that this house was considered to be a fairly respectable dwelling, certainly a cut above the "plain board shanties" that, according to the commentator, sheltered the neighborhood's poorer families. The building's piecemeal growth by means of additions was so common a practice that it is rare to find a mid-nineteenth-century wood-frame house that survives in its original, diminutive, one-story condition. In expanding urban areas such as St. Paul, it was only a matter of time before the price of land exceeded the value of original construction, even with additions. New owners generally could afford to start over, building a new house better suited to their comfort and station.

The city's purest surviving example of a modest, one-story, wood-frame house is the **William and Catherine Dahl House** of 1858, originally situated at 136 Thirteenth Street (Figure 1.5). Built in the northern outskirts of Lower Town by the English-born printer William Dahl and his Irish-born wife, Catherine, the house remained in the Dahl family for the next eighty years. In the mid-1970s, the building narrowly escaped demolition by state authorities, who had hoped to use the site for underground gasoline storage tanks servicing an adjacent state motor pool. The building won a reprieve, and a new life a few miles away, only because of the concerted efforts of St. Paul preservationists, who succeeded in having it moved to a new site in Lower Town, 508 Jefferson Avenue. At first glance, the Dahl House may not look like a building worth fighting for, but its unassuming appearance is the key to its historical importance. Spare, gabled, and rectangular, the building graphically illustrates the simplicity of most wood-frame residential construction in antebellum St. Paul. Showing its broad side to the street, it measures thirty feet across and twenty-three feet deep, with a brick chimney surmounting the roof at each end. The entrance at midfacade indicates the central-hall floor plan, two rooms deep on each side.[27]

FIGURE 1.6. Typical early houses and business blocks in a stripped-down Greek Revival style on Wabasha Street facing Fourth Street, 1857. These buildings were among the first victims of the expanding downtown. Courtesy of the Minnesota Historical Society.

As the Dahl House indicates, speed and economy of construction were not conducive to architectural refinement. St. Paul builders of the 1850s, however, were not completely immune to stylistic considerations. Their preferred style was the Greek Revival, which had emerged three decades earlier as the country's first indigenous architectural expression. Opulent examples, especially in urban areas of the eastern seaboard, vied with one another in classical detailing, much of it focused on monumental porticos with towering columns surmounted by a broad triangular form known as a pediment. The overall effect was of a classical Greek temple, which was the source of the style's proportions, detailing, and name. For the most part, the newly settled West lacked the craftsmen and the materials to produce such architectural extravagance, but simplified versions were possible. After a quarter of a century before the public eye, the Greek Revival had been reduced to its basic stylistic elements in numerous widely circulated "carpenter's handbooks," so that builders did not need a tremendous amount of skill or imagination to produce a passable rendition from locally manufactured millwork. Simple pilaster strips served as columns, a flat board across the gable end created a pediment, and a sidelight-and-transom enclosure

of the main entrance suggested the column-and-lintel construction of the prototype temple. No matter how stylistically abbreviated they might be, virtually all "carpentered Greek" buildings proudly exhibited a coat of white paint, a silent homage to the marbled remains of the Acropolis (Figure 1.6).[28]

Well-articulated examples of the Greek Revival are extremely rare among surviving St. Paul buildings. Stylistic fragments are more common. The Dahl House, for example, gives what was probably the most common Greek Revival salute of the period, the display of eave returns. These short horizontal projections across the gable end were meant to suggest a "broken" pediment, a common classical detail. Consider, also, the **Avery and Emma Adams House,** erected near Irvine Park in 1855 (Figure 1.7). Brick mason Avery Ward Adams intended the structure to be the kitchen wing of his family residence, but shortly after occupying this first stage of the construction project, he and his wife were unnerved by a cholera epidemic in St. Paul. They sold the property and fled the city.[29] In later years, the Adams House would be so smothered by small wood-frame additions that the original masonry almost disappeared from view. But peeping out below the eaves is a brickwork dentil

FIGURE 1.7.
Avery and Emma Adams House,
454 North Smith Avenue. The
removal of a front addition, as
indicated by a paint scar on the
brickwork, has left an unimpeded
view of the original Greek Revival
dentil frieze.

frieze that proclaims Adams's original Greek Revival intentions and suggests that his completed residence might have made a polished aesthetic statement.

For the city's best remaining example of the Greek Revival, it is necessary to visit Irvine Park, a small public square donated to the city in 1849 by John Irvine, one of the original proprietors of Upper Town. Located on the edge of the river bluff near the old Upper Landing, Irvine Park was Upper Town's premier residential district, and it still contains a good share of the city's oldest housing stock. Probably because Upper Town failed in its attempt to become the principal business district, these buildings escaped demolition for commercial development, which eventually erased the original residential district of Lower Town.

Irvine Park itself remained in a natural shaggy state for many years, serving primarily as a public grazing ground. Understandably, most of the area's early houses faced the river, rather than the unkempt park. One exception was the **Rodney and Elizabeth Parker House**, built in the Greek Revival style in 1852 by a married couple from New Hampshire who managed one of Upper Town's most successful hotels (Figures 1.8 and 1.9). This residence, originally standing about one hundred yards to the east of its present location, once fronted on the park. Later, in the 1880s, it was turned to face Sherman Street. The building did not regain its original orientation until the mid-1970s, when, in deteriorating

condition, it was moved to its present site in preparation for an architectural restoration based on historical photographs and surviving structural evidence.[30]

In its restored condition, the wood-frame Parker House is a worthy representative of the Greek Revival style in St. Paul. Its massing, proportions, and simplicity of detailing are all authentically in character. Of particular note are the original fluted, Doric pilasters flanking the entrance; they are the building's only ornamental flourish. The reconstructed front porch also merits attention. Although the latticework railing is a speculative re-creation, the porch's two-tiered configuration is documented by an early photograph, which also shows the present French window centered on the second story.

While porches and balconies were fairly common on eastern Greek Revival buildings, the full-length, two-story wood porch of the Parker House may have had a different inspiration. It is reminiscent of French-Creole architecture, whose builders favored wraparound, multi-tiered verandas, or "galleries," for lounging away the summer heat. There are no remaining examples of pure French veranda construction in St. Paul, but the style was readily available for inspection by early residents. The French Canadian settler Joseph Rondo, for example, replaced his "French-plan" log cabin with a "French brick house with a protecting roof and verandas." Two-story French verandas also appeared in full glory on the 1851 **Charles H. Oakes House** (razed), a two-story frame

FIGURE 1.8. Rodney and Elizabeth Parker House, 30 Irvine Park. The house was moved from the park in the 1880s, then returned to a prominent place near its original site and meticulously restored in the 1970s.

FIGURE 1.9.
Entrance to the Parker House. Sidelights and fluted columns announce the Greek Revival style.

residence built for a St. Paul banker and former fur trader who had married into an old French family.[31]

The well-phrased Greek Revival idiom of the Parker House bespoke the fact that its owners were citizens of taste and substance. True architectural pretension, however, was communicated more by material than by style, and in early St. Paul, nothing proclaimed prosperity better than brick. It was sober, it was solid, and it was very expensive. The city's finest remaining example of early brick construction is the two-story **Simpson-Wood House,** constructed by government surveyor James Hervey Simpson in 1853 and enlarged with a matching rear addition about ten years later by the second owner, Charles Wood, a railroad agent who was brought to trial for stealing $10,000 of company funds (Figures 1.10 and 1.11). Apparently, Wood accidentally dropped the money in the Mississippi River, an admission that saved him from conviction but not from scandal. To the extent that architecture serves as a character witness, the Simpson-Wood House helped restore his good name, for its design is both honest and intelligent.[32]

Originally located a short distance away on Sherman Street, the Simpson-Wood House was moved to its present site at 32 Irvine Park in the late 1970s. Its location next door to the Parker House is fortuitous for purposes of comparison. Unlike its neighbor, the Simpson-Wood House is not a Greek Revival building. Its stylistic antecedents are even older, harkening back to the first two decades of the nineteenth century, when wealthy East Coast merchants looked to England for the latest fashions. Since this monied elite formed the backbone of the nation's conservative Federalist Party, their choice in architecture is often called the Federal style.[33]

Like the later Greek Revival style, the Federal style also relied heavily on classical details, which sometimes makes it difficult to decide where one style "stopped" and the other "began." Perhaps the main difference is that the Federal style delighted in classical embellishment for its own sake, particularly preferring delicate attenuated ornament, as previously popularized in England. These graceful flourishes served to soften the bold massing of exterior masonry facades, for brick was the preferred material of Federal-style construction. Unlike the Greek Revival, which held the Parthenon in reverence, the Federal style was not interested in replicating exotic ancient temples. Its dwellings were meant to look like the homes of sensible conservative men of commerce, as in fact many were.

With all this in mind, let us look closely at the Simpson-Wood House. Capped by a shallow-pitched hip roof, it presents a picture of no-nonsense sobriety. Yet its austerity is lightened by a wood frieze below the eaves topped by a delicate dentil cornice. And the first-floor windows of the front facade are elegantly elongated, being almost the same length as the front doorway. This entrance is thoroughly Federal in character. With its narrow sidelights and fluted mullions sculpted into slender Doric pilasters, the doorway assumes a fragile grace that is completely different in tone from the broad, robust classical detailing of the Greek Revival Parker House entrance.

FIGURE I.10. Simpson-Wood House, 32 Irvine Park (moved from its original site on Sherman Street).

FIGURE I.11.
Entrance to the
Simpson-Wood House,
displaying the refined
proportions and detailing
of the Federal style.

FIGURE 1.12. Benjamin and Martha Brunson House, 485 Kenny Road (originally Partridge Street), 1896. By this date, railroad tracks sprawled across the nearby Trout Brook–Phalen Creek corridor, virtually encircling the once-secluded Brunson House neighborhood, later dubbed "Railroad Island." Courtesy of the Minnesota Historical Society.

The Federal style also influenced the general design of other hip-roofed brick dwellings, such as Irvine Park's **Eaton-Mylar House** at 53 Irvine Park of 1853 and the 1855 **Benjamin and Martha Brunson House** (Figure 1.12), which at the time of construction stood on the city's eastern fringe of settlement, bordering the Trout Brook–Phalen Creek valley. But the style's snobbish aristocratic associations limited its popular appeal and made it unacceptable for public buildings in frontier towns such as St. Paul. As long as politics had been controlled by the wealthy few, the Federalist Party and the Federal style held a place in the public arena. But both were swept away by the increasing democratization of American society, which during the 1820s and 1830s extended the vote to virtually all adult white males. The "Age of Jackson" demanded new democratic architectural symbolism, and in a curious way, the Greek Revival answered the purpose.

Americans had often identified their own democratic aspirations with those of the ancient Greek city-states. During the 1820s, this identification became something of a national obsession, partly because modern-day Greeks were at that time fighting a courageous war of independence against the Ottoman Empire. Believing that their own Revolutionary War was being replayed in Europe, Americans fervently embraced the Greek patriots' cause. They donated money to the struggle, expressed their sympathy in prose and poetry, and liberally sprinkled the national soil with new settlements named "Athens," "Sparta," and "Utica." Intellectually and emotionally, Americans were ready to appreciate the democratic symbolism of the new Greek Revival. They stamped its design on virtually every state capitol and county courthouse built between 1830 and 1855.[34]

The **First Ramsey County Courthouse** of 1852 and the **First Minnesota Capitol** of 1853 (both razed) were true to their times, incorporating perhaps the most common Greek Revival feature of midwestern public architecture during that era: a four-column Doric portico with full pediment and unadorned frieze (Figures 1.13 and 1.14). Fulfilling the minimum requirements of Greek symmetry and symbolism, the plain Doric portico had the additional virtue of being cheaper and easier to build than the more elaborately detailed Ionic and Corinthian orders. The first courthouse and the first capitol also incorporated a domed lantern, a classical Roman detail that had been popular with the builders of American public architecture since the late eighteenth century.

In keeping with their civic importance, the first courthouse and the first capitol were both built of brick with stone steps, trim, and columns. On the whole, visitors were kind in their comments, making allowances for the city's infancy and the scarcity of building materials. One New York reporter even declared that the Minnesota Capitol's "noble dome [presents] an outline somewhat similar to the Federal Capitol at Washington." But a local critic was more accurate in comparing the feature to "an inverted wash-basin." The Minnesota Capitol also

suffered from its underscaled portico, which gave the entire building an anemic appearance. The architectural significance of these two government buildings, however, transcends the nature and quality of their designs. The important fact is that they are among a handful of early St. Paul buildings with known designers.[35]

Although the first capitol and the first courthouse were both politically important and prominently sited, neither was the work of a "professional architect," in other words, a trained paid designer who made a living solely by preparing plans and specifications and by superintending construction. The breed did exist in the East but had not yet made its appearance in St. Paul. Instead, the city had a number of carpenters who possessed varying degrees of design skill. The 1850 federal census for St. Paul lists a total of seventy-nine men in this category, constituting the second-largest occupational group, exceeded only by common laborers.[36]

Most carpenters worked for day wages, but a select few had sufficient experience and financial backing to operate as independent contractors with crews of their own. Since their clients often expected them to provide working drawings, they generally kept on hand a few stock sketches that could be adapted to the present purpose by adding decorative details gleaned from published handbooks. They were also adept at copying buildings that caught their clients' fancy, resulting in numerous press announcements that a new structure would "have a front finished similar to the building erected by [so-and-so] last season." In serving as both designer and

FIGURE 1.13. The First Minnesota Capitol (razed), Tenth and Wabasha Streets, ca. 1860, displays a standard Greek Revival statehouse design of the period. Photograph by Whitney & Zimmerman; courtesy of the Minnesota Historical Society.

contractor, these men earned the title of "master builder," although sometimes the term "architect" was used.[37]

This general profile of a master builder seems to fit a Connecticut-born carpenter named A. C. Prentiss, whose plan for the First Minnesota Capitol was selected in 1851, over three other Greek Revival designs, by the legislatively appointed Board of Commissioners of Public Buildings. In the 1850 census, Prentiss is listed as fifty years old, which made him the second-oldest carpenter in the city. Nothing is known of his background and training, except for his own declaration that he had "thirty years of experience" in his trade. Although Prentiss received $50 for his design, he recognized that the project's greatest financial reward lay in securing the actual construction contract, which eventually exceeded $31,000. To that end, Prentiss formed a contracting partnership with the Upper Town businessman John Irvine,

trained in his youth as a plasterer. The low bidder, however, was another master builder named Joseph Daniels, whose own design for the capitol had been unsuccessful.[38]

Daniels also served as the contractor for the First County Courthouse, implementing the design of David Day. Day was not a master builder. Indeed, his interest in architecture derived from a completely different tradition, for Day was what the nineteenth century called an "educated gentleman." In the words of his contemporaries, he was "quiet, moderate, decisive, metaphysical, thorough"—"a diligent student of questions and problems in social science, philosophy and political economy." Born in Virginia in 1825, Day received a medical degree from the University of Pennsylvania in 1849 and then immediately moved to St. Paul to practice his profession. Successfully branching out into the drug business, he retired from active business life in the mid-1860s.

Thereafter he devoted himself to community service, holding several political appointments. In the 1880s, he served on the board of commissioners that supervised the construction of the **Second Ramsey County Courthouse** (razed), also located in downtown St. Paul. Into his old age, architecture remained his "hobby by day and night."[39]

It was not long after the completion of the first capitol and first courthouse that St. Paul welcomed its first professional architects. Augustus F. Knight, fresh from an architectural apprenticeship in Buffalo, New York, settled in the city in 1857. That same year also saw the arrival of another New Yorker, Abraham M. Radcliffe, who had most recently worked in an architect's office in Chicago. Neither man was overwhelmed by immediate success. In fact, both left St. Paul after only a few years, Knight going to St. Louis, Missouri, in 1859, and Radcliffe to Winona, Minnesota, in 1862. But both also

soon returned to St. Paul and established thriving practices that continued into the 1880s. No early buildings by Knight or Radcliffe survive in St. Paul, but the two men's contribution to the city's architectural history was never strictly a matter of bricks and mortar. For many years, they were virtually the only professional role models of their discipline in St. Paul, and Radcliffe, in particular, was responsible for training a whole generation of local architects who came to prominence later in the nineteenth century.[40]

Although master builders and architects were undoubtedly responsible for the major public and private buildings erected in early St. Paul, they by no means had a monopoly on design. A number of structures owed their existence and appearance to a different sort of tradition that has come to be called "vernacular construction," or "folk architecture." Such buildings were the work of

FIGURE 1.15.
Frederick Spangenberg
House, 375 Mount Curve
Boulevard, ca. 1910. At this
time it was still part of an
operating dairy farm.
Courtesy of the Minnesota
Historical Society.

men and women who did not have formal craft training, although they often knew a good deal about putting up a building, just as they might know a good deal about fixing wagons, making cheese, carding wool, or breeding livestock. Relying on skills learned at an early age from family and friends, they constructed their own homes and barns out of economic necessity, perhaps hiring a carpenter or mason to help them with the work. Since they were most comfortable with familiar techniques and materials, their buildings usually were "traditional" in the truest sense of the word.[41]

Given the conservative nature of early St. Paul architecture and the lack of information concerning the origins of most buildings, it is difficult to identify definite examples of owner-built vernacular construction. An excellent candidate, however, is the **Frederick Spangenberg House** of the mid-1860s (Figures 1.15 and 1.16). This residence is the sole surviving building of the Spangenberg dairy farm, which once occupied eighty acres of bluff land bordering the Mississippi River about five miles west of downtown St. Paul. The owner, Frederick Spangenberg, was a German immigrant, and his dwelling appears to reflect his ethnic heritage. Standing two stories tall with a one-story kitchen wing, his gable-roofed limestone farmhouse displays the generous proportions and

rough rubble-masonry construction of the German countryside. Similar stone farmhouses were built by German immigrants of the mid-nineteenth century elsewhere in Minnesota, as well as in other midwestern states. During the 1920s, the Spangenberg farmstead became part of the new Highland Park residential district, and the old farmhouse was remodeled with an "American Colonial" entrance to keep abreast of its recently constructed period-revival neighbors.[42]

Teutonic fondness for stone construction also reveals itself in three modest limestone dwellings in the West Seventh Street neighborhood of Upper Town, once the center of St. Paul's German-speaking community. These buildings are the **Johan and Maria Magdalena Schilliger House** of 1859, the **Anton Waldman House** of ca. 1864, and the **Martin Weber House** of 1867 (Figures 1.17, 1.18, and 1.19). The Weber House is the work of German-immigrant stonemasons Jacob Amos and Christian Rhinehardt, who equipped the rubble-masonry structure with eave returns and a blocky transom over the front entrance. The Waldman House has a similar transom but features more precise, coursed-ashlar masonry. Still more refined ashlar stonework is found on the Schilliger House, which has a dentil cornice and quoins. This dwelling also displays an entrance with narrow transom and sidelights.[43]

FIGURE 1.16. Spangenberg House after the stylish remodeling of its entry portico in the American Colonial style in the 1920s.

The architectural detailing of the three houses is in keeping with the Greek Revival, but a definite stylistic attribution is perhaps unwise. During the first quarter of the nineteenth century, Germany had championed its own architectural version of a classical revival, so that many German-immigrant builders were presumably familiar with classical motifs before they set foot in St. Paul. Depending on how one wishes to argue the matter, the three houses could be either "German" or "American" in their architectural inspiration. It may also be the case that the Greek Revival style allowed German immigrants to express their Americanism without losing their sense of cultural identity.[44] In 1859, for example, St. Paul's largest German cultural society, the *Leseverein*, decided to build a *Deutsches Haus* for community meetings and German-language theatricals. The group named the building the "**Athenaeum**" (razed),

gave it a full-pedimented design that could easily have passed for Greek Revival, and then dedicated it according to the old German custom of the *Richtefest:*

> At the highest point of the structure a large bouquet of flowers was attached, the contractor of the building spoke a few words in praise of his trade, whereupon one of the members of the society, J. Betz, drank a toast to the success of the society and the building, tossing the empty glass to the sidewalk below. The *Leseverein* then extended an invitation to all members and friends to gather at a nearby restaurant for a light luncheon.[45]

As a general rule, architecture in early St. Paul was not a strong vehicle for nationalist sentiment. The vast majority of first-generation immigrant housing was

FIGURE 1.17.
Johan and Maria Magdalena
Schilliger House, 178 Goodrich Avenue
(moved from 314 North Smith Avenue).
This home was finely crafted by a
Swiss-German stonemason for his
own family.

FIGURE 1.18. Anton Waldman House, 445 North Smith Avenue, 1936. This view was captured by Depression-era photo-documentarian A. F. Raymond. Courtesy of the Minnesota Historical Society.

FIGURE 1.19. Martin Weber House, 202 McBoal Street. This tradesman's house hints at Greek Revival in the "broken pediment" formed by short eave returns.

indistinguishable from dwellings occupied by native-born residents of similar economic status. St. Paul's early German-speaking community, however, did produce one major building with indisputable Old World antecedents. Not surprisingly, it was built under the aegis of religion, which was often an outlet for ethnic assertion among nineteenth-century immigrant groups.

Although St. Paul's German population represented virtually all regions and religions of the fatherland, it contained a particularly large contingent of Catholics, many from Bavaria. When they first arrived in the early 1850s, they found the city's single Catholic parish already ethnically divided into French and Irish factions. They quickly formed a third camp: "The French Catholics celebrated mass at 7 o'clock on Sunday mornings and listened to a sermon in their language. They were followed by the German[s] to whom Father Keller preached in German; and at 11 o'clock the English speaking Catholics were edified with a sermon in their vernacular."[46]

In the mid-1850s, the Diocese of St. Paul permitted the German Catholics to form their own parish. Named in honor of the Assumption, the new parish was appropriately placed under the supervision of the Benedictine Order, whose widespread missionary work among German-Americans had been strongly supported by the Bavarian royal family. The first **Assumption Church** (razed), erected in 1856, was a plain wood-steepled stone building on West Ninth Street at the northeastern edge of Upper Town. Parish membership steadily increased over the next decade, so that by Christmas 1869 the original chapel could accommodate only half the faithful. "The church was too small," remarked the local German-language newspaper, "and the building of a new one [is] an urgent necessity."[47] Considering the importance

FIGURE 1.20. St. Paul Custom House and Post Office (razed), Fifth and Wabasha Streets, engraving, 1876. This was the most expensive building in the city on its completion.

of the undertaking, there undoubtedly was considerable discussion about designing the new edifice. Unfortunately, parish records silently leapfrog all these preliminaries. The only thing known with certainty is that in the spring of 1870, the parish pastor, Father Clement Staub, had in his possession a set of plans prepared by Eduard Riedel, a fifty-seven-year-old Munich architect in the employ of the Bavarian Court.[48]

Riedel's predecessor and mentor at the court was the eminent Bavarian architect Friedrich von Gaertner, who had been among the first to reject the classical revival dominating German architecture in the early nineteenth century. Instead, Gaertner had sought inspiration in the post-Roman building tradition of the early Middle Ages, especially as revealed in the churches of his own country and northern Italy. Working from these historical models, Gaertner helped inaugurate an extremely influential architectural movement known as the Romanesque Revival. His masterpiece, constructed in Munich during 1829–44, was the Ludwigskirche, a striking twin-towered basilica with boldly framed exterior planes broken by arcaded Roman arches on slender colonnettes.[49]

By the 1840s, the Romanesque Revival had crossed the Atlantic to the United States, where it assumed a number of names for what were essentially similar forms: "Romanesque," "Old Roman," "Norman," "Round Style," "Lombard." Adopted by the federal government for the new Smithsonian Institution Building, completed in Washington, D.C., in 1849, the Romanesque Revival eventually became quite popular for public buildings. Its blocky proportions had all the dignity of the Greek Revival, while its arcaded windows provided superior light and ventilation. A typical government example of the style appeared in the **St. Paul Custom House and Post Office** (razed), a $350,000 project completed in 1873 (Figure 1.20). Although this building aroused local interest as the city's first instance of granite construction, its design was uninspired. Ponderous without being powerful, it had none of the austere majesty of Riedel's **Assumption Church,** which was formally dedicated in October 1874, following five years of construction (Figures 1.21 and 1.22).[50]

At the time of the dedication ceremonies, observers clearly were fascinated by the European lineage of Assumption Church. As one newspaper reporter enthused, "The magnificent church . . . is built strictly after the drawings of a church which has a world wide reputation,

and which is located in Munich, Bavaria." The implication was that Riedel had presented the St. Paul congregation with a replica of the Ludwigskirche.[51] Although Gaertner's building may indeed have been the model for Assumption Church, Riedel's design was not a slavish copy of the original. For Assumption Church, Riedel retained the general Roman-arched detailing and twin-towered basilica plan of the Ludwigskirche but eliminated the extended arcades, compressed the massing of the front facade, and strengthened the horizontal lines of the towers. These alterations transformed Gaertner's highly ornamental design into an almost hauntingly ascetic composition, appropriately clothed in St. Paul's craggy native limestone. A similar austerity pervaded the church's three-aisled interior, which was surmounted by broad groined vaults springing from massive square columns. With justice, the St. Paul press lauded Assumption Church as "the most imposing church edifice in Minnesota, and perhaps, with one or two exceptions, in the entire Northwest."[52]

Costing nearly $200,000, the construction of Assumption Church almost bankrupted the German Catholic parish and sent its pastor into seclusion with a nervous breakdown. It also seems to have caused a certain amount of consternation among neighboring Protestant congregations who, in an age not known for its ecumenical spirit, were scarcely pleased to see their city's skyline dominated by a foreign Catholic shrine. It fell to the First Baptist Church, oldest of the local Protestant congregations, to redeem the honor of the Reformation. In the spring of 1872, while the walls of Assumption Church mounted steadily heavenward, the Baptist deacons announced their own plans to build "one of the most splendid church edifices in the West." The German Catholics might pride themselves on their European architect, but the Baptists went straight to Chicago. There they secured the services of William W. Boyington (1818–1898), a successful young architect who was busy rebuilding the city after its Great Fire of 1871.[53]

A prolific designer of hotels, churches, and railroad stations, Boyington is perhaps best remembered in his native city for a stone water tower erected near the downtown district in 1869. Still rearing its fantastic turreted battlements above Michigan Avenue, this structure belongs to a school of architectural enchantment known as the Gothic Revival, which first developed a following in the United States during the 1830s. Like the novels of Sir Walter Scott, which helped inspire the vogue, the Gothic Revival romantically blended valid medieval forms with beguiling nineteenth-century fictions. Popularized through the plan book designs of such American architects as Alexander Jackson Davis and Andrew Jackson Downing, the style challenged the measured order of the Greek Revival by championing an irregular floor plan, asymmetrical massing, bold vertical lines, and the angular Gothic arch. These picturesque features were said to harmonize more properly with the natural landscape, and to this same end, proponents urged the use of muted earth colors for buildings instead of the prevalent Greek Revival white.[54]

FIGURE 1.23.
Henry M. Knox House,
26 Irvine Park. This simple
version of the Gothic Revival
style was popular in eastern
suburbs during the mid-nineteenth
century but rarely seen in
St. Paul homes.

The Gothic Revival left its imprint on villas and cottages throughout the United States, but it never achieved the popularity of the Greek Revival for residential architecture. Despite all the arguments of its adherents, Gothicism remained vulnerable to charges of fanciful excess and literary eccentricity. The style seems to have been especially unappealing in newly settled regions like St. Paul, where people believed they were already living far too close to nature and expected architecture to provide a remedy. According to this perspective, white Greek Revival buildings did not disrupt the landscape, they civilized it. Only one Gothic Revival residence survives in St. Paul, the **Henry M. Knox House,** erected in 1860 by brothers J. Jay and Henry Knox, both local bankers (Figure 1.23). Although a severely plain example of the style, the building does have a characteristic steeply pitched gable with a pointed-arched window. Its most interesting feature, however, is its wood siding: the subdued green color is original, as is the board-and-batten construction, which often was used on Gothic Revival

buildings to suggest the vertical thrust of true medieval Gothic design.[55]

There also was an ecclesiastical version of the Gothic Revival, which had a far greater impact on American architecture. Chronologically and aesthetically, it overlapped the secular development of the style, but its origins and aims were quite different. It sprang from the religious convictions and historical researches of a group of English architects, churchmen, and scholars who during the 1830s and 1840s were intent on purifying the forms of Anglican worship. These reformers believed that Christian architecture had reached a pinnacle of perfection in the Gothic English churches of the Middle Ages and that other styles were spiritually debasing for church purposes. Through both their publications and construction projects, they stimulated a revival of Gothic church design that eventually infiltrated virtually all Protestant sects in England and the United States and lasted well into the twentieth century. The movement's impact was felt in St. Paul as early as 1851, when the city's Episcopal

congregation selected a "pointed" design for the small, board-and-batten **Christ Episcopal Church** (razed; Figure 1.24).[56]

By the early 1870s, when St. Paul's First Baptist congregation approached Chicago architect Boyington about planning their new church, it was a foregone conclusion that he would deliver a Gothic Revival design. Boyington's original drawing of the front facade still exists, and it presents a nicely balanced composition incorporating elements of fourteenth-century English church design, a style commonly called Decorated Gothic. A bold, four-staged tower with octagonal spire is offset by a steeply pitched, gabled block embracing a pointed-arched tripartite window with quatrefoil tracery. Directly below the window, a small porch echoes in miniature the gable end.[57]

Apparently, the First Baptist congregation was not completely satisfied with Boyington's work. It seems that they wanted a grander building. Although they retained the basic massing and detailing of his design, they raised the front gable fifteen feet and the steepled tower sixty feet above the original dimensions. These alterations were effected by master builder Monroe Sheire, a member of the congregation who served as both supervising architect and general contractor. When the **First Baptist Church** was completed according to this revised plan in 1875, the top of its spire rose a full 190 feet above the street, which was still 25 feet shy of the twin spires of the German Catholic Assumption Church (Figure 1.25). Overlooking this minor shortcoming, admirers of the new church asserted that "its massive tower [is] surmounted by the highest and most beautiful spire in the city."[58]

Unfortunately, the weight of the tower eventually caused serious problems in settling, which necessitated the removal of the spire and porch in 1945. A stubby replacement for the spire, added in 1967, does not do justice to the building.

Assumption Church and the First Baptist Church marked a turning point in St. Paul architecture. Unlike the crude, hastily prepared designs of the first capitol and first courthouse, these two buildings were self-assured, aesthetically assertive statements that took their role as public landmarks quite seriously. Their construction reflected the city's growing architectural sophistication as well as its expanding financial base. The First Baptist Church, for example, handsomely benefited from the generosity of Horace Thompson, who had settled in St. Paul in 1860 and amassed a fortune in banking,

railroading, and insurance. Initially underwriting the purchase of the church site, Thompson also contributed over one-third of the $120,000 construction cost.[59]

Like several other business luminaries of the 1860s, Thompson built his own residence on the extreme northeast edge of Lower Town in the exclusive, newly developed Lafayette Park district. Rejecting the egalitarian simplicity of the Greek Revival, Thompson selected an unabashedly patrician style known as the Italian Villa. Patterned after English interpretations of Italian country estates, the Italian Villa became popular in the eastern United States during the 1840s, appealing to the same romantic cravings that had inspired the secular phase of the Gothic Revival. But unlike the Gothic Revival, which seemed too artfully contrived for the tastes of most American home builders, the Italian Villa projected

FIGURE 1.26. Horace Thompson House (razed), 33 Woodward Avenue, early 1880s. This was typical of the rugged limestone Italianate Villas that once dotted Lower Town. Courtesy of the Minnesota Historical Society.

a straightforward elegance that managed to be both picturesque and sedate at the same time.[60]

Designed and constructed by local master builder J. D. Pollock in 1860, the **Horace Thompson House** was a classic masonry example of the Italian Villa style (razed; Figure 1.26). Its romantic qualities stemmed from its irregular massing and plan, its sweeping piazzas, and its boldly bracketed overhanging eaves. Its dignity derived from its tall corner tower, its aristocratically elongated windows with ornamental hoods, and its careful balancing of vertical and horizontal lines. At least two of Thompson's wealthy neighbors—Henry S. Sibley (elected Minnesota's first governor in 1858) and Elias F. Drake (president of St. Paul's first railroad)—also adopted the Italian Villa style. Unfortunately, the entire Lafayette

Park neighborhood was eliminated by twentieth-century freeway development.[61]

Two Italian Villas, however, survive in other parts of the city. They are the limestone **Burbank-Livingston-Griggs House** of 1863 and the wood-frame **Jacob Hinkel House** of 1873 (Figures 1.27 and 1.28). Both buildings substitute a central lantern for the side tower, a common variation. The Hinkel House is the simpler of the two designs. It was built for the St. Paul ice dealer Jacob Hinkel, who almost immediately would lose both his fortune and his house in the national economic meltdown of the mid-1870s. Located about two miles north of downtown St. Paul, the Hinkel House originally occupied a remote rural site. Although intended to be a picturesque country estate, the building has an unassuming

ST. PAUL'S FOUNDING YEARS **30** 1840–1875

FIGURE 1.27.
Jacob Hinkel House,
531 Brainerd Avenue. This
ice dealer's house sports a
cupola, as popular for farmhouses
as for suburban residences in the
pre–Civil War era.

FIGURE 1.28. Burbank-Livingston-Griggs House, 432 Summit Avenue, 1964. The sprawling Italianate porches were replaced at the turn of the century by simple neoclassical porticos. Photograph by Paul Iida; courtesy of the Minnesota Historical Society.

four-square quality. Without its lantern (which, in fact, is a restoration of the original feature), the Hinkel House would resemble those modest urban homes of the period that put on a few architectural airs—a cluster of brackets here, an irregular roofline there—as a pretense to the grand villa style.

The Burbank-Livingston-Griggs House is quite another matter. It is dramatically and persuasively an Italian Villa—or at least an American romanticized conception of one. When the building was completed in 1863, the local press praised it as a "splendid architectural ornament" that "would grace the finest streets of New York or any American city." The reference, in a way, was curious, since the new domicile was not truly on a street at all. At that time, Summit Avenue was a crooked carriage path threading the most distant of the city's bluff lines, high above and far removed from the riverfront bustle of the downtown district.[62] The building's original owner, James C. Burbank, was a classic American success story. Born in Vermont in 1822, Burbank had journeyed through several occupations in New York and Wisconsin before alighting in St. Paul in 1850 "without money and without friends." Recognizing that transportation was the key to St. Paul's future, he organized a small, packet-boat express business, added a few stage-coaches, and soon established a virtual monopoly on mail delivery and passenger travel in the state. Wisely, he sold out his interests before the railroads became serious competitors. Similar shrewdness prompted his purchase, in 1861, of a one-and-one-half-acre site on Summit Avenue,

which would become the most prestigious residential boulevard in St. Paul.[63]

On this secluded wooded spot, Burbank arranged to build an extraordinary country estate, spending over $20,000 in the process. Plans were drawn by Chicago architect Otis Leonard Wheelock, who at the time shared a practice with William W. Boyington.[64] Construction was supervised by J. D. Pollock, who had previously worked on Horace Thompson's Italian Villa. Displaying an irregular, asymmetrical plan that alternated sunshine and shadow on the rusticated stonework, the building embellished its bold cubiform planes with delicate detailing: slender round-arched windows with quoined surrounds, a richly bracketed cornice with pendants, and a finialed lantern resting lightly on the rooftop like a crown.

Burbank's fondness for lavish architectural statements seems to have extended into his commercial ventures. While president of the St. Paul Fire and Marine Company, for example, he oversaw the construction of a new company headquarters in the downtown district. Completed in 1870, the **St. Paul Fire and Marine Company** (razed; Figure 1.29) combined a mansard roof—then at the height of fashion—with a Venetian Gothic entrance arcade, giving a decidedly exotic flavor to the intersection of Jackson and Third Streets.[65]

More commonly, the mansard, or "French," roof was allied with Italian Villa detailing, as in the **Monroe Sheire House** (razed; Figure 1.30), designed and built by Sheire for his own family in 1866. Even before working on the First Baptist Church, Sheire had established a

FIGURE 1.31. Alexander Ramsey House, 265 South Exchange Street. A solid statesman of a house, as respectable and staid as the Minnesota governor who was its original owner.

reputation as the city's most successful master builder, and at least two of his residential designs have survived. They are the **Alexander Ramsey House** of 1872 and the **Anthony Yoerg House** of 1875 (Figures 1.31 and 1.32). All three buildings incorporate Italianate detailing, ranging from the stylish piazza of the Ramsey House to the minimal cornice bracketing of the Yoerg House. All also display an unfortunate squatness, accentuated by their mansard roofs. Sheire was perhaps more prolific than gifted as a designer.

The Ramsey House is noteworthy for its historical associations, being the family home of Alexander Ramsey, who served Minnesota as territorial governor, state governor, and U.S. senator. Open to the public as a historic site, the mansion retains its original fifteen-room interior plan, as well as many of its original furnishings.

The Yoerg House recalls a tradition of another sort. It was the residence of Bavarian immigrant Anthony Yoerg, who in 1848 opened St. Paul's first brewery near the Upper Landing, digging caves in the soft, sandstone river bluff to lager his brew. By 1871, Yoerg had at least ten local competitors, who primarily catered to the city's large German population. To expand his own operations, Yoerg moved across the river to the "West Side" and built a new brewery (razed) just below the bluff-top site of his future home. By the end of the century, the Yoerg Brewing Company had become one of the state's largest producers of beer, and it remained a family-run enterprise until its demise in 1952.[66]

The growth of St. Paul's brewing industry was only one of many signs during the 1870s that at some unheralded point the city had passed from a frontier village

FIGURE 1.32. Anthony Yoerg House, 215 West Isabel Street. A "French" roof was almost an architectural requisite for the prosperous home builder of the 1870s. The assertive neoclassical veranda is a later remodeling.

into a true metropolitan center. Gone were the trees from the riverbank, the log cabins of the first settlers, the sense of limitless space. In 1876, J. Fletcher Williams presented to the public his *History of the City of Saint Paul,* noting that "the old pioneers of our city and State were, one by one passing away, and the events of our early history, if not soon gathered and placed on permanent record, would be lost." A similar nostalgia filled the local press, which even bemoaned the fact that the city's parks—once notorious for their wild state—were unable to support a respectable squirrel population.[67] It was, indeed, the end of an era, more so than people suspected at the time. During the next decade, St. Paul would enter a period of such profound economic and architectural transformation that the 1870s themselves quickly faded into quaint and brittle remoteness.

CHAPTER 2

St. Paul Comes of Age

1875 – 1920

In 1873, the year after Jay Cooke's Northern Pacific Railway extended across Minnesota, his financial empire collapsed. A run on eastern banks ensued, bursting the speculative bubble that had simultaneously fueled railroad expansion and swollen western land values. The following economic depression held eastern cities and farmlands in its grip through the remainder of the decade.

In spite of the woes of its eastern backers, St. Paul's transformation from prairie town to metropolis continued to move forward. Writing in 1876, J. Fletcher Williams noted that the financial revulsion "was scarcely felt here, beyond a slight stringency of the money market and a dullness in real estate. . . . Few or none were in debt, and all in a condition to laugh at panics." The city's development did in fact slow for the next few years, but eastern observers registered constant surprise at the continuing population surge of the midwestern cities at the heart of the real estate and railroading bubble. Between 1870 and 1880, St. Paul's population doubled from 20,030 to 41,473, with a third of that coming in the latter half of the decade. In the next three years, with eastern money beginning to loosen up, the figure would double again.[1]

The expansion of the city's geographic area was equally explosive. Early maps of St. Paul and Minneapolis show two cities separated by a broad crook in the Mississippi River and a ten-mile overland route. In the mid-1880s,

St. Paul almost tripled in size, annexing thirty-five square miles of new territory and pushing its western limit to the border of an equally expansive Minneapolis. Now standing shoulder to shoulder, the two rivals were indeed "Twin Cities" (Map 2.1).

One of the most revealing signs of St. Paul's transformation from village to metropolis was the rapid escalation of its wholesale trade. This was a mark not only of its internal growth but of the increasing reach of its businesses into the developing areas of the Northwest, particularly along the new rail lines. In 1876 civic leaders boasted that they would one day join New York and Chicago as "the third great city of the future." Yet total sales of St. Paul jobbers barely exceeded $20 million. By 1890 sales exceeded $120 million, and the boast courted reality.[2]

Young commercial centers on the midland prairies led the way out of the depression in large part because of their positioning in the burgeoning rail network. Many of them—Omaha, Kansas City, and Wichita, as well as the Twin Cities—were perceived by investors uncowed by current economic conditions as the great metropolises of the future, with Chicago invariably cited as the model. Each continued to attract streams of settlers and money from eastern cities whose banks, factories, and commercial establishments showed few signs of life in their home states.

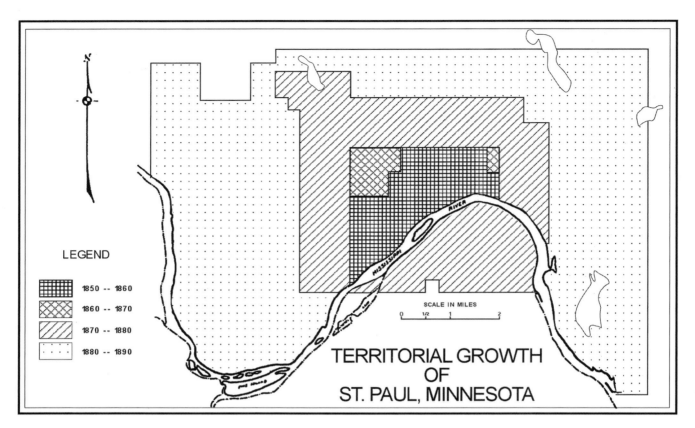

LEGEND

▦	1850 -- 1860
▨	1860 -- 1870
▨	1870 -- 1880
⋯	1880 -- 1890

SCALE IN MILES
0   1/2   1   2

TERRITORIAL GROWTH
OF
ST. PAUL, MINNESOTA

MAP 2.1. An adaptation of Calvin Schmid's map in *Social Saga of Two Cities* (1937), showing the extension of the city's boundaries into farmland and as yet unsettled wilderness in the 1880s. Courtesy of the Minnesota Historical Society.

St. Paul had the benefit of two great rail systems: Jay Cooke's Northern Pacific and the St. Paul, Minneapolis, and Manitoba, created from the ashes of the St. Paul and Pacific in 1879 and soon to be reorganized again as the Great Northern. The rails constructed by these companies created a continuous link between the factories of the East, the warehouses that were already displacing one of St. Paul's earliest residential neighborhoods, and the farms and cities of the West. Both lines eventually paid tribute to the same master, St. Paul entrepreneur James J. Hill, who ruled his transcontinental empire from an office in Lower Town.

When Hill first alighted in St. Paul as a clerk for a steamship company in 1857, the term *Lower Town* applied to the entire residential and commercial community associated with the "Lower Landing" at the foot of Jackson Street. During the 1880s, Lower Town acquired a more restricted sense of purpose and place. It evolved into a pure warehouse district, eventually embracing a section bounded by Jackson Street, Olive Street, Third Street

(renamed Kellogg Boulevard), and Seventh Street (Map 2.2). In this district, according to eastern observer Conde Hamlin, were "some of the largest houses in the country" for drugs, hardware, dry goods, groceries, boots, shoes, fur goods, hats, gloves, harness, and saddlery— "massive structures [that] well nigh shut the sunlight out of the narrow streets on which they stand."[3]

In 1875, 70 percent of St. Paul's residents lived within a mile's walk of Lower Town. But as the downtown area became increasingly commercial during the 1880s, old settlers and new immigrants alike boarded a recently expanded streetcar system for outlying residential neighborhoods in Dayton's Bluff to the east, Arlington Hills to the north, Frogtown to the northwest, and "West" St. Paul across the Mississippi to the south. The wealthy congregated in swelling numbers on fashionable Summit Avenue and on the surrounding "Hill District" immediately to the west of downtown. A few adventuresome souls were even so bold as to settle four and more miles away from the urban core in the railroad

"suburbs" of St. Anthony Park to the northwest, Burlington Heights to the southeast, or Merriam Park dead west of downtown (Figure 2.1), or in the exclusive Como Lake community of Warrendale. All of these were in the corporate city limits, but each was an island of settlement surrounded by as yet undeveloped land.[4]

The city's ascendant position in what was then known as the Northwest set the stage for its dramatic emergence as a major urban center. But the stage would have remained empty, or at best offered a chaotic show of haphazard and makeshift construction, if St. Paul had failed to make significant improvements in both the size and the capabilities of the local architectural and engineering professions. Indeed, the story of St. Paul's maturation as a built environment is largely the story of how those professions grew up.

The first generation of buildings in each of the nascent urban centers of the Midwest emanated from tradesmen and master builders with little or no architectural training. A master builder, simply defined, was a carpenter or mason who designed his own projects. Historically, master builders have often preceded architects in social and economic circumstances that could not yet sustain a profession charged exclusively with building design and supervision. In much earlier and less frenzied times, master builders had created some of the great monuments of Western civilization. But in the frontier midwestern American economy, where all classes of buildings were

in a constant shortage, the master builder rarely had time to devote to anything other than the practical necessity of fulfilling an immediate need. Apart from the perusal of plan books and a visual inspection of the buildings within a day's carriage ride, his education took place with a tool in hand.

In St. Paul's frontier period few of its residents would have cared about or even recognized the benefits of hiring one person to design a building and another to erect it. The Sheire brothers' rugged rendition of the toney Second Empire style out of the bedrock on which the city sat pleased the Alexander Ramsey family well enough, just as their paring down of the style into a wooden box for Anthony Yoerg must have satisfied the West Side brewer's desire for a modicum of taste.

As St. Paul's building stock grew, the most ambitious of the master builders achieved enough wealth and reputation to rise in progressive stages above their bricks-and-mortar beginnings. Some began to assume a largely managerial role, with employees doing the hands-on work. By the end of the post–Civil War boom that ushered in the Ramsey House commission, Monroe Sheire had achieved this stage. Master builders with a strong suit in design could then take a second step, which involved considerable financial risk: severing construction from the firm's operations altogether. This was achieved by numerous master builders in the 1870s, with E. P. Bassford leading the way. Anyone who followed this

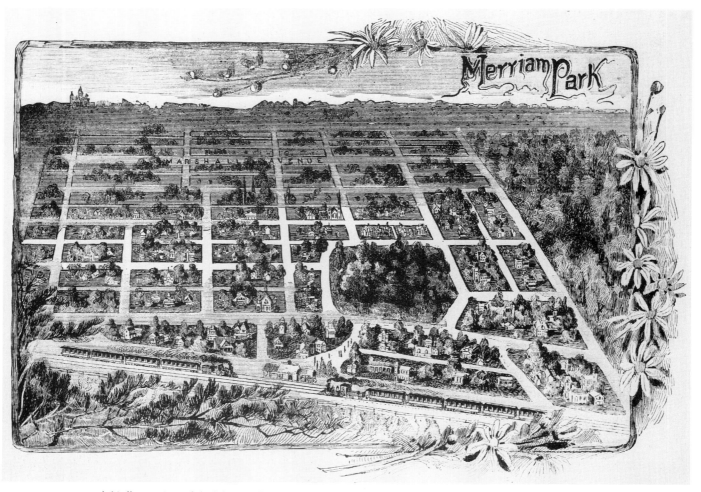

FIGURE 2.1. A bird's-eye view of the Merriam Park plan, published in the regional promotional tabloid *Northwest Magazine* in 1886. Courtesy of the Minnesota Historical Society.

route became an "architect" in the parlance of the day, even though that professional position could be attained simply by narrowing one's line of work rather than by achieving real expertise in all the tasks required of an architect.[5]

To grasp the difference between what was accomplished by these early master builders and the trained architects who would follow in their wake, we have only to look at the city before and after the great building boom of the mid-1880s. In 1892, at the brink of yet another severe depression, a local booster bent on convincing an eastern skeptic of the city's unstoppable progress might have taken him on a downtown stroll through three decades simply by walking away from the river. Beginning just above the Lower Landing at the foot of Jackson, Third Street (now Kellogg Boulevard) offered

a view of the city in its architectural infancy: rows of coarsely ornamented store and shop buildings whose character was primarily determined by the rough local materials (Figure 2.2). The piling up of limestone and iron exuded a certain elemental strength, often more than the construction in fact possessed, but little sense of artistic arrangement or association. These were buildings that did not linger on the drawing board and would not linger on the city's streets, either. Though trumpeted during their construction as the city's first "permanent" buildings, nearly all would be gone by the turn of the century.[6]

Fourth Street, particularly its long brick rows between Sibley and Wacouta Streets, showed a few more rudiments of architecture at work (Figure 2.3). A gable jutted upward to break the monotony of the long, flat roofline,

FIGURE 2.2.
The north side of
Third Street from
Minnesota to Robert
Streets, 1862. Most of
these buildings (all razed)
were constructed of local
Platteville limestone or
of brick imported from
Chicago or St. Louis.
Courtesy of the
Minnesota Historical
Society.

FIGURE 2.3.
An elevated view of the north
side of Fourth Street between
Wacouta and Sibley Streets, ca. 1900.
A continuous wall of three- to
five-story warehouses lined many of
Lower Town's streets (all those
pictured razed). Courtesy of the
Minnesota Historical Society.

stocky towers anchored a couple of corners, and each building had its own distinct combination of colors, window openings, and applied ornament. Architectural "devices" leaped across the faces of the buildings, but they were not yet driven by a trained artistic sensibility. A product of the nascent stages of the 1880s building boom, they were an easy target for eastern critics, who perceived them as "very rationally constructed but most irrationally ornamented," and went on to bewail the condition of the local architectural profession. Many of these buildings persevered until the Modernist rebuilding of the city core in the 1960s, though in a much-altered condition. Only fragments, most of them below grade or behind new facings, survive today.[7]

If our local jingoist had been astute enough to skirt the western edge of Lower Town at Sibley or Jackson, when he got to Fifth, or even better, Sixth, he could have shown off the city in all its Gay Nineties glory (Figure 2.4). A solid march of commercial buildings vied in sophistication, if not in size, with the best of New York and Chicago. Each building displayed the pride and confidence of the architectural hand behind it, but more than that, it breathed with some of the personality of its designer. These were buildings that offered such an embarrassment of riches that until the past few decades the jury was out on whether the emphasis belonged on the first or last word of the phrase.[8]

So far, our eastern skeptic has been led by exclusively commercial buildings. The scales are off but one of his eyes. To remove the other, our booster would only have to take a stroll down Summit Avenue, which remains today the most intact Victorian boulevard in America.

FIGURE 2.5. Norman W. Kittson House, Summit and Selby Avenues, 1886. The most lavishly appointed mansion in the city was torn down barely twenty years after completion to make way for the Cathedral of St. Paul. Courtesy of the St. Paul Public Library.

Initial construction on the avenue was simple enough, consisting largely of wood cottages in bucolic surroundings, many of them second homes for the wealthy who still crowded into Lower Town. But with the explosion away from the riverfront in the late 1870s and early 1880s, Summit Avenue quickly became a select address.

The architectural climax of the avenue's early years was the lavishly appointed **Norman W. Kittson House.** Colonel Kittson, as he liked to be called, built his mansion on the magnificent elevated site where the Cathedral of St. Paul now stands (Figure 2.5). The house exemplified high architectural style in the early 1880s, before the great influx of trained architects into the city. Its design bristled with French Renaissance "features": an elaborately sculpted entry, densely ornamented window hoods, and a mansard roof well stocked with dormers and chimneys.

Farther up the avenue, during the same years that Kittson was memorializing his entrepreneurial success, rising young architect LeRoy S. Buffington (1847–1931) introduced Summit Avenue to the full-blown Queen Anne style in the **Shipman-Greve House** (Figure 2.6). This was an epoch-making style in American architecture. Though rooted in the Old World, it signaled the beginning of an emancipation from European fads; for many the style also signaled the end of an era of bad taste.[9]

The birth of the Queen Anne style took place in England, but it was England in the sway of the Arts and Crafts movement, stressing simplicity in design, honesty in construction, the use of local materials, and the dignity of artistically guided labor. A romance with medieval domestic imagery pervaded this movement on both sides of the Atlantic, but the imagery proved adaptable to a great range of modern settings and purposes.

Among American architects and builders, the Queen Anne style, particularly a suburban variant of it with beetling gables and broad plaster and wood surfaces, came to typify the new aesthetic. It first reached mass public attention at the Centennial Exposition in Philadelphia in 1876. The "Queen Anne" buildings that dominated that exposition thus simultaneously celebrated America's historic ties with England and its aspirations to carve out its place as an independent culture.[10]

The Queen Anne fashion overwhelmed American domestic architecture just at the time that the first wave of trained architects washed into the Northwest. They were quick to exploit its two-faced association with American individualism and patrician, Old World traditions and wealth. An air of informality was one of the telling marks of the Queen Anne style in this country; its multiple gables, juxtapositions of diverse materials, and sprawling plan permitted the architect to dispense with both the balanced compositions and the rigid, processional floor plans of the classically inspired styles. It was also permissible for a finished house to show off its rough materials. The extensive exposure of stone, brick, timber, and shingles constituted an aesthetic statement in itself and was a key moment in the development of a distinctly American language of expression out of the raw materials of construction.

The Shipman-Greve House remains the finest local expression of this aesthetic. Even while it was under construction, neighbors sprang up about it that treated the forthright, natural complexion of the Queen Anne style as a paste makeup to which every exoticism and historicism in the American architect's design kit would soon adhere. Yet the new emphasis on the expressiveness of the materials per se and the informality of the floor plan would remain.[11]

A third house on Summit Avenue captures the climactic mood of the city's boom years. Architecturally, it sits comfortably with the Jackson Street commercial row. In 1887 railroad magnate James J. Hill hired Boston architects Peabody and Stearns to design a house for him in the American Romanesque manner introduced by eastern architect H. H. Richardson. The **James J. Hill House** displays the rough and massive stonework, great low-sprung arches, carefully contained Romanesque and Byzantine carving, and monumental treatments of every projection that were signatures of the style (Figure 2.7). The design that came out of Hill's autocratic consultations with the architects was a triumph of understated magnificence amid the more flagrant displays of artistic prowess going up around it.[12]

The story of St. Paul's transformation from the crude structures of its river streets and the pomposity of the

FIGURE 2.7.
James J. Hill House,
240 Summit Avenue.
The stone as well as the
architectural firm was
imported from New England
to assure that the outcome
would meet eastern standards—
a rare practice in St. Paul.

Kittson mansion to the grand elevator buildings of Fifth and Sixth Streets and the sophisticated monumentality of the Hill House is at its base the story of individual designers and their work with an increasingly wealthy and sophisticated clientele. Together they produced the mercurial landscape noted by a writer for *Northwest Magazine:* "A traveler who comes to St. Paul only once a year must every time get his bearings afresh, the landmarks alter so fast."[13]

St. Paul's city government played a seminal role. It would not boast its own architectural office for another generation, but the bisection of the city by both a broad river and a complex rail network forced it to establish an engineering office as early as 1873. The Common Council established a Board of Public Works with five commissioners to handle contract lettings and to oversee the operation of a city engineer's office. Appointed by the mayor and confirmed by the council, the commissioners were not required to have professional engineering training, but their office staff most certainly was. In the 1880s, under chief city engineer Leonard W. Rundlett, this office made its mark in a series of spectacular bridges that introduced travelers to the city growing at their foot.[14]

The Seventh Street Improvement of 1883–85 is arguably the clearest example in the city's history of an engineering challenge elevated to artistic accomplishment. During the 1870s, St. Paul's expansion to the east had been hampered by the lack of a suitable crossing over the Phalen Creek–Trout Brook valley separating the downtown district from Dayton's Bluff. By the end of the decade the problem was exacerbated by the evolution of the valley into the city's main rail corridor, which meant that future road construction would require a system of viaducts. The Seventh Street Improvement, proclaimed "the heaviest piece of public work ever attempted in the city," escorted the new highway across the valley. It consisted of four major elements: a roadway embankment 80 feet high, 640 feet long, and 66 feet wide; a 320-foot iron truss bridge across the tracks of one railroad; and a double-arch stone bridge across the tracks of another.[15]

The **Seventh Street Stone Arch Bridge** was the climactic component of the project (Figures 2.8 and 2.9). Its design was the work of assistant city engineer William Albert Truesdell (1845–1909), an 1867 graduate of the University of Wisconsin who had apprenticed with the St. Paul, Minneapolis and Manitoba Railway. Truesdell faced a number of challenges. Since the bridge crossed the tracks at a sharp angle, it required a skewed design, which placed special demands on engineer, stonecutter, and mason alike. The problems common to skewed construction were compounded by the fact that "nothing of this kind had ever been built in this western country," so that "very few of our masons in St. Paul had ever seen one, and no one knew anything about the stone-cutting necessary."[16]

FIGURE 2.8.
Seventh Street Stone
Arch Bridge as it appears
today, near the entry
to parkland that has
replaced the Trout
Creek railroad gulley.

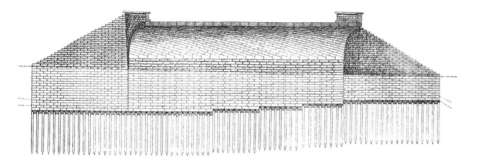

FIGURE 2.9.
A longitudinal section of
the Seventh Street Stone
Arch Bridge, as shown in a
working drawing by
W. A. Truesdell, ca. 1883.
Note the trapezoidal shape
of the stones lining the arches.
Private collection.

Truesdell adopted the "helicoidal," or "spiral," method, in which the arch stones, or voussoirs, are cut with curved surfaces so that they form a series of spiraling parallel courses of great strength and stability. Although fairly common in the British Isles, where the technology was invented, according to an American structural engineer of the period the very study of the subject was considered so "intricate" in the United States that it was usually "abandoned with disgust."[17]

Despite the technical difficulties, Truesdell recognized that the helicoidal method had one overriding practical advantage for the St. Paul project: all of the voussoirs (except for the face ring) are of the same size and shape so "that one set of patterns answers for all . . . and when

the stone-cutters are once taught to cut a stone no further difficulty is encountered." The voussoirs were custom cut at a limestone quarry near Mankato, Minnesota, and the structure was completed without incident in December 1884. On the occasion of Truesdell's death in 1909, his professional colleagues eulogized his contribution to "the most important piece of masonry in the city."[18]

Another Rundlett assistant, Andreas W. Munster, joined the staff while the Seventh Street viaduct was under construction. Born in Bergen, Norway, and educated at the Chalmers Institute in Gothenburg, Sweden, Munster belonged to a generation of Norwegian American engineers who would have a profound influence on

FIGURE 2.10.
Colorado Street Bridge,
ca. 1900. The longest span
masonry-arch bridge in
Minnesota was necessitated
by the dense flow of
commercial traffic that
once drove beneath it.
Courtesy of the Minnesota
Historical Society.

public works in Chicago, Milwaukee, and Minneapolis, as well as in St. Paul. During his first years as city bridge engineer, Munster had the unusual opportunity of supervising the construction of all three Mississippi River roadway crossings in the downtown area: the **Robert Street Bridge** (1886), the **Smith Avenue Bridge** (1888), and the cantilever truss **Wabasha Street Bridge** (1890). All provided several generations of service before being replaced by structures with a greater carrying capacity. One major structure directly attributable to Munster has survived, the skewed stone-arch **Colorado Street Bridge** (1888) on the West Side (Figure 2.10). Anticipating the concrete construction of the future, he utilized a cost-effective way of constructing the arch out of rubble held together by the adhesive power of the mortar. This experiment was particularly bold in view of the fact that the structure's seventy-foot span was (and still is) the longest masonry-arch highway bridge in the state.[19]

Within the city's nascent architectural community, two men, Abraham Radcliffe and Augustus F. Knight, had practiced their profession from the early years of statehood. But in their prime years—the 1870s—they saw some of the city's plum commissions fall into other hands. Under frontier conditions, the primary role of a local architect was to handle building projects of a size or expense that exceeded the capabilities of master builders. One could expect a local architect's hand in large churches, schools, and civic buildings—with an emphasis

on the word *large*. When, on the other hand, a remarkable design was required, outside talent more often got the call. That is precisely what happened in most of frontier St. Paul's moments of real architectural splendor (see Figures 1.25 and 1.28). They were the joint effort of outside architects and local master builders.

Ultimately, all of Radcliffe's and Knight's major buildings—including Radcliffe's widely publicized Kittson mansion—shared the ignominious fate of the humbler structures around them; they came down with scarcely a note of their passing. All that survived demolition was a handful of interior set pieces cannibalized for new construction. The lasting contribution of Radcliffe and Knight to a city that so readily discarded their buildings would be an indirect one, found in the legacy of the score of draftsmen who came to work for them in their twilight.[20]

LeRoy S. Buffington deserves some mention here because of his activity in St. Paul in the early 1870s. He began as a young associate of Radcliffe but by the time of his independent practice (1874) had moved to Minneapolis and begun to concentrate most of his energies in that city. The 1881 State Capitol was the best known of his St. Paul designs.[21]

Radcliffe and Knight supplied the cultivating medium for the local profession by attracting and training a pool of draftsmen/designers who would remain in the city after establishing their own practices. By 1886, a local publication could justly claim that "one-third of the architects of St. Paul and Minneapolis graduated" from Radcliffe's office alone. For most, this would be the only training from which they would "graduate." Many arrived just out of eighth grade and would begin as clerks and errand boys. Others were former builders who knew something about design, ultimately leaving Radcliffe's office as designers who knew something about building.[22]

Among the converted master builders, only a single man, Edward Payson Bassford (1837–1912), succeeded in bridging the gap from mud town to metropolis. Son of a prominent house builder in Calais, Maine, Bassford began as a carpenter but showed enough early promise that his father sent him to Boston to apprentice under architect Charles Painter. After a short stint in the Civil War, Bassford returned to Maine to enter a brief partnership with Thomas J. Sparrow in Portland. In 1866, he moved to St. Paul, where he would remain for the rest of his professional life.[23]

After first settling in to the work he still knew best, contracting and building, Bassford advanced his architectural training by joining Radcliffe as a draftsman. By 1875, he was competing with him for major commercial commissions, and in a few years had eclipsed the career of his mentor. The Fourth Street retail and warehouse district was almost entirely of his (and his draftsmen's) creation. In fact, all of the buildings on the northwest side of the street between Wacouta and Jackson Streets came out of Bassford's office.[24]

When Bassford's independent practice was just getting under way, money often determined not only which style the builder got but how much. For example, round- or elliptical-headed windows were in vogue even for the most pedestrian of buildings. Under a limited budget, the builder laid up a simple stone arch over the windows; with a few more dollars, the individual stones in the arch could be cut rather than hewn, so that they had a smooth face; but neither treatment made much of a stylistic statement. More money yet, however, would buy an enlarged, projecting keystone at the top of the arch, or individual stones with deeply recessed margins ("rusticated"), giving a hint of the Italianate style. Or the arch could be provided with a protruding hood and side pilasters to produce a vaguely French Renaissance look. At the top of the economic scale, the arch could spring from miniature columns and elaborately carved capitals, in a version of the Gothic or Romanesque. It was all money; the more the builder had, the more style he got.

By the time of Bassford's ascendancy, fine materials and stylistic character were no longer regarded as extras. Except in the most utilitarian buildings, a long array of choices became an assumed part of the building's conception. The materials began to be exploited for their color or texture or historical associations, with much less regard to cost once the hurdle of masonry had been crossed. In Bassford's succession of blocks on Fourth Street, bricks were color matched to Lake Superior brownstone, long belts of buff limestone and sills broke

FIGURE 2.11.

John Armstrong Double House in its present location at 225 Eagle Parkway, near the foot of Chestnut Street. Though nearby, this site is quite different from its original setting in a tangle of densely populated streets just north of where Xcel Energy Center stands today.

up uniform red walls, rectangular windows were interspersed with arched ones, and iron was cast or pressed into a pattern looking like carved wood or assembled masonry units.

Bassford was probably the first architect in the city to practice a thorough-going eclecticism. Current styles for Bassford, whether Italianate, French Renaissance, Queen Anne, or Romanesque, opened infinite design and material possibilities while imposing no restrictions whatever regarding their "proper" combination. He cobbled together whatever mix seemed to fit the building requirements and his aesthetic whims and left describing the overall result to newspapermen and the architectural historians of the future.

Two clarion examples survive of Bassford's eclecticism. The **John Armstrong Double House** of 1884 (now commonly known as the Armstrong-Quinlan House) is the last remaining vestige of the grand residences that once lined Summit Avenue's descent to the downtown. Ironically, it has been moved at great expense to an inauspicious site at the edge of the Irvine Park neighborhood a half mile away (Figure 2.11). It could, in the expanded and vague use of the term today, be called Queen Anne on account of its gables and irregular profile. But its turrets and carved ornament drew from the current Romanesque Revival vocabulary, and the brickwork was laid up

in patterns common to vernacular commercial buildings of the period.

The other survivor is a calmer and later design, but it is equally diffident of stylistic boundaries. Near the northern edge of Lower Town, Bassford erected a three-story store and flats building for Louisiana investor Vincent Walsh in 1888. The **Walsh Building** has a proper neoclassical cornice adorned with "modillions," a succession of barlike projections; the cast-iron supports that run through the ground-floor storefronts are either evenly turned columns or flattened and ridged ("fluted") piers; and the second-story windows are arched to collectively form something like a classical arcade (Figure 2.12). All of these are loosely inspired by the Italian Renaissance. However, zigzag decoration like nothing that came out of Rome or Venice crowns the piers, and the windows are tied together with carved brownstone drip caps recalling medieval, not neoclassical, decoration.

In the climactic years of his career, when Bassford was in his fifties, he began to design in a manner more akin to that of his increasingly scholarly younger peers. The **Merchants National Bank** (now the **McColl Building**) of 1890 is as close to stylistic purity as the architect was ever to achieve (Figure 2.13). It is also the sole surviving fragment of the magnificent Jackson Street row of office buildings and warehouses noted earlier. Built of

FIGURE 2.12.
Walsh Building, 191 East Eighth Street,
now stands in solitary splendor on a street
once lined with large business blocks.

FIGURE 2.13.
Merchants National Bank,
366 Jackson Street, as it
appeared in the first edition
of *Gibson's Souvenir of
St. Paul*, ca. 1902.

rock-faced Portage Entry brownstone and elaborately detailed with acanthus leaf carvings, it is an energetic if somewhat chaotic local example of the Richardsonian Romanesque style then being given a stricter treatment in the James J. Hill House.

Bassford's outstanding achievement was the **Germania Life Insurance Company Building** of 1889, a massive high-rise that stood at Fourth and Minnesota Streets (razed; Figure 2.14). Of the scores of historic buildings demolished during the Capital Centre project of the 1960s, it was one of the few whose demise was publicly lamented. Bassford melded Romanesque and classical forms together in a manner much like his contemporaries in Chicago but with his own colorful sense of material combinations. This seminal design completed Bassford's transformation from master builder with indifferent artistic skills to an architect of genuine distinction.

Bassford's greatest legacy, like Radcliffe's, would consist not in that fragment of his building production that survives but in the corps of draftsmen who cut their teeth as designers on his commissions. The closest to him in spirit was German-born, Wisconsin-raised Augustus F. Gauger (1852–1929). Like Bassford, Gauger arrived in St. Paul with a smattering of architectural experience behind him; in Gauger's case it consisted of a few years with an unidentified architect in Chicago. After working for Bassford in the mid-1870s, Gauger launched into his own career in 1878. By the early 1880s, he was doing for contours what Bassford did with surfacing materials: exploring every conceivable way to combine them.[25]

FIGURE 2.15.

Schornstein Grocery and
Saloon, 707 Wilson Avenue,
an architectural selling point of
the East Side in *Picturesque
Dayton's Bluff* (1905).
Courtesy of the Minnesota
Historical Society.

The outlines of Gauger's buildings jump restlessly from roof to dormer to chimney and tower. His residential designs in particular seem to have been elaborated with little thought of what havoc wind and snow might wreak. As a result, though a great many of his houses survive, most of them have been shorn of their most characteristic elements. Among the more intact is his own house and several of its neighbors built for the Warrendale Improvement Company on what is now West Como Boulevard.

Following Bassford's lead, Gauger stubbornly clung to Italianate detailing in the old 1870s manner—fanciful brackets, window hoods, carved capitals wherever they could be squeezed in—as the last word in ornament. His most ambitious designs have the look of an old-timer who bought an up-to-date suit but stuffed it with the collars and ties already in his closet. Gauger's commercial designs have fared somewhat better than his residential

projects, as they tend to keep their ornamentation within the general contour of the building. His 1884 **Schornstein Grocery and Saloon**, a National Register property in Dayton's Bluff, is among the finest examples of his particular brand of architectural exuberance (Figure 2.15). Sober cast-iron storefronts on the ground floor give rise to a profusion of projecting bays, pilasters, dormers, towers, and chimneys growing out of the second and third stories.

Existing local architectural offices could provide only a small patch of the fabric required for a city that aspired to the architectural garb of a Chicago or a St. Louis. At the beginning of its building boom, St. Paul simply lacked the depth of local talent and training opportunities to propel the city into its burgeoning opportunities. Outside help was the answer, and in the early to mid-1880s architects arrived in the city from every potential source of architectural talent: established architectural

FIGURE 2.16.
W. W. Bishop House,
513 Summit Avenue. This
house shows a grafting of
Germanic neoclassicism
onto the American
Queen Anne style.

offices, architectural schools, and the increasingly skilled immigrant population. Their arrival spelled the dawn of a new age—some might say the Golden Age—in St. Paul building.

First to make a mark among the new breed of architects was George Wirth (1851–1921). Born in Germany, Wirth immigrated to the United States at the age of eighteen. In 1871 he enrolled at Cornell College (now Cornell University), which in that year became the third school in the country to offer an architectural curriculum. After Cornell, Wirth returned to Europe for further study and an architectural tour of the sort that would soon become a fashionable necessity for architects in this country.[26]

As a result of these experiences, Wirth arrived in St. Paul in 1879 with two feathers in his cap that no other local architect could boast of: academic training and the benefit of European travel and observation. He was quick to capitalize. Within four years, ten mansions of his design went up on Summit Avenue alone. Unfortunately, history has been singularly unkind to the prolific work coming out of both his St. Paul office and the highly successful Duluth office to follow. The two St. Paul buildings that became his calling card, the **National German-American Bank** at Fourth and Robert Streets and the **Rufus Jefferson House** on Summit Avenue (both built in 1883), have long since disappeared, along with

his other major commercial projects and all but a handful of his houses.[27]

One of Wirth's Summit Avenue mansions remains close to its original state. The **W. W. Bishop House** of 1887, designed during a brief partnership with Abraham Haas, displays Wirth's skill in organizing very complex compositions (Figure 2.16). The house has no fewer "features" than many of Gauger's designs, but they are drawn from a unified and distinctly Germanic vocabulary, and none overshadow the imposing outlines of the overall design. Family connections and the downturn in St. Paul building drew Wirth to Duluth in 1892, where he sustained a successful practice for several more years.

Not long after Wirth's arrival in St. Paul, an architect set up local shop with nothing in the way of credentials apart from a few years of apprenticeship with his father. In this respect he was little different from the master builders that preceded him. But J. Walter Stevens (1856–1937) soon set himself apart from the self-taught and office-trained architects of St. Paul's pioneer years by an uncanny ability to attract and utilize the talents of a host of peripatetic draftsmen circulating through midwestern cities. Harvey Ellis (1852–1904), revered by many then and now as one of the greatest architectural artists of his era, drifted through in 1886–87, and Stevens's designs suddenly turned both more monumental and more engaging. Many of Ellis's projected schemes proved a bit too

FIGURE 2.17.
Noyes Brothers and Cutler Wholesale Drug Warehouse, Sixth and Sibley Streets. At the time of its completion in 1908, this was the largest drug warehouse in the world.

fantastic for St. Paul tastes and pocketbooks and went no further than the drafting board and the trade journals. But with the support of Ellis and his peers, Stevens also produced a score of commercial buildings that would become some of Lower Town's defining monuments.[28]

Of the half dozen remaining Stevens buildings in Lower Town, each remarkable in its own way, at least one may well have engaged the talent of Ellis: the mammoth **Noyes Brothers and Cutler Wholesale Drug Warehouse** fronting Mears Park (Figure 2.17). No other building in the city would acquire so powerful a succession of ground-floor arcades nor so engrossing an interplay of stone and brick. "If present plans are carried out," crowed a St. Paul newspaper at the end of 1887, "its new store and warehouse will be the finest in the United States used in the wholesaling of drugs and chemicals."

Two years passed, however, before construction began, and then only to a considerably reduced plan. The building expanded to the rear during the Panic of 1893, but it had to wait until 1908 for its final bays facing the park.[29]

Several other Lower Town projects carrying Ellis's stamp as a designer were built in 1887, most notably the triptych of florid **DeCoster** and **Mayall Blocks** on Jackson Street (razed; Figures 2.4 and 2.18). Two of these were rendered by draftsman William McLaughlin in an imitation of Ellis's style; all were demolished in the Modernist enthusiasm of the Capital Centre project with little recognition of their merit. McLaughlin would go on to create some of the most distinctive Richardsonian Romanesque monuments in Sioux City, Iowa, but in 1887 and 1888 he was busy with the flood of commercial commissions coming into Stevens's office.

FIGURE 2.18.

Mayall Block, 381 Jackson Street (razed). William McLaughlin's picturesque 1887 rendering was published in *American Architect*, the nation's foremost architectural journal.

Only one major project of McLaughlin's brief tenure with Stevens still stands: the eight-story **Germania Bank Building** at Wabasha and Fifth Streets (Figure 2.19). Although obviously inspired by H. H. Richardson's forms and imagery, it terminates with a flat roof and an overhanging, modillioned cornice more akin to Renaissance palazzi than to the gabled rooflines of Richardson's buildings. Similar revisionist uses of Richardsonian Romanesque were occurring in Boston and Chicago, but 1888—the year the Germania Building was designed—is surprisingly early for the appearance of such a hybrid in St. Paul. Like all of Stevens's Richardsonian designs

in the city, it has been credited to Ellis on few grounds other than its quality and style. The nation's foremost architectural journal, *American Architect*, published a beautiful but unsigned rendering of it in 1892.[30]

Stevens's houses were equally dramatic during this first great flowering of his long and successful career. The most characteristic possess oddly scaled and proportioned towers and dormers, with windows arranged in unusual patterns as well. Because the idiosyncrasies of his firm's designs failed to converge into a common pattern, they appear to be highly individualistic responses by his draftsmen to the client and project at hand.[31]

THE·GERMANIA·BANK·BVILDING
SAINT·PAVL·MINN·
J·W·STEVENS·ARCH
A·D·1888·

FIGURE 2.19.

J. Walter Stevens's competition entry for Germania Bank, 6 West Fifth Street. This anonymous rendering was published in *American Architect* in 1892.

The contributions of Wirth and Stevens to the fledgling architectural community in St. Paul went well beyond their buildings. Wirth was so struck by the low availability and poor quality of affordable housing in the city that he returned to Europe to study recent developments in tenement design and construction. He also took an active part in the formation of the renegade Western Association of Architects in Chicago, an effort to raise pride and professionalism among the growing number of architects several days removed from the East Coast base—and bias—of the American Institute of Architects. Stevens was more active on a local level, earning the lasting respect of his peers for his vociferous stand for high professional standards. In 1885 he tendered his resignation from the Architectural Association of Minnesota because several of its members halved their fees to win

commissions, then took a cut from the contractors to whom the construction contracts were let. The association rejected his resignation and in the following year set up an ethics committee with Stevens as its chair.[32]

With professionalization of the local architectural community under way, St. Paul attracted a number of architects carrying extensive portfolios in independent practice. Denslow W. Millard, William H. Willcox, H. R. P. Hamilton, and John Coxhead arrived from Chicago in 1881, 1882, 1885, and 1887, respectively; Havelock Hand came from Buffalo, New York, in 1882; Emil Ulrici arrived from St. Louis, Charles T. Mould from New York, and Walter Ife and H. Sackville Treherne from England in 1882; Charles E. Joy immigrated from Dover, New Hampshire, Allen H. Stem and his two partners arrived from Indianapolis, and Emil Strassburger came from San Antonio in 1884; Herman Kretz arrived in 1886, bearing a German architectural degree and several years of American practice in New York, Chicago, and Bismarck; and in the same year the redoubtable upstate New Yorker Harvey Ellis began to wander through the Twin City's leading architectural offices. All of these architects had a sizable body of work already attached to their name, yet each came to St. Paul with few if any local commissions actually in hand. It was enough that new construction was still erratic in the East, failing to live up to its earlier promise in points farther west, but booming in St. Paul.[33]

The St. Paul building boom ultimately attracted architects and builders from a diversity of European countries as well as from the East Coast and Canada. Minneapolis had barely a handful of foreign-born architects, led by German Norwegian Carl Struck and Scotsman Alexander Murrie, while St. Paul could boast of at least seventeen, many of them settling in Minnesota after practicing elsewhere in the country. Of those whose countries of origin have been identified, seven were German, three English, three Norwegian, one Swedish, and three Canadian. Half would be gone by 1895 but would remain long enough to weave vital components of the city's growing architectural fabric.[34]

The trained architects who flooded into the city in the 1880s differed greatly among themselves in professional training and perspective. Some were primarily artists in outlook and temperament; others were transfixed by the economic opportunities, the latter class in particular inspiring Stevens's wrath. Initially, however, it was the artists who had the greatest impact. By and large, the architects who built the city in the 1880s achieved a modicum of financial success without letting go of their artistic ideals. Their success in imposing a strong personal stamp on their projects while struggling to build a practice from scratch gave the city its first generation of mature architecture.

Nineteenth-century architects who regarded their work as an art first and foremost were often accomplished in freehand drawing and painting, skills that served them well in the production of presentation drawings used to market their work. But their artistic ambitions went well beyond the drafting table. The most avid of them conceived of architecture as an umbrella for all of the other visual arts, much as opera embraces all of the performance arts. Designing was only the first step in the process; developing a network of visionary clients and first-rate artisans was the second; creating an enduring legacy was the culmination. This was the idealism taught at the École des Beaux-Arts in Paris and the eastern architectural schools based on the French model, tirelessly preached and practiced by Louis Sullivan, John W. Root, and their many associates in Chicago, and brought to St. Paul by the architects that streamed into the city from other midwestern urban centers, the East Coast, and abroad in the 1880s.

William H. Willcox (1832–1929) was the first architect to move into the state with a portfolio of completed projects worthy of a national reputation. After several years

FIGURE 2.20.
Frederick Driscoll House,
266 Summit Avenue. The home
was featured in *Artistic Country
Seats*, a lavish subscription
portfolio published in 1886–87.

of practice in Brooklyn, he had moved to Chicago to become an associate and sometime partner of Dankmar Adler and Edward Burling. He had scores of large churches, schools, and residences to his credit by the time he arrived in St. Paul at the age of fifty in 1882.[35]

Willcox's first major residential commission in the city was a flamboyant Summit Avenue mansion for *St. Paul Pioneer Press* manager Frederick Driscoll. Though the design of the **Frederick Driscoll House** might appear a bit overloaded today, even to a fancier of historic styles, many of the exterior complexities expressed intricate interior arrangements and requirements (Figure 2.20). Willcox gave each of the rooms its own distinctive level of privacy, exterior lighting scheme, and outlook into the yards. For example, the half-round window at one end of the street facade brought filtered light into the dining room while retaining the privacy of the diners. Willcox would have been aghast at the accusation that any element of his designs lacked utility, if the preachment of his office brochure against the "wilful disregard of fitness and truth" is any measure of how he approached his practice.

In the hands of skilled architects, the Queen Anne style offered matchless resources for dressing functional requirements with complex exterior embellishments. But the same architects who had brought the style into the Midwest soon began to shy away from its frequent excesses. Even Willcox, whose buildings were hardly paragons of restraint, lambasted the fashion for its "useless finery" and the frequent absurdity of Queen Anne–inspired window placements and fireplaces "regardless alike of comfort, convenience, and health."[36]

These last three considerations were at least as strongly vocalized a concern of the architectural profession as design excellence, inspiring countless windy articles in local trade journals. One of the commonest sales arguments offered by the new breed of architects was that their services were needed to ensure that the client's practical needs were not neglected in favor of eye-catching "skin jobs." Ornate styles could be tolerated only to the extent that they served practical requirements.[37]

In 1886, Willcox joined rising young architect Clarence Johnston (1859–1936) in a partnership that was to last four years and produce some of St. Paul's most refined late Queen Anne designs. For all its increasing sense of discipline, perhaps Johnston's contribution to the partnership, their work together was every bit as pictorial as Willcox's solo commissions. The finest survivor is **Riley's Row** (also known as Laurel Terrace) just north of Summit Avenue. A magnificent sequence of broad, low arches marks the separate apartment entries, while a rhythmic march of identical gables provides each unit with its own crown. As with Bassford's Merchants National Bank, the spirit of American Romanesque master H. H. Richardson can

FIGURE 2.21.
Frank B. and Clara Kellogg
House, 633 Fairmount Avenue,
1910. A ponderous design for a
rising public figure. Photograph
by Ingersoll; courtesy of the
Minnesota Historical Society.

be seen lurking behind the shapes of the arches and gables, but unlike their less tutored predecessor, Willcox and Johnston also captured some of Richardson's sense of quiet horizontality.

During his last year in St. Paul, Willcox independently created a truly astonishing mass of masonry and wood in the **Frank B. and Clara Kellogg House** (Figure 2.21). The first floor and a half of the house are of pink quartzite brought in by rail from the southwestern part of the state, and the upper floor and a half are covered with shingles. A great swollen tower and a polygonal dormer present an impressive face to the street, but the most remarkable elevation is at the garden side. Two enormous gables sweep above a long attic arcade, a two-story projecting bay, and a profusion of oval windows. This was Willcox's last major project before moving on to Tacoma and Seattle in 1891. Kellogg would continue to hire local architects to modify and add to the house during his long and distinguished career as senator and international diplomat.[38]

Willcox's strong artistic orientation and mastery of the latest eastern styles marked out a distinctive place for him among the city's architects when he first arrived. It was not to remain unique for long. Clarence Johnston arrived on Willcox's heels, and Cass Gilbert came the next year. Both architects were fresh from training at the Massachusetts Institute of Technology (MIT) and important eastern apprenticeships, and each had taken or was about to take extended European sketching and note-taking tours.[39]

At this stage in their careers, Johnston and Gilbert were fast friends. They had discovered each other in Radcliffe's office soon after their eighth-grade graduation, they roomed together at MIT, and they joined forces to help charter the Architectural Sketch Club of New York. But more disparate personalities could not be imagined. Gilbert was the dreamer, the great water-colorist, the driven romantic who saw himself in a great procession of artist-architects beginning in ancient Greece and Rome, a man who never perceived St. Paul to be a fitting venue for his vision or his talent. Johnston was the pragmatist, the "prompt and thorough" professional, the man of patience and endurance who found fulfillment in whatever work was at hand.[40]

The contrast in their personalities would await their maturation as architects to find expression in their respective work. On his arrival Johnston was as visionary a designer as any in the city. Born in a pioneer settlement in

FIGURE 2.22.

Addison G. Foster House,
490 Summit Avenue. The
home was pictured in *Artistic
Country Seats* in 1886, when its
lot was still devoid of trees.

Waseca County, Johnston grew up in St. Paul and re-turned to the city to apprentice under Bassford when his family's economic situation forced him to drop out midway through his first year at MIT. The head of the school's architectural program, William Ware, was, how-ever, so convinced of his talent that he drew him back East to work for the famed Herter Brothers decorating firm in New York City. Johnston immediately fell under the spell of Charles B. Atwood, widely regarded as one of the front-rank architectural designers in the country.

With three years' apprenticeship under his belt, John-ston returned for the final time to his home state in 1882. He had the unusual opportunity to begin his practice with a sequence of mansion-class houses. At least one of these, the **William Merriam House** on the hill behind the present State Capitol, was drafted while he was still at work for the Herter Brothers. His first Summit Avenue projects, the Chauncey W. Griggs and Addison G. Foster mansions, have retained much of their picto-rial strength through a series of remodelings. The **Addi-son G. Foster House** in particular is a delicious collage of stylistic contradictions, beginning with stick-work porches and terminating in an attic story that jumps from a Romanesque open gallery to a stepped gable in the Flemish manner to a chimney recalling Tudor England (Figure 2.22). Behind all these late-Victorian bells and whistles lurk the regimented window and wall compo-sitions that became a Johnston trademark, but in this

early design, the sobriety of the building surfaces makes their appendages all the more fantastic.[41]

The products of Johnston's instantly successful part-nership with Willcox we have already sampled. The still-young architect who came out of that partnership four years later immediately set to work in the scholarly vein that has come to be associated with his name. Two row houses across the street from each other on Summit Avenue near Dale Street, both known as **Summit Ter-race**, display the force of that transition (Figures 2.23 and 2.24). Designed in 1889 and 1890, they straddled the partnership dissolution. The older, commonly referred to today as Fitzgerald Row for its connection with the young F. Scott, was designed by Willcox and Johnston in the "New York style," that is, each unit given a dis-tinctive character in the manner of the posh row house districts of eastern cities. Across from it arose a severe, though still vividly pictorial, rectangular realization of the north Italian Renaissance. Even when continuing to dabble in medieval exoticism, as he would for other Sum-mit Avenue commissions, Johnston's work took on an increasing sense of balance and order.

Cass Gilbert (1859–1934) was born in Zanesville, Ohio, but like Johnston moved with his family to St. Paul in his childhood. Committed to an architectural career by the time he was thirteen, he suspended his formal edu-cation to work for Radcliffe. After a few years, his rest-less spirit asserted itself, and he did fieldwork for a civil

FIGURE 2.23.
Summit Terrace I,
587–601 Summit Avenue, 1891.
The "New York–style" row
was featured in *Northwestern
Builder and Decorator*. Courtesy
of the Minnesota Historical
Society.

FIGURE 2.24.
Summit Terrace II, 596–604
Summit Avenue, 1892. This
picture from *Northwestern
Builder and Decorator* shows
the increasing formalism
of row house design.
Courtesy of the Minnesota
Historical Society.

engineer before matriculating at MIT. Exhausted by the rigors of his first school year, he abandoned formal education once again, choosing instead to seek employment with an eastern civil engineering firm while shaping his plans to begin his architectural career in Europe.

After spending much of 1880 in France, Italy, and England, where he arduously sought and failed to find a position, Gilbert returned to New York City with no apparent prospects. But with the support of his MIT professors and an unusually mature portfolio of drawings,

he soon found work with the rising young firm of McKim, Mead and White. Discouraged by White's domination of the firm's expanding practice, Gilbert returned to St. Paul late in 1882. Failing to convince his New York employers to set up a local branch, he launched into independent practice with no commissions in hand other than a house for his mother.[42]

The core of Gilbert's architectural talent lay close to his skill as a watercolorist. He was a phenomenal manipulator of colors and surfaces. In his hand, even the most

FIGURE 2.25. Elizabeth Gilbert House and Frederick Jackson House, 471 and 467 Ashland Avenue. These houses are important for pairing very early designs by Cass Gilbert and his eventual partner, James Knox Taylor.

pedestrian shapes and stultifying symmetries—which he was not above employing—could be transformed into wonderful essays in light and hue and texture. The demands of a particular style were never more than vehicles for this power, and he seemed equally at home in almost all of them.

The **Elizabeth Gilbert House**, at which he resided for the first few years, has the sweeping side elevation and closely integrated walls and roofs of the Shingle style, but it also draws on the medieval and neoclassical imagery associated with H. H. Richardson and colonial America, respectively. It is a wonderful side-by-side companion to the **Frederick Jackson House**, designed a year earlier (1882) by another old St. Paul friend, James Knox Taylor, who would soon join him as a partner (Figure 2.25).

Gilbert continued to work in a highly pictorial vein for several years, borrowing freely from Richardson as

well as drawing on the recorded experiences of his first European trip. His churches in particular inspired his imagination to wander freely over a broad range of archaeological (and geological) materials. A handwritten note on the permit application for **Bethlehem German Presbyterian Church** at the foot of Ramsey Hill specifies that the stonework was to be as rustic as possible to make it look as if the tower grew out of the bedrock (Figure 2.26).[43]

With few exceptions, Gilbert failed to enjoy Johnston's success in Minnesota, either as an independent or in practice with Taylor. Prior to the State Capitol commission, he lost every major competition he entered, in spite of the acclaim given his designs and their renderings. His greatest patron, Henry Endicott, lived in Boston, and the lion's share of his commercial commissions came through the Boston and Northwest Realty Company, of which

STUDY FOR THE LITTLE STONE CHURCH AT THE FOOT OF THE HILL
FOR THE BETHLEHEM PRESBYTERIAN SOCIETY · ST PAUL MINN=
=ESOTA · GILBERT & TAYLOR · ARCHITECTS ·

FIGURE 2.26.
Cass Gilbert's rendering of
Bethlehem German Presbyterian
Church, 311 Ramsey Street,
1890 (published in *American
Architect* in 1891). The tower
was supposed to look "grown
rather than built."

Endicott was a principal. The **Endicott Building** was the first of Gilbert's projects to gain national notice (Figure 2.27). Built in the boxy, strictly symmetrical, multi-layered Italian Renaissance manner that McKim, Mead and White (and Gilbert's close friend in their office, draftsman William Wells) had introduced into America, it displays all of his mentor's skill in enlivening the surface with elegant ornament and variegated materials.

Gilbert was equally at home in the historic American neoclassical mode, usually identified as "Colonial Revival." McKim, Mead and White helped to introduce the retro style into American building practice while Gilbert was still in their offices. In 1886, Gilbert brought their version of the Colonial Revival into St. Paul. The **Charles P. and Emily Noyes House** has all of the expected symmetries, along with the shuttered windows, side chimney, and rooftop captain's walk mandated by this version of the style (Figure 2.28). But the exposed rock-faced foundation, very thin columns, and variably scaled dormers also announced the restless hand of an artist who was not held down by the strictures of any particular fashion.

When Gilbert reverted to the heavy Romanesque manner still popular for masonry residences, he imposed the same rigorous ordering of the surface that the Renaissance and Colonial Revival styles demanded. In the **William H. and Carrie Lightner House**, the front is even made symmetrical (Figure 2.29). But that did not prevent Gilbert from romancing with the stones, particularly on the secondary elevations; window sizes and shapes shift dramatically, large hollowed-out areas appear, and stocky columns inserted into the hollows dramatize the enormous weight of the walls. The house remains one of the outstanding architectural monuments of Summit Avenue.[44]

Gilbert's grandest commission, the new **Minnesota State Capitol**, announced to the nation that St. Paul had come up to the level of eastern tastes and had done so through the accomplishments of a local architect (Figure 2.30). So much has already been written about that building and its design that we will only touch on it

FIGURE 2.28. Charles P. and Emily Noyes House, 89 Virginia Street, 1890. This Colonial Revival came complete with picket fence. Photograph by Haynes; courtesy of the Minnesota Historical Society.

FIGURE 2.29.
William H. and Carrie
Lightner House, 318 Summit
Avenue. Gilbert and Taylor's
Young-Lightner double
house is to the west. This
photograph by Binner was
published in the short-lived
Architectural Reviewer in 1897.

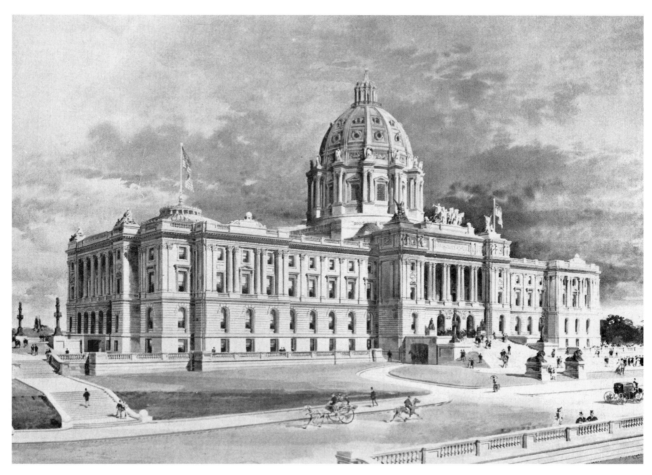

FIGURE 2.30. Minnesota State Capitol, 1895. A halftone of a rendering created by Cass Gilbert's office was published innumerable times on postcards and in city promotional literature; this example of it surfaced in *St. Paul: History and Progress* in 1897.

lightly here. Neither of Gilbert's historic sources—the Renaissance palazzo and the dome of St. Peter's—were novel usages, nor was the general layout of the building, a long horizontal mass centered by a raised dome. All of the other prizewinning entries in the 1895 competition, including those by Minneapolis competitors Harry Jones and W. B. Dunnell, were substantially similar to Gilbert's in the latter respect. What distinguished Gilbert's exterior design was the elegance of its composition. In the distance, Gilbert's building is a gleaming white fusion of pavilions spreading out from the central golden cap; from midrange, clear horizontal divisions begin to appear, the same kind of upward layering that created such a splendid effect for the Endicott Building; while up close, the uniform white surface dissolves into swirls of variegated marble and richly carved ornament. It was a design clamoring for a grand approach, and Gilbert would ultimately add a succession of ever more ambitious planning schemes to provide just that.[45]

A comparison of the haunts and hobbies of Bassford and Gilbert gives us as clear a sense of how the local profession was evolving as a look at their work does. Bassford was an avid fisherman; Gilbert was among the city's first golfers. Bassford's closest friends were builders; Gilbert hobnobbed with eminent artists and sculptors. Bassford spent off-hours regaling newspapermen with choice stories; Gilbert put up his heels at the Minnesota Club and the Town and Country Club. In his prime, each man was at a pinnacle of his profession in the state. It just was not the same pinnacle.

Johnston and Gilbert were the first architects to achieve national renown for their work in Minnesota, and Gilbert has in recent years become something of a post-Modernist icon of American neoclassicism. But in their early years they were hardly alone in either talent or ambition. Foremost among their young peers was Allen H. Stem (1856–1931). Born in Van Wert, Ohio, Stem was educated at Indianapolis Art School. Such schools often offered the only ready means for an aspiring architect to receive academic training before architectural curricula were established in state colleges and universities. Stem then worked as a draftsman in the offices of his father, J. H. Stem, until becoming a partner in 1880. In 1883, the partnership expanded to include draftsmen Edgar J. Hodgson and Charles A. Wallingford. A year later the three young men moved to St. Paul to set up their own firm.[46]

Stem's gift for rendering surfaced early in an exhibit at the American Art Galleries in New York, in which Stem and Gilbert each displayed renderings of designs for a "Rural Home." Like Gilbert, Stem continued to do renderings for publication of his firm's projects even after the size of his office had grown past the point where he was required for such duties. As the other half of his public persona, Stem also matched Gilbert in knowing the right people to choose as sporting companions.[47]

Stem's forte as an architect was an imaginative sense of form. His design with Hodgson of the **Horace P. Rugg House** of 1886 is a monumental upright L swollen outward in the middle of one side to form a broad tower

FIGURE 2.31.
Horace P. Rugg House,
252 Summit Avenue.
This early-winter view was
published in *Northwestern
Builder and Decorator* in 1891.
Courtesy of the Minnesota
Historical Society.

between massive chimneys (Figure 2.31). Even without further ornament this stone and brick house would be a stunning design, but Stem turned the screw another rotation. The wide entry arch is decked with elaborately carved human figures, most of them nude, and purple-spotted bricks are set into the base of the second story. The latter had been introduced by Richard M. Hunt for his Tiffany house in New York and immediately acquired the name "Tiffany brick." Gilbert, a master of disciplined surface ornament in his early years, might have blanched at either of these ornamental devices.

Stem's love for picturesque profiles and skill in manipulating volumes turned him quite naturally to the Shingle style. Of the many notable designs he executed in this vein, two of the finest have come down to us: the **William and Martha Horne House** at 993 Lincoln Avenue and the **Charles W. Schneider House** in the Hazel Park neighborhood (Figure 2.32). Both are arresting components of older neighborhoods. The Schneider

house in particular expresses in compressed form the love of boulder and shingle construction that eastern architects put to such expansive effect in the rocky New England terrain.

In commercial design Stem struck a Renaissance path (with both an Italian and an English track) in the early 1890s and never wandered from it for the rest of his career. Of his many nineteenth-century projects of that stamp, the only monument to survive is the **Palazzo Hotel** (since dubbed The Colonnade after its conversion to apartments) at the head of St. Peter Street. Decapitated by a fire in 1955 and defaced by a succession of remodelings in the 1960s and 1970s, it has recently returned to a semblance of its former self on the four stories (of six) that survived the fire. Though shorn of its tiers of arcaded balconies that visually united the residential towers at each corner, it still shows Stem's predilection for monumental design elements distributed over much of the building surface.

FIGURE 2.32.
Charles W. Schneider House,
750 Ames Place. This view of
the showpiece of the fledgling
East Side suburb of Hazel
Park appeared in *Northwestern
Builder and Decorator* in 1890.
Courtesy of the Minnesota
Historical Society.

Below the lofty financial scale of Summit Avenue, the most important Queen Anne residential architects in the city were Norwegian-American partners Omeyer and Thori. Didrich Omeyer (1850–1907) immigrated to St. Paul in 1883 and spent his first four years in the city apprenticing under Radcliffe and Gauger, who would have done nothing to hold back his predilection for ornamental exuberance. Martin P. Thori (1864–1905) immigrated to Minneapolis with his family while still a young child and went to work as a carpenter in his teens. By 1884, he had developed into a contractor and builder, and in the following year called himself an architect and builder in the city directory, the sure signature of a master builder. In 1887, Omeyer joined with Thori in a partnership that was to produce over eight hundred buildings before its dissolution seventeen years later.[48]

Omeyer and Thori had two great specialties: within the city, deliciously ornamented Queen Anne houses, and outside of it, sophisticated, small-scale commercial blocks, especially Main Street banks. Their greatest talent was in the creation of porches, gables, and cornices that endowed each of their designs with great charm and individuality. The wonderfully intact **William H. and Ida Garland House** and its neighbor (also for the Garland family) west of Crocus Hill typify the firm's work at its most effusive (Figure 2.33). Irregular contours and profiles are held in careful balance, so that the designs are not dependent on ornamental camouflage for a good "read." Ornament was in fact put to the purposes taught at the eastern schools: to center attention on important areas, to accentuate the depth of protruding and receding parts of the building, and to create a visual unity out of the diversity of shapes expressive of the building's plan. The many survivors of Omeyer and Thori's extensive St. Paul practice show their work to be of an absolutely uniform quality, an astonishing achievement for a small firm, neither of whose principals received academic training.

Apart from Omeyer and Thori, German-Americans were far and away the most important immigrant group in shaping the architectural legacy of St. Paul. A foursome of German-born architects came to the city between 1883 and 1887, each exemplifying a distinctive path to success in the New World, and each leaving behind him a characteristic body of work. Emil W. Ulrici (1857–?) arrived with seventeen years of practice behind him in Milwaukee and St. Louis. His work never quite fell into American stylistic molds, carrying throughout his career the Germanic signature imposed by his early experience

FIGURE 2.33.
William H. and Ida Garland
House, 846 West Fairmount
Avenue. A typically florid
production of Norwegian
Americans Omeyer and Thori.

and training. Many of his clients were of German ori-gin. Very little mention was made of him or his projects in the press, his name surfacing today principally through isolated buildings that have undergone sympathetic res-toration. The **O'Connor Block** at 644–66 East Seventh Street, one of the few iron-fronted buildings ever built in the city, carries its massive dormers as a skyline adorn-ment much like countless neoclassical commercial build-ings arising on midcentury German city streets. His most significant remaining residential project, the cream brick **Justus Ohage House** in Irvine Park, bears many more similarities to the eclectic Round Style of his native country than it does to the brand of Romanesque Revival then current in America (Figure 2.34).[49]

Equally Germanic in his initial St. Paul work was Saxon-born architect Emil Strassburger (1854–?). After beginning his practice in his homeland, Strassburger immigrated to San Antonio, Texas, which had a large German community, before coming to St. Paul. One of the few nineteenth-century architects to settle on the West Side, Strassburger has left a sizable legacy in that section of the city. Much of his work was in the same ponderously ornamented style that Ulrici and Wirth had imported. One particularly persistent trait was the rhyth-mic breaking of the skyline with blocky elements such as dormers and short, thick chimneys. Wirth's German-American Bank and Ulrici's O'Connor Block had just such rooflines; Strassburger carried the tendency forward in his **Grady Flats** erected at 46–48 West Delos Street in 1891. By that time, however, the architect's work was beginning to conform more closely to mainstream Amer-ican practice, and his ensuing work adopted finer detail-ing and less agitated surfaces.[50]

Saxon architect Albert Zschocke (1859–92) took Strass-burger's absorption of American designing and building practices one step further. Arriving fresh from a German

FIGURE 2.34.
Justus Ohage House,
59 Irvine Park. This house
shows the same fusion of
German and American
styles as the Bishop House
on Summit Avenue
(Figure 2.16).

architectural school and a short stopover in Wisconsin, he at first worked in the offices of George Wirth and William Willcox successively. His idea was not simply to serve an apprenticeship but to get "a better idea of what class of architecture was needed in the Northwest." His own practice, established in 1885, was instantly successful, perhaps in part because of his mastery of American building methods and tastes. The **Owen Apartment House** and the mighty **Barteau**, his greatest local accomplishments, fell to the Capitol Mall clearance of the 1950s, and many of his other signature buildings have disappeared as well. But such surviving residential designs as the **Peter Giesen House** at 827 Mound Street in Dayton's Bluff and the **Lucy Miller Double House** at 156–58 Farrington Street show his grasp of the picturesque possibilities of the Queen Anne and Richardsonian Romanesque styles. Zschocke's death in 1892 at the age of thirty-three robbed the city and the nation of an architect of extraordinary promise.[51]

In 1887 the last of the notable German architects to arrive in St. Paul set up his practice. Herman Kretz (1860–1931) brought with him a technical training equal to anyone working in the city at that time. Though artistic "devices" sprouted from all sides of his buildings, his

FIGURE 2.35.
Blair Flats, 165 North Western
Avenue. The size and ornateness
of the building astonished the
city. This anonymous engraving
was published in *Northwest
Magazine* in 1888. Courtesy
of the Minnesota Historical
Society.

The Blair Flats.

reputation ultimately rested, as Bassford's had before him, on the soundness of his structures and their mechanical systems. Like Zschocke, he moved freely among American design idioms, but he never quite achieved the compositional strength and stirring profiles of Zschocke's work. Rather than developing a distinctive approach to design, he became a master of three specialized building types: in the cities, massive apartment buildings and midsize commercial blocks, and in small communities throughout the region, Catholic churches. His first major project, the **Blair Flats** (successively renamed the Albion and the Angus before returning to its original name as the Blair House), went up the year of his arrival, and the density of its ornamentation and sheer size caused something of a local sensation (Figure 2.35).[52]

Among native-born architects, the most forward-looking of the period were largely men with little or no academic training. Two of the most successful of these, W. H. Castner and C. E. Joy, did for the Shingle style what Omeyer and Thori did for the Queen Anne: adapted it to small lots and made it accessible to the average pocketbook. Originally devised for rugged, semi-rural settings, the Shingle style house was set onto a high stone foundation, wrapped in a continuous sheath of shingles, and spread out into its environs with dramatic sweeping roofs and large open porches. The challenge for the urban architect was to make these ideas work on crowded city parcels.[53]

In a number of St. Paul designs, William H. Castner (?–1892) succeeded in capturing much of the rugged spirit and all of the flowing lines of the style within the confines of the forty-foot lot. How Castner came about his ideas is unknown. He apprenticed briefly with Radcliffe before joining Knight as a partner in 1883. Neither of those architects, both approaching the end of their careers, so much as dabbled in anything as avant-garde as the Shingle style. But by 1887, Castner was designing in that mode almost exclusively, at least for residential projects, and continued to do so until 1890. Among his many surviving designs, the most interesting are the adjacent **William Moran Spec Houses** in the Summit-University district (Figure 2.36). The houses appear almost to be in conversation across the narrow green space and drive that separate them.[54]

Just south of Dayton's Bluff along the Mississippi, a commuter suburb sprang up that briefly promised to be a regional haven for Shingle style design. The principal architect of the suburb, Burlington Heights, was

FIGURE 2.36.

William Moran Spec Houses,
1048 and 1050 Hague Avenue.
The often-sprawling Shingle
style was here confined to
forty-foot urban lots.

Charles E. Joy (1837–1905), a New Hampshire native who began his professional life as a printer. He had practiced architecture for ten years by the time of his arrival in St. Paul in 1884. After working his way through a number of offices and partnerships, he finally settled in with D. W. Millard (an 1881 arrival) in 1888. Best remembered today for his ice castles, Joy's most promising local commission was for seventy houses in the Burlington Heights development. Fewer than a dozen of those were built, but all that can be traced to Joy, most notably the **Harry I. and Anna Weikert House**, show some degree of fidelity to the Shingle style and an effort to create a dramatic appearance from the road below the bluff (Figure 2.37).[55]

A number of talented architects of the 1880s and 1890s worked in so many veins that it is difficult to isolate their particular talent. One of the most prolific of these was Charles T. Mould (1854–?). When he emigrated from New York in 1883, he was already a mature designer. Shortly after his arrival he entered and won a highly publicized competition for the prestigious **Minnesota Club**. This was also Cass Gilbert's first effort in an architectural competition, which he lost—as he would many others—principally for his lack of experience. While Gilbert proposed a faithful essay in Richardsonian Romanesque, Mould utilized his signature combinatorial style, drawing on elements of the English Renaissance as well as the current Queen Anne and Romanesque fashions. His prolific residential output, both in individual practice

and in partnership with Robert McNicol, was equally eclectic. A single outstanding exception arose in 1886 when Harvey Ellis came into his office for a few months. Ellis's hand can be clearly perceived in the **John L. Merriam House**, a lost masterpiece of Richardsonian Romanesque that for many years housed the Science Museum of Minnesota.[56]

More typical of Mould's approach to current styles were a number of houses in Woodland Park harmoniously melding what architectural historians now identify as the Stick and Shingle styles with the Queen Anne. In partnership with McNicol he also pursued a vein that defies stylistic categorization. One particularly eccentric example survives. The **Alvin Krech House** of 1888 registers Mould's (or McNicol's) unique take on Richardson shortly after Richardson himself had died (Figure 2.38). Picturesque elements abound—a corner bay, expansive porches and loggias, a sculpted cornice, and a bevy of chimneys—but all are subjugated to the discipline of the cube.

The last of the artistically gifted architects to arrive during St. Paul's great building boom was John H. Coxhead (1863–1943). Born in New York City and educated at Columbia University, Coxhead apprenticed for seven years with architects in New York, Boston, Chicago, and Sioux Falls. In 1886 he joined prominent school architect F. S. Allen in Streeter, Illinois, and the following spring moved to St. Paul to set up practice

FIGURE 2.37.
Harry I. and Anna Weikert
House, 770 South Brookline
Avenue. Broad porches
overlook the railroad and
river below.

FIGURE 2.38.
Partial side elevation of
the Alvin Krech House,
314 Dayton Avenue. An
eccentric local effort to
squeeze H. H. Richardson's
Romanesque vocabulary
into a cube.

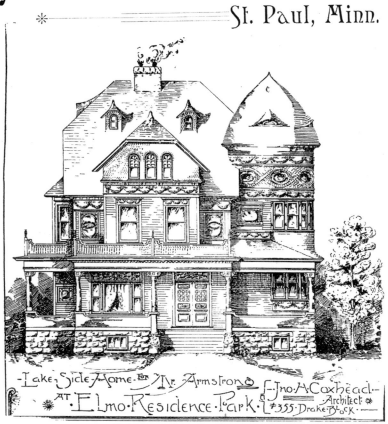

Architect. Jno. H. Coxhead,
St. Paul, Minn.

-Lake-Side-Home-For-Mr. Armstrong -Jno.H.Coxhead-
AT-Elmo-Residence-Park. #355-Drake-Block. Architect

Professional Advice on All Classes of Buildings,
— ACCURATE AND RELIABLE. —

JNO. H. COXHEAD,
ARCHITECT, 355 Drake Block.

FIGURE 2.39.
Advertisement for popular
local architect John Coxhead
in *St. Paul City Directory*, 1890.
Courtesy of the Minnesota
Historical Society.

independently. Coxhead was a gifted draftsman and retained his membership in the Chicago Architectural Sketch Club through the first two years of his St. Paul practice (Figure 2.39).[57]

Coxhead's forte was interior design, particularly of casework. Much of his identified surviving work shows a disconcerting affinity on the exterior with the kind of scaling and detailing we would normally associate with interior fittings. A matched pair of double houses on Laurel Avenue typifies the idiosyncratic flavor of Coxhead's residential output (Figure 2.40). They are very difficult to place on a stylistic map. Yet Coxhead's work is in its own way as much an artistic expression of the

possibilities of wood-frame design and construction as the more mainstream work of Omeyer and Thori, Castner, and Joy.

A host of other capable architects helped to create the remarkable streetscapes St. Paul could boast of in the 1880s and 1890s. Many of their names have all but passed from public record, even in the wake of the extensive historic site survey work of the past two decades, because the lion's share of their buildings has disappeared. Among those about whom we possess some biographical information, Englishman H. Sackville Treherne (1855–?) established the city's first architectural association, the St. Paul Architectural Sketch Club, at the end of 1882.

FIGURE 2.40.
Charles Carman Double House, 534 Laurel Avenue. This was one of many Coxhead designs with canted, oval corner towers.

Although as well respected and successful as any of his peers, he had the misfortune of winning St. Paul commissions in or near the downtown area. All but a few outlying houses have been demolished. Another early organizer of local architects, Denslow W. Millard (1841–c. 1910), created a large stock of school buildings throughout the state, along with a great number of houses and commercial blocks. One of the latter, the old **First National Bank**, was revered as the city's finest monument on its completion in 1882. But the bank and all of his known schools failed to survive into the 1950s; only a warehouse and a scattering of residences, most of them in partnership with C. E. Joy, testify to his once familiar presence in the city.[58]

We have concentrated on St. Paul's own architects but cannot really leave the city's first great building boom without an appreciative glance at the creative efforts of outsiders. Three of the grandest structures of nineteenth-century St. Paul were designed by out-of-state firms. Each utilized idioms that combined the exuberant styles of the late 1880s with the controlled academicism that was beginning to dominate the major architectural centers of the East Coast.

First among these monuments in sheer magnitude is the **U.S. Courthouse and Post Office**, begun in 1892 but not completed until 1902 (Figure 2.41). Rechristened

Landmark Center after its restoration in recent times, it owes its design to countless hands in the Office of the Supervising Architect of the Treasury. Richardson and his French Romanesque sources inspired most of the guiding ideas, but the building is capped with a profusion of small towers and gables recalling Renaissance châteaus. The normally rugged surfaces of the American Romanesque style were also dressed smooth, subjugating the raw force of the Romanesque to the patrician elegance of the Renaissance and marking a transition that would soon overtake American public building.[59]

Equal in architectural importance, but nearly forgotten today, was the spectacular office building of the **New York Life Insurance Company** (Figure 2.42). Later in style but earlier in construction than the U.S. Courthouse and Post Office, this elegant structure beat Cass Gilbert's Endicott Building by a nose in the race to copy New York's craze for Renaissance Revival office blocks. New Yorkers Babb, Cook and Willard won the much-ballyhooed 1887 competition against such locals as Hodgson and Stem (who also submitted a design of Renaissance pedigree) and J. Walter Stevens (whose draftsman, Harvey Ellis, produced a design fantasy that can only be called High Eclectic). The winning design was an asymmetrical double tower layered in the conventional Renaissance Revival fashion but surmounted by

U.S. Courthouse and Post Office
(now Landmark Center),
75 West Fifth Street. In the
words of a local critic, "one of Uncle
Sam's fearfully and wonderfully
designed structures."

FIGURE 2.42.
New York Life Insurance Company
Building, 395 Minnesota Street,
ca. 1900 (razed). Respected historian
and critic Russell Sturgis selected this
building as a premier example of
modern architecture in *How to
Judge Architecture* (1903).

FIGURE 2.43.
Pioneer Press Building,
334–36 Robert Street, 1888.
This anonymous engraving
introduced the subscription
volume *The City of St. Paul and
State of Minnesota*.

an elaborately decorated attic and a stepped gable on each of the facades. In 1903, eminent architectural historian and critic Russell Sturgis singled it out for praise as "one of the best things in modern original design," but it failed to survive urban renewal in the 1960s.[60]

A far more functionalist design was ordered for the **St. Paul Pioneer Press Building** in 1888 (Figure 2.43). The architect, Solon Beman, was an important member of the Chicago School. This "uncompromising parallelopiped of brown brick," as critic Montgomery Schuyler described it, uses a vocabulary of long exposed piers and discreetly placed terra-cotta ornament to dress but not obscure the underlying steel frame. A rare survivor among the city's nineteenth-century high-rise buildings, it probably owes its survival to local reverence for Cass Gilbert, whose Endicott Building wraps it on two sides.[61]

What makes St. Paul architecture of the 1880s so invigorating is the evident artistic freedom that its coterie of architects, including those invited into the city, possessed. The demand for artistically conceived buildings was so high and so constant that the cost-conscious, management-oriented way of running an architectural office was, for the moment, pushed to one side for all but the cheapest or most utilitarian classes of building.

The leading architects of St. Paul's boom years still had to be sound businessmen in order to do well, but their being artists, or having a bevy of artists in tow, was a major component of their success.

In the early 1890s, all of this began to change, as St. Paul's architectural community underwent a shift in focus and direction at the threshold of the new century that would be as dramatic as the changes wrought by the booming 1880s. This time the catalyst was not a local or regional condition but a change in the economic and architectural outlook of the nation as a whole. The two faces of the change, economic and architectural, ultimately joined together, but we shall look at their separate character first.

The Panic of 1893 ushered in the most severe depression the country had faced since 1873. This time St. Paul had no great surge of immigration or investment to insulate it from the national economic chill. As soon as the incredible boom of 1884–89 had begun to die down, the young architects who had flooded into the city scarcely a decade before began to look elsewhere. Stevens, Johnston, Stem, and Kretz would remain until their deaths many years later. But by the mid-1890s, Wirth, Willcox, Ellis, Zschocke, Ulrici, Castner, Joy, Mould, Coxhead, Treherne, Millard, and Strassburger had gone, Gilbert had one foot out the door, and Omeyer and Thori were devoting most of their energies to commissions outside of the city.

The remaining architects survived the financial fallout largely by letting go of the individualistic artistic impulses that had once been their principal source of identity. Johnston moved on to institutional building, and even some of his houses began to acquire a vaguely institutional look. Stevens lost the last of his superb line of artistic draftsmen and turned increasingly to standardized renditions of the Chicago School. Even Stem, whose public persona continued to hover somewhere just short of Inigo Jones, joined up with engineer-architect Charles A. Reed (1857–1911) and began to shift his practice to railway and hotel projects that required less design per square foot. These three architects kept their offices intact during a period of nationwide retrenchment principally by finding a niche in building types that would remain in demand whatever the financial woes of the community. In the process, the city's first management-oriented, mega-architectural practices were born.[62]

Ironically, the way to the future had been pointed in the late 1880s by immigrant architect Herman Kretz. Though he would never match the opulence of his first great commission, the Blair Flats, he repeated its basic type in several dozen brick-and-stone flats buildings throughout the city. Eighteen such buildings were reported in the regional architectural press in Kretz's first ten years in St. Paul, and the Ramsey County Historic Sites Survey unearthed several more. Each cost in excess of $20,000 (the price of a mansion-class house in St. Paul), and several approached or exceeded $100,000. Many had identical or nearly identical plans. Kretz continued his specialties in commercial buildings and country churches, but these were a whisper to the roar of his

FIGURE 2.44.
Thomas B. Scott House,
340 Summit Avenue. This
partial, oblique view displays
a wealth of neoclassical
ornament.

apartment construction projects. He was the first architect in the state to carve out an upscale specialty that
invited replication. Kretz had found his métier and pursued it with great success right through the depression.[63]

There were many exceptions to this general picture,
of course. In particular, Stem continued to design a select
number of houses and occasional business blocks with
some of the élan of his early St. Paul buildings. The
Thomas B. Scott House, for example, imposed a very
imaginative window scheme on the kind of Renaissance
Revival design that was often little more than a sequence
of reiterated but gorgeously tricked-out holes punched
into a large rectangular solid (Figure 2.44).

The surface simplification dictated by shrinking bud-
gets also actually strengthened Stem's quasi-medieval designs. He created a darkly dramatic effect for the **Horace
and Maude Stevens** house in 1895 by focusing the design
energy on the flat profile of chimney and gable, reiterated by the centered entry. The scant windows exaggerated further the gaunt power of this great contoured slab
wall (Figure 2.45).

By the mid-1890s the economic shakedown was complemented by a careening of American tastes away from
the hodgepodge of historical styles and toward the
neoclassical manner taught in the academies. Thus, the
extraordinary material combinations, restless forms, and

FIGURE 2.45.
Horace and Maude Stevens
House, 530 Grand Avenue.
The austere, planar design
shows how Reed and
Stem responded to new
architectural currents.

ornamental excesses of the late-Victorian styles began to lose their popularity just as they lost their economic viability. The catalyst of change in the Midwest was the Chicago World's Columbian Exposition of 1893. That exposition presented row upon row of glistening white buildings, all tricked out in the columns and arcades and domes of the Roman Renaissance manner. Millions of Americans who were soon to build commercial blocks and residences, as well as to support bonds for ambitious public buildings, flocked to the exposition.

Academic training in architecture had stressed the superiority of classical tastes and styles for nearly a generation. The model for every architectural curriculum in the country, and there were as yet only a handful, was the École des Beaux-Arts in Paris. Architectural discipline in a Beaux-Arts curriculum meant working with classical proportions and prototypes: aesthetic order meant classical order; historical precedent meant the Renaissance and Baroque monuments of Italy and France and their antecedents in ancient Greece and Rome. The study of the medieval building traditions that had inspired so much nineteenth-century architecture—particularly neo-Gothicism—was relegated to student exercises and lesser projects such as rural churches and village railroad stations.

As this brand of academic training became the norm for aspiring architects and the trade periodicals began to fill with examples of Beaux-Arts classicism, the colorful array of late-Victorian styles began to look more and more like a Gorgon's head of gaudy, contorted, incongruous forms. Every architectural firm in St. Paul, like their counterparts throughout the country, ultimately had to come to terms with the officially sanctioned ideals of the "new" American architecture, and most leaped immediately into some variant of classicism or another. English Gothicism, particularly the kind of late-medieval, early-Renaissance mix of England's parish churches, still prevailed as the norm for Protestant church design, but every other high-style building type leaned increasingly in the direction of classical prototypes. Even the humblest house could be fronted with a tiny neo-classical portico, and in the houses of the wealthy these porticos stretched to the full height of the front wall or frankly imitated a well-known design from colonial times.

This double shift in the country's economic conditions and its tastes ended up working very well together, for the image-obsessed Romans and the financially strapped American colonialists had practiced an identical piece of wisdom, how to create the effect of art cost-effectively. Uninterrupted walls of brick or near-white stone and

FIGURE 2.46. E. L. and Susan S. Welch House, 785 Dayton Avenue, 1894. The family sits beneath the giant portico. Courtesy of the Minnesota Historical Society.

symmetrically placed windows now became exemplars of good taste rather than gaps in artistic inspiration. Replicating the effect and even the detail of another period's building became an achievement rather than a mark of laziness or the product of a tight schedule.

The classical fetishism that found its way into the mainstream of American architecture was an easy target for ridicule by progressive architects. To Louis Sullivan and his followers, its pomposity and callow glorification of the masterpieces of another era seemed absurdly out of place in a country still struggling to discover and establish its own architectural identity. But the concerted effort to find modern meaning and application for the most ancient architectural forms in the Western tradition also produced many monuments of real strength and, within the limits of the styles, originality. The Germania

Building, Endicott Building, New York Life Building, and Pioneer Press Building were each among the finest achievements of their respective architects, and each owed much to the first wave of resurgent classicism.

Architects who survived the 1890s by becoming expert managers, such as Johnston and Stevens, also found in the limited parameters of the new classicism a means of refueling their creative energies. It is no accident that Johnston's Colonial Revival structures from the mid-1890s, such as the **E. L. and Susan S. Welch House** of 1894, have an air of easy elegance (Figure 2.46), while his Gothicizing designs appear increasingly forced. The same can be said of Stevens's commercial work of the late nineteenth century. Stripped-down versions of his earlier work look like a penny-pincher's Chicago, while a new type of building that introduced Renaissance motifs

FIGURE 2.47.
Fairbanks, Morse, and Company, 220–26 East Fifth Street. The building reveals its modernity by compressing ornamental detail nearly to the building plane.

and principles of organization, such as the **Fairbanks, Morse, and Company Warehouse** of 1895, breathes with fresh confidence and vitality (Figure 2.47).

The economic cataclysm of the 1890s also had an effect on the ways architects did business. When the members of the local profession regrouped at the end of the century, it was no longer quite the same small band of individualists. The profession had begun to splinter into specialists distinguished not so much by the character of their designs as by the type of work they took on. After 1895, there were no dominating architectural firms in the city, only a welter of dominating public needs and the ebb and flow of popular tastes.

Much of early-twentieth-century architecture in America can be understood as a marriage between Beaux-Arts classicism and a rising interest in building economy and efficiency. The warehouses, office buildings, and houses in nineteenth-century St. Paul that crossed most easily into the next century, and even into our time, were largely classical in inspiration. The reasons for this had little to do with grand columns, high arched windows, or any of the rest of the paraphernalia of borrowed antiquity. It had to do instead with simple lines, controlled ornament, the forthright expression of structure, and an acceptance of the aesthetic of rectilinear organization and form. All of these were cost-effective ways of organizing and

FIGURE 2.48.
Gideon and Mary Ivins House,
625 Marshall Avenue. The house
combines a familiar New England
form with gold-hued limestone
from the Mankato area.

composing a building. Often trumpeted as "modern" in local newspapers and the regional architectural press, this approach to building design was in fact a harbinger of Modernism as we know it today.

One of the most graceful local transitions into an updated classicism was made by Thomas Holyoke (1866–1925) just as the new century arrived. Born in Massachusetts, Holyoke received nearly all his office training with Cass Gilbert. In 1890, with his employer's financial assistance, he took a year off to study in Paris and travel in Europe; then, once more with Gilbert's blessing, he found employment in New York City. After four years, he returned to Gilbert's St. Paul office as his chief assistant. When Gilbert himself relocated to New York in 1899, Holyoke remained to manage the remaining St. Paul work on an on-call basis while establishing his own practice.[64]

Holyoke immediately developed a strong suit in two specialties: English Gothic Protestant churches and Colonial Revival houses. His most characteristic designs were rendered in a colorful buff, rock-faced limestone mined near Mankato, Minnesota. He thus straddled the vivid pictorialism of one era and the scholarly exactitude of another without missing a beat. In such designs as the **Gideon and Mary Ivins House**, Holyoke's use of rugged stonework, painstakingly laid up, created a picturesque effect of great age without sacrificing anything in the way of historical scholarship or formal clarity (Figure 2.48).

Another post-Victorian apostle of clarity in the guise of classicism was Louis Lockwood (1866–1907). Born in London and educated at King's College, he received his architectural training in London architectural offices during St. Paul's great building boom. In 1888 Lockwood immigrated to Winnipeg and soon thereafter came to St. Paul, continuing his apprenticeship under various architects until setting up his own practice in the unpromising year 1893.

Lockwood managed to be successful during a period when so many of his peers were at loose ends by devising formulas that could be applied to a limitless variety of houses and commercial buildings. Starting around 1895, he began creating a long line of neoclassical houses that fit loosely into the Colonial Revival fashion. This allowed replication of plan without necessitating a loss of individual character. Novel dormer placement and decoration, the doubling of stone pier and classical column on the porch, and several startling appearances of oval and half-round shapes added up to designs that defy classification, though they are undeniably neoclassical in mood as well as detail.[65]

In 1904 Lockwood broke free from his endless variations on Colonial Revival themes to design a house that stands alone in his work, both in style and in quality. The **Jared Howe House** on Oakland Avenue (now an extension of Grand) combines English Arts and Crafts,

FIGURE 2.49.
Jared Howe House,
455 West Grand Avenue.
A powerful and idiosyncratic
design by Louis Lockwood,
an architect not otherwise
known for his originality.

Gothic, Colonial Revival, and totally personal detailing into a formal composition that is held together by a rigid spatial discipline (Figure 2.49). The building could not be called classical in any literal sense, and yet there is a classical spirit in its arrangement. The symmetry of the design on each of its sides, the steady rhythms of the piers and the brackets, and the careful framing of the dormers by much taller chimneys are all the sort of lessons one could learn by studying classical monuments. It is these devices that hold the idiosyncratic detailing in check, transforming what could easily be a crackpot experiment into a highly imaginative domestic design.

Omeyer and Thori's chief draftsman, William Linley Alban (1873–1961), brought the firm into the new century with several sparkling examples of Beaux-Arts design. The best of them, like Holyoke's, managed both functional honesty and the air of an ageless monument. The **First Methodist Church**, for example, produced by the short-lived successor firm of Thori, Alban, and Fischer, recalls a Roman temple or treasury house (Figure 2.50). But the raised basement, accessible from street level, and the banks of windows along the side also manifest the intensely social nature of this denomination's work. The mighty screen of front columns addressing the street lends an air of importance (perhaps even a hint of immortality) to a design that is otherwise quite plainly functional.[66]

The American neoclassical fervor also had its academic, archaeological side. Emmanuel Masqueray (1861–1917) was the only local architect to push this aspect of the Beaux-Arts movement to its hilt. In the major cities of the East his work would have fit quite clearly into a larger developmental context. But in St. Paul Masqueray stood alone, as a general in a battle in which no one else enlisted for more than occasional duty.

Masqueray was a special case from the beginning, for he was both born and trained in France. A star pupil at the École des Beaux-Arts in Paris, he was lured to America in 1887 by fellow student John Carrere to a succession of tenures in leading New York City firms, ultimately starting his own atelier modeled on those of his French instructors.[67]

In 1903, Masqueray achieved national renown for superintending the design of the Louisiana Purchase Exposition. This was a task for which he was uniquely suited because of his mastery of the baroque architectural styles insisted upon by the other designing architects. Although Masqueray complained considerably about the excesses of his fellow designers, the exposition brought him into contact with the most important client of his career, St. Paul's Archbishop John Ireland.

The occasion of Masqueray's coming to St. Paul was his invitation to design the new **Cathedral of St. Paul**

FIGURE 2.50. First Methodist Church, 43 North Victoria Street, ca. 1910. The raised basement for office and classroom use is clearly visible from the side. Photograph by Charles P. Gibson; courtesy of the Minnesota Historical Society.

(Figures 2.51 and 2.52). Masqueray's grand scheme united a familiar Renaissance plan (said to be based on St. Peter's) and general appearance, meant to blend with the new State Capitol, with Masqueray's personal composition of baroque towers and domes, then connected the interiors with the flowing spaces of a French Romanesque pilgrimage church. The engineering and aesthetic problems in seamlessly joining architectural ideas from these three periods into one building while remaining faithful to each are mind-boggling. Yet this was the sort of task to which Masqueray returned again and again for churches inside the St. Paul bishopric as well as a number of other churches and cathedrals throughout the upper Midwest. Masqueray's achievements must have produced a combination of awe and diffidence in his

St. Paul contemporaries. Perhaps few of them even wanted to know what Masqueray knew or how to do what he was able to do.[68]

Catholic church architecture in general caught the archaeological fervor sponsored by Beaux-Arts training and influence. Even local priests and builders with very little architectural training frequently sought out European prototypes for their new churches, particularly if they were to be of large size. **St. Agnes Church** is a premier St. Paul example (Figure 2.53). Located north of University Avenue at the heart of Frogtown, it soars above a working-class neighborhood of two-story frame and brick cottages. In the early 1900s, St. Agnes's parishioners began an ambitious scheme to erect a Baroque Revival building mimicking those of their German

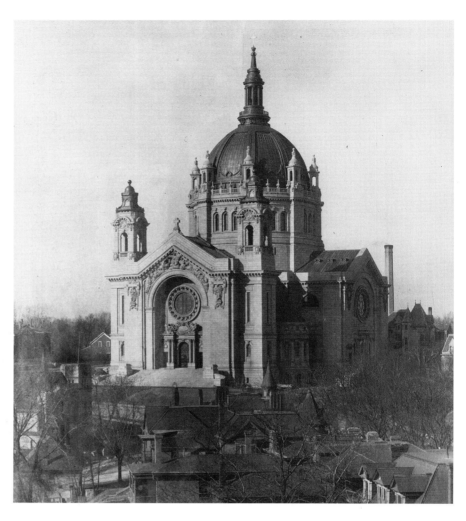

FIGURE 2.51.
Cathedral of St. Paul, Summit and Selby Avenues, ca. 1915. Capitol area clearance and highways later replaced its residential bridge to downtown. Courtesy of the Minnesota Historical Society.

FIGURE 2.52.
Emmanuel L. Masqueray's rendering of the interior of the Cathedral of St. Paul. Created in the light-filled, awestruck manner common to late-nineteenth-century depictions of European cathedral interiors, this illustration was published in *Western Architect* in 1908. Courtesy of the Minnesota Historical Society.

homeland. Their architect through the twelve-year construction process was George Ries, a German immigrant whose difficulties with the English language forced him to begin his career as a bricklayer.

At the other end of the spectrum, in 1905 the northside parish of St. Bernard's hired a Viennese-trained architect to design a building that was anything but an echo of a European past. John Jager (1871–1959) had come to Minneapolis in 1903, where his primary energies were spent in city and residential planning. His gift to St. Bernard's parish was not nostalgic references to the European experience but an expressive exploitation of the latest European concrete framing technologies. These permitted him to develop unbroken interior spaces while treating the shell as an independent design unit. Like St. Agnes, **St. Bernard's Catholic Church** became an

instant icon and enduring presence in a working-class neighborhood (Figure 2.54).

Between the turn of the century and World War I, a dozen or more churches with obvious and intentional links to the European roots of their congregants arose in St. Paul. This was part of a larger, regionwide trend toward ethnic self-expression. The frame and brick cottages, business blocks, and small churches erected by first-generation immigrants tended to follow American building practices and fashions. Even the brick cottages scattered about St. Agnes Church, though a valued part of the city's architectural heritage, carry few marks to separate their German builders from the Scottish, English, and New England builders of other parts of the city. But once firmly in place, the German-American community had only to wait for a favorable economic climate to seek

FIGURE 2.54.
St. Bernard's Catholic Church,
197 West Geranium Avenue.
The avant-garde Viennese Secession
arrives in the American Midwest.

an architectural expression of its European background. Recovery from the Panic of 1893, which in St. Paul did not arrive until 1901, brought to the city its largest stock of buildings bearing conspicuous links to northern European architecture.

Most of St. Paul's German- and Scandinavian-influenced monuments from the turn of the century were churches. But they had a strange bedfellow with equally proud Germanic roots: the brewery industry. Innovations in brewery technology led to the rebuilding of two of the city's premier breweries, Hamm's on the East Side and Stahlmann's on West Seventh, at the end of 1901. Jacob Schmidt, a former brewmaster at Hamm's, bought the Stahlmann property and immediately hired a Chicago architect, Bernard Barthel, to build a new plant around the old malt houses.[69]

While the Germanic pieces of Hamm's Brewery architecture have been supplanted or overwhelmed by new construction, **Schmidt Brewery** still carries the air of a medieval fortress (Figure 2.55). Turrets, battlements, and round-headed windows abound, and the setting above the Mississippi River enhances the romantic association with Rhineland castles. The multiplicity of building shapes, roof heights, and fenestration schemes that Barthel compacted into a single block adds to its commanding appearance. The effect is of a city within a city.[70]

In commercial design, the commonest way to resolve the American Beaux-Arts dialectic between functional honesty and historical fidelity was to divide buildings into zones. The middle of the building would read clearly and functionally, while the top and bottom could display the learning of the architect and the fine taste of

FIGURE 2.55.
Schmidt Brewery, 882
West Seventh Street.
This fanciful nighttime
depiction was published
in the subscription
volume *Book of Minnesota*
in 1903.

his client. Reed and Stem's **St. Paul Hotel** of 1910 was an eloquent expression of these opposing forces within the American Beaux-Arts movement (Figure 2.56). The building is divided into three horizontal zones, a high basement of rusticated stone, a long midsection faced with glazed terra-cotta, and a two-story attic and penthouse crowned with a gaudy, precipitously overhanging cornice. This was a common Beaux-Arts formula for high-rises, creating divisions that roughly corresponded to the parts of a classical column: the base, shaft, and capital.

A modern observer looking up from the foot of the hotel must at the very least feel some sense of bewilderment at the concentration of ornament at the crown of the building over one hundred feet above the ground. Critics contemporary to Reed and Stem had a term for it: designing for the angels. How to finish off the top of a tall building crystallized the Beaux-Arts architect's difficulty in dealing with the new verticality, which required reaching a comfortable synthesis of modern, cost-conscious functionalism with "properly" placed historical embellishment.

With the death of his MIT-trained partner Charles Reed in 1911, Stem reverted to the pre–Beaux-Arts sensibility of his earlier years. In such buildings as the St. Paul Athletic Club, he continued to mine Renaissance, especially English Renaissance, sources but gave little effort to creating a classical composition. Ornament flits from floor to floor, and window sizes and surrounds freely express the use of the spaces within rather than being fit into a properly classical mold. As he had for the Colonnade Hotel twenty-five years earlier, Stem looked to history to enrich his architectural vocabulary without accepting its dictates on how he was to organize what he had borrowed.

The struggles inherent in putting Beaux-Arts principles into twentieth-century American practice were generally reserved for buildings at the upper end of the economic spectrum. The small detached house, on the other hand, continued to evolve with little regard for the clashing aesthetic ideals and utilitarian restraints overhead. Colonial Revival designs of various stripes, such as those by Holyoke and Lockwood, popped up here and there in the city, but for the most part were built with little sense of joining hands with the past or of recovering ancient splendor. Even the ornament and the facing materials were freely treated. More significantly, a pointedly anticlassical housing type made its appearance. The name for that type of house was the bungalow.

Bungalow building was a nationwide phenomenon. It is most often discussed as an architectural component of the Craftsman movement in the United States. The guiding themes of that movement were simplicity, natural materials, honesty in construction, and individual self-expression. These themes were at loggerheads with the Beaux-Arts movement, or at least that is what its apologists believed. But the housing types shared many

THE SAINT PAUL HOTEL, ST. PAUL, MINN.

FIGURE 2.56.
St. Paul Hotel, 363 St. Peter
Street. This postcard pretends
that the street corner is defined
by broad boulevards rather
than narrow city streets.

ideological underpinnings. That aspect of the Beaux-Arts movement that supported Colonial Revival design also inspired respect for simplicity and honesty in construction, initially providing a haven for disciplined expression among architects bewildered by the chaos of late-Victorian design.

The fundamental difference between the Beaux-Arts and the Craftsman movements was more a matter of association than of principle. The one movement was epitomized by a monumental civic building that wore its historical trappings proudly and self-consciously, the other by a small suburban residence that had little or no regard for its ancestry. One is an image of power and expense and represents a sizable public interest; the other is humble and inexpensive and expresses the tastes and needs of a single family. Simplicity, honesty in construction, even individuality have quite different meanings in contexts so widely separated by historical associations and building programs.

A bungalow roughly considered is a one- or one-and-a-half-story house with a low roof and broad overhang, open porches, an abundance of windows (often connected in pairs or threes), and some of its structural members and materials exposed. Within those general guidelines, there is enormous latitude. The house can be faced in clapboard, shingles, brick, stone, or, most often, some combination of those. It can be square in plan, L- or T-shaped, or a prolonged rectangle stretching away from the street. It can be trimmed out with an attention to detail rivaling the Queen Anne house, or it can be left little more than a porched box. It can be devoid of historical detailing or borrow extensively from Colonial Revival, Tudor Revival, or even Mission Revival ornament and surface treatment.

The uniqueness of the bungalow was its expression of a multifaceted architectural type not derived from the styles adapted to larger building types. For the first time, American families unable to afford a high-style house could build a dwelling with a character specifically reserved for buildings of small stature. The bungalow was not a shrunken down or simplified mansion, nor was it a plain vernacular structure à la the mechanic's cottages of the 1880s and 1890s.

From the owner's and builder's standpoints, the place of the bungalow in a larger aesthetic movement was an irrelevance. For St. Paulites who actually built and lived in them, the design of the bungalow probably instilled no nostalgic longing for a simpler world, registered no protest against formalism, expressed no particular love for nature. The house alone was the thing, and that was enough.

Comparison of a typical bungalow with the standard middle-class tract housing that preceded it demonstrates the enormous appeal of the new building type. The simple housing of the late-Victorian era, whatever its size, had very little stylistic or individual character. It looked like what it was, a pared-down version of some more complete house, and it was buried among neighbors of similar noncharacter. The bungalow, on the other hand, exuded character and was very rarely, at least in St. Paul,

put next to another of identical design. There were hundreds of designs available, and new ones could be readily generated by alterations to porch, roofline, window arrangement, or facing materials without touching the plan or appreciably affecting the cost.

St. Paul's bungalows came from a wide variety of design sources: lumberyard plans, pattern books, independent carpenters and developers, even mail-order companies, which shipped precut lumber packages and instructions together over the rails. Though architects were often the ultimate source of these plans and skilled draftsmen invariably produced the illustrations that spurred their sale, names of either draftsman or architect were seldom attached to them.

Mail-order packagers such as Gordon-Van Tine in Davenport, Iowa; Aladdin Homes in Bay City, Michigan; and Sears, Roebuck in Chicago all made significant inroads into the Twin Cities. Except for the piers and rafters of their open front porches, most of their bungalow designs were unremarkable in both street presence and detailing. St. Paul contractors (and their Minneapolis peers) nearly always adapted the plans by enclosing the porches, thus closing the curtain on the only significant moment of drama presented by the plans. This was not a response to weather alone. The so-called northern bungalow was as much a creature of fashion and economy as it was of harsh winters. The street-addressing veranda lost its appeal as the carriage was replaced by the automobile, and pulling the porch into the plan of the house was an economical way to add a room.

The best of the local bungalow plans came from the offices of speculative developers, who would retain control over their product by not releasing the names of their design sources to the public at large. Because the bungalow masked similar plans under an enormous variety of guises, it was a natural for this class of builder. In 1910 real estate tycoon Dennis E. Lane, St. Paul's self-proclaimed "own your own home" man, published a romantic rendering of the bungalow being built for him and his brother in the local newspaper. Nothing as sophisticated as the **C. A. and D. E. Lane House** ensued (Figure 2.57), although Den Lane built considerably cheaper variants of it throughout the Macalester-Groveland neighborhood. After a brief hiatus following World War I, Lane would resurface in the Highland Park neighborhood as a sponsor of two-story houses in his own subdivision, this time pressing for period-revival styles.

Perhaps because it was so exceptional a design, the developer allowed the name of his architect to be published. Mark Fitzpatrick (1866–1955) was the son of a local builder and a past master at cloning buildings of every conceivable type and pedigree, from the Chicago School houses of George Maher to the neoclassical commercial blocks of Cass Gilbert. This time around, Fitzpatrick

seemed to have Southern California in mind, specifically the low rooflines and showy rafters of Greene and Greene's work in Pasadena.[71]

Among the many speculative developers whose architects are not known, George W. Blood stood out for the sophistication and originality of his plans. Bungalows were his first specialty. Accepting porch enclosure at the outset, his plans had to find other places for ornament to roost. In the **Linwood Avenue Spec Bungalows**, erected between 1908 and 1914 just east of Lexington Avenue, imaginative variations in roofline, footprint, wood slat-on-stucco design, and glazing patterns give each house its own picture-perfect appearance yet create a neighborhood of utter cohesiveness (Figure 2.58). As principal partner in a real estate and house construction business, Blood went on to construct some of the first concrete block and structural tile houses in the city, in each case masking the wall material with a veneer of stucco.[72]

Apart from plans sold to developers and lumberyards, few bona fide architects bothered to generate bungalow designs. In fact the most prolific of St. Paul's bungalow designers was not an architect at all but a civil engineer with drafting skills. Born to a carpenter in Norway in 1866, Jens Pedersen immigrated to St. Paul with his

FIGURE 2.58. G. W. Blood's Linwood Avenue Spec Bungalows, 1042, 1048, 1054, and 1058 Linwood Avenue. The porch designs have been adapted to a winter climate.

family while still an infant. He did not graduate from high school until he was thirty, and rose very slowly in the city civil engineering department until embarking on his own as a house designer in 1912. But all along he had been spending the off-season at the drawing board. The result of his labors was a business that sold plans for hundreds, perhaps thousands, of bungalows in the upper Midwest. His means of sale was a brochure with a color lithograph picturing each house, a fanciful description, and a price tag for the complete set of plans.[73]

For the most part, architects stuck to larger commissions than the bungalow could offer, but their work after the turn of the century clearly showed the rising influence of the Craftsman movement. The better firms generally took some pains to impart a kind of historical flavor and consistency to their designs. Clarence Johnston, for example, designed what could be regarded as an oversized bungalow for Olaf Lee on the North Side in 1905. He was able to create the effect of a bungalow in quite a large house by organizing the floors in the picturesque manner of a Swiss chalet. The second story

huddles beneath the grandly bracketed overhang of the attic, and the veranda sprawls out into the yard. On an even grander scale, Johnston's **Samuel W. and Madeline Dittenhofer House** on Summit Avenue utilizes much the same horizontal, picturesque Craftsman vocabulary as the more informed of the bungalow builders but clothes the design with a sense of majesty that leaves no doubt of its manorial English pedigree (Figure 2.59).[74]

Bits and pieces of Elizabethan and Jacobean England, first brought back into vogue by the Queen Anne style, lie buried in many bungalow designs. While Johnston was content to Americanize them, other architects endowed these pieces with a genuinely English sensibility. Reed and Stem, of whom one would scarcely have expected it, did about as nostalgic and pastoral an English piece as there was in the city before the quaint styles of the 1920s set in. Tucked away behind the dense woody growth at the top of Grand Avenue, the **Goodkind Brothers Double House** of 1910 stretches from one end to the other of its lofty site (Figure 2.60). Its segmental alternations of stucco, wood, and stone suggest the

FIGURE 2.59.
Samuel W. and Madeline
Dittenhofer House, 807 Summit
Avenue. A modern American plan
was placed into a shell recalling
early-seventeenth-century English
country houses. Courtesy of the
Minnesota Historical Society.

FIGURE 2.60. Goodkind Brothers Double House, 5–7 Heather Place, ca. 1915. A country estate on a capacious city lot. Photograph by Juul-Ingersoll; courtesy of the Minnesota Historical Society.

FIGURE 2.61.
Ward and Bess Beebe House, 2022 Summit Avenue. One of only two Prairie School designs on the avenue, this home imports English Arts and Crafts influences as well.

connections of farmhouses with their outbuildings in some late-medieval English village, a far cry from the grand hotels and railroad stations that had become the firm's primary specialty.

Whatever historical resonance the Craftsman bungalow might have had to an informed architect and client, a major element of its appeal was its presentation of structural forms and natural materials for their inherent beauty without reference to prior usages. This is the aspect of the Craftsman movement that connects it to the Prairie School. Spawned in the suburban Chicago offices of Frank Lloyd Wright and his early associates, Prairie School houses stood midway between the stolid rectilinearity and axial plans of Beaux-Arts practice and the broken contours and informal plans of Craftsman bungalows.[75]

The Prairie School first crept into St. Paul via a single project by the Minneapolis firm of Purcell, Feick and Elmslie, the **Ward and Bess Beebe House** on upper Summit Avenue (Figure 2.61). The stunning clarity of the design is a mark of its debt to Wright, but for all that, the Beebe house picks out of the same grab bag of sources as the bungalow movement. The half-round attic window is Colonial Revival in inspiration, while the steep gables and tied windows draw on the same currents in period English suburban architecture as the Goodkind and Dittenhofer houses. None of this diminishes the stature of the design, for the Beebe House remains an ornament of the city. But its telling achievement, like that of all Craftsman architecture, has nothing to do with stylistic purity, whatever that had become, and everything to do with the melding of diverse sources into unified, workable, and buildable designs.[76]

Protestant church architecture during this period asserted an equally strong and considerably more consistent tie to late-medieval English building types and their modern English incarnations. By the end of the nineteenth century, English Gothicism had become the accepted mode for most Protestant denominations, and the resurgence of neoclassicism did nothing to offset the trend. Masqueray himself, in fact, used English Gothic parish churches as models for his Protestant churches, just as Gilbert had done in the 1890s. A modern is likely to find Masqueray's **Bethlehem Lutheran Church** in St. Paul more accessible and its scholarship less burdensome than the architect's more famous cathedral commissions (Figure 2.62). Yet its rationalism remains a far cry from the informal and nostalgic air of Gilbert and Holyoke's stone churches with the same precedents.[77]

A fitting place to close this architect-dominated exploration of St. Paul's first great generation of building is with the man who became the first St. Paul city architect.

FIGURE 2.62.
Bethlehem Lutheran Church,
655 Forest Street, 1964.
Emmanuel Masqueray reveals
a more ingratiating, human-
scale mood here than in his
cathedrals. Photograph by
Eugene Debs Becker;
courtesy of the Minnesota
Historical Society.

Between 1913 and 1918, Charles A. Hausler (1889–1971) succeeded in drawing around him all of the various intertwining and clashing tendencies of American architecture in the first two decades of the twentieth century. The scores of important buildings put up during his tenure and under his many partnerships in private practice drew on every available stylistic mode, in much the same way as they exploited the full range of ready material and technological resources. Exploring the breadth of Hausler's connections and legacy provides an encompassing summary of where St. Paul architecture stood at the time of the country's entry into World War I.

Charles Hausler was educated in the St. Paul public schools. After a few years at Mechanic Arts School, he dropped out short of graduation and finished his teenage years drifting through an astonishing sequence of distinguished architectural offices: Clarence Johnston in St. Paul, Harry Jones in Minneapolis, and Solon Beman and Louis Sullivan in Chicago. By the time he was twenty-one, he had assumed some design responsibility in the local firm of Peter J. Linhoff. For the next ten years he continued to maintain close professional ties with architects possessing a high order of design skills.[78]

Hausler's appointment as the first city architect under the new commission form of government was a bold move, to say the least. As a designer he was still very much a work in progress. But he knew how to pull the best young talents of the city around him, and that is what he immediately did. While his city office was struggling without funding or a clear operating structure, Hausler ran a private practice with a succession of gifted designers as partners: W. L. Alban in 1913, Percy Dwight Bentley in 1914, and Ernest Hartford in 1915. Each very likely contributed to the work of the office until the Civil

New Saint Paul Public Library
and the J. J. Hill Reference Library,
Saint Paul, Minn.

Service Commission provided Hausler with a full staff in the fall of 1915.[79]

The first project overseen by Hausler as city architect was also the greatest to arise during his tenure. As early as 1901, the City of St. Paul had approached Andrew Carnegie about funding a new library for the city. Gilbert had been particularly solicitous through his New York contacts in hopes of landing the commission for himself. But Carnegie refused to offer the city a grant for its main library, believing that James J. Hill had the means and the obligation to finance it without recourse to outside assistance.[80]

Hill ultimately yielded to the pressure on the condition that the new library be conjoined to one containing his business papers and collections. The new **St. Paul Public Library and James J. Hill Reference Library** would span a full block facing into the city's central green space, Rice Park (Figure 2.63). Prominent New York architect Electus Litchfield won a competition to design it, producing a plan reminiscent of Florentine palazzi in both outline and elevation. But unlike many of the recent American houses based on palatial European precedents, the entire expanse exuded an air of serene, even subdued dignity. How much if any influence Hausler had on the practical working out of the plans we do not know. But as city architect, he was the project superintendent responsible for enforcing the designing architect's plans in the latter's absence. More importantly, the impact of the building on other civic projects and its pivotal role

in the architectural development of the downtown would be immediate and far-reaching.[81]

The first important buildings to emerge from the city architect's office represented the best that small-scale Beaux-Arts design had to offer. The **St. Anthony Park Branch Library** and the nearly identical **Riverview Branch Library** funded by Carnegie grew up in St. Anthony Park and on the West Side. Wrapped with splendid molded arcades, they present an inviting face to the public and open to interior spaces flooded with natural light (Figure 2.64). Although the creator of the underlying design is unknown, its sparkling formal clarity, freedom from academic contrivances, and subtle color scheme could easily have emanated from either of Hausler's two closest associates at the time, Alban and Bentley, or even his gifted on-again, off-again draftsman, Harry Firminger.

William Linley Alban, who had helped to shape the transition from Queen Anne to neoclassicism in the Omeyer and Thori office, was Hausler's first partner. Alban was a graduate of an architectural school in Chicago and, like Hausler, fell under the spell of Louis Sullivan. His tastes and skills ran to formally ordered but materially expressive designs. Even bungalows were not exempt from Alban's demand for formal clarity. The material combinations of the **Alban and Hausler Spec Bungalow** on Lexington Avenue might be as complex as its California prototypes, but the design is firmly framed by buttressed piers that gesture toward Sullivan's aesthetic (Figure 2.65).[82]

FIGURE 2.64.
St. Anthony Park Branch
Library, 2245 Como Avenue, 1925.
The first and best sited of
St. Paul's Carnegie libraries.
Photograph by Charles P. Gibson;
courtesy of the Minnesota
Historical Society.

FIGURE 2.65.
Alban and Hausler Spec
Bungalow, 130 South Lexington
Avenue. This design is unusually
complex in outline and detail
for a St. Paul bungalow.

Hausler's second partner was a devotee of the Prairie School, in fact one of the finest designers in that idiom outside of Wright's office. Percy Dwight Bentley (1885–1968) was a rarity among American architects of the time, a man who seemed to thoroughly understand Wright's work without, so far as can be determined, ever having met him. Trained at the Armor Institute in Chicago, he began his practice in La Crosse, Wisconsin, then moved to St. Paul just as the first city building requests came through Hausler's office. The two began a partnership that served them both, and the cities of La Crosse and St. Paul, very well.[83]

At least three St. Paul area houses from the Bentley and Hausler partnership remain. The first of these, the

FIGURE 2.66.
Albert and Austia Wunderlich
House, 1599 Portland Avenue.
This little-known Prairie
School gem substitutes a
"living porch" for the usual
street-side veranda.

Frank and Rosa Seifert House of 1914, occupies a prominent lot at Chatsworth Street and Osceola Avenue. It has been noted and illustrated in several surveys of the city's historic architecture, though generally without proper attribution. A less known project from the following year, the **Albert and Austia Wunderlich House,** typifies Bentley's predilection for living rooms hidden from the street and corner-lit bedrooms (Figure 2.66). Its wide overhangs, casement windows, lateral entry, and terraced brick and stucco exterior are all dramatic devices common to most Prairie School practitioners. They would be taken up in somewhat subdued form by dozens of pattern book and contractor-designed wood and stucco boxes scattered around the city.[84]

As Bentley's later work in St. Paul would demonstrate, he was as lively a designer working in period revival idioms as he was in following Wright's lead. He is thus as likely a candidate as Alban to have had a hand in the St. Paul branch library designs. A more definitively Bentleyan contribution, however, was a series of park structures built in 1915 and 1916. The **Phalen Park Streetcar Station** (razed), the **Como Park Comfort Station**, located immediately south of the amusement park, and the **Mounds Park Pavilion** were all tiny gems of Prairie School design. The first went the way of the streetcars, but the latter two have managed, with recent help from the city, to hold on to enough of their integrity to prove that even the least expensive of physical amenities—a shelter against the rain—can reflect and celebrate its landscape (Figure 2.67).[85]

Hausler and his partners' skipping about from style to style was not capricious. Their practice followed a commonly accepted wisdom of their day, that style served the purpose of the building rather than the purpose trying to adapt to style. In a way, it was a broad interpretation of the Chicago School dogma that "form follows function." A single architect could consistently use Colonial Revival for houses that called for a formal plan, some variant of the Prairie School when the fireplace was to be centrally located and the staircase set off to one side, and the bungalow if living area, kitchen, and bedrooms were all to be contained on the ground floor. Similarly, a building enclosing open, brightly lit public spaces might call for the grand arcades of a Renaissance design, whereas a two-story store and flats building was a natural for the simpler detailing and horizontal effects of the Craftsman movement.[86]

A clockwise walk around Rice Park, from the U.S. Courthouse to the St. Paul Hotel to the Public Library, gives a fair view of what the city's progress over the last generation might have looked like to the gentleman whom we led through the downtown and up Summit Avenue in the 1880s. If he had a flair for metaphor, he might have imagined his walk to follow the course of a clock's hour hand, with the top of the clock positioned nearest the river. At six o'clock, with the summer sun

FIGURE 2.67.
Mounds Park Pavilion,
a perfect image of shelter
and civilized gathering place
in a riverside parkland.

young but fully risen, the great U.S. Courthouse went up. It shows some Beaux-Arts discipline in the window arrangements, an anticipation of the sophistication to come, but still relies for its impact on a monumental stockpiling of late-Victorian historicisms. The St. Paul Hotel, built in midmorning, takes modern principles more seriously, but with its vivid polychromy and beetling cornice has not quite let go of the Victorian penchant for the picturesque and the overwhelming. The Public Library, erected at twelve o'clock, brings the dramatic horizontal expanse and the glistening stone facings of the Florentine palazzo up to date and into the heart of the American Midwest. This was St. Paul architecture at high noon.

The building of the Public Library signaled completion of St. Paul's inner city. From here on, new buildings in downtown, Lower Town, and the inner ring of residential developments would by and large no longer fill gap sites or replace shoddy early construction. Their erection would follow or even necessitate the demolition of buildings originally designed and intended for permanence. The powerful new aesthetic forces, evolving building programs and technologies, and redevelopment pressures that brought these changes about are the subject of the next two chapters.

CHAPTER 3

From the Picturesque to the Moderne

1920 — 1940

At the turn of the twentieth century, a common vision haunted the labors of artists and art critics throughout the United States. The "Great American Novel," the first truly American symphony or opera, a distinctively American kind of ballet, poetry that breathed with an identifiably American spirit—these were all aspects of a broadly shared vision that the American people would at last become leaders rather than followers of European culture.

In architecture as in the other arts, the precise content of the vision varied considerably from dreamer to dreamer. Many years earlier, while still in his twenties, Cass Gilbert articulated the historical and European connections that would invigorate the duration of his practice:

> This is pre-eminently an age of thought and learning. And now in all our research and investigation into things of the past we find that we have gotten together so much material that like the Goths and Vandals of old dwelling in the midst of the classic it is difficult to utilize it all without confusion. . . . [We] forget the good things we might do ourselves if we would but accept the principles on which they worked as well as the results they produced.[1]

At the other pole was Louis Sullivan and Frank Lloyd Wright's following in the upper Midwest, to whom the architecture of Greece and Rome—and the neoclassical

spin-offs admired by leading American practitioners—were anathema both to individual artistic expression and to any hope that Americans had of outgrowing their European roots. Their vision embraced what they believed to be a wholly new way of looking at buildings and their relationship to their site, as emancipated from the American past as it was from any period of European architecture.

In between the two extremes, where most of American architectural practice actually occurred, was an intentional, one might even say principled, eclecticism. The so-called Queen Anne style had at the end become a carrier of whatever historical trappings or current novelties the architect or builder had the skill and knowledge to attach to it, and the bungalow had quickly proved to be a developer's dream, able to grow or shed with a few flicks of the pen any stylistic touches the designer or client desired, with no alterations to its program or floor plan.

Beneath this diversity in ideals and practices was a widespread belief that some great American synthesis was in the offing. Beaux-Arts and progressivist practitioners were equally driven by the hope—if not the conviction—that American invention and the academic tradition would ultimately converge in a great flowering of the American architectural profession. This was often referred to as an American Renaissance. Gilbert himself dreamed (and perhaps truly believed) that this would overshadow the fifteenth-century resurgence of the arts in Italy. The fruit would be a distinctive body of architectural work that would take its place among the monuments of Western civilization.[2]

World War I and its aftermath made short shrift of this grand vision. Full analysis of its demise is beyond the scope of this book. But we cannot begin our consideration of the nostalgic pictorial styles of the post–World War I period without coming to terms with some of the reasons that American building practice strayed so far from any of the paths laid out by prewar idealism.

The force of defeat most often cited by disappointed progressive architects was the retreat of public taste into clichéd territory. The interest of the American public in progressive architectural design proved to be short-lived and geographically limited. Even the small band of devoted Prairie School architects (with the exception of Wright himself) survived by working simultaneously in traditional styles. After a flurry of enthusiasm just before World War I, the public proved itself intractably bound to the romance of its English cultural ties (if not ethnic heritage) and the stirring associations of its colonial past. In the 1920s Americans returned en masse to the architectural forms associated with late-medieval England and the Georgian beginnings of their own architectural heritage with a devotion far more impassioned and nostalgia-laden than the flirtatious backward glances of the Queen Anne and Colonial Revival styles in the 1870s and 1880s.[3]

The war experience itself played a part in the breakup of anything approaching a new architectural synthesis on this side of the Atlantic. Entry of millions of American soldiers into the European arena flooded the national consciousness with images of centuries-old buildings at a level far beyond that afforded by the occasional whirlwind tours of the nineteenth-century gentleman-architect. American doughboys and reporters stayed in English cottages, trooped past French farmhouses, and surveyed the remains of Rhenish cities to return home with stirring memories of picturesque silhouettes, accretive architectural forms built up over centuries of use, and environmental settings as architectonic as the buildings themselves.[4]

Finally, rapidly rising building costs on the heels of the war put out of reach the proliferation of grand monuments that was supposed to bring the American Renaissance to fruition. For the first time since the rise of academic architectural training in this country, qualified architects turned to small-house design—not for individual clients but for professional organizations. The pattern books of the past had largely been generated by single individuals or architectural firms; those of the 1920s came out of nationwide associations that drew on the services of a large, geographically diverse pool of architects and designers. These designs trickled down to lumberyards, real estate companies, and homeowners. Foremost among the pattern books in local influence and use were the White Pine Series of Architectural Monographs documenting the houses of colonial America and the many diverse publications of the Architects' Small House Service Bureau (ASHSB). The latter was established as a nonprofit service of the American Institute of Architects (AIA).

Hundreds of American newspapers, the *St. Paul Pioneer Press* among them, regularly published ASHSB designs, all generated by AIA members and running the full gamut of stylistic options. This time the American architectural establishment not only set the example but provided the design base for the approved array of period styles. Manifestos for the new, history-based pictorialism frequently accompanied locally published ASHSB designs. The following appeared in the real estate section of the *St. Paul Pioneer Press* in 1926:

> Our streets and countrysides would indeed be monotonous if every one elected to build a square or rectangular house. It is fortunate that there are many who prefer homes of pleasantly irregular outline, houses that ramble picturesquely over the lot and are charmingly unconventional in their room arrangements. In the old country the houses which have inspired much of the recent small home building in America have gained their picturesque qualities often from having been built bit by bit as the years went along, a wing added here, a bay projected there.[5]

Imitating the rambling quality of small European houses not only produced a picturesque effect but also imported to the new neighborhoods of a still-youthful nation the impression of age-old use. A house that "extends into bays and angles" also "bears the mark of successive generations that have passed through it." Such statements as these provided a gloss for artistically rendered sketches and floor plans with their geographical and/or historical pedigree attached. The American architectural establishment thus lent explicit approval to a renewed reliance on European and early-American precedents.[6]

In imbuing their designs with the requisite picturesqueness, architects frequently appealed to standards of design set outside of their immediate professional circles. For example, St. Paul architect (and Norwegian immigrant) Magnus Jemne looked to the French for models of excellence, whether he was creating in a historicist vein or grappling with Modernism. His peers Edwin Lundie and William Ingemann aspired to a level of craftsmanship in their buildings that vied with their eighteenth-century American forebears. Even the building contractor took pride in his ability to create something in the proper "Georgian" or "English" or "Spanish" manner, no matter how confining the budget.

Engulfed in this geographically and historically diverse sensibility, American building as a whole emerged from the post–World War I lull with an architecture that was thoroughly American in planning and engineering, but in *looks* American only in the sense of not collectively being anything else. The latter half of the nineteenth century had witnessed a sequential ordering of style, Greek Revival shading into Italianate shading into Second Empire or Queen Anne shading into Shingle Style or

Colonial Revival, and all of them yielding to Beaux-Arts or Craftsman variation and invention. By the end of World War I, this sequence had given way to a static offering of all the current styles at once. A hundred-year parade of fashions was compressed to a block of department store windows.

The great nineteenth-century battle of the styles, particularly the conflict between Classicists and Gothicists, disappeared in the process, for all styles came into equal favor, so long as they proved amenable to modern building, living, and working conditions. For most architects and builders, even modern and distinctively American design, rather than setting itself against the diversity of styles, lapsed into one of the stylistic options. One could create in the spirit of the "New American Architecture" or not, with no censure either way.

Single-family residences were the first to capture the full range of pictorial styles and remained its central showcase through the 1920s. The diminutive Prairie School houses of St. Paul architect Charles S. Elwood (1883–1960) are a good starting point, for they show how clearly even a breakthrough, quintessentially American style could become a shop window item. Elwood was a postwar arrival trained through a correspondence course and by work in half a dozen architectural offices, most notably those of Wright's Oak Park protégés William Drummond and John S. Van Bergen. Before coming to St. Paul he also put in several years as a draftsman-designer for prefabricated building companies. After his arrival, many of his renderings found their way into the local newspaper as well as *Fruit, Garden, and Home,* the precursor of *Better Homes and Gardens*.

Elwood's cryptic residential essays in St. Paul capture both ends of his professional background; quaint, compressed, and rarified, they reduce the Prairie School idiom to its bare essentials, each wall looking as if it could have rolled out of a railcar and been snapped into place. This does not diminish the significance of Elwood's designs, which are surely numbered among the architectural treasures of the city. But their snapshot quality clearly locates them in the mainstream of the picturesque styles of the 1920s rather than at the cutting edge they would have occupied a decade earlier.[7]

Elwood's many published renderings place his houses in charming tree-framed settings and endow them with genteel, countrified names of English origin: "Low Gables," "Shadycrest," "Beyond Avalon," and the suitably named "Wee Haven." Minnesota versions of all of these were built, with one, **Wee Haven**, going up in Urbana, Illinois, as well as St. Paul (Figure 3.1). Elwood himself occupied **Shadycrest**, which still perches, though in somewhat altered condition, on a high earthen embankment at 1240 Goodrich.[8]

Anglicisms are not hard to find in many of the designs. The climactic work of his brief independent career was the 1925 **James M. and Mae Shiely House** (Figure 3.2). Though thoroughly Prairie School in plan and detail, it is crowned with a dramatic cat slide roof that would have been perfectly at home in the late Arts and Crafts designs then populating the London suburbs.

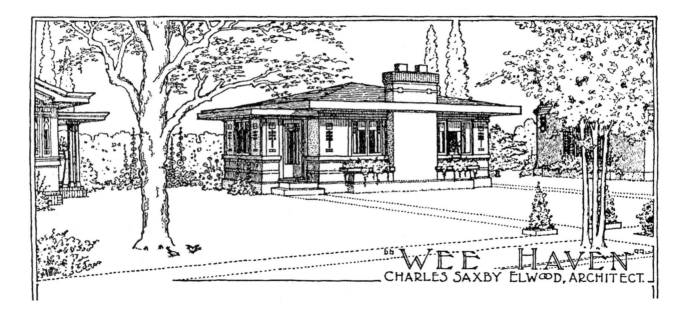

FIGURE 3.1. "Wee Haven" prototype of the Leo S. Hugo House, 1286 Dale Street, 1924. This rendering by Charles S. Elwood was published in *Fruit, Garden, and Home*, precursor of *Better Homes and Gardens*.

FIGURE 3.2.
James M. and Mae Shiely House, 1460 Ashland Avenue. This house demonstrates a striking melding of Prairie School motifs with the clipped eaves and long diagonal lines of the English Cottage.

A melding of sentimental associations with clearly delineated geometrical forms was but one expression of the precarious balance between progressivism and tradition typical of post–World War I domestic design. The dyed-in-the-wool Modernists of the following generation tended to ignore all but the backward glance of the pictorial styles, dismissing them in toto as the last gasp of a dying picturesque tradition initiated by Downing and his peers nearly a hundred years earlier. But confrontation with modern conditions and requirements was as much a concern of the period revivalists in the 1920s as it is today. The modernity of a house in function, materials, and technology was not sufficient to free it from historical trappings.[9]

Charles Hausler's final Prairie School designs, created during and just after World War I, show the late Chicago School in a guise quite different from Elwood's quaint pictorialism. While he continued to dabble in the historical styles for most of his clients, the more adventurous among them received designs stripped of anything that could be identified as ornament, even ornament in a Wrightian or Sullivanesque vein. His own home, the **Charles A. and Philomena Hausler House**, though it has been moved from its original West Seventh Street location, is the best preserved of these severe attempts at a style without historical dress (Figure 3.3). As in Elwood's houses, its interior spaces are diminutive, but

its angular geometries, beetling cornices, and dark tones have a brooding atmosphere that invites neither sentimental attachment nor imitation.

Whatever inherent interest Prairie School design might have had, St. Paul's lingering experiments in that direction never made it into the mainstream. Its very freedom from historical resonances counted against it with a public enamored with the past, the foreign, even the exotic—at least so much as could be dragged onto a city lot. Easiest to market of the emerging pictorial styles was one generally identified with England and marketed as a "cottage." A description accompanying an ASHSB house design published in 1926 outlines the English Cottage style before proceeding to its pitfalls:

> The distinguishing characteristics of English architecture are informality and picturesqueness. The plan is irregular; the rooms are not symmetrically arranged; the windows and doors locate themselves largely where they happen to be convenient. The exterior is also irregular with steep roofs, sharp gables, large chimneys, and varying combinations of materials like wood, stone, brick or stucco.[10]

Some of the city's first creations in this new, purportedly English manner were also its most lavish. Lying at the termination of Summit Avenue by Mississippi

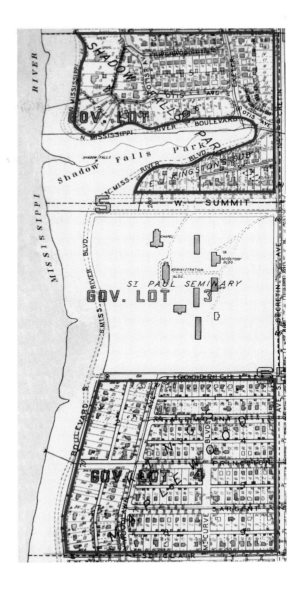

River Boulevard, they helped jump-start a new subdivision with the romantic moniker **Shadow Falls Park** (Map 3.1). At the top of the charts was Clarence Johnston's **Archibald C. and Florence Jefferson House** on Otis Lane (Figure 3.4). Built for a second-generation lumber magnate, it was one of the two most expensive houses to be erected in the city in 1925. Its formal approach and scholarly detailing betray lingering connections to the firm's many manorial houses of the prior two decades. But the massing is so pointedly, one might even say perversely, irregular that it has the appearance of having gone through several construction periods. This effect is enhanced by an abrupt change from stone to half-wood between house and garage; all this was from a firm distinguished for its strictly ordered compositions.[11]

The **Edwin S. and Amy Binswanger House** next door, designed by the foremost scholar among the regional pictorialists, Edwin H. Lundie (1886–1972), breathes with a different spirit altogether (Figure 3.5). Rather than stretching out before the road, it retreats into an idyllic woodland setting. The siting, the layout, and the landscaping all emanate a romantic reverence for natural scenery, from the garden enclosed by an elliptical drive to the irregularly faced stonework to the building contours themselves, which become increasingly informal as the house retires from the street. Houses displaying this informality in outline and faced in rough-cut stone frequently carried the moniker "Cotswold Cottage," extending the romantic resonances to the West Country of England at the time of Shakespeare.[12]

Lundie stood apart from his contemporaries in his lifelong reverence for tradition. What was a 1920s fad for many remained his lifeblood as a designer throughout his career. He worked in many of the current historical idioms, with the New England Colonial style his commonest choice for the outlying urban lots where most of his local clients lived. The house on Otis Lane was an exception. By creating the semblance of a rural setting near the western edge of the city, the landscaping of the Binswanger property allowed Lundie to indulge in a picturesque mode ordinarily reserved for his lakeside cabins and country houses.[13]

Important as they are as individual designs, these two houses had too steep a budget and too manorial a presence to typify the English Cottage style in St. Paul. Most home builders had neither the will nor the resources to carry forward the grand material assemblage of the Jefferson House or the rich and complex relationship of Binswanger's stone-faced dwelling to its setting. Broad, planar stucco surfaces were far more economical while

FIGURE 3.6.
Carroll and Corinne Lewis
House, 44 Otis Avenue.
This building shows very
few of the Modernist tendencies
that the architect-owner
would soon adopt.

equally conducive to a picturesque profile and the proper resonances with Ye Olde England.

Shadow Falls Park abounds with houses that achieved the English Cottage style in this manner. Among the earliest is the **Carroll and Corinne Lewis House** of 1924 (Figure 3.6). Designed by Carroll Lewis (fl. 1923–29) for his own family, it incorporates a dizzying diversity of shapes, textures, and historical references. Lewis's career, which was just beginning, would go in the opposite direction from Lundie's. Within a few years, his firm, Lang, Raugland and Lewis, would emerge as a leader in the movement toward architectural Modernism in the Twin Cities.[14]

Whatever their occasional involvement in mass-produced design (such as those generated by the ASHSB), established architects for the most part continued to eschew custom small-house commissions because of their low profitability. This left a large opening for young talents with a facility for fast-track design. One particularly precocious talent stepped forward in 1921, an architect whose training is unknown. Kenneth B. Worthen (1899–1947) graduated from Shattuck Academy in Faribault,

Minnesota, in 1917. According to one family tradition, he then worked as a ship's architect. Around 1920 he resurfaced in St. Paul as an employee of Twin Cities Telegraph and Telephone Company (the predecessor of Northwestern Bell). A year later he opened an architectural office. Still barely twenty-one years old, he began to create some of the city's most distinctive period-revival homes. He was so successful that within two years he was supported by a corps of some of the city's finest draftsmen, Charles Elwood and Harry Firminger among them. Worthen became both specialist in and master of period-revival design for the midsize house of 1,500 to 3,000 square feet, a position he would occupy for the duration of his nine-year St. Paul career. Over one hundred of his commissions have so far been identified, with the list nowhere near complete.[15]

Worthen's first residential project to achieve wide public notice was the **Louis A. Mussell House** at 322 North Mississippi River Boulevard. Although its craggy stone entry and sprawling overall shape indicate movement toward the English variant of 1920s-style picturesqueness, the clean break from stone to half-wood and the long,

FIGURE 3.7.
The second Kenneth B.
and Francis Worthen House,
221 Woodlawn Avenue.
This "Cotswold Cottage"
was supposed to be reminiscent
of Shakespeare's time and place.

horizontal casement ribbons betray a lingering fidelity to the earlier Craftsman style.[16]

By 1923, Worthen had discarded the Craftsman look altogether and begun to design in the irregular, additive fashion identified with the English Cottage. He designed a succession of three houses for his family, each larger and more elaborate than the preceding. The second **Kenneth B. and Francis Worthen House** went up in 1925 in **King's Maplewood**, a small subdivision near the Mississippi River just below St. Paul Seminary campus (Figure 3.7). The Worthen house struts out the most compelling charms of the Cotswold Cottage: irregular native stone facings, picturesquely placed chimneys and gables, sweeping rooflines, and a gracefully curving front sidewalk. Its neighborhood quickly evolved into another preeminent St. Paul venue for lot-to-lot, street-to-street period-revival design.[17]

To an outsider, the three generations that lapsed between the founding of the city and the settlement of some of its most beautiful residential properties must

have seemed a peculiarity. In the 1880s, landscape architect Horace Cleveland had tried to set apart the western sector of the city as an area ideal for country houses and estates. Had St. Paul's social climate been more favorable to remote, pretentious estates, the Mississippi River Boulevard and its parallels would likely have achieved residential density along the lines of Cleveland's vision by the turn of the century, just as St. Louis's covenanted neighborhoods filled up well before the grid that connected them to the center of the city. But in St. Paul, the wealthy were content to settle on arteries running directly away from the urban core, in particular on and around Summit Avenue. As a result, one of the most picturesque areas of the city ideal lay empty and waiting in the 1920s, ripe for the multiplication and rejuvenation of historical styles.

While the American Institute of Architects officially frowned on architects acting as contractors for the construction of their designs, many architectural offices of the post–World War I era in fact functioned as design-build

FIGURE 3.8. Axelrod's Bungalow Court, 1657–67 Randolph Avenue, 1925. This rendering by the architect was published in the *St. Paul Pioneer Press.* Courtesy of the Minnesota Historical Society.

firms. This was the only way most architects could hope to make a living in the small-house market. Jay Axelrod (fl. 1915–29), one of the most successful of the local designer-builders, presided over the St. Paul incarnation of the English Cottage variant known as the "bungalow court." The fashion flew into the city in 1925, fluttered about for three years in the city's western neighborhoods, particularly on and around Cleveland Avenue, took on increasingly Mediterranean airs, then winged its way out. **Axelrod's Bungalow Court** on Randolph Avenue, the first of six he would build in the western part of the city, remains among the best of the lot (Figure 3.8). Four distinct buildings are clustered around a garden court open to the street, suggesting a miniature English village.[18]

Builders' magazines and newspapers often singled out one particular variant of English-inspired design with the term *Norman.* Generally speaking, the label was applied to designs that borrowed and miniaturized pieces from medieval fortified farmhouses, whether or not these technically belonged to the Norman period in England. In American usage, the "Norman" house was usually anchored to its site by a deeply engaged tower, but that could also be abbreviated into a faceted, projecting entry. The Norman house frequently bore dormers rising directly from the face of the wall to pierce the steep roof,

was sheathed in purposely careless stonework, and was penetrated by round-headed windows or slotlike attic lights, all of which conveyed in varying degrees the image of the house as quaint refuge from foe and foul weather, the latter (rather than marauding invaders) constituting the chief enemy to the comfort of a Minnesota resident.

Most of St. Paul's houses in the Norman style were small cottages whose design origins are difficult to establish. The **Samuel D. and Miriam Krueger House** in King's Maplewood is one of the most delightful of these (Figure 3.9). Constructed in 1927 by prolific house builder John L. Wilson to an unknown architect's plans, it attaches a short entry tower to a picturesquely pierced and trimmed front wing. Its compact aspect from the street is belied by a sizable price tag for the area ($12,000), the result of the plan's deep penetration of the lot.

One of the city's most complete examples of the Norman mode waited for the opening years of the Great Depression. Built on Woodlawn Avenue in 1932, the **Albert and Anna Shapira House** elevates flush dormers and decidedly unflush masonry to a high style, and salutes the corner with a faceted tower engaged in the crossing of the wings (Figure 3.10). Curiously, the second story of the tower houses the bathrooms, which are

FIGURE 3.9.
Samuel D. and Miriam Krueger
House, 2252 St. Clair Avenue.
Another Cotswold Cottage,
this time tailored to the grassy
expanse and central entry favored
by most Americans in the 1920s.

lit by the requisite round-headed windows. Like scores of its nineteenth-century kin, the house was instantly dubbed "The Castle," a name by which it continues to be known in the neighborhood. It was designed by the Minneapolis firm of Liebenberg and Kaplan (1921–80), one of the few firms of that city that won many St. Paul commissions during the 1920s and 1930s. Though renowned today for their Art Deco theaters from the 1930s, they achieved their reputation as midsize-house designers in the pictorial styles of the 1920s.[19]

A third European-based pictorial style was identified as French, using as its point of departure either vernacular French houses or French neoclassical monuments, appropriately scaled down to a fifty-foot lot. In the nineteenth century, building "in the French manner" often meant little more than capping a formally planned, classically detailed design with a two-sloped mansard roof.

No particular understanding or love of French architecture and building practices was implied; the style simply mimicked what the English were doing in the wake of the rebuilding of Paris at midcentury.

By contrast, the 1920s house "of the French type" was inspired by buildings that were seen, studied, and sketched by American visitors abroad. Buildings creating the most interest tended to lie outside the major cities and dated considerably earlier than the Second Empire architecture imitated in Victorian times. The signature design element was a steeply pitched roof, the eaves of which commonly occurred approximately at the midsection of the story beneath. This meant that the window heads were either set right against the cornice or rose slightly into it. The remainder of the house could be as simple as a rectangular block with large, formally arranged windows.

FIGURE 3.10.
Albert and Anna Shapira House, 299 Woodlawn Avenue. A Norman cottage with enough medieval overtones to be locally dubbed "The Castle."

Architects and builders often passed off informal versions of the style as "French farmhouses," and some may indeed have been inspired by the World War I experience in Normandy. As a writer for the trade magazine *Building Age* put it, "Many soldiers brought back with them from France pleasant recollections of the inherent beauty of French farmhouses to be seen in that old world country. Some of these men were themselves architects and builders, and their creative impulses have been spurred to new endeavor by what they have seen."[20]

However rural its roots, the "French type" in an academically trained architect's hands was the most disciplined of the foreign-based period-revival styles. Its most complete St. Paul exemplars were the creation of two architects who were in the process of establishing regional reputations: Magnus Jemne and William B. Ingemann. In 1921 Jemne (1882–1967) built the house he would occupy until his death some forty years later. The life and career of this key figure in the city's history will be detailed later in connection with his more frankly Modernist work. But even his early essay in the old French manner, erected on a well-treed lot at the edge of King's Maplewood, displays how a nostalgia-laden style can tilt toward Modernism by evincing a keener interest in formal geometry than in historical paraphernalia. The Gallicism of the **Magnus and Elsa Jemne House** is confined to its roof type and contour and the formal, though asymmetrical, elegance of its fenestration

scheme (Figure 3.11). His house was also among the first in the city to use the locally manufactured Andersen casement windows.

Jemne deserted the historical styles altogether in the late 1920s, but his peer and friend William B. Ingemann (1897–1980) hung on. Ingemann was a St. Paul native who apprenticed with Electus Litchfield, the architect of the St. Paul Public Library, and studied at the American Academy in Rome before setting up a local office in 1925. He made a significant splash almost immediately by helping to establish the St. Paul Art Museum (now the Minnesota Museum of Art) and walking away with nearly all the honors in two widely publicized house design contests in 1926.

In the first of these contests, sponsored by the Master Builders' Association, Ingemann won first prize in three of four categories. In keeping with our display-window image of the historical styles, mock-ups of the prize-winning houses were eventually erected and opened to the public on the fourth floor of the Golden Rule Department Store in 1932.[21]

The impact of the second contest was more immediate, and that is where Ingemann's French manner came into play. In March 1926, the Better Homes Committee of St. Paul staged a contest for house design with separate prizes for wood, stucco, and brick veneers. The contest was locally significant for a number of reasons. Directed by the city architect's office, it was supervised

FIGURE 3.11.

Magnus and Elsa Jemne House,
212 Mount Curve Boulevard.
An urbane and modern American
takeoff on French farmhouses.

by the St. Paul Chapter of the American Institute of Architects, judged by a panel including Frederick Mann (chairman of the Architecture Department of the University of Minnesota), and exhibited to the public in the St. Paul Auditorium.

Most important from the standpoint of the city's development, the Better Homes Contest was financed by developer Den E. Lane. After World War I, Lane had shifted his focus from bungalows on small lots in the Macalester-Groveland area to the more expansive pictorial styles and the larger lots available in his own Highland Park development. This is where the winning contest entries went up. Lane's Highland Park addition was the first area of Highland Park to achieve density, and it did so largely by the building of smaller or simpler versions of the period-revival houses going up in Shadow Falls Park and King's Maplewood (Map 3.2). Houses similar in style and scale went up throughout the city, but nowhere else did they form so great a concentration or occupy lots that gave a high degree of visibility to three of their four elevations.[22]

Ingemann's winning stucco house was designed in what the neighborhood paper announced as the "Versailles type of the French style." The French reference cast an obvious cloak of elegance over what was at heart a very humble design, consisting of little more than a hip-roofed rectangular solid with a smoothly troweled surface. The only efforts at exterior ornament were arched window heads swelling above the eave line and stucco work set out from the wall plane around the door and along the corners to create a semblance of quoining. But the design must have raised some eyebrows, for it took three years for Lane to find a speculative builder willing to execute it. By that time an inset coat of arms had been substituted for the central window above the entry.

In 1930, the year after its completion, the troubled project came back into the spotlight as a **Better Homes Week Demonstration House,** when it finally found a buyer willing to live in it (Figure 3.12). In the meantime Ingemann had built his own version of a French farmhouse, the **William and Dorothy Brink Ingemann House,** at 2 Montcalm Court, in an upscale part of Highland Park well away from both the Ford Plant and the streetcar line.[23]

Cozier versions of the French style proved more amenable to St. Paul tastes. In the mid-1920s Worthen's restless imagination wandered onto French territory, with immediate success. His essays in what was purported to be a French mode were rendered in materials akin to the English Cottage. The finest of these was also the most wildly eclectic, a third house for his family, this time in Shadow Falls Park with approaches to both Mississippi River Boulevard and Otis Avenue. In the third **Kenneth B. and Francis Worthen House,** the roof is

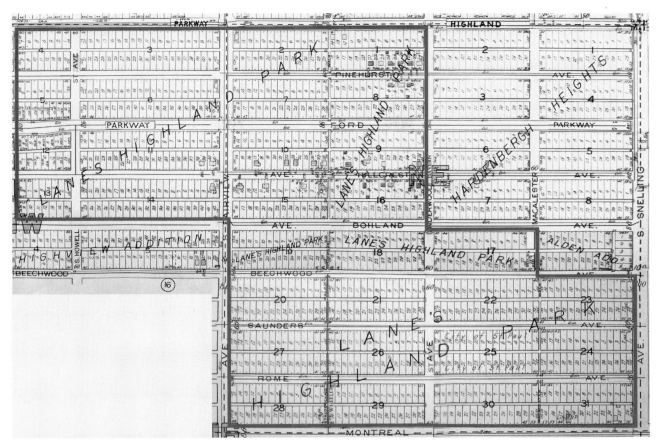

MAP 3.2. Lane's Highland Park. Assembled from Hopkins's *Plat Book of the City of St. Paul* (1928).

FIGURE 3.12.
Better Homes Week Demonstration House of 1930, 1712 Highland Parkway. A smidgen of Versailles arrives in St. Paul.

FIGURE 3.13.
The third Kenneth B.
and Francis Worthen House,
54 North Mississippi River
Boulevard. This was the most
effusive design of St. Paul's
greatest pictorial architect.

as tall as the two stories beneath the eaves, and the stone-clad walls sport a variety of iron, copper, and wood attachments that vies with the most ornament-laden designs of the prior century (Figure 3.13). Numerous design elements, such as the exaggerated scale of the roof, the eave-piercing arched window heads, and the brickwork surrounding the windows and rising into the chimney, all hint at French pedigree with no pretense at any actual French precedent. When appraising the property for the first time, the county assessor anticipated the Modernists of the next generation by classifying the house as an "architectural freak."[24]

That so few St. Paul houses were erected in fidelity to a thoroughgoing French style showed how little resonance French architecture had compared to early English and American colonial building types. Its formalism also worked against it; the most sought-after European-based revival styles expressed a taste for the informal and the

picturesque. St. Paul homeowners that favored the kind of balanced elegance that the French style offered (in hands less intransigently pictorial than Worthen's) opted for something more homegrown, usually a variant of Colonial Revival.[25]

Because of their predominantly stucco facings, simplified variants of the English cottage and French farmhouse played well into a rising fad in local construction, the so-called winter-built house. Temporary insulating walls and portable heat sources allowed contractors such as Highland Park's Conrad Hamm to continue exterior construction through the year. With local newspaper features providing free advertisement, Hamm developed a method combining concrete block, wood frame, and plaster veneer. The result was invariably a gabled box, but adorned with enough wood stripping, brick quoining, and other pictorial paraphernalia to create a semblance of style. Hamm called on erstwhile Prairie School

Located at
1814 Hillcrest Ave.,
Corner Fairview,
Lane's Highland
Park.

Open to the Public
February 12th to 25th
from 2 to 9 P. M.

Ample Parking
Space With Police
Protection.

Street Car Service---
Randolph-Snelling
to Otto.

Randolph-Hope,
Cleveland to
Ford Road.

Drive Any of These Routes---
Snelling to Ford Road;
Cleveland to Ford Road;
Fairview to Hillcrest

You Are Cordially Invited to Visit

ST. PAUL'S WINTER-BUILT DEMONSTRATION HOME NO. 2

FIGURE 3.14. The second Winter-Built Demonstration Home, 1814 Hillcrest Avenue, 1927. This advertisement appeared in the *St. Paul Pioneer Press*. Courtesy of the Minnesota Historical Society.

luminary Percy Dwight Bentley (1885–1968) to design his second **Winter-Built Demonstration Home**, which was featured in several issues of the *St. Paul Pioneer Press* and went up at the corner of Hillcrest and Fairview Avenues in early 1928 (Figure 3.14). Referred to by Hamm as an example of the "French type of architecture," its geometric clarity and simple lines have equal affinities with the French farmhouses that inspired Jemne and the New England cottages then just coming into popularity.[26]

The most complexly sourced of the styles that swirled through St. Paul in the 1920s combined elements derived from villas of coastal Spain, France, Italy, and even North Africa with bits and pieces of vernacular Hispanic building in the southwestern United States. The composite style was generally advertised as "Spanish." It had already been anticipated by the California-based Mission Revival that had given St. Paul a scattering of bungalows, apartment houses, and service stations. But after World War I, the Hispanic material was supplemented with features and motifs drawn from largely transatlantic sources: a low-pitched red-tile roof, trowel-textured stucco walls, a mix of arched and rectangular openings, and decorative wrought-iron balconies. Some architectural historians have tried to break down the style into subtypes, for example, Mediterranean Revival, Late Mission Revival,

Adobe Revival, and so on, but this presumes a kind of archaeological precision that neither the architects nor their builders sought, particularly when dealing with a mode of building to which neither the designer nor his client had historical ties. In common practice, Hispanic, North African, Mediterranean, and inland Spanish sources were all in the same grab bag. As most of the Moorish sources crept into Spain, the period designation of the eclectic style as "Spanish" ends up capturing the most of any single label.

For a brief period in the mid-1920s, real estate columns, the ASHSB, trade magazines, and lumberyards pushed the Spanish Style nationwide as much as they did its less exotic picturesque peers. On first blush, this may appear anachronistic for a style whose prototypes were never built in a northern climate and whose cultural base had little with which St. Paul residents of the 1920s could identify. But the Spanish Style possessed several unique advantages. For one thing, it placed no restrictions on the floor plan; the rooms could be located and interrelated in any way that struck the builder's or the home owner's fancy. As a result, some of the more innovative plans of the period found their way into Spanish-looking shells. Step-down living rooms and open floor plans were common; so were dining rooms overlooking

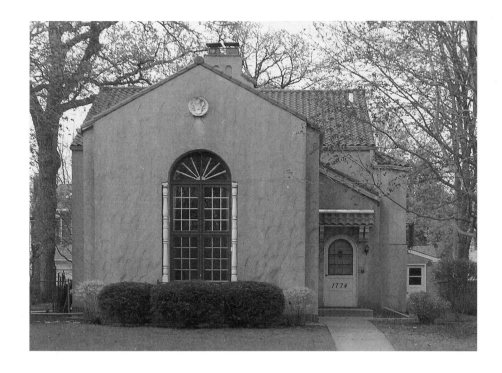

the front yard, and comfortable spaces at the rear that today would be called family rooms. If ornament was kept to a minimum, Spanish Style exteriors could also be quite practical in a northern climate because of their lack of exposed wood and overhanging cornices.[27]

The **Edward L. and Nell Murphy House,** just east of King's Maplewood, was the first full-blown Spanish Style house to be built in St. Paul (Figure 3.15). Designed in 1922 by Percy Dwight Bentley, it showed just how far a Prairie School devotee could wander from the avant-garde enthusiasms of his youth. Like Jemne and Ingemann working in a French vein, Bentley seemed more fascinated with the broad stucco facings and bold geometries permitted by the style than with its historical detailing. But the out-scaled arched front window, the sequence of tile roofs, and such conspicuous ornaments as the turned colonnettes flanking the front window all clearly announce a "Spanish" presence.

The Murphy house also introduced St. Paul to a gaudy stuccoing technique known as "jazz plastering." Popularized by builders in Southern California, it had two important elements: a deep, agitated surface texture, often invented by the plasterer himself; and the use of multiple pastel tints in the finish coat. The technique could not have been better named. Picking up on an article in the *Southwest Builder and Contractor,* the locally published

Improvement Bulletin condemned the fad for "mixing things up in an appalling way" that was a "travesty upon real Spanish or Italian architecture." Disparagement by the press did little to curb the enthusiasm of local builders and home owners, as even so distant a city as St. Paul boasted many examples of jazz plastering. Nearly all have been overpainted, but the great variety of deeply troweled, swirling and leaping stucco textures remain.[28]

Spanish-inspired architecture never infused whole neighborhoods in St. Paul as it did in the northern suburbs of Los Angeles. In the upper Midwest, that honor was reserved for the English Cottage and the American Colonial house. Instead, the style was loosely scattered through the city's 1920 neighborhoods, often popping up in surprising places. Across from Cherokee Park on the West Side, the **Henry Schroeckenstein House** concentrates the Spanish paraphernalia around two projecting bays, one that embraces the entry and one that sends a balcony out from a second-floor bedroom (Figure 3.16). Its architect was Myrtus Wright (1881–1960), like P. D. Bentley an early aficionado of the Prairie School. A broken roofline, suggestions of symmetry compromised by an irregularly shaped lateral wing, quirky overhangs and window shapes, an abundance of rope-shaped moldings—these are all borrowings from some source that could be linked to Spain. Perhaps because of Wright's lingering

FIGURE 3.16.

Henry Schroeckenstein House,
656 Chippewa Avenue.
The city's best theater architect
of the 1930s created this
Mediterranean fantasy.

sympathies with his famous namesake, the ground-floor plan is as open as any that came out of the Prairie School, but broad Moorish strokes and Colonial Revival detailing arrest the eye in every direction.

In a little-traveled western corner of the city just north of Shadow Falls Park are two houses that express the polar extremes of design in the Spanish Style. Both were commissioned by members of the Brewer family, with the William M. Linden Company as the designer-builder of record. The first of these, the **Francis A. and Alice Brewer House** at 544 Desnoyer, is at base an ornamented cube. This was the brand of so-called Spanish architecture most often presented in the real estate section of local newspapers. Broad, planar stucco surfaces (this time without jazzed finish) are relieved with numerous stylistic touches: tile shelf roofs, wrought-iron fittings, stepped water tables and window surrounds, and a bell-shaped parapet.[29]

On a raised corner lot a short distance to the north, famed local artist Nicholas Brewer put up the free-form opposite, a dizzying amalgam of Spanish and Moorish motifs affixed to an irregular plan and approached via a curving, parapeted walk. The crowning touch of the **Nicholas R. Brewer House** is a horizontal arrangement of loglike timbers suspended above a part of the roof in fanciful reference to a common Moorish construction

device (Figure 3.17). The building's sizable $12,000 price tag is supported by a plan with a larger footprint than appears from either street. Brewer himself had a hand in the finish work and perhaps some of the design as well. As a reporter described it in 1932, "Entering the living room one is immediately impressed with the large windows, the great fireplace and the interesting woodwork. The unusual finish on the woodwork was Brewer's own idea. After much persuasion he induced the workmen to go over all the woodwork in the room, including the beamed ceiling, with a blow torch, burning off the softer part of the surface." The artist lived there only during the summer months, and his hillside fantasy spent a decade waiting for its first permanent occupant.[30]

The Spanish Style always had a hint of opulence, linked in the popular mind to the entertainment palaces of Hollywood. But it was not reserved for the wealthy. During their brief period of popularity, St. Paul's bungalow courts often took on Hispanic overtones, together with the economical, cold-weather expedient of connection into a single, U-shaped plan. The **Samuel Grodin Bungalow Court** on Cleveland Avenue is a particularly well-preserved and finely detailed example of the bungalow court in Spanish dress (Figure 3.18). A near-clone of the Grodin triplex farther down Cleveland Avenue

FIGURE 3.17.
Nicholas R. Brewer House,
510 Frontenac Place. One of
the city's few Moorish Revival
houses is tucked behind trees
on a steep hillside lot.

FIGURE 3.18. Samuel Grodin Bungalow Court, 93–97 Cleveland Avenue. This project pushes the English village motif of the bungalow court toward a Mediterranean villa.

FIGURE 3.19.
James H. and Blanche Nolan
House and George and
Sadie von Nieda House,
151 and 145 Woodlawn Avenue.
These homes show a strangely
compatible pairing of an
eccentric Prairie School design
with an eclectically detailed
English cottage.

still possesses a faded rendition of the multiple-tinting sponsored by the jazz-plastering rage. It is hard to ascertain at this date how many of St. Paul's Spanish Style houses might have once had this Technicolor treatment.

In spite of its complex and interwoven historical base, most of the residential architecture of the 1920s maintained fairly clear stylistic boundaries. It is as possible today as it was eighty years ago to assign the labels English, Norman, French, and Spanish to the period-revival houses with European affinities. There were, however, a number of designs that pointedly defied stylistic boundaries, creating a kind of combinatory architecture that truly deserves the label "eclectic." Houses of this character juxtaposed sweeping curves with sharply defined geometrical shapes, formal window arrangements with irregularly shaped walls, historical borrowings with aggressively modern innovations.

King's Maplewood has several splendid examples of this brand of eclecticism. At the same time he was building the **James H. and Blanche Nolan House,** a modified Prairie School design of Charles Elwood's, carpenter-contractor Eric Fridholm put up a neighboring house for a Minneapolis druggist that defies classification under any category other than "eclectic." The swooping roof and projecting, columned entry of the **George and Sadie von Nieda House** are the antithesis of Elwood's rectilinear geometry and quietly recessed approach, yet

the two form a strikingly picturesque pairing (Figure 3.19). A perfect microcosm of the two contrasting but complementary styles can be found in their garden gates. The simple slatted Nolan House gate sits between posts with "capitals" of stacked squares, while the von Nieda gate is curved across the top and sports a miniature balustrade. Such yard and landscape features were common and important accompaniments to period-revival houses, though their preservation has been far more vulnerable to the whim of successive property owners than has conservation of the house itself.[31]

Shortly after the Nolan–von Nieda pair was finished, a stunning miniature of stylistic anarchy went up down the street. For the **Edward G. and Emily Bremer House,** Kenneth Worthen combined a classical, pedimented entry with a chimneylike, truncated tower, an arched window (complete with projecting keystone), random rubble facings, and a cat slide roof (Figure 3.20). A drawing of the design was published in the local newspaper with three others carrying the great pictorialist's signature. As with all period-revival essays in the hands of a capable designer, the mix of historical sources fails to mar the unity or quality of the finished design.[32]

More often than not, the basic scheme of 1920s ventures into eclecticism was some variant of the English cottage, or at least the prevailing design sources were English. The **Jerome Hirsh House** at 1800 Bayard

Avenue in Highland Park is one of the more ingratiating examples. Selected by the *St. Paul Pioneer Press* as the "June Bride Home" for 1930, it requires no great imagination to see a young couple tripping out through the music box entry. An irregularly faced chimney is balanced (in an offhand sort of way) by a cat slide roof and arched entry to one side and a dormer and two-story faceted bay to the other. All are bunched like bosom companions, their historical and formal dissimilarities masked by the play of multicolored stone across their surfaces. Inside, the naive eclecticism is preserved, for the dining room was furnished with walnut paneling supposedly based on eighteenth-century precedents, while the bedroom was appointed in early American maple. Built by prolific contractor John S. Brenny, the architect of the house has not been identified.[33]

By the onset of the Great Depression the boundaries of the foreign-based styles had begun to blur so badly that the eclectic spirit often invaded the plan as well as the exterior treatment. The 1933 **George F. and Jessie Beatty House** on Woodlawn Avenue, designed by Minneapolis architect Carlton W. Farnham, perfectly integrates the picturesque look and informal floor plan of the English cottage with colonial American propriety (Figure 3.21). The south half of the house, containing the informally arranged living spaces, is a hodgepodge

of swooping roofs, rippling chimney wall, and irregularly sized openings, while the north half, containing a formal dining room and the master bedroom, is capped with a hipped roof, ordered with absolute symmetry, and fenestrated in proper Colonial Revival manner.

Up to this point, we have alluded only incidentally to styles of American origin. This is as it should be, for our initial focus has been on the European-sourced picturesque tradition as it resurfaced in the 1920s, and neither the emphasis on symmetry nor the thirst for American roots of the Colonial Revival fits within that tradition. In addition, the type of colonial American building resurrected in the 1920s and 1930s was ordinarily quite restricted in range and degree of inventive possibilities. Its prototype was the Massachusetts Bay or Connecticut Valley house reduced to a standard format of three or five equal window bays, side gables, and a central, pedimented entry.

Yet this one housing type was of such extraordinary popularity, particularly among formally trained architects, that it deserves some attention here. By the early 1920s, the ascendance of the Colonial Revival was so taken for granted on the East Coast that the major architectural periodicals covered little else in the way of domestic design. Of 571 house designs surveyed by a writer for the *Architectural Record* in 1925, 24 were classified

FIGURE 3.21.
George F. and Jessie Beatty
House, 459 Woodlawn Avenue.
A side-by-side marriage of
English Cottage and Colonial
Revival appears here.

as "English" in inspiration, 51 "Spanish," 31 "French" (including both farmhouse-inspired and formal Renaissance Revival designs), and a whopping 231 "American Colonial." In the upper Midwest at mid-decade, the allotment of English would have greatly exceeded Spanish and French, even vying with American Colonial in popularity, but by the onset of the Great Depression American Colonial would reign supreme.[34]

Even while the English Cottage was at its apogee, the Colonial Revival made significant inroads in the picturesque, countrified settings above the Mississippi River that we have been exploring. Probably the best-known St. Paul example of 1920s American Colonial Revival, the house now owned by the University of Minnesota for the use of its president, is also one of the most complex renditions of the style in the city. Designed by Clarence Johnston Jr., who had by this time taken over the domestic branch of his father's practice, it was built for a lumber manufacturer in 1921 and sited on a huge parcel directly overlooking the river.

Although the main facade of the **Edward and Markell Brooks House** is built up with proper Colonial detail, the building sprawls out onto its lot in a manner befitting the picturesque tradition (Figure 3.22). Every bay and wing of the house is infused with the classical proportions and refined vocabulary of the style's New England

origins, and yet each of these appears as a separate pavilion joined almost haphazardly to the main mass.

Typically, the New England Colonial style of the 1920s and 1930s presented a single symmetrical rectangular mass, broad side to the street. More often than not, the chief individual marks of distinction were the treatment of the entryway and figurative, fret-sawn shutter ornament. A particularly well-sited and pristinely preserved specimen of proper Colonial style sits on Woodlawn Avenue flanked by houses designed in the English Cottage and Prairie School modes. Worthen's **Herbert R. and Elsie Galt House** presents an absolutely symmetrical facade to the street, and this is reinforced by its formal landscaping, including a central walkway flanked by a tall hedge (Figure 3.23).

As the building that arose on the side lot shows, neither scholarship nor symmetry succeeded in killing the pictorial spirit. Nestling into the rear of the flower beds is a garage presented to the street side as a quaint summer house. Built by a succeeding property owner, Twin City Motor Company executive W. E. Schulke, the **Walter E. and Elizabeth Schulke Garden House and Garage** has lost its environing gardens but remains a charming testimony to how a properly detailed version of the New England Colonial style could wander into the picturesque, even when pressed into utilitarian service (Figure 3.24).

FIGURE 3.22.
Edward and Markell Brooks
House, 176 North Mississippi
River Boulevard. This Colonial
Revival estate was designed
in the piece-by-piece manner
of incessantly remodeled
English country houses.
Courtesy of the University
of Minnesota Archives.

FIGURE 3.23.
Herbert R. and Elsie Galt
House, 157 Woodlawn Avenue.
A picture-perfect Colonial
Revival house.

One of the asymmetries regularly tolerated by the original colonial builders was a side porch or, if enclosed, a library wing. In the 1920s, this theme was taken up many times by architects and builders across the country. New lifestyles dictated that the old library wing now serve as an extension of the living room into a "sun porch," or as it was first called, a "living porch."

With the introduction of the automobile, this wing also became the ideal location for a tuck-under garage. The **James E. and Phillippina Niemeyer House**, designed by prominent local architect James Niemeyer (1890–1957), shows how readily a scholarly take on the Dutch Colonial architecture of New York could make this adaptation (Figure 3.25). Niemeyer exploited the full range of current

FIGURE 3.24.
Walter E. and Elizabeth
Schulke Garden House and
Garage, 157 Woodlawn Avenue.
High style could suffuse even
a garage, as one wall becomes a
garden retreat.

FIGURE 3.25.
James E. and Phillippina
Niemeyer House, 1075 Lombard
Avenue. The architect
incorporates the automobile
into Colonial Revival design.

styles but seemed more interested in the range of geo-metrical compositions and planning options that the styles offered than in their picturesque possibilities. The 1920s had room for both picture painters à la Kenneth Worthen and protomodernists like Jemne and Niemeyer.

One local architect probably did more than any other to establish both the strictures and the minute variations available within the American Colonial style: Edwin Lundie. Though best known locally for his work in University Grove in Falcon Heights just outside of the city limits, Lundie's hand can be seen in dozens, perhaps scores, of meticulously detailed Colonials throughout the city whose designs he had worked out for a major lumber company and a prominent builder.[35]

Of Lundie's Colonial Revival work in St. Paul proper, one of the most picture-perfect is also the smallest: a Cape Cod cottage for Kathryn Spink just west of the College of St. Catherine. Built in 1938, the **Kathryn L. Spink House** has all of the antique charm imputed to this building type by the trade magazines without losing the sense of sturdiness and weight that infuses all of Lundie's work (Figure 3.26). One can almost imagine heavy timbers behind the clapboards and shingles, rather than the light framing skeleton of the modern house. The attached garage echoes the lines of the house but in a lighter voice.

Many city neighborhoods experienced rapid residential development in the 1920s: Como to the west of the lake, the North End south of Lake Phalen, the East End in the vicinity of Hazel Park, and Highland Park north of Montreal. Of these areas, Highland was the last to move forward. While Lane's Highland Park division filled with houses in the mid-1920s, the remainder of the area developed slowly and erratically. Yet the area as a whole held on to the pictorial styles of the 1920s with unusual tenacity, developing a housing stock that would remain cohesive for another generation.[36]

The emergence of Highland's distinctive architectural environment was closely bound to the decision of Ford Motor Company to locate a major plant on the St. Paul side of the river. Between the time the decision was publicized in January 1921 and the opening of the plant for production in May 1925, a dirt road had been transformed into Highland Parkway, with a streetcar line that ran to the river; a major new hydroelectric plant was in operation; and a new commercial artery culminating in the great Ford Parkway Bridge was under way.[37]

In the fifteen years following the opening of the Ford Plant, new residents moved in fits and bursts into the residential development now opened up between Highland Park and the river. After the initial surge of the mid-1920s, what they built more often than not was a compendium of revival styles reduced to their bare essentials and grouped into stylistically uniform clusters. The result is tract housing of a sort, but it is tract housing that never quite abandons the careful craftsmanship, scholarly detail, and historical resonances of the Roaring Twenties, and above all it is tract housing with enough visual interest to create an expansive but cohesive neighborhood.

Much of the appearance of Highland Park was shaped by city planners, who took pride in Highland Park as "the first area in the Northwest to be laid out along city planning lines." This was a slight exaggeration, even in St. Paul; except on the West Side, most of the city's residential neighborhoods were already laid out in east-west blocks one-eighth of a mile in length and one-sixteenth of a mile in height, rather than the standard one-twelfth of a mile square. The intent was to reduce the number of intersections leading to the heart of the city. In much of Highland Park, this plan was stretched further, so that the blocks were made a full quarter mile long.[38]

Zoning restrictions brought city planning most visibly into play. Businesses were confined to Ford Parkway and Snelling Avenue. The absence of corner groceries or drugstores, mechanics shops, or even churches from residential streets—particularly when coupled with large lots and deep setbacks—created a length of unbroken green space reminiscent of the garden suburbs being planned for eastern cities. Yet downtown was less than five miles away.

The most common housing type to emerge on these expansive lots was also the least costly on a square-foot basis: a two-story, three-bay, six-room American Colonial. Entire blocks of this type of house went up, often differentiated by little more than whether the door pediment was curved or straight, or the design jigsawn into the shutters was a Christmas tree, a sailboat, or a candle. All were detailed in the fashion locally perfected a decade earlier by Lundie, Ingemann, and their peers and advertised with the often-repeated assurance that they would "remain in good taste as long as the house endures."[39]

For the builder of the truly small home, the upper story of the American Colonial house could be cropped, leaving a housing type that would soon become a symbol of post–World War II recovery. This was the so-called Cape Cod. In its first appearances in the city, the Cape Cod had been dormered, elaborated with fine detailing in the eaves and window heads, and crowned with a central chimney. Lundie continued to design in this manner through the remainder of his career. But by the time the Cape Cod began to proliferate in Highland, the chimney was allowed to pop out wherever it would, and all of the historical associations were packed in around the doorway.

The more vividly picturesque styles did not play so well in the economic hardships of the 1930s. However, a standardized version of the English cottage developed that occasionally acquired enough density to create neighborhoods of real character. One such row, the **1977 to 1999 Scheffer Avenue Houses**, took five years and five different builders to complete, a testimony to the occasional achievement of aesthetically cohesive neighborhoods through owner incentive alone. Each of the houses is distinctive in plan and materials, but each is designed around a street facade with an offset chimney and a complex, broken roofline.

At the brink of World War II, the Highland neighborhood continued to fill up with period-revival houses. Many of them ignored the call of economy and standardization, presenting to the city the final breath of the nostalgia-laden picturesque tradition in residential design. Colonial Revival continued to reign supreme but was often imbued with formal and material quirks reminiscent of the style's French and English peers. Just as often,

FIGURE 3.27.
Joseph P. and Eleanor Strigel
House, 1771 Highland Parkway.
Although Colonial Revival
in detail, this house inches
toward Modernism.

novel materials and a desire for more window exposure pushed the designs away from the 1920s styles altogether. The **Joseph P. and Eleanor Strigel House** of 1940, for example, places the entry within a Norman arch, uses a brick veneer reflective of a distinctly modern palette, and displays to the street two broad window bays more reminiscent of shop front than of residential design (Figure 3.27). Yet for all its nuances, it carries a distinctly Colonial air and was probably labeled as such by both its builder and architect.

The other period style that barely made it through the Depression was French. The **Martha E. Hagstrom House** of 1935 (Figure 3.28) neatly packages the windows and scrubs down the surfaces of the French château, but the corner tower is still there, and the beetling roof and brick-arched door. The architect of this house, like that of the Colonial house just described, remains unknown. Both cost in the neighborhood of $10,000, well above the $6,000 norm for two-story housing during the Depression. With Modernism waiting in the wings, a higher price still continued to bring a more fully elaborated period style.

One of the least known, but in some ways most telling, products of 1920s architectural sensibilities was the wall-to-wall period remodeling. Many received so much publicity as to become a kind of local sensation. This kind of remodeling worked only if the original house had a visual character that could be subsumed under some period fashion. Then every effort was made to shoehorn a style and period into the house that would complement the original shell, perhaps better than its original interiors.

In 1910, John Ordway bought a simple Craftsman Tudor house designed by local architect James MacLeod for a large lot on Summit Avenue. Within a year, he hired Reed and Stem to design a two-story addition, and the **John G. and Charlotte Ordway House** was off and rolling in the direction of the transitional English Medieval–English Renaissance (the "Jacobethan" style as some refer to it today) hinted at by the exterior (Figures 3.29 and 3.30). For nearly two decades, terminated only by the decline in Stem's health in 1927, new wings and walls and roofs piled up around the old as if the house were growing from within, with scarcely a hint of stylistic change. A famous New York decorator is said to have thrown up her hands at the crude materials— cypress paneling and rough plaster—of the Gothic living room. But what did she know? This was history brought to St. Paul.[40]

A. H. Stem spent the waning years of his career engaged in just this sort of reoutfitting of older houses. The **Frank B. Kellogg House** on Fairmount Avenue and the **Mrs. C. W. Griggs House** on Summit Avenue are two among many of the city's landmark residences on

FIGURE 3.28.

Martha E. Hagstrom House,
1755 Highland Parkway.
One of the last turreted houses
built in St. Paul before the
advent of the rambler.

Summit Hill for which Stem created lavish remodelings in the 1920s. In each case, new interiors and landscape structures enhanced the medieval or Renaissance resonances that the property already possessed. The cost of these enhancements often exceeded the price of the most expensive new King's Maplewood homes.

Edwin Lundie launched into the remodeling market with a spectacular follow-up to Stem's work for Mary Griggs. In 1930 Mrs. Griggs hired Jemne to design a ballroom for the basement in the current French fashion; then she proceeded to purchase entire rooms from French and Italian houses of the seventeenth and eighteenth centuries. Lundie took over Jemne's work and shared with Mrs. Griggs and a Venetian antique dealer the job of selecting the rooms and getting them to fit into the existing spaces, including those produced by the extensive 1884 and 1925 remodelings already noted. This required cutting the materials down or in-filling with

matched material as the spaces required. Most of the refitting occurred outside of Venice, in spaces that duplicated the Griggs house rooms. No exterior walls were changed, no windows were filled in or punched out; in fact, absolutely no evidence exists from without that the building was not still a Tuscan Villa with Beaux-Arts updating of its porches and terraces. But the interior spaces flowed from one period and country to another as if they were always designed that way. The result has been called a "modern apotheosis of architectural eclecticism."[41]

Occasionally, extensive additions to an exterior were so skillfully done that the real history of the house would fool modern observers. In 1929 Clifton C. Daily acquired an 1860s Italianate house of the simple bracketed-cube, side-hall type. Its original owner, William Davern, was the first permanent settler in the area just south of what would become King's Maplewood. The house was magnificently sited on a large, well-treed hill but had nothing

FIGURE 3.29. John G. and Charlotte Ordway House, 485 Summit Avenue. After its conversion into an English country estate, the home was featured in the high-style magazine *Golfer and Sportsman* in 1933. Courtesy of the Minnesota Historical Society.

FIGURE 3.30.
Living room of the Ordway House.
The steep Gothic ceiling was briefly
fashionable. From *Golfer and
Sportsman* (1933). Courtesy of the
Minnesota Historical Society.

FIGURE 3.31.

FIGURE 3.31.
St. Paul Pioneer Press–Dispatch
Demonstration House,
1749 Princeton Avenue.
Edwin Lundie updates an
ordinary suburban house of the
mid-1880s into a properly
Colonial Revival "farmhouse."

approaching its age or style for blocks around it. Rather than start from scratch, the **Clifton C. Daily House** at 1173 Davern Street duplicated the south two bays of the original house on the north, creating a central-hall plan and a main facade reminiscent of the New England Colonial type. Carpenter Robert Elholm was so successful in redesigning the doorway and reiterating the old bracketing that modern surveys have dated the current appearance of the house to its original construction in the 1860s rather than to a 1930 period-revival remodeling.[42]

With the onset of the Great Depression, new building starts slowed dramatically, adding an economic edge to the remodeling boom. Modernizing through remodeling became a mantra of the real estate industry, and its greatest public booster, the local press. Scores of articles and books were written urging home owners to update the style of their homes at the same time they added a room or modernized its mechanical systems. Through the early years of the Depression, local papers published a constant stream of "before" and "after" photographs, most of them

showing a conversion so complete that the original style was obliterated. More often than not the outcome was, like the Daily House, some version of Colonial Revival.

In St. Paul, the growing taste for wholesale makeovers acquired an official voice as early as 1930, with the creation of the St. Paul Building and Modernization Bureau. Its first public splash was a model project in Macalester Park that "demonstrated the practicability of transforming out-of-date homes into modern dwelling." This remodeling encapsulated the ways that an older house could be brought up to date in style, planning, use of materials, and mechanical systems.[43]

Known as the **St. Paul Pioneer Press–Dispatch Demonstration House**, the abandoned dwelling of 1884 stood in the middle of a large lot at 1749 Princeton Avenue (Figure 3.31). Still in sound condition, it was carefully inspected, scale drawings were made up, and state-of-the-art mechanical systems were installed. After twenty full-page feature articles exploring every possible kind of modernization that the house was putting in place,

FIGURE 3.32.
Harry Firminger House,
1883 Stanford Avenue. A local
concrete company showed
the unlimited plasticity of
its material.

the newspaper finally announced Edwin Lundie as the designing architect. Lundie turned the plan of the house sideways on the lot, creating a stylized informality meant to recall a New England Colonial farmhouse. Sequences of boxy rooms became interconnected, flowing spaces, and Lundie's penchant for storage nooks, American Colonial imagery, and bold craftsmanship had free rein.[44]

For all of the emphasis on updating its old housing stock, St. Paul took on Modernism slowly in residential design. The initial impetus came from the engineering rather than the aesthetic side. This is amply demonstrated by a frequent emphasis on modern construction and mechanical systems in the advertisement of houses with period-revival designs, but even before that by the kinds of designs that anticipated Modernist structural and engineering developments.

On the basis of geometric simplicity alone, it would be natural to look for some variant of the four-square house or a Colonial-inspired gabled rectangle to pave the way for the purist vocabulary and expanded structural innovations of Modernism. As a matter of fact, the opposite was true. The standard wood-frame basis of colonial-inspired, rectilinear house forms was never seriously threatened by experiments with newer materials, and the classical ordering of the Colonial Revival facade rarely got simplified or reconfigured in a Modernist direction. Then and now the style remained rooted in its neoclassical composition and a modicum of historical detail;

without that, it failed to create the resonances with Early America that were so essential to its appeal.

Ironically, the experimental use of steel and concrete and the use of structural detail as aesthetic form commonly began not with the squarish houses we associate with early Modernism but with houses of the most picturesque character. Nationwide, the many experiments with cast-in-place concrete houses dating back to 1906 nearly all echoed English rather than American design elements and motifs. The most famous of these, the garden suburbs created on Long Island by Grosvenor Atterbury, was a conscious attempt at imitating the new industrial suburbs of England. Steel framing also found its way more frequently into large-scale designs of English inspiration largely because of the span required for the "Great Hall" at the heart of the building.[45]

For the small, custom-designed house, the complexly contoured surfaces of the "English" cottage also invited a number of attempts at concrete construction in order to cut costs. By the 1920s, concrete block had replaced cast-in-place construction. Manufacturing and setting up the steel forms for pouring had proved too expensive to be practical. St. Paul got a taste of the new type of building in 1925, when the Formless Concrete Construction Company erected several houses in Macalester-Groveland, among them the **Harry Firminger House** (Figure 3.32). On first glance, these appear to be little more than spec houses in an English vein. However,

FIGURE 3.33.
Pierce and Hilda Butler House,
5 Edgcumbe Place. The house
is an essay in geometry as
much as a specimen of the
English Cottage.

each of the wall openings is modularly scaled and shorn of wood casings, and the eaves are clipped nearly at the wall, creating a composition of simple solids and voids of strikingly modern appearance. The effect is enhanced by such features as stepped chimneys and boldly outlined parapets, which emphasize sculptural form above surface detail.[46]

Trained architects did not hesitate to exploit the opportunities the English style gave for geometrical display. At the northeast corner of Highland Park, Minneapolis architects (and soon to become Modernists) Lang, Raugland, and Lewis gave the **Pierce and Hilda Butler House** an English Cottage look by reducing the style to two gabled wings punctured with geometric shapes and joined to a tubular chimney (Figure 3.33). The sympathy for bold combinations of rounded and angular shapes suggested by such designs paved the way for the French-inspired Modernism that would explode in the downtown area at the beginning of the next

decade. In the meantime, the area of Highland Park in which Butler built, dominated by Edgcumbe Road, would emerge as the venue of some of the city's showiest housing during the transition from period revival to Modernism.

The self-consciously modern house finally appeared in the city in 1935. So many variants of it burst on the scene at the same time that it is tempting to look for a massive external stimulus. There certainly was one close at hand. In 1933, Chicago held a Century of Progress Exposition featuring experimental houses built and serviced with the latest technologies. The designs of these houses pointedly defied both the classical and the picturesque traditions. Neither the call of history nor a romance with bucolic environments was any longer relevant; the ideals that now mattered were all bound to the technological achievements, increased efficiencies, and aesthetic possibilities embodied in the new structural and mechanical systems.

FIGURE 3.34.
Richard M. and Mathilda Elliot
House, 1564 Vincent Street.
Though preceded in St. Paul
by a dozen other flat-roofed
houses, this was the only
one that had steel casements
and shunned all historical
references.

The Century of Progress streamed into St. Paul's residential neighborhoods via four quite independent channels: the architectural community, a construction products company, a builder-developer, and an electrical appliances company. All of them obviously had an economic stake, or hoped they did, in the new fad. In University Grove, Rhodes Robertson and Roy Childs Jones, both affiliated with the School of Architecture of the University of Minnesota, designed a brick and steel sequence of interpenetrating cubes for psychology professor Richard Elliot. It was perhaps the first house in the city to make the garage the dominant element of the design from a pedestrian point of view. All the windows of the **Richard M. and Mathilda Elliot House** are steel casements with ladder mullions, and the walls are unadorned except for flush belt courses of contrasting color running above the window heads (Figure 3.34). Although the house spawned no other known designs, it remains a landmark of early Modernism in residential construction in the St. Paul area.

While the Elliot House was under way, steel home construction made its St. Paul debut with great fanfare. Sited in the midst of period-revival housing in King's Maplewood, the **Steel Construction Products Company "All-Steel Home"** was an obvious progeny of the Century of Progress (Figure 3.35). The manufacturer had just opened a local branch, intending the house to be "the first of a series of pre-fabricated homes which the company will build in St. Paul, each one to be individual in plan and appearance, yet all to be built on modern lines." Company manager Bernard Rand further boasted that the design assured almost perfect sound insulation, coolness in the summer, and warmth with low fuel consumption in the winter. In spite of these assurances, no similar all-steel homes were constructed in the city, although the company did build another, much simpler steel-frame house in King's Maplewood.[47]

Designed by associated architects Raphael Heime, Eugene Lund, and Walter MacLeith, the "all-steel" house on Woodlawn Avenue actually utilized a variety of materials. The floors were sheathed with plywood and finished off with oak, and the exterior panels were set off by narrow aluminum bands. Whether the latter provided "a decorative motif carrying out the streamline effect" or simply a high-tech equivalent of masonry joints depends entirely on one's point of view. The company in fact offered a variety of surface treatments as options. The one chosen for their house on Woodlawn was apparently unique at the time: a matte surface porcelain-coated steel. Fittingly enough, the first owner of the house was iron ore magnate Emmett Butler, who moved in sometime in 1937.[48]

FIGURE 3.35.
Steel Construction Products
Company "All-Steel Home,"
265 Woodlawn Avenue. This
project, sheathed in porcelainized
steel, displays a curious assortment
of historical motifs.

Always at the forefront of national building trends, Conrad Hamm immediately piggybacked on the Steel Construction Products foray into the city with his Fabricated Home Company. His **All-Steel Demonstration Home**, now much altered, went up at 1969 Jefferson Avenue in the midst of Craftsman and period-revival houses. Its walls and roof were sheathed with a copper-alloy steel, and insulation and innovative window design were claimed to cut heating costs by three-fourths. However, behind the steel shell lurked a wood frame, and the vaunted fireproof exterior was further compromised by all-linoleum flooring. The experimental house was also intended to show how quickly latest-technology houses could be put up, but the construction schedule grew from the advertised few weeks to the sixty-day standard for small-house construction. Apparently the alloy sheathings also failed to live up to expectations, for the house has since acquired an aluminum and fiberglass veneer.[49]

The last 1935 design to push the steel-house construction fad was the local winner of a national architectural competition sponsored by General Electric Company. St. Paul architect Kenneth Fullerton (1891–1960) drew up the plans, Jackson Investment Company footed the bill, and Highland Park afforded the site for the **General Electric Company "New American Home"** (Figure 3.36). It, too, was intended to be the first in a series, all of

them "super dwellings" with steel posts four feet on center. Steel panels were affixed to the outside of the posts, and wood paneling lined the interiors. Most important from the standpoint of the sponsor, the heating and air-conditioning as well as the kitchen appliances were all electric. Yet for all of the house's vaunted advances in design and comfort, it waited over a year to find an occupant. It has since suffered the ironic indignity of a shingle-and-plywood overlay, exactly reversing the wood-to-metal direction of the normal 1950s and 1960s facelift. What is more, the sheer sides and flat roof gave way to a mansard arrangement that creates the appearance of a 1970s updating of the neighborhood's period-revival styles, rather than the bold, stand-alone Modernism of the original design.[50]

The difficulty two of the three experimental houses had in finding an occupant, in spite of considerable free publicity in the local newspapers, was indicative of how small an impress the publicity surrounding the Century of Progress and its aftermath made on the local mind. Except for one other Steel Construction Products Company house in King's Maplewood, the three demos remained the only known steel houses erected in St. Paul before World War II.

A fourth futuristic demo went up two years later by yet a different sponsor, and it too failed to gather enough

FIGURE 3.36.
General Electric Company "New American Home," 1819 Bohland Avenue. The Modernist design now hides behind a mansard roof and wood sheathing. The anonymous rendering was published in the *St. Paul Pioneer Press* in 1935. Courtesy of the Minnesota Historical Society.

interest to generate offspring. The **Cemstone Products Company "House of Tomorrow"** was a manufacturer's attempt to expand into the home-building field with a concrete block product (Figure 3.37). Conveniently located near the company's East Side plant, the model home was a builder's mix of period revival and Modernism.

Advertisements claimed the Cemstone house to have been "applauded by thousands," but it was ultimately occupied by the vice president of the company, and few if any others followed in its wake. Like its three predecessors in experimental steel housing, Cemstone had anticipated a feeding frenzy, but the combined result of their efforts was two sharks already in tow.[51]

For all of these faltering attempts to reach a mass market during the Great Depression, St. Paul did succeed in building two upscale, forward-looking residential designs of real distinction. Neither quite achieved the austerity of their immediate Century of Progress–inspired predecessors; they can be classified as Moderne (in Ada Louise Huxtable's term, *modernistic*) rather than Modernist. The first, a little-known masterpiece erected in 1937–38, was designed by Magnus Jemne. Since Jemne was such a pivotal figure in the city's slow and cautious embrace of architectural Modernism, we will take a look at the man and his career before peering more closely at this particular design.[52]

Trained first in Cass Gilbert's St. Paul office during its final days in the city and then at the University of Pennsylvania under famed Beaux-Arts exponent Paul

Cret, Jemne had as much exposure as anyone in the city to the neoclassicism of the academies. His early partnership with fellow Gilbert draftsman Thomas Holyoke had also given him ample opportunity to flex his classical training.

After partnering with Holyoke for five years, Jemne launched an independent practice in 1925. Shortly thereafter he became a staunch advocate of a brand of Modernism that grew out of the famed 1925 Exposition Internationale des Arts Décoratifs et Industriels Modernes in Paris. More popularly known today as the birthplace of Art Deco, that exposition also gave Le Corbusier and his contemporaries their first international exposure. Following the lead of that exhibition and its tremendous American press exposure, Jemne preached and practiced a modern approach to architecture that was more romantic and less formally strictured than the Modernism that ultimately took hold. His pre–World War II work would thus be classified today as Moderne rather than Modern.

The Depression confined much of Jemne's work to high-style remodeling, in which he was ably assisted by his wife, Elsa Jemne, an estimable artist in her own right. Most of this important work remains unidentified and unlocated. One of his few published designs from that period illustrates a house with a complex array of setbacks and recesses, all contained within a roughly cubical shape. It bears many similarities to the single known Jemne-designed residence of the era that has come down

FIGURE 3.37.
Cemstone Products Company
"House of Tomorrow,"
1345 East Minnehaha Avenue.
This was the East Side's most
highly advertised venture
into 1930s Modernism.

to us: the **Robert S. and Freda Ahrens House** just east of Highland Park (Figure 3.38). Although the lot faces east, the building is planned so that all of the major rooms have broad southern exposure, an expression of Jemne's belief that "all life should be geared to the sun." Jemne was able to achieve this by contouring the south and east walls in a sequence of monumental rounded and faceted bays, creating the effect of a single great wall reaching out in ripples toward the sun. As with the Women's Club building before it, Jemne makes free use of the gold-hued Mankato-Kasota stone, this time complemented with a clay yellow brick. His loyalty to and romance with this native stone was perhaps his single noteworthy inheritance from Holyoke.[53]

The other great Moderne house in St. Paul is far better known to local residents, although its designer has lapsed into an undeserved obscurity. In 1939, furrier Abe Engelson commissioned the recently formed partnership of Firminger and Purtell to design a house for him in the heart of the Highland Park neighborhood. The **Abe and Mary Engelson House** represents the flip side of Modernism from Jemne's work: rather than carefully crafted surfaces, broad sweeps of industrial material; rather than a clear expression of interior planning requirements, a single great, curving wall; rather than carefully ordered modular openings, a fenestration scheme employing surface penetrations of every shape and size (Figure 3.39). By far the dominant element in the design is a giant, stepped glass-block window mounted across the wall curve. Rather than lighting a staircase or a single large room, it washes light through the house.

Harry Firminger (1889–1961) was a modern version of the peripatetic nineteenth-century draftsman, a Harvey Ellis in a business suit. He began his career with journeyman architect E. J. Donohue, then skipped through a succession of architectural offices that had Prairie School affinities—Alban and Hausler, Bentley and Hausler, the city architect's office, Hartford and Hausler, and Olin H. Round—before setting up an independent practice in 1919. In the 1920s, he continued to do work for other

FIGURE 3.38.
Robert S. and Freda Ahrens House,
1565 Edgcumbe Road. This little-known
jewel from Magnus Jemne appeared
in a cement advertisement in
Northwest Architect in 1935.
Courtesy of the Minnesota
Historical Society.

If you want the perfect mortar material that —

Bonds perfectly with all types of masonry units

Has been approved for work in all government departments

Will not cause efflorescence

Assures the mix you specify

Will not fade mortar colors

Is uniform in color *Specify-*

Is economical

Carney Cement for Masonry —

FIGURE 3.39.
Abe and Mary Engelson House,
1775 Hillcrest Avenue.
St. Paul's best-known and most
theatrical Moderne house.

FIGURE 3.40.
This "Model Village House"
was a competition entry
submitted by Harry Firminger
in 1914 and published in
Western Architect. It was built for
R. C. Ashby at 1423 Chelmsford
Street. Courtesy of the
Minnesota Historical Society.

architects, Kenneth Worthen among them, returning at last in 1928 to Charles Hausler, whom he served as chief draftsman/designer for the next six years. He took up independent practice again in 1934, this time combining architectural work with civil engineering.[54]

Firminger first made a local mark with his **"Model Village House"** entry in a Minnesota State Art Society Competition in 1914 (Figure 3.40). Rendered in the manner of Marion Mahony's superb drawings of Wrightian projects, a modified version of it was constructed the following year in St. Anthony Park for R. C. Ashby. That design merits mention here because it combines Prairie School with English cottage motifs in a manner more akin to the overt geometries of Art Deco than to the picturesque tradition to which its materials belong. Its bewildering array of window shapes and sizes also anticipates the eccentric fenestration scheme of Firminger's Moderne house twenty-five years in the future.

Adapting the intimate, human scale of period residential design to larger buildings presented a difficult challenge to architects and builders. But apartments were in high demand. In spite of a nearly fifty-year tradition of promoting home ownership, St. Paul realtors and financiers could not buck the national trend toward multifamily residences. In the 1920s, the proportion of the American population living in apartment buildings nearly doubled, to a high of 62 percent. The result in St. Paul as elsewhere was a booming market in apartment building

that happened to coincide with the rising demand for heavy architectural stylization.[55]

Apartment building developers responded with versions of all of the styles, whether period revival or Art Deco, that not only flattened them out but forced them into the same mold. In St. Paul, the typical apartment building of the 1920s and 1930s had three stories including a raised basement, three bays demarcated by setoffs, and windows grouped in twos and threes within the bays. All the styles were molded to fit into that basic format.

The **Realty Service Company Apartments** of 1925 typify the English style as it was expressed in the midst of the city's densest area of new apartment development on Grand Avenue west of Syndicate Street (Figure 3.41). Four apartment buildings just west of Syndicate parcel out elements of the style among the three front bays: crenellated parapets, stone-trimmed Tudor arches, half-wood panels, and false gables. The resulting designs express some of the picturesque silhouette and detailing of the English residential style but repackage it into a format that transforms formal nuances into eccentric attachments.

Underneath the stylish wrap, the Grand Avenue apartments were marketed as specimens of the "finest building construction in the world," fully soundproof, "absolute proof against fire," equipped with "every known modern appliance," and destined to last three to five hundred years. The units were also sold rather than rented, with

FIGURE 3.41.
Realty Service Company
Cooperative Apartment Building,
1280 Grand Avenue. Kenneth
Worthen designed six of these
buildings, all of which were
variations on the same English
Cottage themes stretched over
a three-story surface.

the common facilities and grounds managed on a cooperative basis, much like the modern townhouse or condominium. Architect of the four buildings, in an unusual venture from small-scale design, was Kenneth Worthen.[56]

A particularly elegant attempt to make the same scheme work in a Moderne mode occurred near the west end of Grand Avenue, this time by an unknown architect. The approach walk, entry, and address medallion of the 1939 **Kieffer Brothers Apartments** are a wonderful set piece of Art Deco design, with a sculpted tower element affixed to one side and a setback of the other completing the stylistic package (Figure 3.42). The Moderne style has here lost its radical pretenses and linked arms with its period-revival predecessors. In fact, this building, like so many of its Art Deco companions, appears not so much to toll the bell for the picturesque movement as to sing its swan song.

In the 1920s, the New England Colonial style had been the least picturesque of all the revival styles. But by the 1940s, apart from a few scraps of Old England around the doors and rooflines, it was all that was left in the way of historical styles. Colonial America, not medieval England, became the visual model for the most ambitious development of the period between the wars, **Highland Village Apartments** (see Figure 4.4). This vast residential and service complex, completed under an FHA loan in 1939, was the most expansive blending

of natural scenery and a nostalgic building type in the city. Twelve buildings housing 256 families were spread over twenty-two acres filled with gardens, trees, and playgrounds. Total control of the parcel assured freedom from the noise and congestion of the commercial district arising to the north, while large, closely placed windows brought in ample fresh air and exposure to the parklike setting.

Commercial architecture of the 1920s and 1930s had a shorter distance to travel to Modernism than the erratic course taken by residential architecture. But it was infused with some of the same pictorial interest. Coming out of World War I, nearly all of St. Paul's large-scale commercial and public buildings showed the formalizing influence of Beaux-Arts training. Clear exposure and surface elaboration of the main vertical supports (whether piers or columns), rhythmically ordered facades, and repetitious, simplified neoclassical detail were all marks of that influence. But a gradual shift was occurring, away from structural exposition and toward a surface play and material richness that were of one piece with the pictorial sensibility of period-revival design.

The French academy's final dance in St. Paul was initiated by the finishing of the **Hamm Building** (Figure 3.43). Begun in 1915 as a speculative office building, it stood as a bare steel skeleton for three years until a new investor came aboard in the person of brewing potentate

FIGURE 3.42.
Kieffer Brothers Apartment
Building, 1947 Grand Avenue.
A Moderne facade is affixed to
an apartment type developed at
the turn of the century.

FIGURE 3.43.
Hamm Building, 408 St. Peter
Street. This building, with
the largest terra-cotta surface
in the Twin Cities, is shown
shortly after its completion in
1920. Photograph by Charles P.
Gibson; courtesy of the
Minnesota Historical Society.

FIGURE 3.44. A manufacturer's photograph of a terra-cotta panel for the Krank Manufacturing Company Building, 1885 West University Avenue. Courtesy of the Northwest Architectural Archives, University of Minnesota Libraries.

William Hamm. Hamm hired the rising young firm of Toltz, King, and Day, and the building soon began to adorn a steel skeleton with the most expansive terra-cotta skin in the city. Its designer, Roy Childs Jones (1885–1963), was a university professor who was rapidly making a name for himself as a design associate of Toltz, King, and Day.

In an issue of the terra-cotta trade periodical *Common Clay* entirely devoted to the building, Jones gave his rationale for the design of the terra-cotta facings. It is a clear exposition of the blending of Beaux-Arts academicism and the pictorial sensibility of the 1920s:

Here there was a frame work of steel lines that had to be closely followed. The outside face of the building becomes thereby a skin more or less tightly drawn about the steel bones underneath. The resulting composition is one of lines rather than surfaces. But the treatment of these terra cotta lines offered an interesting chance to express the material as the historic examples have shown it should be expressed. By repeated ornamental motifs, by various details of section and jointing, a surface pattern of low relief has been developed. This ornamental pattern does not

exist so much for its own sake, as for the creation of a totality of light and shade texture into which all the individual motifs merge.[57]

Jones returned to a more straightforward expression of structure for the **Krank Manufacturing Company** in 1926 (Figure 3.44). The march of strip pilasters across the front is its primary motif. But above the pilasters is a frieze of elaborate brickwork, and connecting them at the height of the door heads is a spandrel clad in gaily colored terra-cotta. The terra-cotta work was an appropriate expression for Krank's main product, cosmetics. Its swirling floral shapes and colors pose an effective counterpoint to the martial order of the facade.

Shop-front architecture was also quick to indulge in the spirit of Beaux-Arts refinement gone picturesque. Sculptor Lawrence Brioschi and painter Carlo Minuti were Italian immigrants who had done work for Stanford White before establishing a partnership as "St. Paul's first architectural sculptors" in 1910. Minuti himself designed the building they moved into in 1922, the **Brioschi-Minuti Studio and Shop** on University Avenue (Figure 3.45). It is a simple composition of brick piers and large show windows. Those on the second floor illuminated

FIGURE 3.45.
Brioschi-Minuti Studio and Shop,
908–10 West University Avenue, ca. 1935.
The company's handiwork is clearly displayed
to the street. Photograph by Charles P. Gibson;
courtesy of the Minnesota Historical Society.

their studio as well as showing off its products to the street in the manner of the elevated automotive showrooms of the period. Relief sculpture is set in to all available blank spots, and decorative urns pierce the skyline at either end.[58]

When the budget allowed, church design also took hold of this distinctive combination of form-as-structure and eye-catching pictorial detail. By the end of World War I, English parish Gothicism was losing its exclusive hold on ecclesiastical design. The architectural profession was gaining increasing expertise in other archaeological strains as well as responding to the pull of the commercial styles. Romanesque work in particular enjoyed a brief resurgence, probably because it so naturally supported the Roaring Twenties fascination with the interaction between roughly blocked-out forms and finely executed detail.

The **Church of St. Luke** on Summit Avenue, built in 1925, clearly tosses in both directions at once (Figure 3.46). Its sheer limestone walling, vast stretches of un-ornamented surface, and simple tagged-on volumes are almost factory-like in their severity. But the elaborately carved front echoes the triptych portal of St. Gilles-du-Gard in southern France, and behind the doors stretches one of the truly magnificent architectural spaces in the city. Emmanuel Masqueray's death had passed the design of St. Luke's on to his successors, Slifer and Abrahamson (fl. 1919–36), and they continued their master's forays into archaeology-based design hung onto modern American structural systems.

Herbert A. Sullwold's (fl. 1914–30) **Chapel of Our Lady of Victory** at the College of St. Catherine shares St. Luke's two-faced sensibility (Figures 3.47 and 3.48). The 1924 design is a tour de force of eclectic archae-ologizing held together with distinctively American craftsmanship. The tower, side wall treatment, and gable detailing derive from various sources in northern Italy, and the portal is drawn from St. Trophime at Arles, France. But the extraordinary way the stone is cut and laid up, in a mix of rectangles and trapezoids, appears to be the architect's own invention, as is the terra-cotta

FIGURE 3.46.
Church of St. Luke,
1079 Summit Avenue.
This commission, first awarded
to Emmanuel Masqueray, was
completed in the 1920s by his
successor firm and others.

finish of the portal and the elaborate tile work of the interior. The church is a romantic commingling of ancient European memories with modern factory-based technologies.[59]

When Gothicism emerged triumphant once again in the late 1920s, it was with quite a different spirit than the scholarly re-creations and domestically scaled neighborhood churches that dotted small towns and city residential neighborhoods before the Great Depression. As late as 1937, **Nativity of Our Lord Catholic Church** erected a surprisingly elaborate example of the Gothic Revival at Stanford and Prior Avenues, just to the east of King's Maplewood. The familiar bias toward parish versions of late English Gothicism can be seen in the great mullioned windows, strongly vertical silhouette, and vividly contrasting stonework. But architects O'Meara and Hills were working with poured concrete and steel, and every convolution of the sanctuary's profile shows it.

The march of thin lateral buttresses clearly marks the regular intervals of a steel frame, and the stone hangs on to the sides like a single great carved ornament.[60]

Small-scale commercial architecture never quite got into the Beaux-Arts swim of things, nor did it have an acknowledged master like Gothicist Ralph Adams Cram in church architecture. As a result, architects with small commercial commissions after World War I quickly absorbed and put into play all of the various styles and devices developed for other building types.

In 1926, Charles Hausler showed how expansively the English Cottage could be treated in the **Kessler and Maguire Funeral Home** on West Seventh Street (Figure 3.49). Hausler (and his chief draftsman, Harry Firminger) came up with an apparition of a sprawling English village inn, complete with stone arches, an "Old English fountain," and a host of other equally nostalgic paraphernalia. The effect of a country inn was not entirely

FIGURE 3.47. Chapel of Our Lady of Victory, College of St. Catherine, ca. 1925. A design of French Romanesque inspiration is put to modern American service. Courtesy of the St. Paul Public Library.

FIGURE 3.48.
Interior of Chapel of
Our Lady of Victory, ca. 1925.
Woodwork, ceramics, and fixturing
were all custom designed to meld
with the ancient form of the
barrel vault. Courtesy of the
St. Paul Public Library.

FIGURE 3.49. Kessler and Maguire Funeral Home, 640 West Seventh Street. A miraculously intact assembly of medieval English church, country house, and village square, all miniaturized and rolled together. The overhead electrical sign is also original.

FIGURE 3.50.
Eric Fridholm Office Building,
1795–97 St. Clair Avenue.
Contractor Fridholm erected
this little office suite for
himself and a tenant.

gratuitous, for the plan included a kitchenette apartment for mourners who intended to stay overnight.[61]

Occasionally, the English Cottage style also served a direct advertising purpose for its occupants. In 1928, the diminutive **Eric Fridholm Office Building** gave a speculative builder a venue that clearly showed his residential clients both the manner and the quality of what they would get from him (Figure 3.50). Its architect, Kenneth Worthen, also designed many of Fridholm's other construction projects, particularly in Macalester-Groveland and King's Maplewood. Two years later, the **Red Wing Stoneware Company Store and Offices** provided a major pottery manufacturer with a St. Paul branch in the Midway district. In the understatement of a contemporary

FIGURE 3.51.
Hancock Oil Company
Filling Station, 716 South
Mississippi River Boulevard,
1925 (demolished). This
advertisement in the *St. Paul
Dispatch* lauds the aesthetic
virtues of the service station.
Courtesy of the Minnesota
Historical Society.

ANNOUNCING

*The opening of the most unique and attractive
gasoline and oil filling station ever opened
to the service of the motoring public.*

newspaper description, it was "a departure from the average type of business structure." But its tile roofs (now replaced) clearly linked the building to its product, and its cottage form reinforced the company's sometime image (never quite true) as a producer of handcrafted ware. One of the first projects of local luminary Kenneth Fullerton, it shows how far the tastes and even the technical knowledge of architects would have to move from the pictorial work of the 1920s to the gradual absorption of novel forms and innovative technologies during the Great Depression.[62]

English Cottage touches brought style and panache to the most pedestrian commercial buildings, with automotive filling stations leading the way. The intersection of Mississippi River Boulevard and Highland Parkway once boasted the picture-perfect **Hancock Oil Company Filling Station**, a purveyor of Pure Oil products, intentionally designed to blend with the garden suburban ethos of its residential neighborhood (Figure 3.51). An ad released at the time of the facility's opening in 1925 described it as "an unusual architectural beauty" and gave the rationale for its design:

> Set back amid a grove of stately oaks and maples this gabled cottage of true English design, with its broad curbed drives, artistic lanterns and old fashioned

watering-well centered on a broad expanse of lawn, is not suggestive of commercial enterprise, but blends in colorful harmony, as intended, with the quiet dignity of the surrounding community.[63]

Cottage designs continued to capture the fancy of the automotive service industry for nearly two decades. St. Paul once had four that even sported Dutch windmills, the product of a 1922 Superior Refining Company initiative. At the beginning of World War II, the fashion was still carrying on, though the picturesque roofs, chimneys, and doorways of the English style were more often than not mixed with colonial Americana. Pure and Skelly oil companies placed their versions of filling station cottages in small towns and outlying urban neighborhoods across the country. St. Paul has one that has survived virtually intact, the 1940 **Gratz Pure Oil Station** at Snelling and Blair Avenues.[64]

Forward-looking commercial building types had clear predecessors, in general appearance if not in detail. This contrasted markedly with the discontinuities between St. Paul's housing stock and the local spin-offs from the Century of Progress. The latter were advertised by their promoters and reviewed by the papers as "totally new" and "revolutionary," and dismissed by the public for those very reasons. Innovatively styled commercial buildings, on

FIGURE 3.52.
Northwest Distributors Building,
370 Dayton Avenue. A small
business block points the way
to the window walls and pure
rectilinear forms of the future.

the other hand, were accepted and lauded from the start, in large part because they were comprehensible extensions of building methods and types already in existence.

The simplest of these early modern building types was the one-story display-window building, in recent times given the typological label "enframed window wall." Shortly after World War I, young architects began to strip their storefront designs of all historical references and ornate brickwork and concentrate instead on decorative elements that would reinforce the basic lines of the building. The buildings that most consistently received this treatment were often related to the automobile, perhaps in large part because of the associations of automotive use with a distinctively modern lifestyle. Display-window fronts also permitted automotive showrooms to be fully visible from the street.[65]

In 1919 H. A. Sullwold, who was as knowledgeable as any of period-revival styles, designed an elegant example of this type just west of the Cathedral of St. Paul. Originally designed as a truck parts and repair shop, the **Northwest Distributors Building** is almost equally divided between glass display window and brick frieze articulated into three bays (Figure 3.52). A continuous strip of transom lights, minutely divided into squares of translucent glass, softens the transition from plate glass to brick, and the brick has inlaid rectangles and surrounds of glazed tile. This close interaction of masonry and glass surfaces is the primary decorative motif of the building, as its simple division into rectangular bays is its primary formal device. So much refinement in the

service of so modest a design was a harbinger of things to come.

A building of equal sophistication was erected in 1927 on Grand Avenue, this time for the display of Studebaker automobiles. The **Byers-Prestholdt Motor Company** designed by John Alden (fl. 1912–40) expresses the same relationship between brick and glass as its predecessor but frames each of its five bays with buff Mankato stone and surmounts the central and largest bay with a flared false gable (Figure 3.53). The historical overtones of the gable are muted by a reiteration of the triangular theme in several brick inlays and the carving of the limestone piers. All are clear anticipations of the type of ornament that would soon distinguish the Zigzag Moderne style that introduced Art Deco motifs to the nation's skyscrapers.[66]

With a pair of industrial supply houses near the western edge of the city, the evolution of the Moderne storefront was complete. Both designed by the Minneapolis firm of Lang, Raugland, and Lewis, the **Frigidaire Warehouse and Showroom** and the **Borchert-Ingersoll Machinery Company** sprang up on a stretch of University Avenue that had become the city's commercial transportation hub (Figure 3.54). Each uses a careful arrangement of brick to create the effect of fluted pilasters without diminishing the overwhelming presence of the great windows themselves.[67]

A second building type that naturally bridged into Modernism was the factory. Manufacturing buildings with few or no elements of style had been erected since

FIGURE 3.53.
Byers-Prestholdt Motor Company, 850 Grand Avenue, 1928. The Studebaker showrooms are clearly captured in this view. Photograph by Charles P. Gibson; courtesy of the Minnesota Historical Society.

FIGURE 3.54.
Borchert-Ingersoll Machinery Company, 2375 West University Avenue, 1931. The building was cleverly designed with a two-story showroom and an office mezzanine at the rear. Photograph by Norton and Peel; courtesy of the Minnesota Historical Society.

post–Civil War days. As the wall and window composition gradually became accepted as the sole essential ingredient of facade design, factories began to take on an increasingly sophisticated appearance. By 1923, it was possible for the popular press to praise the aesthetics as well as the efficiency of Albert Kahn's new **Ford Motor Company Plant**, which had little ornament of any sort apart from the shaping of the strip pilasters dividing the windows (Figure 3.55). The straightforward expression of concrete and steel framing was by then regarded as a stylistic assertion in itself.

Appending a tower to the middle of the factory block fostered the transition from utilitarian-as-expedient to utilitarian-as-beautiful. Once more, the basic form dated to post–Civil War days, when it had first become popular to advertise the presence of low-lying buildings by giving them a vertical element. Generally, the tower was treated with more detail than the main block and even dressed with the rudiments of high style, as if the designers wanted at least one part of their creation to be "architectural." By the 1920s, the stylistic separation of vertical and horizontal elements had become a thing of

FIGURE 3.55. Ford Motor Company Plant, Ford Parkway at Mississippi River Boulevard, 1936. For many years this was the largest and most straightforward exposition of concrete framing in the Twin Cities. Photograph by Norton and Peel; courtesy of the Minnesota Historical Society.

the past. Historical detailing dropped off of the tower, and in its place emerged a high-rise vocabulary that did little more than stretch the themes of the horizontal building upward.

The Midway area of St. Paul acquired an extraordinary cluster of buildings of this type during and after World War I. The first, the **Brown and Bigelow Company**, was begun in 1913 and acquired a major addition in 1925. Designed by Minneapolis architects Kees and Colburn, its central tower elements were simply prolongations of the corner pavilion designs that locked the building to its site. The second, a mammoth catalog house for **Montgomery Ward**, boasted a seventeen-story tower said at the time to be the highest reinforced concrete structure in the world. Its designers, however, chose to simplify standard period-revival elements rather than simply carrying upward the utilitarian design of the plant sprawling beneath.[68]

Both of these monumental buildings sat within expansive parks: Brown and Bigelow even offered a "mashie and putter" golf course. The parks have long since disappeared, along with the tower of the Brown and Bigelow plant. Long after the store itself closed, the Montgomery Ward tower persevered as the dominant landmark of the area until it too fell to the wrecking ball in 1995.[69]

The most sophisticated and best preserved of the Midway's towered commercial designs was erected in 1922 for the **St. Paul Casket Company** (Figure 3.56). Architect A. H. Stem set out the corners with monumental piers in a manner superficially similar to stock factory building design. But these perch on a clearly articulated basement story and are pierced with vertically dimensional windows. Rather than anchoring the building to the ground, the corners propel the design upward, reinforcing the vertical thrust of the central tower. The tower itself is set

FIGURE 3.56.
St. Paul Casket Company,
122 West University Avenue.
The building was designed with
a small office park and setbacks
to preserve the residential
scaling that ruled most of the
avenue's development through
the 1920s.

within stepped corner piers, clearly anticipating the great setback designs of the near future.

Stem was not always so attuned to the future. As late as 1927, he proposed enclosure of the projected Highland Park standpipe in a three-bay Gothic tower. Fortunately, the design was controlled by the city architect's office, and they had at their disposal the insight and skills of an architect who would soon become a major figure in modern public works design. Clarence W. Wigington (1883–1966), at the time a little-known draftsman in the city architect's office, had been trained under Omaha Beaux-Arts architect Thomas Kimball. His **Highland Water Tower** (Figure 3.57) instantly became the most popular as well as the most visible landmark in the emerging Highland Park community, though Wigington himself was late in receiving credit for it.[70]

The Highland Water Tower has a special significance in the city's architectural history for its anticipation of the PWA (Public Works Administration) projects in which Wigington would play a major part. Period-revival themes are not hard to find in the tower: the 1920s Spanish or Mediterranean Revival style in particular lurks in the corbeled belt courses and the open cap, the latter reminiscent of a mission bell tower. But these are so severed from their ordinary context that their nostalgic associations lose their pull, and the tower looms as a new creation. The upward, eight-sided expanse of warm-hued brick and stone is the principal carrier of the design, and the decorative components simply a way of giving it grace and texture. Art Deco monuments of the 1930s were to do exactly the same thing with motifs of ancient or exotic origin.

All of these precursors of Modernism have one thing in common: a long ancestry in utilitarian buildings whose aesthetic character had largely escaped notice. But there was a type of utilitarian structure with much more respected parentage. Great bridges have been regarded for their beauty since ancient times. Engineering and cost requirements alone often dictated a balance between strength and lightness, massiveness and transparency, that produced work of stunning visual force.

In the 1920s, the rise of automotive transport gave St. Paul the opportunity to build three large bridges using the latest concrete and steel technology, and all three proved to be masterful examples of architecture wrought from engineering. The first was built on Robert Street in 1924–26. Its designers were Toltz, King, and Day (fl. 1919–32 under the original partners). The **Robert Street Bridge** is a hybrid design joining conventional spans with a dramatic 264-foot rainbow arch centered

FIGURE 3.57.
Highland Water Tower,
Snelling Avenue at Ford Parkway,
ca. 1940. The rise of the reservoir
is visible behind the tower.
Photograph by Donaldson
Photo Company; courtesy of the
Minnesota Historical Society.

over the main river channel (Figure 3.58). Geometric patterns were cast into the rails and the main piers, creating just that complementary relationship between strong distant profile and ingratiating surface detail that was to distinguish the Art Deco monuments at the horizon. Yet the engineers could honestly declare that "no money has been spent to beautify the bridge." A newspaper reporter commented on completion of the central arches, "The new span depends on its massive proportions and graceful lines rather than particular decorations for its aesthetic appeal."[71]

The Robert Street Bridge was shortly followed by the **Ford Parkway Bridge**, first known as the Intercity Bridge, and the **Mendota Bridge**. Both have open spandrels with concrete ribbing connecting the arches to the road platform. The distinguishing mark of the Ford Parkway Bridge was a unique rib design created for the sole purpose of making all parts of the bridge readily accessible for walk-through inspection from either side of the river, proving that even a peculiar intercity political process could generate interesting design (Figure 3.59). The distinction of the Mendota Bridge is more dramatic: as

the longest continuous-arched concrete bridge in the world, its great curves stride across the commencement of the Minnesota River.[72]

In St. Paul as elsewhere, the Moderne movement that preceded Modernism took on several guises. Commercial building types fell rather neatly into two distinct patterns of dress. The first was consciously and often assertively anticlassical and was generally reserved for small to midscale buildings such as clubhouses, restaurants, theaters, and neighborhood businesses. It led toward considerable formal freedom, an inventive use of materials, and an early demise in the onslaught of a stricter brand of Modernism and the cost-efficient climate of the post–World War II period. The second Modernist dress stole shamelessly from the classical tradition and was the garb of choice for public and commercial buildings of monumental scale. Its progenitor was the branch of the Chicago School that cursed at Beaux-Arts academicism but passed on some of its leading principles: an outwardly expressed frame, a clearly articulated foot and crown, and an emphasis on balance and proportion, often to the point of absolute symmetry.

FIGURE 3.58. Robert Street Bridge, 1926. The interweaving of the platform with the arches is dramatically shown in this view. Photograph by K. L. Fenney Company; courtesy of the Minnesota Historical Society.

FIGURE 3.59. Ford Parkway Bridge, 1927. This bridge is still one of the great rainbow-arched crossings over the Mississippi River. Photograph by C. J. Hibbard; courtesy of the Minnesota Historical Society.

FIGURE 3.60.
Women's City Club,
305 St. Peter Street, 1931.
Etching by Theodore Haupt;
courtesy of the Minnesota
Historical Society.

St. Paul's acknowledged masterpiece, then and now, of the Moderne style in its romantic guise is Magnus Jemne's **Women's City Club** of 1930–31 (Figure 3.60). Crammed into a very difficult downtown site, the building presents a play of materials and a foil for the movement and patterning of natural light that a more classical ordering would never have permitted. Said Jemne, "The building had to be fitted into a sweeping view of the river. There was no way I could get the building's peculiar shape and my special window arrangement into any established style. So I let the style evolve out of the given conditions. . . . An architectural effect was obtained through extreme simplicity rather than ornamental embellishment." Ted Haupt's contemporary charcoal rendering beautifully captured the relationship of the design to its natural setting, nature in this case being reduced to its sweeping views of the river and the shifting effects of sky and light across the surface of the building.[73]

The interiors were also treated as theaters of suggested natural movement with terrazzo and parquet designs of windswept trees, swimming fish, and the zigzagging of modern dance steps, and a lighting scheme of reflections and interactions complementing the ever-changing patterns of natural light. On the day of the opening, exulted a Women's Club member, "Nature herself went obligingly modern. . . . She sent the sun to cast just the right highlights and shadows through the great bow windows onto the walls and ceilings to carry out the proper feeling for geometrical pattern."[74]

Much of the best Moderne work in St. Paul was born of collaboration, and the Women's City Club was no exception. Jemne designed the interior disposition of the spaces but had little to do with their finish or contents. The wall coverings, color and lighting schemes, and fittings and furnishings, including the light fixtures themselves, were all the work of young Minneapolis interior architect Frank Post. Elsa Jemne did the decorative floor designs. This kind of collaboration was becoming increasingly common for upscale buildings, as interior design was evolving into an independent profession. The year of the Women's City Club completion (1931) was marked by the establishment of the first professional

organization of interior designers, the American Society of Interior Decorators. The organization is still known as the ASID, but the last word is now "Designers."[75]

Though Jemne and his collaborators would have been loath to acknowledge it, their approach to Modernism owed much to the picturesque tradition. Buildings such as the Women's City Club may not imply a pastoral environment, but they continue to play with its basic elements. The interiors are as instilled with natural suggestions and effects as the most nostalgic images of the English countryside. Moderne architecture in this vein was also an architecture of surprises—unexpected juxtapositions, novel material uses, unusual spaces—and in this respect is more closely linked to the accidental compositions of nature than to the abstract, idealized compositions of the classically ordered architectural mainstream.

Nature was not the only source of romance among the free-form Moderne designers, however. There were also theater and the movies, where "anything goes." Russian-born set designer Werner Wittkamp (fl. 1930–54) brought years of experience in Berlin and Hollywood with him when he came to St. Paul to design the **Cinderella Cosmetics Factory** in the Midway in 1930. At the grand opening, a curtain covering the entire facade was drawn by a current movie star, and the building's 500,000-candlepower lighting system suddenly turned on. Unfortunately, the cosmetics factory proved to be a front for a bootlegging operation and soon went to seed, but Wittkamp himself continued to find work during the Depression designing restaurant and hotel interiors in

the manner of Hollywood movie sets. The most impressive of these, a redesign of the **Lowry Ballroom** undertaken around 1935, elevated the interior to the same level as its exterior shell (Figure 3.61). Once one of the finest Art Deco spaces in the state, it is on the brink of restoration after years of use for storage.[76]

Three important fragments of Wittkamp's work survive in some form or another. The remodeling of the Kaiser Restaurant into the **Tip-Top Tavern**, still standing, at 1415 West University Avenue in the mid-1940s playfully thrusts stacked, marqueelike slab-canopies out toward the street. Its bar and Streamline Moderne ceiling treatment are still as Wittkamp designed them, but the native limestone facings have been painted. Mortuaries were also a specialty of Wittkamp's. This is not as strange as it may seem at first, for providing a quiet kind of theater is one of their main functions, and Wittkamp evidently took the handling of their interiors as a challenge. The Willwerscheid family hired him many times between 1942 and his death in 1973, and the **Willwerscheid Mortuary** on Grand Avenue retains some of his work (Figure 3.62). The building itself was designed by Kenneth Fullerton, who had distinguished himself a few years earlier as architect of the city's most elaborate tribute to the Century of Progress. Though anticlassical in scale and massing, the mortuary is closer to the hybrid Modernism of local PWA work than to the exuberant romanticism of Jemne and Wittkamp.

Immigrants Jemne, Post, and Wittkamp may have been the three most talented local hands at the kind of

Moderne design that emphasized emotive power over compositional balance, but St. Paul actually got more buildings in that vein out of homegrown talent. Charles Hausler, Myrtus Wright, and Toltz, King, and Day (TKD) were its most active exponents. They created some of the most distinctive buildings of the Depression era in the city.

Hausler's first uncompromisingly Moderne design was a comprehensive remodeling of the **Minnesota Milk Company** at 378–80 University Avenue in 1931. The new plant skillfully blends the concrete slab-and-pilaster look of Albert Kahn's factories with the chevron friezes and ziggurat tower of Zigzag Moderne. It illustrates the facility with which a leading designer of the period (once again, draftsman Harry Firminger) could move from the picturesque historicism of the 1920s styles into the severe geometries of the newer fashions.[77]

Four years later, TKD rebuilt **Pilney's Market** on West Seventh Street, creating a Streamline Moderne image with a theatrical edge (Figure 3.63). This time the tower element is stepped horizontally as well as vertically, its irregular profile drawing attention to the acute corner into which the building fits. The main facade is invigorated by wide, flat, contrastingly colored belt courses and copings to create the streamlined effect.

After his brief partnership with Hausler, Myrtus Wright and his architectural practice were largely taken up with houses and large, rather characterless apartment buildings. But in the 1930s Wright emerged as a movie theater designer, and the hints of Moderne geometries in his earlier work took center stage. The **Grandview Theater**, erected in two phases between 1933 and 1937, served the end of the city's most important between-the-wars apartment district (Figure 3.64). Farther west, the **Highland Theater**, erected in 1939, arose on Cleveland Avenue at the edge of a new shopping area serving the city's newest residential area and the soon-to-be-completed Highland Village Apartments. With their unexpected juxtapositions of volumes, brilliant color combinations, eccentric fenestration, and suave graphics, the two theaters are eminently successful designs without quite achieving the suave cohesiveness of Minneapolis architects Liebenberg and Kaplan's statewide theater work.

One last expression of free-form Modernism deserves mention: the fondly regarded, factory-produced piece of roadside Americana known as **Mickey's Diner**. Built to standardized plans in New Jersey and shipped (how else?) by train, Mickey's Diner is a populist version of the romantic Moderne sensibility. The railroad theme of the restaurant takes over its form, dictating much of its interior planning as well as its exterior appearance. Railway travel becomes a form of theater, and architecture the means of giving the theater permanence.

The Moderne in classical dress had clear continuities with the neoclassical principles and building types espoused by Beaux-Arts education. Temple fronts and palazzo-style office buildings had clearly met their demise, but their underlying themes of visual order, structural clarity, and vertical organization hung on.

An early expression of the Moderne in classical dress deserves mention by way of anticipation. It pursued a

FIGURE 3.63.
Pilney's Market,
1032 West Seventh Street.
Its Moderne setbacks create
an arresting street corner.

FIGURE 3.64.
Grandview Theater,
1830 Grand Avenue. This
is one of Myrtus Wright's
two memorable Art Deco
theaters in St. Paul.

course quite different from the developing mainstream but is of interest in its own right. Three years before Hausler designed the Minnesota Milk Company Building, he and Firminger designed the first high-rise to be erected in the city since the end of World War I. This structure, the **Minnesota Building**, may also have been the first local office tower to dispense with the cornice (Figure 3.65). The attic story was a blind frieze of checkered stonework, terminating in a toothy skyline formed by the rise of the piers above the parapet. The spandrels beneath were cast in a geometric pattern and—here is the design's chief distinction—set nearly flush with the piers, spreading the checkered motif downward across the entire facade. This contrasts sharply with the vertical emphasis common to both historicizing and Moderne high-rise design. A penthouse addition at the

FIGURE 3.65.
Minnesota Building, Fourth and
Cedar Streets. Originally designed
in a conservative manner, the
building adopted increasingly
Moderne language as it rose.

top has toned down the once-arresting skyline, but the decorative motifs and surface articulation of the facades continue to be unique in the city.

At the onset of the Depression, public school designs nationwide drifted from increasingly simplified renditions of Collegiate Gothic to a version of the Moderne. First off the drawing boards in St. Paul was **Horace Mann Elementary School** in Highland Park, designed in the city architect's office by Carl Buetow; it would be followed by an equally distinguished design for **Chelsea Heights Elementary School** by Clarence Wigington. Like much of Moderne work, each school building draws on stylistic fashions already in play. A procession of piers marches across the front, arranged and scaled in much the same manner as the Krank Manufacturing Company and other classically inspired industrial buildings of the 1920s. The location and proportions of the limestone trim, on the other hand, highlight openings and corners in much the same manner as Collegiate Gothic practice.

The innovative imagery of the Moderne style is withheld from all but the ends and edges of the building elements, where stepped corners and triangular motifs adorn the piers and trim work.

The Moderne in full classical dress arrived with one of the great architectural landmarks of the city today, the **St. Paul City Hall and Ramsey County Courthouse** of 1930–31 (Figures 3.66 and 3.67). Situated between Fourth Street and the newly widened and upgraded Kellogg Boulevard, the new seat of local government captured every element of classical Modernism: tall vertical windows set in from the wall plane; dark, geometrically ornamented spandrels; a broad, stepped "plinth" of three stories forming the foot of the tower; and a barely marked termination in a thin frieze, as if the building might momentarily resume its vertical growth.

The Advisory Courthouse Commission decided very early in the process to combine the services of a national and a local architectural firm. Many of the local architects

FIGURE 3.66.
St. Paul City Hall and
Ramsey County Courthouse,
15 West Kellogg Boulevard,
ca. 1933. One of the great
Moderne monuments in the
nation. Photograph by
Wright Studios; courtesy of the
Minnesota Historical Society.

FIGURE 3.67.
Atrium of St. Paul City Hall
and Ramsey County Courthouse, 1938.
Its theatrical lighting and the onyx
God of Peace are prominent features
of the building. Photograph by
Norton and Peel; courtesy of the
Minnesota Historical Society.

whose names have become familiar to us appeared before the commission: Ellerbe, Hausler, Ingemann, Johnston, Lundie, Stem, Worthen, and Toltz, King and Day. Though the Chicago firm of Holabird and Root was apparently a shoo-in as lead architects, Tom Ellerbe had a great deal of maneuvering to do before his company won the commission as the local architect. By his own account, the crucial move was installing a public exhibit of his firm's work in its offices occupying half a floor of Hausler's recently completed Minnesota Building.[78]

Ellerbe and Company's role in the ad hoc partnership began with supervisory work, but as the job became increasingly complicated, the firm began to take charge of many of the design details. Every fitting and fixture in the building was ultimately modeled or assembled to carry Art Deco themes, from the door handles and mailboxes to the stair railings, furniture, and light fixtures. The crowning touch was a darkly lit interior concourse forty-one feet high, leading to a monumental onyx image of a Native American God of Peace by famed Swedish sculptor Carl Milles.[79]

Complementing the new city-county building were a number of changes and additions to blocks in its immediate vicinity. In 1929, the block across Fourth Street from the new City Hall had three major high-rise buildings, the old Germania Bank of 1889 at Fifth and Wabasha Streets (then known as the Pittsburgh Building), the Medical Arts Building of 1911 on St. Peter Street, and the Lowry Hotel of 1926 at Fourth and Wabasha Streets. But in between was the same hodgepodge of endlessly

remodeled structures that occupied the site of the new municipal building. Minneapolis transportation magnate Horace Lowry, who owned the entire block except for the Pittsburgh Building, transformed or razed all of the intervening structures just as the Depression settled in. Each project was designed in some variant of the new Classic Moderne style: a **Lowry Medical Arts Annex** (now the City Hall Annex), a complete remodeling of the **Field-Schlick Store** wrapping the old Germania Bank corner, the **Lowry Garage**, and, most important from a design standpoint, the **Lowry Hotel Restaurant and Ballroom Addition** on Wabasha Street. Though severely damaged by fire in 1982, the ballroom front retains its Zigzag Moderne lines as well as its finely carved relief panels of Mankato stone.

The other plot ripe for redevelopment in 1930 was the former city hall block across Wabasha Street from the Lowry Hotel. The Morris T. Baker Company of Minneapolis proposed to erect a mammoth office building in the same Gothic-tinged Moderne spirit as Eliel Saarinen's famed entry to the Chicago Tribune competition. The Depression halted this ambitious scheme, but not before Baker had achieved a partial bailout by selling the one corner of the parcel that could be immediately built to a local utility.[80]

The resulting **Northern States Power Company** building (now Ecolab Global Communications Center) is the Ellerbe version of Classic Moderne, shallowly sculpted and staidly composed but elegantly detailed (Figure 3.68). Its material combinations became the local standard for

the style straight through its waning years in the early 1950s: a base of polished Morton gneiss (a native, finely grained granite with a swirling texture), walls of buff Mankato stone, and spandrels and window frames and/or architraves of dark patinated bronze. As in the city-county building then still undergoing construction, its Art Deco sensibility intensified with the interiors. The stone materials were carried into the main lobby, the canted exterior corner was reiterated in the octagonal section of numerous freestanding interior piers, and the bronze ornament became denser and more geometrical.

The onset of the Depression was also responsible for St. Paul's first genuine skyscraper in the new fashion. In 1929, the Merchants National Bank was absorbed into the First National Bank, and an ambitious new building immediately got onto the drawing boards. The Chicago firm of Graham, Anderson, Probst, and White (fl. 1917–36) designed a thirty-two-story setback-style skyscraper, which instantly became the identifying feature of the St. Paul skyline. Not to be outdone by the slightly taller Foshay Tower just completed in Minneapolis, the owners crowned the new **First National Bank** with a four-story electric sign bearing the simple pronouncement "1st" (Figure 3.69).[81]

Even Clarence Johnston's architectural firm, among the most conservative in the city, got into the Modernist swim, first with the Lowry Medical Arts Building addition, then with the **Tri-State Telephone Company** in 1936 (Figure 3.70). Both were largely the work of Stirling Horner, who took over the commercial end of the firm's work as Johnston's health failed. As one might expect, the firm's designs appear to have discovered orthodoxy in the midst of revolution: all parts of the buildings are scaled in a Beaux-Arts hierarchical manner, and even the cast and sculpted detailing is cribbed from the classical lexicon. Their backward glances notwithstanding, both buildings remain important contributing elements to St. Paul's outstanding cluster of Classic Moderne designs.

FIGURE 3.71. 3M Company Headquarters, 900 Bush Avenue. This design utilizes another severe rendition of Moderne, this time pushing toward a thoroughgoing Modernism.

The last major monument in the style was also the most abstract: the **3M Company Headquarters** on the East Side (Figure 3.71). Albert Kahn worked with local architects Toltz, King, and Day to produce a design that strips classicism to its bones. All significant exterior contour is eliminated except for the vertical reveals of the windows. Piers and frieze are flush, the base and cornice only slightly stepped out. The result is an utterly abstract composition of voids and solids, or more precisely, a single rectangular solid pierced by repeated vertical voids. The materials and scaling of the structure maintain a tenuous link to the Classic Moderne style of the 1930s, while the uniformity of its surfaces and openings points to the office buildings of the 1950s.

The monumental spirit of the Classic Moderne was also carried forward by a number of smaller structures. In Minnesota, these were typically built with Public Works Administration financing, which has led some writers to call the style as a whole PWA Moderne. The **Como Park Zoological Building** (1936), **Holman Field Administration Building** (1939), **Hamline Playground Building** (1940), and **Harriet Island Pavilion** (now Wigington Pavilion) (1941) are progressively less formal versions of

the Moderne in classical dress (Figures 3.72 and 3.73). City Architect Charles Bassford is the architect of record for each of these buildings, but the architect in charge of all but the first project was the lead draftsman in his office, Clarence Wigington.[82]

The smallest building type of all to express the Moderne spirit of the 1920s and 1930s illustrates how little size had to do with monumental effect. Oakland Cemetery erected half a dozen monuments in the Classic Moderne manner, each as imposing in their way as the miniature Greek temples that preceded them. The best of these, the **George S. McLeod Mausoleum** erected in 1933, opposes massive corner piers and a blank setback frieze to a finely detailed entry of stepped reveals and exquisitely cast bronze doors.

Since the advent of high-style commercial design in the city, style-defining elements had often been restricted to the street facade. At first, this was largely a matter of convenience or even necessity, for Main Street buildings generally shared their lateral walls with others. But after World War I, the confinement of style to facade gradually became elevated from a matter of expedience to a stylistic assertion in itself. Buildings faced in the current

styles began to have more in common among themselves than they did with other buildings that carried their particular styles deeper into the structure.

The phenomenon of style-as-face has already been traced in apartment building design. But the between-the-wars fixation with stylish exterior dress was not always or even primarily a matter of new construction. Transformation of commercial fronts became commonplace, particularly for buildings whose businesses implied imagery that was both topical and modern. Theaters, restaurants, and building supply outlets became strange stylistic bedfellows in their common concern to present a constantly updated image to the public.

Completion of the **St. Paul Union Depot** in 1920 was the catalyst for St. Paul's first long linkage of commercial properties with a visually unified facade. A miscellany of industrial and commercial buildings of varying styles and heights faced the new depot. Under a city mandate to widen the street but keep as much of the buildings intact as possible, a group of downtown businessmen seized the opportunity to tear off the hodgepodge of street fronts, replacing them with a design of "solid, modern appearance." Clarence Johnston's 1926 solution for the new **Fourth Street Facade** (partly razed) picked up stylistic and material elements of the solemn new building that it addressed (Figure 3.74). The finished

product lacks the sophistication of Johnston's original design, but it remains the first local essay in large-scale design whose principal point was harmonizing with extant modern structures.[83]

On a smaller scale, theaters were the first class of buildings to apply new sidewalk-to-skyline facades in step with current fashion. The **Victoria Theater** at 825 University Avenue is a fine surviving St. Paul example. Franklin Ellerbe had designed a very simple, commercial-style facade in 1915. Then the Roaring Twenties arrived,

and with it a thirst for high style. An elegantly detailed brick facade was applied, and this was adorned with ornamental light fixtures and a new marquee (since removed).

From the standpoint of sheer visual impact, the most remarkable street-front transformation of the era occurred downtown, when **Elvgren Paints Store and Warehouse** took over a newly remodeled warehouse and store near the corner of Seventh and Robert Streets (Figure 3.75). Seventh Street was widened by twenty-six feet in 1930,

FIGURE 3.76.
Hyman Margolis Tire Shop,
740 Grand Avenue.
A hodgepodge of buildings
are melded under a continuous
Streamline Moderne skin.

and the building owners hired Toltz, King, and Day to create a thematically unified sequence of new facades. The four-story rise of stone, glass, and metal alloy at the eastern end of the project is one of the finest early glass-wall designs in the city. Utility and elevator shafts are cleverly indicated by deeply set slot windows at either side, and the decoratively molded alloy panels that form the parapet are scaled to the glass window units and set flush with them to create the effect of the wall itself piercing the skyline.

During the trying years of the Great Depression, updating properties built up through several periods by giving them a unifying face was a common economic expedient. Occasionally designs of genuine distinction resulted. By covering the phases of a growing tire operation on Grand Avenue with a continuous new skin, in 1937 Harry Firminger turned a hodgepodge of building structures into a prolonged essay in the Streamline Moderne mode for the **Hyman Margolis Tire Shop** (Figure 3.76).

The Midway district was a favorite location for Moderne makeovers during the Depression, as the long commercial strip attracted an ever-richer array of commercial uses. One of the finest examples occurs in the recently created University-Raymond Historic District at the west end of University Avenue. When the Specialty Manufacturing Company decided to install a small restaurant in one corner of their plant, they opted for the Streamline Moderne style. The **Ace Café and Box Lunch**, designed by Ellerbe and Company, was a kind of retrofit kit intended for insertion in existing commercial buildings (Figure 3.77). The arresting Mankato-Kasota stone facings and aluminum-mulled windows of its St. Paul location have survived a period of office use to function once again as the front for a restaurant.[84]

Nearly all of the city's increasing number of facade alterations in the 1930s reflected changes in client base or function as well as a desire to modernize. They were in fact a symptom of a much larger phenomenon in the city, that of property redevelopment. In most cases, the buildings altered were less than thirty years old and in decent enough condition, but they lacked panache or an imagery calling out a modern use, or simply no longer fit into what their neighborhoods had become.

Several new downtown buildings in the 1930s were also a part of this phenomenon. The land chosen for the new city-county building in 1930 was already filled with masonry buildings, many of them of recent construction and all of them intended as permanent city structures at their inception; Tri-State Telephone Company's predecessors on its site were brick automobile garages of the 1910s and 1920s. Choice empty land was simply no longer available, and the growth of the city underwent a shift from outward expansion to rebuilding of the commercial

FIGURE 3.77.
Ace Café and Box Lunch,
2356 West University Avenue.
The restaurant introduces high
style to the corner of an old
furniture warehouse.

core. The demolitions and face-lifts of the 1930s set the tone for urban renewal programs of the 1950s and drew the lines for the restoration-versus-replacement battles that emerged in the 1970s. Nobody in recent times has thrown down the gauntlet for preservationists more decisively than the director of the Better Housing Exposition did at the 1937 Minnesota State Fair:

Regarding modernization, there are two points of view. In some cases, the owner looks upon his property as a possible landmark, valued for its historical associations. The collective viewpoint of the better house movement is that too many historic landmarks retard progress, create architectural misfits in an environment that is rapidly becoming modernized, and stand as potential menaces to life and property.[85]

CHAPTER 4

Planning the Modern City

1940 – 1985

Minnesota sent 275,000 sons and daughters off to World War II. In the ranks of the returning veterans marched St. Paul humorist Max Shulman, who recounted a fictional homecoming in his first published novel. In outward appearance Minnesota had changed very little during the war, but Shulman's hero noted with approval a new, and very determined, sense of order. "War has shown us what we can do," he said. "While some of us assured our country's destiny on the battlefields of the world, others stayed home and builded our future. An inventory was taken. The perspective of time revealed our old errors. . . . Strong, healthy, and wise, we stand on the threshold of tomorrow." Eager to claim his just reward as "Postwar Man," Shulman's protagonist asked himself—just as so many American citizens were to ask themselves in ensuing decades, though often with less enthusiasm—"What had the planners planned for me?"[1]

The perception that the average citizen had a stake, perhaps even a role, in city planning was a new phenomenon in St. Paul. Since the establishment of the City Planning Board in 1918, urban planning activities had reflected the concerns, and disagreements, of special interests, as espoused by a number of overlapping and sometimes competing groups. The local Amherst H. Wilder Charity, for example, was interested in slums. After instigating a housing survey in 1917, the charity

called attention to the social evils and abysmal living conditions in the city's dilapidated tenements, some of which were encroaching on the downtown area. The St. Paul real estate lobby was divided in its response. While it sympathized with any effort that promised to stem the erosion of property values, it feared do-gooder solutions that might affect property ownership and rental profits. For the most part, the municipal planning board tried to stay clear of the debate. It focused its energies on accommodating the rapid increase in automotive use, arguing the merits of street widening, grade reduction, parking lots, and curbside lighting. Meanwhile, supporters of the City Beautiful Movement tirelessly promoted the virtues of redesigning the approaches to the Capitol area.[2]

The only planning proposal to receive funding on a consistent basis was street widening, popular for serving the dual purposes of opening up traffic lanes and clearing out decaying building stock. One such project, the widening of Third Street along the Mississippi River in the downtown district, produced a short boulevard and park in 1931, a self-conscious exercise along City Beautiful lines.[3]

The scheme longest before the public eye was Cass Gilbert's Capitol Approach Plan (Figures 4.1 and 4.2). Gilbert, who had been selected to design a new state capitol in 1895, first broached the subject of a grand

boulevard leading to the statehouse steps in 1903, while the building was still under construction. In Gilbert's original conception, the main Capitol approach was a spacious, arrow-straight, north-south mall, almost a mile in length, cutting diagonally across much of the existing street grid on the western edge of downtown. Roughly at midpoint, the mall opened into a monumental plaza memorializing the state's Civil War dead. In successive enrichments of his plan in 1906, 1907, and 1909, Gilbert placed imposing ranks of public and private buildings around the plaza, in an arc before the Capitol, and along diagonal axes flanking the mall, each symmetrically arrayed and stylistically appointed to form an appropriate architectural honor guard for the Capitol itself. The proposed mall would terminate at "Seven Corners" in the West Seventh Street commercial district, thereby creating the city's first grand boulevard vista.[4]

The St. Paul City Planning Board, which held its first meeting in 1920, endorsed Gilbert's scheme but then turned its energies to more practical matters, such as zoning and traffic routing. The first official city plan, published in 1922, adopted the same strategy. Composed by Chicago planning consultants Edward H. Bennett and William E. Parsons, it simply copied Gilbert's axial boulevards onto the city's existing street grid without discussing implementation. Most of this plan's recommendations dealt with relieving traffic congestion en route to and within the central business district.[5]

Perhaps the greatest obstacle to the realization of Gilbert's approach plan was a continuing dispute between the city and the state over the funding and maintenance of the proposed Capitol improvement. In 1929, Governor Theodore Christianson inadvertently breathed new life into the project by attempting to dispatch it altogether. Disregarding Gilbert's emphasis on architectural symmetry and decorum, Christianson attempted to push through a proposal that would erect a hulking, utilitarian brick building for state offices on high ground behind

FIGURE 4.2.
Cass Gilbert's plan of a boulevard from
West Seventh Street to the State Capitol.
From *Plan of St. Paul* (1922). Courtesy of
the Minnesota Historical Society.

the Capitol. Civic outrage united business groups, the city council, the municipal planning board, and the Ramsey County Board of Commissioners. This coalition invited Gilbert to return to St. Paul for a final exposition of his vision. Gilbert lambasted the "back yard" location for the office building and projected an even grander mall in front of the Capitol, extending the axial boulevard all the way to the Mississippi River. The immediate result was that the proposed office building was given a respectable granite mantle and a new site in front of the statehouse. The rest of Gilbert's scheme continued to gather dust.[6]

At the outbreak of World War II, the Capitol Mall was barely a block long, with only one dignified edifice on each side, the **Minnesota Historical Society Building** (690 Cedar Street) of 1918 on the east and the recently contested, newly erected **State Office Building** of 1932 on the west. The remainder of the proposed approach was largely filled with older commercial buildings

and tenements, many in deteriorated condition. The plight of the Capitol Mall might simply have remained cause for intermittent storms of local controversy if *Fortune Magazine* had not elevated it into a matter of national embarrassment.

In 1936, *Fortune* ran an in-depth profile of Minneapolis and St. Paul, in which St. Paul came off much the worse for the comparison. Under the heading "Epitaph for a City," the magazine's reporter penned what he called "an autopsy on St. Paul":

> St. Paul is cramped, hilly, and stagnant. Its streets are narrow and its buildings small. . . . Its slums are among the worst in the land. . . . The hotels are not very good. Among the people there is less breeziness, less cordiality. . . . Above all, there is the atmosphere of a city grown old. . . . St. Paul is what Minneapolis has been fighting not to become: a city economically obsolete.[7]

FIGURE 4.3.
The State Capitol and its
surroundings depicted in a
watercolor by Ludwig Bemelmans
published in *Fortune Magazine*
in 1936.

This description was accompanied by a watercolor illustration of the Minnesota statehouse, framed in the foreground by two rundown buildings (Figure 4.3). The caption stated: "Cass Gilbert Designed the Capitol; The Slums Got There Unaided."

Even without the poisonous comparison to Minneapolis, the *Fortune* piece would have touched a raw nerve in the St. Paul body politic. It appeared during a revived debate about the existence of slums and their proper remedy. In 1934, the federal Bureau of the Census had conducted a housing survey in St. Paul that revealed crowded conditions in 14 percent of the housing stock, representing about 9,400 dwelling units. The situation was most severe for low-rent properties, where 40 percent of the units were judged to be "inadequate for decent living conditions." Marshaling these data, the St. Paul City Planning Board applied for a federal Public Works Administration (PWA) grant to replace the worst slums in the Capitol area with a low-income public housing project. According to the board's director, George H. Herrold, the grant was rescinded after initial approval because Washington decided "there was too much opposition to public housing in St. Paul." Apparently, the most outspoken critic was the St. Paul Apartment House Owners' Association. When Congress established a program in 1937 to distribute construction money to the states for low-income public housing, the St. Paul association led the successful lobbying campaign in the Minnesota

statehouse to block passage of the required enabling legislation. As a result, Minnesota was one of only nine states that failed to participate in the federal housing program before World War II.[8]

The only government-backed housing constructed in St. Paul during this period was the **Highland Village Apartments**, completed during 1939–40 (Figure 4.4). This venture received its subsidy in the form of a mortgage insured by the Federal Housing Administration (FHA), the first in the city. Ironically, Highland Village looked very much like a New Deal housing project, even though it was built for middle-income residents. To facilitate FHA approval of the twelve-building, 256-unit complex, owner-and-builder Walter Butler Construction Company of St. Paul adopted a basic PWA design that clustered three-story apartments with attached two-story row houses in a broad-lawned, campuslike setting.[9]

It was not until World War II that the groundwork was laid for a municipal planning effort that would ultimately unite the many factions pressing for change. In 1941, newly installed mayor John J. McDonough, elected on the local Progressive-Labor ticket, reached out to the business community for help in charting St. Paul's future. With the backing of forty-six commercial, professional, and civic organizations, McDonough organized the United Civic Council, an informal parliament consisting of twelve committees, each dedicated to studying a major urban issue, such as tax structure, property

valuation, zoning, and public transportation. The chair-men of the various committees inaugurated the project by meeting in mid-December 1941, only a few days after Pearl Harbor. It was understood from the beginning that their planning looked "ahead to post-war readjustments."[10]

Implementing any of the plans to come out of these committees required enabling legislation for city prop-erty condemnation, as well as the establishment of a downtown tax district. This fell into place during the spring session of the 1943 Minnesota Legislature with the creation of the Central Business District Authority. Meetings continued, but progress was minimal. Early in 1944, with the end of the war believed to be imminent, Mayor McDonough warned the city council that St. Paul "must speed preparation of plans for post-war work or be left far behind by other communities getting ready to obtain federal help." Meanwhile, in February 1944, the private sector formed still another citizens' committee, with the mission of drafting an omnibus "St. Paul loop improvement plan." One of the first mandates of the new group was to raise $25,000 for a study of ways to improve the downtown. The money appeared in short order, and the committee immediately hired the most successful consultant available, Raymond Loewy Associ-ates, with main offices in New York City and Chicago.[11]

Like Herrold and many of the other members of the St. Paul City Planning Board, Loewy was trained as an engineer. But his outlook went far beyond the public works perspective that had so far hamstrung city devel-opment efforts. Emigrating from France to the United States in 1919, the twenty-six-year-old Loewy first found work as a fashion illustrator. As the economy sank into depression, Loewy correctly surmised that manufacturers could be persuaded to restyle their products to improve sales. His foothold in American industry was assured by his appointment in 1929 as art director for Westinghouse. Through a mixture of brazen self-promotion and Gallic charm, he rounded up clients and, with a handful of peers, virtually created the field of industrial design. Loewy's particular gift lay in streamlining European Modernism for American popular taste, creating mass-produced de-signs that managed to retain a certain aura of exclusive sophistication. During the 1930s, he turned out a string of products and packaging that would become essential icons of American material culture, including the Sears, Roebuck Coldspot icebox, the Greyhound Silversides motor coach, and the Lucky Strike cigarette pack.[12]

Reflecting his general interest in the psychology of merchandising, Loewy expanded his firm's services in the late 1930s to include department store planning and design, which became the specialty of staff architect William T. Snaith, recently a student at New York Uni-versity and the École des Beaux-Arts in Paris. Marketed as "combined retail store, architectural and city planning design," the new division helped Raymond Loewy Associates weather the lean years of the war. The firm's proposal to prepare a downtown plan for St. Paul emphasized the architectural component, explaining that the study would suggest "means of improving existing buildings by minor superficial changes . . . of combining single buildings into group building facades of distinctive appearance . . . of making store fronts more attractive." The final plan would incorporate "features of glamour and interest needed by a growing city so that its public relations may enable St. Paul to become nationally known."[13]

Loewy presented his downtown development plan in January 1945. The study showed a great deal of political acumen. It supported proposals that already had public backing, such as a new design for the Capitol Mall, reduced from Gilbert's grand axial boulevard to a truncated fan-shaped concourse radiating outward from the Capitol, with a new veterans' service building and war memorial at the far end, facing the Capitol. Instead of choosing sides on divisive issues, Loewy attempted to build consensus for solving problems. In regard to slum housing, for example, his study recommended the replacement of "sub-standard buildings" between downtown and the Capitol with a public park surrounded by "a residential development for middle or low income groups." The question of public-versus-private ownership simply was not addressed.[14]

Above all, Loewy assured the St. Paul business community that there was nothing intrinsically wrong with their city's economy or management. Instead, the threat to downtown St. Paul was largely external, rooted "in the downtown area of another city"—unnamed in the report but clearly Minneapolis. "The proximity of this competing city," Loewy explained, "heightens the danger of the situation, for it is virtually as easy for the people of St. Paul to visit their neighbor's downtown area as it is to visit their own."

For Loewy, St. Paul had a textbook opportunity to seize the advantages of industrial design. This opportunity presented itself whenever customers had the choice of two products of similar performance and cost. In such a situation, as Loewy was fond of telling manufacturers, the buyer would generally choose the product that looked better. Adapting this maxim to city planning, he advised his St. Paul clients that "a more efficiently laid-out and beautified downtown area will make it easy, comfortable and inviting for residents to . . . patronize its services rather than those of an easily accessible competitive city. . . . A program of revitalizing and modernizing the loop area is vital to the economic health of the community."[15]

Loewy's recommendations for modernization covered both new construction and remodeling. New facilities included riverfront apartments on Kellogg Boulevard, a luxury tourist-and-convention hotel "adjacent to the main shopping area," and multistory parking garages on the loop periphery. These garages would convey shoppers across intervening streets by means of "pedestrian cross-overs" connected to the second-story level of

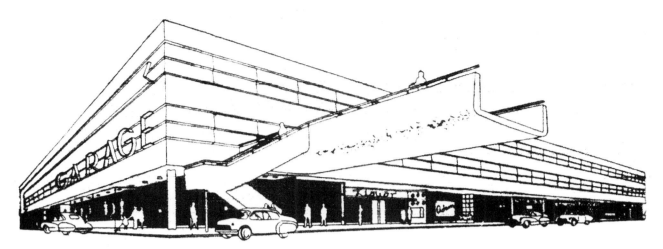

FIGURE 4.5. The plan of Raymond Loewy Associates for second-story pedestrian walkways, prefiguring the skyway system of the 1960s. Published in the *St. Paul Pioneer Press* in 1945.

neighboring buildings, an arrangement that promised to increase "the sales potential of the floor connected" (Figure 4.5). Loewy's suggestions for remodeling struck the contemporary press as equally innovative. Arguing that the relative shortness of the city's downtown blocks created too many traffic-snarling intersections, he proposed "joining pairs of east-west blocks and eliminating every other north-south street." But even more startling was his prescription for a "general face-lifting program" to add the "necessary ingredients of glamour and beauty" to the downtown area.

In former decades, St. Paul had prided itself on the architectural splendor of its Queen Anne, Richardsonian, and various historic revival buildings. In Loewy's eyes, however, this old-fashioned mixture of styles and ornamentation was a major stumbling block to a modern, marketable downtown. As he explained elsewhere:

Multiplicity being the essence of confusion, the designer will endeavor to eliminate or combine parts, supports, or excrescences whenever possible. This technique I would call "reduction to essentials." He will then take into consideration colors, textures, and finishes as well as materials themselves and submit them to the same simplification treatment. When every component part has been stripped down to its simplest form, every duplication ruled out, projections and asperities reduced or eliminated, colors and textures

simplified, the result is bound to be aesthetically correct. . . . Besides this tribute that design pays to aesthetics, it pays in some other ways too. It is good business, as it sells the product.[16]

To achieve such desirable simplification in downtown St. Paul, Loewy recommended stripping all offending facades, removing "ugly and superfluous architectural detail, such as cornices, pediments and rococo ornaments." The outer surfaces could then be "evened up with the same materials and painted for unity of design," or "dressed up with facings which reflect the character of the individual store." At the same time, "exposed upper parts of the remodeled buildings should be veneered with a new material such as architectural terra-cotta tile, marble and limestone." In product design, Loewy unabashedly called this resurfacing technique "a wrapper or shell treatment," and he justified it whenever "a given product has been reduced to its functional best and still looks disorganized and ugly." So that his St. Paul clients could better appreciate the benefits of face-lifting and shell treatment, he presented them with two photographs of Seventh Street between Cedar and Minnesota Streets, one showing the building facades in their current condition and the other retouched to show the recommended improvements (Figure 4.6).[17]

Loewy's study was never intended to be, and never became, an official city planning document. But as planning director Herrold noted in the mid-1950s, the report

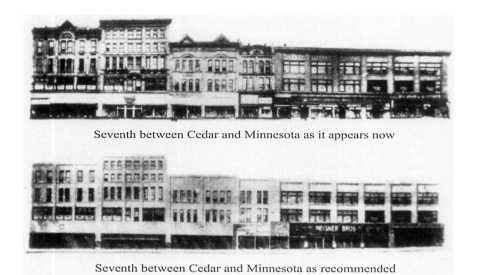

Seventh between Cedar and Minnesota as it appears now

Seventh between Cedar and Minnesota as recommended

FIGURE 4.6.
Proposed modernization of Seventh Street storefronts by Raymond Loewy Associates. Published in the *St. Paul Pioneer Press* in 1945.

FIGURE 4.7.
Frank Murphy store, Fifth Street between Wabasha and St. Peter Streets, 1948. This view of the remodeling of the Schlick and Lowry Blocks appeared in the *St. Paul Dispatch*. The fronts have recently been removed.

wielded "great influence on the thinking in the business district." Twenty years later, when St. Paul finally did embark on a massive program of downtown reconstruction, several of the highly touted new design features, such as "skyways" and "superblocks," had clear antecedents in Loewy's recommendations. Loewy's greatest influence, however, was probably in the area of storefront remodeling, which was familiar terrain for downtown business owners. Throughout the city's history, shopkeepers had been remodeling their businesses according to whatever aesthetic they (or their designers) found appealing. Even

without a city planning study, such activity would have continued. In 1948, for example, clothier Frank Murphy, who catered to the carriage trade at the southeast corner of West Fifth and St. Peter Streets, wrapped his two-story shop front in a French Quarter fantasy, replete with moss green, wood-paneled balconies fringed by iron grillwork imported from New Orleans (removed during Lowry Building restoration; Figure 4.7). Two decades earlier, historical architectural themes had been the norm, but, as Murphy himself acknowledged, his remodeled storefront was risking a "different" look. The

difference was that most Americans, having just lived through the privations of the Great Depression and the horrors of World War II, no longer found the past to be particularly charming. Part of Loewy's appeal was that his remodeling recommendations thoroughly erased the past. During the late 1940s and 1950s, many other architectural apostles of shell-treatment Modernism would find receptive clients throughout urban America, but Loewy was the most articulate of the group. No other designer so persuasively and on so many levels combined an aesthetic stance with a marketing strategy.[18]

The typical remodeling of the early postwar period—as exemplified by the **Golden Rule Department Store** on its East Seventh Street front in 1950—entailed the installation of large, aluminum-framed display windows on the ground floor, with the sheathing of adjacent surfaces in polished granite or dressed limestone (Figures 4.8 and 4.9). Some businesses, such as the **West Publishing Company,** preferred to wrap their store fronts in porcelain enamel steel panels, which readily accommodated advertising graphics. According to its local distributor, the material also had the virtue of giving "the

modern look to all buildings—old or new." This comment is particularly revealing, for it goes to the heart of the entire face-lift program of the late 1940s and 1950s.[19]

When contemporaries described this remodeling effort as a way of "modernizing" the downtown, they did not merely mean that store owners were sprucing up their buildings. They were also affirming that these alterations were, in fact, Modern architecture. As the *Pioneer Press* said of one of the city's more expensive face-lifts, "Remodeling Will Make Golden Rule Ultra-Modernistic." Since previous architectural styles had derived their identity from the design of facades, it seemed perfectly reasonable to assume that the Modern style was also a matter of surface treatment.[20]

True Modernists found this assumption appalling. A basic tenet of their movement held that the "new architecture," as it was sometimes called, broke with the past precisely because it did not believe in dressing up facades. Instead of concealing what lay beneath, a building's exterior was supposed to express interior functions and methods of construction. How this was done often depended on the temperament of the designer, especially among the founders of the Modern movement.

A romantic like Frank Lloyd Wright, for example, created buildings that looked very different from the work of classicists Walter Gropius and Ludwig Mies van der Rohe, two influential German-born architects who were advocates of what became known as the International style. Fond of traditional materials and committed to an intensely personal vision, Wright saw architectural form as a flowering of interior space, most successful when it seemed to be a natural extension of the site itself. Gropius and Mies, on the other hand, envisioned a Modern architecture of anonymous machine-made parts, so effortlessly supported by new high-strength materials that the demarcation between interior and exterior space needed nothing more than a thin glass wall. If Wright's buildings blended with the earth, those of the International style tended to dissolve against the sky. In either case, architectural form disappeared as an end in itself. Supporters of Wright's organic architecture often criticized the International style for being regimented and boring, and they, in return, were chastised for indiscipline. But these were battles over aesthetic interpretation. Both sides were equally committed to the same underlying functionalist aesthetic.

Loewy was fully aware that Modernists considered his face-lift program to be a complete breach in design integrity. There were cases, however, when it was possible to muster a plausible-sounding functionalist defense. In 1957, the management of the **Emporium Department Store** announced the most ambitious face-lift yet attempted in downtown St. Paul (Figures 4.10 and 4.11). Not only would the ground floor of the block-long building be

remodeled with new windows and stone veneer, but all four upper stories of all four facades would be encased in beige plastic panels, changed in the final design to aluminum siding. The result would be a "functional" windowless box.[21]

A staple of postwar American retailing, the windowless department store was itself something of a Loewy innovation, first implemented by the designer in a new store in Houston, Texas, in 1947. Playing on the phrase of the great French architect Le Corbusier that a house was a "machine for living," Loewy contended that a department store was a "machine for selling" and that all aspects of its design should be devoted to getting merchandise on and off the sales floor as quickly as possible. To improve logistics, Loewy filled the perimeter of the sales floor with merchandise storage and handling facilities, giving each sales department immediate access to its own stock. This arrangement made the sales floor dependent on artificial illumination, which Loewy felt was generally superior to daylight for display purposes. Since upper-story windows were unnecessary for illuminating stock areas, they were eliminated from the design.[22]

Of course, there was a world of difference between leaving windows out of a building for functional reasons and covering existing windows up to simulate a functional look. Even the Emporium management seems to have understood the distinction. Although they talked about how the remodeling was "a functional approach to department store design," they were most impressed by the resulting "square modern look," which "emphasize[d] the size of the huge building."[23]

The "square modern look" also influenced new commercial construction in St. Paul during the 1950s. It gave architects and their clients the opportunity to project a contemporary image without sacrificing traditional values. The master of the moment was Ellerbe and Company, an old-line St. Paul firm that had built an enviable reputation with its institutional and commercial commissions for sound engineering, efficient space planning, and dignified architectural design in whatever idiom was currently popular. During the 1950s, Ellerbe almost tripled its workforce to about three hundred employees, and it opened the next decade as one of the country's top one hundred architectural firms in terms of annual value of projects designed. Despite its size and success, the company was still very much controlled by the founder's son, Thomas Farr Ellerbe, a largely self-taught architect who had taken over the family business in 1921.[24]

Ellerbe and Company's early approach to Modern architecture is illustrated by the **Mutual Service Insurance Companies Building** on University Avenue, planned in 1953 and completed two years later in the Midway district (Figure 4.12). Although originally constructed as three stories, the design provided for expansion to five,

the building's eventual height. In discussing this project, as well as other commissions of the period, Ellerbe stressed its commitment to functional design: "Gone are the days of squeezing a plan into a predetermined shape. Now the plan helps to determine the shape." The Mutual Service design most obviously reflected this aesthetic by assigning separate rectangular volumes to entrance, stair tower, and office blocks. To ensure that the final product would communicate "the dignity and obvious quality" of the client, Ellerbe faced the entire building in stone. As a company spokesperson explained regarding a similar project of the mid-1950s, the use of stone "will symbolize the [client's] reputation of strength and reliability." On the Mutual Service Building, the result was a series of masonry boxes, only slightly relieved by a horizontal glass stripe across the entrance. In its way, the Ellerbe design was almost as much of a "shell treatment" as the Emporium face-lift, for which Ellerbe also prepared the final plans.[25]

To appreciate better the conservative nature of the Mutual Service Building, it is helpful to compare it to the **Veterans' Service Building** at the south end of the Capitol Mall, opposite the Capitol (Figure 4.13). When state authorities announced a national architectural competition for the Veterans' Service Building in 1945, they laid down two general rules. First, the new building "should harmonize" with the existing Classical Revival architecture of the Capitol complex, "having the scale, proportions, dignity, and exterior materials that will make it seem at home in its surroundings." Second, it should provide office space for state officials and veterans' groups responsible for administering veterans' affairs, while also incorporating a memorial component honoring the state's war dead. Although these requirements could easily have been the prescription for a very traditional building, the winning design was Modern in the truest sense of the movement. Its author was W. Brooks Cavin Jr., a little-known architect, barely thirty years old, living in Washington, D.C.[26]

A Philadelphia native, Cavin had received an undergraduate degree in engineering from Harvard in 1937. He then stayed on for an advanced degree in architecture, studying under Gropius, who had just taken charge of the Harvard program. After four years, Cavin emerged a confirmed Modernist who, by his own admission, knew very little about architectural history or historic revival styles. It was partly because of his ignorance of these matters that he was intrigued by the St. Paul competition, which seemed to require a sympathetic historical understanding of the architecture and landscaping of the

FIGURE 4.13.
View from the State Capitol
to the Veterans' Service
Building, 1954. Photograph
from *St. Paul Dispatch–Pioneer
Press;* courtesy of the
Minnesota Historical Society.

Capitol complex. He decided that, if nothing else, the competition would be "a good learning experience."[27]

Cavin proved to be an astute student of history. Of the four top-placing entries in the competition, his alone truly complemented Cass Gilbert's design for the Capitol and its grounds. Cavin arranged the new building around a monumental memorial plaza pointing straight at the Capitol about one-quarter mile to the north. On the west side of the plaza, he placed a public auditorium-and-museum wing, and on the east side, an L-shaped office wing intended for the State Department of Veterans Affairs. To provide administrative space for veterans' groups, he linked the two one-story wings with a three-story office block that spanned the plaza on a colonnade. By elevating the central office block, Cavin created an open vista that salvaged something of Gilbert's original conception of a grand Capitol approach, soon to be permanently laid to rest by the construction of an interstate highway across the south end of the Capitol grounds, immediately behind the Veterans' Service Building. The stilting also underscored the building's Modern functionalist aesthetic. Out of respect for the neighboring stone buildings of the Capitol grounds, Cavin specified a granite exterior for the Veterans' Service Building. But this was no ponderous, make-believe, stone-walled design.

Springing upward from its colonnade, the building rejected any claim to true masonry-bearing construction—its granite walls could only be veneer; its support system, skeletal steel.

Although Cavin's design for the Veterans' Service Building was the first important example of Modern architecture in St. Paul, it had relatively little impact on either public taste or architectural practice. Its influence was muted by an interminable piecemeal construction process, the result of various bureaucratic delays concerning site clearance and funding. The two one-story wings were completed in 1954, but the stylistically crucial three-story office bridge did not appear until the early 1970s. By that time, Cavin's design, although not quite a historical curiosity, was certainly no longer in the city's architectural avant-garde. During the hiatus, Cavin himself gradually shifted his orientation from ground-breaking Modernist to a leader in the field of historic preservation, a logical outcome, at least in retrospect, of his study of the Capitol grounds.[28]

Two postwar designs for religious buildings introduced quite a separate strain of Modernism into St. Paul, each originating from an architect at the end of his career who had achieved early international renown for highly personal versions of expressionism. Chicagoan Barry Byrne's

FIGURE 4.14.
Church of St. Columba, 1327
Lafond Avenue. The design,
by Modernist master Barry Byrne
of Chicago, is an ode to the
plasticity of concrete.

first ecclesiastical work, done in the 1910s, had pressed the functionalist ideology of his early mentor, Frank Lloyd Wright, into the service of a contorted, highly evocative Gothicism. By the time of his commission for the **Church of St. Columba** in the Hamline neighborhood, he had shed even these skewed references to the traditional architectural garb of Catholicism for a more radical spatial symbolism (Figure 4.14). Built in 1949–51, the Church of St. Columba was designed in the shape of a fish, the earliest symbol of Christ. In form and detail, the church conveys the sense of a reality utterly distinct from the orders and shapes of conventional expectations. It is also a tour de force of concrete as the most plastic of all structural materials.

For **Mount Zion Temple** on Summit Avenue, German-born architect Erich Mendelsohn created a substantially more austere essay in Modernist composition (Figures 4.15 and 4.16). The Jewish congregation had hired him largely because of a Reform philosophy that accommodated nontraditional building. Yet when it came time to

select a design, they rejected a model with canted sides and a highly imaginative succession of gabled parapets in favor of a serene nest of rectangular volumes. Mendelsohn was forced to confine the formal elasticity that was his trademark to the shaping of the interiors. The spaces of the sanctuary, foyer, social hall, chapel, and school hover and soar to an ever-changing succession of ceiling heights, and the back wall of the sanctuary was formed of a folding screen to permit inclusion of the foyer and social hall within a single unitary space.[29]

For all the national notice they received, the Church of St. Columba and Mount Zion Temple had little local influence. They remained curiosities throughout the 1950s, specimens of what outside architects were doing rather than stimulants for St. Paul's own embrace of Modernism. Unlike earlier architectural movements and styles, Modernism in St. Paul was not seeded by newcomers and visitors, such as Cavin, Byrne, and Mendelsohn. Nor did it spring from well-entrenched St. Paul firms like Ellerbe and Company. For the first time in St. Paul's

history, innovative architecture found its most influential champions in new homegrown companies, in this case, established and staffed by alumni of the University of Minnesota in Minneapolis.

Formal architectural training at the University of Minnesota dated to 1913. In that year, Frederick Mann, an 1892 engineering graduate from Minnesota, left his position as head of the architecture department at the University of Illinois to organize a new program for his alma mater. In keeping with his own architectural training at the Massachusetts Institute of Technology (MIT), Mann imbued the Minnesota curriculum with the Beaux-Arts method, the prevailing pedagogy of American architectural schools until the 1930s. Named for the École des Beaux-Arts in Paris, Beaux-Arts training emphasized the mastering of accepted architectural styles and traditions, particularly the Italian and French Renaissance. Students marked their progress via a series of rigorous design competitions. In this scheme of things, ornamentation was the crowning act of architectural creation. Beaux-Arts aesthetics demanded scholarly precision in historicist detailing, within a larger context of accepted good taste. A building was expected to satisfy efficiently the needs of its occupants, but it was not considered essential to reveal to the street-side observer precisely how it was done, although some Beaux-Arts practitioners did value functional clarity in architectural expression. Still less important was the "honest" exposition of materials and construction. In the eyes of a Beaux-Arts designer, it would be as rude for an important public building to flaunt a utilitarian structural system as for a grande dame to wear a corset over an evening gown.[30]

Most American architectural programs were closely connected to college engineering departments, providing them with a pragmatic bent often lacking in the ateliers of French architects and their direct American offspring. The University of Minnesota was no exception. Despite the laments of the engineering faculty that their architecture students paid "more attention to external beauty than internal utility," Minnesota graduates in fact were known for their proficiency in both design and structural theory, which contributed to their almost legendary success at the nation's most prestigious graduate schools, especially Harvard and MIT.[31]

When Mann retired in 1936, the chairmanship of the program devolved upon Roy Childs Jones, a former instructor under Mann at Illinois and his first appointment to the Minnesota faculty in 1913. Although perhaps best known for his Beaux-Arts work in terra-cotta, Jones believed that the future of American architecture lay with the new movement and that his job was to train students to be part of it. As he explained to the university administration shortly after becoming department head, "both the profession of architecture and the training for it are in a critical period of change. I foresee a complete realignment of school objectives and methods within the next few years." Jones recognized that much of his teaching staff was ideologically aligned with the old regime. He therefore urged that it was "vitally necessary to get in some young blood as soon as possible . . . [to] make

FIGURE 4.17.
Walter W. Coombs House, 375 Pelham Boulevard. This home was a woodsy Modernist intruder into an isolated neighborhood largely built up in the 1920s and 1930s.

for the stimulation of fresh ideas." Although staff retirements and new appointments would not fully transform the school into a Modernist program until after World War II, Jones strongly indicated the future direction by immediately hiring former student Robert G. Cerny in 1936.[32]

Only four years out of the Minnesota program, Cerny had already earned a master's degree in design at Harvard, worked for two years as a staff architect for the Tennessee Valley Authority, and traveled extensively in Europe studying modern housing and town planning. As interested in building as he was in teaching, he would in the postwar period create one of the major architectural practices in the Twin Cities, providing on-the-job training for dozens of his students. His Modernist commitment was clearly demonstrated in one of his earliest Minnesota commissions, a small house completed in St. Paul in 1941 for bank examiner Walter W. Coombs. Containing three upstairs bedrooms over an open-interior, ground-floor plan, the **Walter W. Coombs House** was a simple, flat-roofed, rectangular volume, sheathed in horizontal redwood siding with a wall of glass on the south side (Figure 4.17). Where a historic revival design of the period might have highlighted the entrance with ornamental columns or pilasters, Cerny functionally framed his front doorway with two industrial steel pipes supporting a sheltering overhang.[33]

Cerny's teaching career at the University of Minnesota spanned forty years, but he was probably most influential during the first decade. As a former student remembers it, "he was conducting virtually a one man crusade to develop an interest in contemporary architecture in the metropolitan area. It seemed he was speaking everywhere—in church basements, in museums, at businessman's clubs."[34]

Not surprisingly, Cerny had the greatest impact on his students. By the early 1940s, the first students who had studied under him for the full five-year program were preparing their final theses. Almost without exception, their various renderings of libraries, factories, air terminals, and office buildings were in the severe glass-walled idiom of the modern International style (Figure 4.18). This was an abrupt departure from the Moderne designs that had dominated student work during the late 1930s and that would continue to influence Minnesota architecture well into the 1950s.[35]

By developing a Modernist program at the University of Minnesota, Jones and Cerny placed their school not only in the forefront of American architectural education but also a good deal ahead of regional popular taste. The result was fairly depressing for any recent graduate who dreamed of turning a thesis project into an actual building. As one member of the Minnesota class of 1948 later recalled, the early postwar period "was a time when

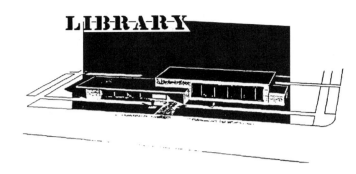

FIGURE 4.18. *Left:* Charles K. Berg's undergraduate thesis, "An Air Terminal," University of Minnesota, 1943. *Right:* Richard F. Hammel's undergraduate thesis, design for Owatonna Public Library, University of Minnesota, 1944. Courtesy of the University of Minnesota Archives.

gifted graduates trained in the contemporary manner could find employment only with architects doing Gothic churches and colonial houses." It soon became apparent to young Modernists that if they intended to build as they had been taught, they would have to establish their own practices, hire their classmates as designers, and create a market for contemporary architecture.[36]

As is common with architectural practices, the new ventures often went through several reorganizations before finding a stable form. In 1949, for example, Louis Lundgren (B. Arch., 1946) left a position with Ellerbe and Company to form a partnership with two other University of Minnesota alumni, Donald Haarstick (B. Arch., 1938), also of Ellerbe, and Grover Dimond Jr. (B. Arch., 1946), then employed with Slifer and Cone, an architectural firm descended from Emmanuel Masqueray's practice and located across the street from Ellerbe in downtown St. Paul. Although the new partnership dissolved in 1951, it gave birth to two of the most successful St. Paul practices of the 1950s and 1960s: Grover Dimond Associates, Inc., and Haarstick, Lundgren and Associates, Inc. According to Lundgren, he and his partners did not consider themselves advocates for any particular aesthetic movement. If they preferred Modern architecture, it was not the result of passionate ideological commitment, but rather because their university training had taught them to think and see in Modernist terms. Their biases were confirmed by one of their first commissions, a subcontract from Slifer and Cone requiring a Romanesque Revival

design for **St. Luke's School** on Summit Avenue. As Lundgren later recalled, "We had to do a hell of a lot of research."[37]

Foreseeing the impact of the postwar baby boom on the state's educational system, Haarstick and Lundgren decided to specialize in school architecture. They launched their business with a letter campaign aimed at every school superintendent in the state. They then spent much of their first year meeting with local school boards. Aggressive promotional efforts coupled with the firm's growing reputation for efficient project management would bring Haarstick and Lundgren more than three hundred school commissions over the next two decades. The City of St. Paul was among their earliest clients. After neglecting the upkeep of city schools for more than twenty years, the citizens of St. Paul in 1950 approved a school bond issue of $9.4 million to pay for badly needed repairs and new construction. Within two years, the St. Paul Board of Education had negotiated twenty-three architectural contracts, all with local firms. Haarstick and Lundgren's assignment was to design a classroom addition for Chelsea Heights Elementary School, a two-story Moderne building originally built in 1932 and then expanded with an addition in 1939.[38]

The **Chelsea Heights Elementary School Addition** was one of several school building projects necessitated by rapid postwar residential development (Figure 4.19). Others included **Mississippi School, Prosperity Heights Elementary School, Eastern Heights Elementary School,**

FIGURE 4.19.
Chelsea Heights Elementary
School Addition, 1557 Huron
Street. This was among the
first St. Paul school designs
to reduce its exterior to the
essentials required to withstand
hard use and Minnesota winters.

and **Highland Park Elementary School**. All of these were located on the city's northern, northeastern, and southwestern edges, which received a large share of the thirteen thousand new dwelling units constructed in St. Paul in the decade following World War II. To ensure that the new elementary schools were planned and built in an economical manner, the St. Paul school board in 1951 hired a staff architect. Their choice was Richard F. Hammel, a University of Minnesota graduate (B. Arch., 1944) with a master's degree in architectural design from Harvard. Just prior to assuming the St. Paul position, Hammel had designed University High School in Minneapolis for the well-known firm of Magney, Tusler and Setter of that city.[39]

Hammel developed a basic program that gave the new St. Paul elementary schools of the early 1950s a consistent look. After studying the physical condition of the city's existing school buildings, he decided that certain types of construction were unsuitable for structures that traditionally had received hard use and poor maintenance in the severe Minnesota climate. His list of taboos included pitched roofs, parapet walls, exposed concrete, skylights, and (because he was a Modernist) "ornamental projections." In general, he favored flat-roofed, one-story, steel-framed buildings with brick facing over concrete block. Hammel was particularly concerned with providing classrooms with adequate controllable illumination.

Based on his work at University High School, he had come to believe that classroom windows were a poor source of lighting, yet he recognized the psychological value of giving students a visual connection with the outside. As a compromise, the St. Paul elementary schools were designed with generous fenestration and an interior lighting system that was independent of daylight. To control glare and solar gain, the windows were shielded by a roof overhang, which also increased the visual interest of the exterior.[40]

The Chelsea Heights project, completed in 1953, was typical of the grade schools built under Hammel's tenure as school board architect. Yet for Hammel, the building had special significance. It renewed his acquaintance with Haarstick and Lundgren's chief designer, Curtis H. Green, whom Hammel had first met while the two were undergraduates at the University of Minnesota. After finishing his studies at Minnesota (B. Arch., 1946), Green took a master's degree in architecture at MIT. There he fell under the spell of the renowned Finnish Modernist Alvar Aalto, one of the more romantic practitioners of the International style. In Green, Hammel found a sensitive designer who shared his own concerns about crafting a total architectural environment. Green approached the Chelsea Heights project, for example, as though he were responsible for the entire site and not just an addition. To promote aesthetic harmony, he found and used the identical brick of the 1930s building and then fretted that because of twenty years of grime, "the darks in the existing building . . . tend to contrast too strongly." He informed Hammel that "the entire building would be enhanced greatly" if the school board would find the money to clean the older masonry. According to Green, the two men met for lunch one day in 1952 and "agreed we knew almost everything about architecture and should set our own destiny." The next year they formed a partnership, opened an office in St. Paul, and began seeking school commissions of their own.[41]

If Haarstick and Lundgren designed in the contemporary manner because it was what they knew how to do, Hammel and Green were Modernists because of what they believed was right. Imbued with a mission to elevate public taste, they wanted to blaze a new direction in regional architecture, bringing the Twin Cities closer to the Modernism of New York and Chicago. This commitment was reaffirmed in 1954 by the hiring of Bruce A. Abrahamson, who would add his name to the company letterhead ten years later.

Like Hammel, Abrahamson had followed the familiar educational path leading from the University of Minnesota (B. Arch., 1949) to Harvard (M. Arch., 1951), and like Green, he had worked for a time in the architectural office of his undergraduate professor Robert G. Cerny. In 1952, however, Abrahamson broke with precedent and moved to Chicago to work for Skidmore, Owings and Merrill, the prestigious architectural firm that was largely responsible for introducing corporate

America to the International style. As a member of the city's architectural elite, Abrahamson found himself in the company of the likes of Mies van der Rohe, who, as head of the architecture program at the Illinois Institute of Technology (IIT), had made Chicago his home since the late 1930s. Perhaps even more important, Abrahamson had the opportunity to study Mies's work, from the earliest designs on the IIT campus to the recently completed glass apartment towers at 860–80 Lake Shore Drive, widely regarded as Modernism's most elegant statement.[42]

Abrahamson returned to Minnesota a devout disciple of Mies. Like his master, he was in quest of the precisely placed, perfectly balanced, hard-edged structural line. He had little interest in concrete, which slavishly went wherever it was poured, adopting the most outlandish postures. For Abrahamson, "it didn't seem pure enough. There was a real logic to steel. But concrete gave you too much license. You could cheat with concrete." If nothing else, Abrahamson was determined to set an honest structural example, even if it meant sacrificing something of his own personal comfort. In the mid-1950s, for example, he set about building a steel-framed, glass-walled house for himself, hoping to prove that "the aesthetic qualities desired could be [achieved] in a cold climate and still not cost any more than the standard and accepted methods of house construction used in this area." After its completion, Abrahamson affirmed that his home cost less than "the unit cost of most builder's houses." He did not add, however, that such economy

FIGURE 4.20.

Advertisement in *St. Paul Dispatch* for the reopening of the W. T. Grant Company Department Store, Seventh and Cedar Streets, after its modernization in 1955. Courtesy of the St. Paul Public Library.

was achieved partly by designing a smaller, more minimalist house than he might otherwise have preferred. But, then, his home was not simply for shelter. "I had in mind," said Abrahamson, "making a strong statement."[43]

In pledging his allegiance to the structural steel frame, Abrahamson took on one of the more interesting challenges of Modern architecture. Although Modernist principles demanded that buildings express the true nature of their materials and construction, it rarely was possible to expose the naked metal skeleton to public view. Building codes generally required that structural steel be encased in fireproofing material. How to reconcile this conflict? The conventional solution was to indicate the internal frame by means of pierlike thickenings in the curtain wall. A somewhat more creative alternative was to draw a picture of the frame on the curtain wall by using contrasting types of cladding, a device adopted by Cerny and his partner Roy Thorshov in their design for the **W. T. Grant Company Department Store** building completed in downtown St. Paul in 1955 (Figure 4.20).[44]

Probably the most sophisticated solutions, however, were worked out by Mies van der Rohe. In his design for Alumni Memorial Hall (1946) at the IIT campus in Chicago, Mies symbolically expressed the building's structural skeleton by embedding in the plane of the curtain wall steel members attached to the supporting steel frame beneath. A few years later in his high-rise apartment towers at 860–80 Lake Shore Drive (1948–51),

Mies further elaborated this symbolic structural vocabulary by pushing what were largely ornamental vertical steel members completely through the plane of the glass curtain wall, so that architectural space seemed the indisputable result of a palpable exterior metal frame—a surface illusion for an underlying reality. There was no denying that this treatment of the facade was a return to ornamentalism. But unlike decorative detailing in the Beaux-Arts period, Mies's purpose was to reveal rather than conceal structure. Whether such ornamental expression was "honest" or not depended on the viewer's attitude toward symbolism in general. In American intellectual circles of the 1950s, symbolism was very much in favor, whether it appeared in a film by Ingmar Bergman, a novel by William Faulkner, or a painting by Pablo Picasso. Indeed, for many academic critics, there seemed to be no better way to reveal inner truth in a world of deceptive appearances.[45]

In time, Mies's symbolic vocabulary was adopted by so many American Modernists that it became a design cliché. But the Miesian approach was still quite fresh when Abrahamson brought it to bear on his first major design project at Hammel and Green, the nine-hundred-student **Highland Park Junior High School** constructed during 1955–57 (Figure 4.21). To express the building's steel structural system, Abrahamson marked the interior uprights with ornamental steel channel sections set in recessed panels in the exterior brick cladding. On extended

FIGURE 4.21.
Highland Park Junior
High School. The design
combines aluminum-ribbed
glass walls with a windowless
classroom block.

areas of glass, vertical aluminum ribbing protruded from the curtain wall, echoing the structural rhythm of Mies's Lake Shore Drive apartments. If the building's exterior detailing was a tribute to Mies, its interior plan was largely the work of Richard Hammel. In his earlier programming for the St. Paul school board, Hammel had bowed to architectural convention, permitting traditional daylight fenestration in classrooms that actually depended on artificial lighting. In the Highland Park Junior High School, however, he attempted to enforce a strict functional honesty in at least one area of the building. The result was a windowless classroom block surrounded by glass-walled corridors. In this scheme, windows served a purely psychological purpose, allowing students a visual connection with the outdoors during period breaks, when they traveled between classrooms equipped with artificial illumination.[46]

Since schools were supposed to be receptive to new ideas, it seemed almost natural for St. Paul's new school buildings to be of Modernist design. In most other circumstances, however, Modern architecture was a decidedly unconventional statement. During the 1950s and early 1960s, it appealed most strongly to those attempting to project an image of exciting innovation. A prime example was the Group Health Mutual Insurance Company, regional pioneer for the concept of providing the insured with medical services rather than simply reimbursements for medical costs. In 1957, the company inaugurated its clinic program in its new **Group Health Mutual Insurance Office** on Como Avenue, designed in the International style by Haarstick and Lundgren. The crisp, glass-and-silicone-panel curtain wall was meant as a pledge that the building's medical facilities were as up-to-date as its architecture (Figure 4.22).[47]

During the 1950s, airport commissions used Modern architecture with a similar kind of intent. In the early years of commercial aviation, airline terminals had been designed with monumental solidity to reassure passengers about the safety of flying. In the postwar period, however, air terminals became soaring structures of lightness and grace. The emphasis was still on safety, but in the more sophisticated public consciousness of the Space Age, safety now was equated with advanced design and technology. The new **Minneapolis–St. Paul International Airport Terminal** was true to its era (Figure 4.23). Designed by Thorshov and Cerny in 1956 and completed in 1961, the building symbolically fused the technologies of architecture and aviation in a boldly serrated roof that mimicked the outline of wings in flight. The distinctive roofline signaled the regional debut of a relatively new reinforced-concrete technology known as folded-plate construction, which dramatically increased the clear spans

MERIT AWARD

Group Health Mutual Insurance Office
St. Paul, Minnesota

Haarstick, Lundgren
& Associates
St. Paul, Minnesota

34

FIGURE 4.22.
Group Health Mutual Insurance Office,
2500 Como Avenue, 1957.
A crisp and clean emblem of
health and modernity. Photograph from
Northwest Architect; courtesy of the
Minnesota Historical Society.

FIGURE 4.23.
Minneapolis–St. Paul
International Airport terminal,
1961. The folded concrete plate
roof construction is emblematic of
wings in flight. Photograph by
Norton and Peel; courtesy of the
Minnesota Historical Society.

FIGURE 4.24. The carousel design for Midwest Federal Savings and Loan branch banks. This illustration is from an advertising brochure, "The Story behind Midwest Federal's Progress and Leadership since 1891" (1966). Courtesy of the Minnesota Historical Society.

previously attainable by conventional slab roofs. Thorshov and Cerny completed their design statement with Miesian-inspired glass walls, prominently ribbed on the exterior with protruding aluminum mullions.[48]

Modern architecture also served the purposes of those who wished to destroy an old image as much as to create a new one. In 1963, for example, the Minneapolis Federal Savings and Loan Association (later renamed Midwest Federal) decided to combat its staid downtown image and expand its market by opening branch banks throughout the Twin Cities. For its new buildings, the company retained a recently established Minneapolis architectural firm consisting of William J. Miller, Kenneth J. Whitehead, and Foster W. Dunwiddie, all previously employed with Thorshov and Cerny. The architects responded with a design for the first truly transparent commercial structure in the Twin Cities, consisting of twenty-eight floor-to-ceiling, plate-glass windows set in thin mullions to give the appearance of a clear glass cylinder. Centered beneath an overhanging circular roof with sunscreen, the banking floor beckoned to the surrounding parking area like a carousel in an amusement park (Figure 4.24). In promotional brochures, the bank itself promoted the new buildings as a "carousel design" that would increase neighborhood accessibility to banking services. Over the next ten years, approximately ten buildings were constructed according to the 1963 prototype,

including one at the northwest corner of Snelling and University Avenues in St. Paul (razed).[49]

If Modern architecture in the mid-twentieth century appealed to a select commercial clientele, its residential market was even more limited. Home construction depended on mortgages, and mortgage bankers were a cautious lot, quick to penalize any untested novelty that might lower resale value. As housing historian Gwendolyn Wright has noted, national banking policy in the immediate postwar period strongly encouraged builders to stick with "Colonial Revival, Cape Cod, Tudor, Spanish, or a safe contemporary look like the ranch house." In Minnesota, the president of the statewide chapter of the American Institute of Architects bluntly warned builders "that to go too modern in design was bad business."[50]

The case of Donald and Elizabeth Lampland of St. Paul is instructive. Since Donald was a trained engineer and part owner of a family lumber company, the Lamplands thought it well within their capabilities to design and build their own home. Lampland Lumber Company had been involved with one of the first housing projects completed in St. Paul after World War II: a two-block development of fifty-six Cape Cod homes off Edgcumbe Road and West Seventh Street in Highland Park. During the late 1940s, the Lamplands themselves had lived in one of these tract homes, and they hoped that their

FIGURE 4.25.
Donald and Elizabeth Lampland
House, 2004 Lower St. Dennis
Road, 1952. Interior walls could
be shifted to suit planning needs.

new house would offer more in terms of comfort and style. To stimulate their imagination, the couple enrolled in a night architecture class with Robert Cerny at the University of Minnesota, and also attended an intensive seminar on new home-building techniques at the University of Illinois. Such preparation whetted their appetites for a Modernist dwelling. But they soon learned that their own preferences were only part of the design equation: "We had to build a house that the bank would loan us money on." Consequently, the Lamplands shelved any ideas they might have had about unorthodox massing or rooflines and built a seemingly conventional, gable-roofed ranch house. The building's construction, however, incorporated a number of devices that made it one of the more innovative houses of its period.[51]

Completed in 1952 in a recently platted area of Highland Park, the **Donald and Elizabeth Lampland House** represented a radical attempt to create a completely flexible, Modernist floor plan (Figure 4.25). Employing a Fink truss configuration recommended by the University of Illinois, the house carried the roof almost entirely on exterior walls. Since only one interior wall had a load-bearing function, the others were designed as temporary partitions, which "may be easily unfastened with a common claw hammer and moved to a new location." The result was an adjustable interior plan, satisfactory to mortgage bankers and modernists alike. As befitted the

owners of a lumber company, the Lamplands finished the house with wood inside and out, brightening the living-dining area with floor-to-ceiling windows on three sides. In their amalgam of conventional ranch house exterior and Modern interior, the couple ended up creating the kind of contemporary house that many Americans yearned for in the early postwar period. As *Better Homes and Gardens* explained after surveying 4,900 families, "Most families want houses that are low and ground-hugging instead of high and boxy.... They want picture windows. . . . They want not imprisoning cells for living rooms but rooms big enough to relax in, entertain in, live in."[52]

Satisfying popular taste did not necessarily mean compromising Modernist principles. After all, there was nothing intrinsically retrograde about a house with a conventional roofline, just as there was nothing intrinsically Modern about an unorthodox appearance. The test was whether or not the overall design truly met and expressed the needs of the occupants and the challenges of the site. As Modernist Norman C. Nagle explained upon becoming curator of architecture at the Walker Art Center in Minneapolis in 1952:

> The urge to design a building which will stand out
> from its neighbors because of a peculiar interpretation
> of the esthetic of modern architecture is strong in
> many of us. Insofar as differences of appearance are

FIGURE 4.26.
Stanley S. Miller House,
320 Stonebridge Boulevard, 1951.
The home is shown shortly after
its construction in the midst of a
Modernist development near
the Mississippi River. Photograph
by Photography, Inc., from
House and Home.

the result of a discipline which requires a fresh look at each new problem, this is a healthy attitude, but the temptation to design something "different" results only in unhealthy exhibitionism. . . . It concentrates attention on irrelevant details while avoiding real investigation.[53]

Nagle may well have been referring to his own temptations while designing a residence for the Stanley S. Miller family in the Macalester-Groveland district of St. Paul. Completed in 1951, the **Stanley S. Miller House** occupies a narrow, severely sloping wooded lot in the Stonebridge subdivision (Figures 4.26 and 4.27). Uneven terrain often invites dramatic treatment, and Nagle investigated the possibility of thrusting the Miller House into the air on stilts. Although this option was economically feasible, he chose instead to notch the house into the hillside, capping the redwood exterior with an extended shed roof that quietly paralleled the slope of the site. This arrangement allowed Nagle to put the drama of his design on the interior, where it could be more fully enjoyed by the occupants. Although the roof creates barely a ripple on the outside, it is high enough to accommodate an arresting, dining loft and two-story living-room space. In comparing the Miller House with eight other recent hillside residences, *House and Home*

magazine noted that Nagle had chosen "the customary way" of solving the problem of a sloping site but had done it "unusually well." Of all the designs featured, Nagle's best illustrated Frank Lloyd Wright's dictum: "No house should ever be on any hill or on anything. It should be of the hill, belonging to it, so hill and house could live together each the happier for the other."[54]

Wrightian harmonies also suffused the work of the partnership of Elizabeth Scheu Close and Winston Close, who first met as architecture students at MIT in the mid-1930s. The daughter of Viennese intellectuals, Elizabeth literally grew up with Modern art: her childhood home in Vienna had been designed by Adolph Loos, an early prophet of the Modern movement. For Elizabeth, the Modernist program at MIT was a confirmation of family beliefs. Winston, on the other hand, grew up in a small Minnesota farming community, and his introduction to architecture was by way of the undergraduate program at the University of Minnesota in the 1920s. For him, Modernism represented a revolution in taste. In 1938, the couple married and established a practice in Minneapolis specializing in housing.[55]

In time, Elizabeth and Winston Close developed a highly personal residential style that had an especially strong impact on a suburban development just north of St. Paul known as University Grove. Within the area of

FIGURE 4.27.
The dining loft and two-story
living room of the Miller House.
Photograph by Photography, Inc.,
from *House and Home.*

a few square blocks, the Closes were responsible for four-teen houses, from the **Tracy Tyler House** of 1939 to the **Walter Heller House**, completed in 1959 (Figures 4.28 and 4.29). Generally, these designs were characterized by simple forms, low profiles, and natural materials, espe-cially cedar and redwood siding, that blended with the site. If a Close house somehow seemed smaller than it actually was from the outside, the interior tended to give an exaggerated sense of space—the result of an open interior plan that skillfully exploited natural lighting, vistas, and changes in site elevation. In the case of the Closes' work in University Grove, the understated qual-ity of their house exteriors had little to do with conser-vative mortgage regulations about Modern architecture. Construction financing in the Grove was arranged by the University of Minnesota, which operated the devel-opment as a restricted housing compound for its faculty. The university's sole stipulation concerning aesthetics was that all plans required the approval of the school's

advisory architect, a position held by Winston Close from 1950 to 1970.[56]

Elizabeth Close once said, "My husband and I are both convinced that you have to use the environment and that it is best used by disturbing it as little as pos-sible." This statement posited an architecture that was not merely harmonious with its site but was virtually invisible—an ideal that the Closes actually approached in a sod-covered rustic cabin in 1941.[57] Even their most assertive designs, however, had a certain mute, retiring air about them. Indeed, it was precisely this unobtrusive quality that linked their work to most other Modern domestic architecture built in the St. Paul area during the 1950s. Whether the result of conservative mortgage policies or environmentally sensitive aesthetics, very few Modernist designs were aggressive enough, or noticeable enough, to challenge conventional taste.[58]

Probably the most striking Modernist statement was Ralph Rapson's design for the **William G. Shepherd**

House, erected in University Grove in 1956 (Figures 4.30 and 4.31). Rapson was a newcomer to the Twin Cities, having arrived only two years before to assume the chairmanship of the architecture program at the University of Minnesota. Rapson had done his own undergraduate work in architecture at the University of Michigan, proceeding to graduate study in urban planning at the Cranbrook Academy of Art in the late 1930s. During the war years, he found a receptive outlet for his innovative designs in journals and competitions, so that by the time he joined the architecture faculty at MIT in 1946, he was already known in academic circles as "a bright and brash designer." Wider recognition came in the early 1950s, when Rapson's designs for a series of American embassies in Europe received international acclaim for their efficient, flexible floor plan and bold Modernist

FIGURE 4.30.
William G. Shepherd House,
2197 Folwell Avenue. This view
offers the street a playful but
secretive glimpse of the plan
behind the facade.

FIGURE 4.31.
The rear of the Shepherd
House. A two-story main
block opens broadly to the
yard and woods at back.

detailing. It was, as Rapson himself was fond of saying, "the first time in our history [that] the United States government officially exported good architecture."[59]

Although Rapson was impressed by the Modern architecture program at the University of Minnesota, he found little in the way of Modern architecture in the Twin Cities. "To do a Modern house wasn't easy," he later recalled, "apart from University Grove," where

Modernism, in his opinion, meant "woodsy contemporary stuff," far removed from his own thinking about residential design. Unlike the Closes, Rapson did not make a virtue out of blending a house into the surrounding landscape, since, as far as he was concerned, most urban and suburban building sites were not that interesting to begin with. Instead, he believed that a "house, more often than not, must create its own environment."[60]

Rapson's houses characteristically showed a dramatic interplay between voids and volumes, revealing unsuspected courtyards, bold overhangs, and intimate recesses. A recurring device was an open breezeway dividing the plan into a main living-area block and a garage block. In the Shepherd House, the two blocks were joined at the top by fascia boards, indicating an unseen linkage below grade, where a recreation room beneath the garage slab opened into the first-floor living-room area of the main block. To emphasize that his design was intended to transform rather than harmonize with the site, Rapson gridded the front facade into gaily painted rectangles of yellow, beige, and white, which, in their own visually shifting patterns of contrast, replayed the thrust and counter-thrust of the breezeway and building.[61]

After the Shepherd House, Modern residential design became more adventuresome both in University Grove and the Twin Cities in general. At the same time, however, residential construction attracted less and less attention in St. Paul, for the simple reason that fewer and fewer houses were being built. By the mid-1950s, St. Paul's boom in single-family home construction was over. The 822 new housing starts of 1956 were only about half the number registered in the postwar peak year of 1950. And the downward trend continued, so that by 1970 barely 100 new homes were under construction. As city officials recognized at the time, the plummeting statistics reflected the growing scarcity of suitable open land for home building within city limits.[62]

Multifamily housing was the obvious solution. But apartment buildings and the dense urban lifestyle they suggested had been slow to catch on in St. Paul. Prior to the Depression, the city's high proportion of single-family residences had been one of its major selling points. However, the combination of a housing shortage and substandard older dwellings forced the city to take a new look at itself. Elsewhere the New Deal vision of federally assisted slum clearance for inner-city rehabilitation had already taken hold. The Minnesota Legislature, after rejecting the program in the 1930s, finally signed up for participation in 1947, thereby linking St. Paul's first public housing efforts with postwar urban renewal. The core of the legislation was an enabling act for the establishment of public housing authorities with broad powers of eminent domain and the right to raise money through bond issues.

St. Paul's about-face on public housing did not necessarily reflect a new awareness about the evils of slums. Instead, it seems to have been inspired by a healthy respect for the political clout of returning veterans, who were encountering the worst housing shortage in the state's history. In St. Paul, housing was in such short supply that the city council in 1946 spent $145,000 to move 240 war-surplus Quonset huts onto neighborhood playgrounds and convert them into double apartments to rent to veterans with families. After this unexpected entrance into the public housing field, the council saw no reason why it should not continue the work in a more orderly fashion with federal funds. In 1948, it took advantage

FIGURE 4.32.
John J. McDonough Homes,
Jackson Street and Wheelock
Parkway. This multifamily
housing project was built to
bring low-income World War II
veterans into a campuslike
setting.

of the new state legislation and created the St. Paul Housing and Redevelopment Authority (HRA).[63]

At first the HRA could do no wrong. With remarkable speed and efficiency, the agency planned and built two major public housing projects: the 320-unit **Franklin D. Roosevelt Homes** at Hazelwood Street and Maryland Avenue, and the 512-unit **John J. McDonough Homes** at Jackson Street and Wheelock Parkway (Figure 4.32). As seemed appropriate for taxpayer philanthropy, the prevailing two-story, row house design at both projects was spare yet humane, featuring no-frills wood siding above concrete block in a campuslike setting. Equally important from a public relations standpoint, the design was completely the work of St. Paul architects. Haarstick, Lundgren and Associates was responsible for McDonough Homes, and Ingemann, Bergstedt, and Cavin for Roosevelt Homes. When the two housing projects welcomed their first low-income veterans' families in the fall of 1951, state and local politicians stood in line to praise the HRA for providing the "space, light and the air necessary for the rearing of families."[64]

These were among the last kind words the HRA was to hear for some time. It soon became apparent that the public was willing to support public housing only if it was built in someone else's neighborhood. The HRA inadvertently had satisfied this criterion by building its first two projects in no neighborhood at all. Both had gone up on largely vacant land in the city's northeast corner, one of the few relatively rural sections remaining within municipal limits. But when the HRA attempted to acquire land for low-income housing in more developed areas, neighborhood opposition became so strident that it reverberated throughout the mayoral campaign of 1952, helping defeat the two-term incumbent Edward K. Delaney, an unabashed supporter of public housing.[65]

Two years later, the HRA sidestepped neighborhood issues by locating a third public housing project, **Mt. Airy Homes**, in an area behind the State Capitol that was isolated from other residential districts by topography and a railroad yard. Yet the agency failed to avoid controversy altogether. After initially retaining Associated Architects and Engineers as architects of the $5-million project, the HRA hired the Butler Company on the basis of that firm's willingness to work on a sliding fee scale at a savings of over $100,000. The result was something less than architecture, stimulating a new line of attack on the HRA, this time from the architectural community as well as the public at large.[66]

The backlash against its public housing initiatives placed the HRA in an awkward position. The agency already had committed itself to an ambitious program of slum clearance in the Capitol area estimated to uproot over 1,500 families. Without additional public housing, some of the dispossessed might literally end up in the street, which in fact almost occurred when demolition got under way in the mid-1950s. By 1957, downtown businessman William F. Davidson charged that demolition in the area between the State Capitol and downtown had forced 15,000 residents out of the loop and into other areas of the city, with no plans on the board to replace any of the housing lost to slum clearance.[67]

The concerns of the downtown business community were not strictly humanitarian. Slum clearance was removing a large number of customers who had previously walked downtown to shop. If the HRA was not going to rebuild the cleared land with housing, as Loewy had recommended, downtown retailers saw the frightening possibility that the HRA might redevelop it as a new commercial district. As Philip Troy of the Golden Rule Department Store put it, "Who wants to put money into the loop when there is the prospect of obtaining cheap, competitive property in the [Capitol] area?" In 1957, the merchants' worst fears came to pass, when the HRA awarded a fourteen-acre tract in the Capitol redevelopment area to Sears, Roebuck and Company for construction of a large, new merchandising center. Outraged that a municipal agency was installing a formidable competitor on their doorstep, downtown business interests attempted to block the Sears, Roebuck project by litigation, which, although ultimately unsuccessful, seriously disrupted the city's urban renewal program for the remainder of the decade.[68]

To a certain extent, displeasure with the HRA expressed itself as distrust of city planning in general. This was unfortunate for the St. Paul City Planning Board, which during the 1950s had worked very hard to gain acceptance for the idea of comprehensive planning to assist orderly municipal growth. Technically, the planning board was governed by a committee composed of eleven city officials and fifteen citizens appointed by the mayor to overlapping terms. In practice, however, the head staff person established the agency's program. For most of its history, the planning board had followed the dictates of George H. Herrold, an 1896 engineering graduate of the University of Minnesota who became the agency's first director in 1920.

A "good-government" reformer of the early-twentieth-century Progressive variety, Herrold had brought national attention to St. Paul's street traffic designs, zoning ordinances, and unrealized city plans through a stream of publications in engineering and city planning journals. Herrold, however, had little talent for compromise and therefore little patience with city politicians, who had repaid his inflexibility by restricting his budget and relying on the city engineer's office for most of the planning studies involving important public works. During the 1940s, Herrold further isolated himself within city government by opposing the construction of an interstate highway through downtown St. Paul along a route laid out by the state highway department and approved by the city council. Herrold feared that the proposed route would, as he later put it, "muss up residential districts." As a matter of principle, he believed that new highways should be built around cities rather than through them.

"After all," he argued," a city is for people. Their standards and values and way of life should be a first consideration. They have a right to be let alone." When set next to the state highway department's engineering statistics, these sentiments seemed hopelessly old fashioned, and the octogenarian Herrold was eased into retirement in 1953. When Interstate 94 finally was constructed along the prescribed route in the 1960s, Herrold's fears about its disruptive impact were to some extent confirmed. The new highway obliterated an established residential neighborhood west of the Capitol along Rondo Avenue, which had been home to much of St. Paul's African American population for over seventy years.[69]

Herrold's successor, C. David Loeks, was of a more pragmatic bent. A recent graduate from MIT, Loeks believed that a planner's philosophical principles were irrelevant if he could not work within the political system to get his ideas accepted—a conviction equally shared by Herbert C. Wieland, who took over from Loeks in 1958. Loeks spoke deliberately, attempted to avoid controversy, lobbied to achieve consensus—and was rewarded by an ever-larger annual budget, which at $115,554 in 1957 was nine times the amount Herrold had worked with in 1950. Part of the budget increase came from the HRA, which in 1957 contracted with the St. Paul City Planning Board to produce a comprehensive city plan, a federal requirement for all cities receiving federal urban renewal funds.[70]

A major component of the comprehensive plan previewed in 1958, in the form of a land-use study of the downtown business district. Representing the first extended analysis of the area's development patterns since Raymond Loewy Associates had completed their work in 1945, the 1958 study began with what had also served Loewy as a central thesis: "Saint Paul's Central Business District must be revitalized in order to meet . . . growing competition," although it was now recognized that such competition was not restricted to neighboring Minneapolis but also extended to "outlying commercial centers"—a thinly veiled reference to suburban shopping malls.[71]

As proof of downtown St. Paul's failing health, the city planners adduced a variety of disturbing symptoms. Between 1948 and 1954, downtown retail sales had slipped more than 15 percent on an adjusted basis. Only six of the thirty-three downtown blocks between St. Peter and Sibley Streets had gained in value since 1930; the remainder had lost on the average about 20 percent of their assessed worth. Downtown St. Paul looked "old," "drab," and "depressing," with "very few examples of nationally acclaimed architecture in either remodeled or new structures." The planners, however, reserved their strongest language for the four-block core of the downtown retail district, bounded east-west by Wabasha and Minnesota Streets and north-south by Fifth and Seventh Streets. This area formed such a "void" in terms of "less intense land use, lower pedestrian volumes, and lower land values" that it deserved to be characterized as "the hole in the doughnut."[72]

If the HRA had not already alienated the downtown business community with its Sears, Roebuck project, it is possible that the planning board's report might have been received with greater equanimity. But downtown businessmen were in no mood to tolerate unpleasant criticisms from public servants who, so it was believed, would better spend their time and public dollars promoting a positive image of the city. The report also was unsettling because it seemed to discount the ability of the business community to solve its own problems, calling instead for some form of public action under the auspices of the villainous HRA:

> Apparently, the sporadic efforts of individual interests have not been able to re-vitalize the Central Business District. There appears to be little factual basis for optimism concerning the ability of individual action alone to bring Downtown up to competitive standards. . . . One major reason private real estate transactions do not always produce desired results in the Central Business District is the fact that small parcels of land are in separate or even multiple ownership. . . . This often prevents potential developers from assembling large enough tracts to be planned, financed, developed, and operated according to present-day requirements of good design and function. The City's redevelopment powers may be required to help solve this problem which currently thwarts desirable private improvements.[73]

The criticism of private initiative was perhaps especially provoking because downtown business interests were in the midst of one of "the sporadic efforts" to prepare a revitalization plan for the central business district. This effort had begun in June 1955 with the formation of a nonprofit booster organization known as Downtown St. Paul, Inc. The original board of directors contained both large and small retailers, as well as First National Bank president Philip Nason, who had promised his own corporate board that he would devote up to a third of his time to "redevelopment projects that would attract business to the city."[74]

At first, Downtown St. Paul, Inc., concentrated on encouraging merchants to modernize their storefronts along the lines recommended by Raymond Loewy Associates a decade earlier. For design assistance, the group turned to the St. Paul Chapter of the Minnesota Society of the American Institute of Architects, where they secured the volunteer services of three ambitious young architects, all trained in the Modern movement and each a principal in his own firm: Brooks Cavin, Grover Dimond, and Louis Lundgren. It was not long before the "Architects Committee," as it came to be called, was recommending bolder measures. "Superficial face lifting is not enough," explained Dimond. Old buildings may have been well designed by the standards of their own age, but the "progress of our civilization has made them out of date." The solution was not cosmetic remodeling but new construction.[75]

In the summer of 1956, Cavin, Dimond, and Lundgren presented Downtown St. Paul, Inc., with a bold plan to make over the central retail district "so people would rather come downtown to shop, in fact, come from miles around to spend their money there and like it!" Their concept, developed in models and schematic drawings, called for clearance of most of a seven-block corridor along Fifth and Sixth Streets between Market and Sibley Streets. The goal was to construct a pedestrian mall with "new shops, outdoor areas, amusement facilities, and continuous air-conditioned walkways," including second-story pedestrian ramps between buildings. According to Cavin, the proposal was not a "definitive plan" but an "illustrative idea," showing what part of the downtown might look like if the community should decide to implement a comprehensive replanning of the central business district.[76]

In occasional details, this plan recalled suggestions made by Raymond Loewy Associates eleven years before, but in overall concept it was far more indebted to another European transplant, the Viennese-trained, California architect Victor Gruen, who in the 1950s brought the compact diversity of the traditional European marketplace to the American suburbs in order to create the country's most successful shopping centers. Starting with the basic premise that shopping should be a recreational activity, Gruen sought to control the shopping environment to maximize both customer pleasure and storekeeper profits. In the Twin Cities, his work attracted the attention of the Minneapolis-based Dayton retailing family, who hired him to guide the expansion of Dayton's Department Store into the suburbs. During his trips to the Twin Cities, Gruen invariably found that the

weather was "either freezingly cold . . . or it was unbearably hot." "From these personal experiences, under which I suffered greatly," he later explained, "I came to the conclusion that a[n outdoor] shopping center . . . would never do. . . . So I carefully prepared the Daytons for the shocking idea of establishing completely weather protected, covered and climatized public areas." The result was Southdale, the nation's first fully enclosed shopping center, which opened in the southwestern Minneapolis suburb of Edina in 1956.[77]

Although Gruen made his fortune in the suburbs, he was an urbanist at heart, and he hoped that downtown retailers would eventually adopt the principles of the suburban shopping center to revitalize the center city. In 1955–56, he attempted to point the way by preparing a redevelopment plan for Fort Worth, Texas. Although the plan was never implemented, it was widely publicized and distributed, and became something of a bible for Modern architects and planners throughout the country. Gruen's prescription for a pleasurable downtown shopping environment was to ban the automobile from the retail district and construct a pedestrian island of new shops and amusements, surrounded by strategically placed parking structures. It was this concept, coupled with the climate-controlled environment of Southdale, that fueled Dimond, Lundgren, and Cavin's redesign of downtown St. Paul as a pedestrian shopping mall with air-conditioned walkways. Under the sponsorship of Downtown St. Paul, Inc., the architects' plan served as the basis for exhibits and panel discussions in 1957,

FIGURE 4.33.
Dayton's Department Store,
Sixth and Cedar Streets, 1978.
The store's construction in 1963
replaced more than a dozen
older buildings with a single
concrete and brick monolith,
heralding the beginning of
downtown urban renewal.
Photograph by Elizabeth M.
Hall; courtesy of the
Minnesota Historical Society.

culminating at the end of the year in the formation of a new, closely affiliated group, Greater St. Paul Development, Inc. This group raised $52,000 and hired the master himself, Victor Gruen Associates, to transform downtown St. Paul into "a shopper's paradise with malls and landscaped gardens."[78]

From the outset, the Gruen team pledged to apply the principles of the Fort Worth plan to downtown St. Paul, but purging the automobile from the Minnesota capital proved an arduous task. For one thing, the state highway department, with full city council backing, had already fixed the route of a new interstate highway along the north edge of downtown, cutting a 300-foot swath between the central business district and the Capitol redevelopment area. In the summer of 1958, Gruen's planners called on the highway department to reroute the interstate above the Capitol grounds, along a course earlier proposed by the City Planning Board as a feeder route for the Capitol-downtown area. This would not only shift the anticipated increase in traffic away from the center city but would allow the downtown commercial district eventually to expand toward the statehouse area. "You can't let the Capitol be on the wrong side of the tracks," a Gruen partner explained. "Instead of splitting the downtown in half, [our] plan would make the area much larger." But the interstate plans were too far advanced to be successfully challenged. Indeed,

opposition to the highway department tended to mark the consultants as impractical dreamers who did not understand the realities of St. Paul politics. In early 1959, Downtown St. Paul, Inc., itself disavowed the Gruen plan and came out in support of the state highway department's route. Although Victor Gruen Associates continued their planning work in St. Paul for another year or so, a final report was never released to the public.[79]

In the end, Gruen had to be satisfied with a single downtown project, the construction of **Dayton's Department Store** on the block bounded by Wabasha, Cedar, Sixth, and Seventh Streets (Figure 4.33). Completed in 1963, the new building was a giant windowless box, as inward-looking as any suburban shopping mall. The store's built-in, continuous-spiral parking ramp—a major innovation for the city's retailing—was an important part of the shopper's hermetic experience. To drive into the Dayton's ramp was to drive out of the city: "Customers arriving by car have elevator access to a main floor, [and they] use [the] store's moving stairways to reach [the] other three sales floors."[80] To emphasize its kinship with Southdale Dayton's, the new downtown store sported the same brick facing in the same interrupted pattern of projecting vertical stripes.

The 1950s ended with St. Paul downtown planning in disarray. The city's two major planning agencies, the HRA and the planning board, had each managed to antagonize the downtown business community, whose own independent planning effort had crashed headlong into the unyielding wall of state highway department priorities. Yet the urgency for downtown redevelopment remained, as measured by continuously falling retail sales and increasing vacancy rates in commercial space. Especially disturbing was the perception that St. Paul's decline was even greater if the city was compared to Minneapolis, which in the late 1950s had secured federal urban renewal funding for a massive rebuilding of about one-third of its downtown area. With the specter of a rejuvenated Minneapolis before them, the St. Paul business community began to reevaluate its long-standing aversion to government subsidy and planning. As First National Bank president Philip Nason observed several years later, it became apparent that "we wouldn't be able to compete unless we got some federal money in here too."[81]

Political leadership for downtown renewal finally emerged from the St. Paul mayoral election in the spring of 1960. Traditionally, the mayor's office had been occupied by a labor-supported politician lacking significant influence with the business community. But this time the winning candidate, George Vavoulis, was himself a member of the downtown fraternity. Reelected to two additional terms, Vavoulis during his six-year tenure as mayor escorted the business community into the municipal planning process and encouraged city planners to be more responsive to business concerns. The outcome was a redevelopment plan that completely transformed the look of downtown St. Paul.[82]

In the fall of 1960, Vavoulis began his assault on downtown decay by appointing yet another committee of businessmen, to be known as the Committee for the Economic Development of Downtown St. Paul. Consisting of seven prominent corporate executives, including banker Nason, this committee had a single mission: to recommend a method of coordinating all of the various plans already in hand, leading ultimately to concrete action. The initial task force would be assisted by an even larger team of businessmen united by a common dedication to downtown redevelopment. The new recruits, about forty strong—all "top level figures in business, labor, industry and the professions"—were ready for work six months later. Organizing themselves as the Metropolitan Improvement Committee (MIC), they hired an executive director with professional city planning experience, Robert Van Hoef, and began hammering out the framework for implementing a program for the revitalization of downtown St. Paul.[83]

At the end of 1961, the City Planning Board began pulling together its own plan for downtown improvement to supersede those of Loewy and Gruen, while pledging to work closely with both the MIC and the St. Paul HRA. According to planning director Herbert Wieland, this time the city would rely on local talent. St. Paul experts would design and develop the plan with the help and consultation of St. Paul businessmen. The strategy began with detailed fieldwork to update the findings of the Gruen study. It culminated the following year in proposals addressing an enormous range of issues,

FIGURE 4.34.
Model of downtown
St. Paul showing projected
Capital Centre development.
From *Northwest Architect*, 1962.
Courtesy of the Minnesota
Historical Society.

from the improvement of traffic circulation and the creation of pedestrian amenities to the recycling of old buildings and the establishment of new or expanded housing, office, and convention complexes.[84]

While the planning board was still airing its intentions, the MIC moved quickly toward a finished product. In December 1961, the Architects Committee of St. Paul Downtown, Inc., consisting of Cavin, Dimond, and Lundgren, sprang back into existence and took charge of designing a four-block area situated in the "hole in the doughnut." Four weeks later the MIC had in hand a design concept and model that would form the core of a redevelopment area thereafter known as Capital Centre. Hiring of an additional team of architects led to the expansion and refinement of the concept in the following months, ultimately producing a plan to raze almost two million square feet of floor space in a twelve-block area and to replace it with $63 million in new construction.[85]

The MIC, City Planning Board, and HRA released their plans together on August 16, 1962 (Figure 4.34, Map 4.1). This time the alliance of commercial interests and architectural Modernists had the full cooperation of local governmental agencies, at least partly because the participants had respected each other's domains. Planning director Wieland spoke for all concerned when he said, "there is no conflict at all" between the Capital Centre

project and his own agency's goals. The City Planning Board had confined its work to an economic study and a master plan, which dealt more with infrastructure and program than with the appearance or precise location of buildings. It was understood that actual redevelopment would be the responsibility of the HRA, the only agency with both the power of eminent domain and access to federal funding.[86]

Although publicity at the time emphasized that St. Paul was preparing "a home-grown plan" "designed and developed by St. Paul experts," the bloodlines were not quite so pure. Cavin, Dimond, and Lundgren were indeed the principals of St. Paul offices, but they were soon joined by architect Cecil Tammen, who had recently been elected head of the Minneapolis Chapter of the American Institute of Architects. Tammen was also a partner in Cerny Associates, the Minneapolis company that had masterminded an urban renewal plan for its native city. Despite his carpetbagger status, Tammen brought needed practical experience to the St. Paul planning effort.[87]

Nor was Tammen's the only outside influence on Capital Centre planning. The spirit of Victor Gruen hovered over the entire enterprise. In public forums, the Architects Committee took pains to disassociate themselves from Gruen's ideas, especially his ban on downtown automobiles, which had proved his undoing in St. Paul.

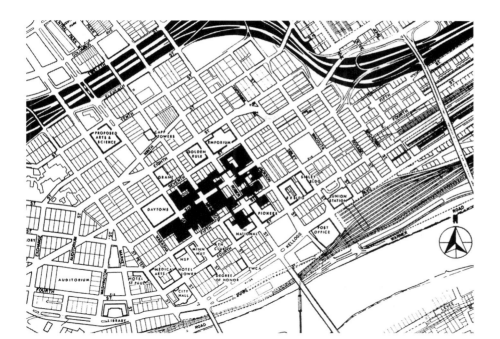

MAP 4.1.
Downtown St. Paul, showing projected Capital Centre development. From *Northwest Architect*, 1962. Courtesy of the Minnesota Historical Society.

"Everyone has been trying to get the automobile out of downtown," declaimed Dimond. "But that isn't . . . the way we live. Our idea was, instead of fighting the car, to bring it downtown and make the driver feel right at home."[88] But in reality, Capital Centre was as firmly rooted in Gruen's theories as the urban renewal proposal tendered by Dimond and his colleagues in the mid-1950s. Gruen's goal of separating pedestrian and vehicular traffic remained primal, as did his aim of making shopping a recreational experience. The authors of Capital Centre hoped to accomplish both objectives by means of an extensive system of elevated, enclosed, climate-controlled walkways, later known as skyways (Map 4.2). In their minds, this pedestrian network would not only insulate the shopper from the distractions and inclemency of the outside world but would be an alluring

MAP 4.2.
St. Paul skyway plan. The system was extended to historic buildings well outside the Capital Centre area.

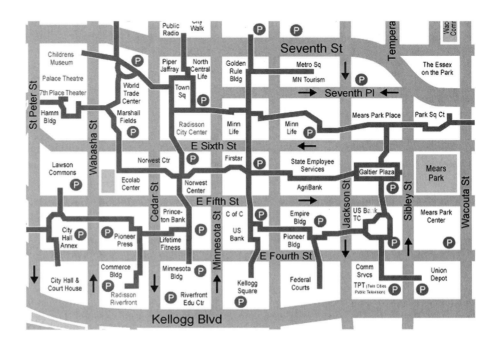

FIGURE 4.35.
Degree of Honor Building,
325 Cedar Street. This was the first
of the bland high-rises that would typify
the Capital Centre development.

novelty in and of itself. According to Lundgren, it would give St. Paul "something unique and worth coming to rather than just a bunch of new buildings." "When the skyway program is completed," enthused one developer, "St. Paul will be one of the biggest shopping centers in the world—all under one roof." This vision was so central to St. Paul's urban renewal effort that the city would eventually assume ownership of the skyways and administer them as public thoroughfares.[89]

Public response to Capital Centre indicated how far St. Paul sympathies had shifted from the distrust of government funding and planning that had stymied earlier initiatives. Prominent businessmen stood shoulder to shoulder with the president of the St. Paul Trades and Labor Assembly and the secretary of the St. Paul Building and Construction Trades Council to praise the new urban renewal plan. Even more significantly, a residential

neighborhood group, the North Central Community Council, voiced its approval, then appealed for the same swiftness in the adoption of an urban renewal program for its area. All that municipal planning and federal funding had so far done for this predominantly African American north-central area was to cut it up with a freeway, yet still its residents were hopeful that the same political processes and governmental monies could be used in rebuilding their troubled district.[90]

Additional planning and the search for developers absorbed Capital Centre energies during the program's first two years. In the meantime, the public's thirst for some evidence of progress was slaked by newspaper features promising that rebuilding was only a heartbeat away. Headlines were interchangeable throughout much of 1963 and 1964: "St. Paul Gathers Speed in Rebuilding Downtown" (*Minneapolis Tribune,* October 27, 1963),

FIGURE 4.36.
Wabasha Court, Wabasha
and Fifth Streets, ca. 1977.
Among the most refined
designs of the 1960s, Wabasha
Court was demolished in 1998.
Photograph by Hammel,
Green, and Abrahamson.

"Downtown to Turn a New Face toward the Future" (*St. Paul Pioneer Press*, January 12, 1964), "St. Paul's Capital Centre Picks Up Speed" (*Minneapolis Tribune*, December 10, 1964). Although the downtown area boasted a half dozen new buildings by the end of 1964, all but one were at the outskirts of Capital Centre. Yet two of them showed significant promise of what the new downtown might look like. The **Degree of Honor Building**, completed in 1962, was a harbinger of the upright, rectangular high-rises that would soon typify the central development (Figure 4.35). Designed by the St. Paul firm of Bergstedt, Hirsch, Wahlberg, and Wold, it clothed a steel frame in polished stone—white granite on the upper stories, black granite on the recessed ground-floor level. For the sake of "honesty," the building's skeleton stood exposed at both top and bottom.

Exposition of structure played an even larger role in a much humbler construction project completed in 1964 in the **Wabasha Court** (razed) retail development, just west of the new Dayton's Department Store (Figure 4.36). On the northwest corner of Wabasha Street and Fifth Street, Bruce Abrahamson of Hammel, Green, and Abrahamson placed a one-story, glass-enclosed, flat-roofed steel pavilion, clasped from behind by an L-shaped pedestrian court. Designed to give its specialty retail tenants a maximum of street-level exposure, the building was yet another tribute by Abrahamson to Mies van der Rohe, who had first explored the simple pavilion

form in the 1920s. Sensitive in detailing and flexible in plan, the Wabasha Court building expressed a degree of refinement unusual for any downtown, although its understated elegance and diminutive scale made it easily overlooked.[91]

Although Wabasha Court was outside the boundaries of Capital Centre, Abrahamson's next contribution would, literally and figuratively, be at the very heart of the urban renewal undertaking. Both spatially and conceptually, the sprawling Capital Centre project hoped to achieve design integration through the unifying function of its new climate-controlled, street-straddling, second-story linkages between buildings; it was Abrahamson's task to design the prototype of these structures. Stripped of promotional rhetoric, the "skyway" was simply a bridge, and to Abrahamson's way of thinking, a bridge was an industrial structure that cried out for a completely honest treatment of materials. Given the designer's Miesian orientation, it might have seemed a certainty that this particular bridge would be some sort of minimalist glass-and-steel passageway. Yet Abrahamson at first toyed with the idea of constructing the skyway from unpainted Cor-ten steel and then allowing it to develop a rough, robust finish by means of natural weathering. While this approach would have created an exceedingly honest bridge, it also would have placed a multitude of rusted constructions over the streets of the downtown district, a design solution entirely at odds with the spick-and-span

image of the Capital Centre program. In the end, Abrahamson settled for an elevated, flat-roofed, glass-enclosed pavilion with an exposed, painted structural-steel frame (Figure 4.37).[92]

A major breakthrough in Capital Centre finally occurred in 1965 with the awarding of a contract to the Davidson-Baker Company for the development of a "superblock" at the heart of the urban renewal project. Plans called for a three-block, $26.5-million complex of nine buildings, with Grover Dimond Associates as the general architect. Now that work was actually in the offing, the respected eastern journal *Progressive Architecture* discovered St. Paul's downtown plans and lauded the city's much-delayed foray into Modern architecture under the headline "St. Paul Sees the Light." The *New York Times* reported on the Capital Centre project as well, beginning its story with a note that 108 downtown buildings were soon to be razed and 371 businesses relocated.[93]

The first phoenix to rise from the ashes would also prove to be the single universally acclaimed architectural accomplishment of Capital Centre. The **Osborn Building**, located on the northeast corner of Wabasha Street and Fifth Street, was the new administrative headquarters of Economics Laboratory, Inc. (later renamed Ecolab), a St. Paul company that had grown to be the world's largest manufacturer of detergents (Figure 4.38). In its

symbolism, the building looked simultaneously into the past and future. A quarter century earlier, another soap maker in another city, Lever Brothers of New York, had erected a sleek glass-box headquarters to promote its image and wares. Twelve days out of every month, a cleaning crew scaled the Lever House and, in full public view, soaped its reflective expanse into a shining advertisement. At a press conference in the fall of 1965, Edward E. Osborn, president of Economics Laboratory, announced that he, too, would erect a "monument to cleanliness" in order "to symbolize our business and to give image and identity to our company."[94] He told St. Paul architect Clark D. Wold:

> Design an office building as modern and handsome as can be found anywhere, one that is flexible, functional, and attractive but with the added distinction of *cleanability*. . . . Do it by the selection of materials, the shapes of surfaces; do it by shutting off the outside world with glass and bringing in filtered air; do it by leaving no place for dirt to hide. Devise, invent, innovate to make the building convey a sense of cleanliness everywhere.[95]

The Osborn Building incorporated several features that had become stylistic conventions of the corporate

FIGURE 4.38.
Osborn Building,
370 Wabasha Street, 1968.
A sparkling view of a detergent
manufacturer's "monument to cleanliness."
Photograph by Economics Laboratory
and Warren Reynolds and Associates of
Minneapolis; courtesy of the
Minnesota Historical Society.

American headquarters. Like the Lever House, which had in so many ways started the trend, it, too, was an International style box on polished stone stilts, set back from the street in a concrete plaza. Wold's design, however, was no foolish imitation or insipid sequel. He gave the Osborn Building a vibrant personality by ribbing its twenty stories of glass with vertical stainless-steel fins, so that the deeply striated facades seemingly rippled—now open, now closed—as the viewer shifted position. In the best Modernist tradition, these gleaming projections were intended to be functional as well as ornamental. In addition to housing ventilation and air-conditioning equipment, the fins were supposed to carry "a mechanical [cleaning] device that will run up and down the face of the building," although this scheme was never put into practice. When the Osborn Building was completed in

1968, there may have been only a few people in the city who fully appreciated its historical antecedents. But almost everyone understood its importance as the herald of a clean, new downtown St. Paul. As the *Northwest Architect* affirmed, "Saint Paul's skyline sparkles with the newly completed Osborn Building . . . , symbolic of the architectural renascence taking place."[96]

Grover Dimond's own contributions to Capital Centre proved to be considerably more bland. First of his projects to go up was the **Northwestern National Bank,** a pairing of horizontal and vertical boxes faced in precast concrete aggregate and glass (Figure 4.39). Completed in 1969, the building was meant to reflect "the solidarity of an institution that has cared for the funds of a community for more than 43 years." More importantly, Northwestern National Bank was a major catalyst for

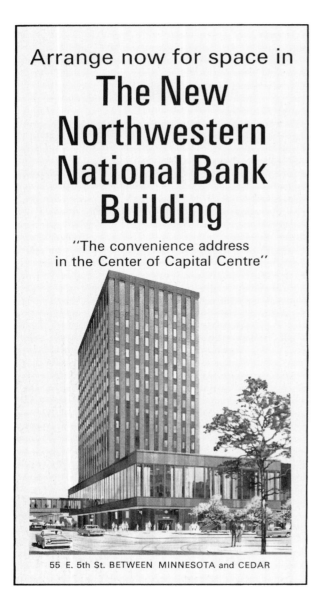

Arrange now for space in
The New Northwestern National Bank Building

"The convenience address in the Center of Capital Centre"

55 E. 5th St. BETWEEN MINNESOTA and CEDAR

development of the Fifth and Sixth Streets corridor. "We weren't content to settle for a new bank," said CEO Roger Kennedy. "We wanted a new neighborhood." In 1970, another Dimond project, the **Skyway Building**, linked the bank tower to the Osborn Building. The lower, two-story volume of the bank was dubbed the Skyway Concourse, indicating its role at the heart of the evolving second-story walkway system.[97]

Immediately south of Capital Centre's Fourth Street boundary, the HRA had earmarked three additional blocks for redevelopment as a part of the 1962 master plan for the central business district. This stretch above the Mississippi River, beginning one block east of the City Hall and County Courthouse, had long been targeted by city planners as a government services corridor. The 1962 plan added a luxury high-density residential component to serve anticipated office and retail development to the north. The area also was slated for hotel development, an essential part of a larger scheme to build a new convention center to the west. In consonance with these plans, a new **Federal Courts Building** (316 North Robert Street) arose at the eastern end of the three-block area, while a new hotel, the **St. Paul Hilton** (11 East Kellogg Boulevard), and a high-rise apartment building, **Kellogg Square,** went up between the city and federal buildings (Figure 4.40). Along the south side of Fourth

FIGURE 4.40.

Kellogg Square, Kellogg Boulevard
and Robert Street, 1975.
This product of four architectural
teams and four years of construction
offered the city 426 apartments and
30,000 square feet of office space.
Photograph by Steve Plattner;
courtesy of the Minnesota
Historical Society.

Street, a handful of midrise structures from the 1920s were permitted to survive, more as the product of incomplete redevelopment than as a matter of preservation interest.[98]

First of the projects to be completed in the southern sector was the St. Paul Hilton, which proved remarkable for its cost alone, a $13-million figure far exceeding the price of any single project in Capital Centre. The Federal Courts Building approached it at $11 million, but for all its tonnage of white marble facings, it failed to draw critical praise or even much in the way of public attention. Kellogg Square fared much better. Its design was the product of a partnership between the MIC's four consulting architectural firms, and its $12-million cost was the lowest of the projects considered by the HRA for the site. All but $2 million was expended on a thirty-two-story tower containing 426 apartments, 385 parking stalls, and nearly thirty thousand square feet of commercial space. The balance of the money finished off the project with fourteen town houses, which filled out the block at the third-story level. Kellogg Square took nearly four years to complete, but by the spring of 1973, its commercial spaces were 90 percent committed, while its residential occupancy was projected to reach a similar figure in December.[99]

As the southern corridor gradually filled with new buildings, the press, the downtown community, and the public at large slowly shifted their gaze northward until their eyes fell on the huge gaping holes at the center of the city. "Gads, The City Has Been Bombed," announced a headline in January 1966. Facetious at first, such comments soon took on the strain of battle fatigue as the nation's money supply tightened and new construction faltered. One year later the press delivered a good news/bad

news verdict. The good news was that previous financial commitments had so insulated St. Paul from the
nationwide building slowdown that the city had captured
70 percent of the state's new construction during the first
nine months of 1966. The bad news was that high interest rates had closed the door on developers not already
committed.[100]

Although boosterism of Capital Centre continued un-
abated, two of the three blocks on the northern edge
remained completely empty. Other blocks that retained
existing structures begged for developers. In spite of
continuous reportage of developments whose time had
come, the only new project in the urban renewal district
since 1967 had been the much-delayed Kellogg Square.
In the early 1970s, however, the **First Federal Savings
and Loan Building** went up on Cedar Street (Figure
4.41). From a distance, the building seemed to be simply another midrise glass box, yet it emphasized street-
level design by means of a two-story, concrete and glass
extension along Cedar Street, which provided welcome
visual relief to the slab-tower massing of most of the
new downtown construction. Further progress occurred
in 1973 with the completion of Grover Dimond Associates' sixteen-story **Capital Centre Building** (Figure 4.42),
built but never occupied by the Northern Federal Savings and Loan Association. Sharing a small concrete plaza
with the Osborn Building, the reflective glass block
held up a mirror to its gleaming neighbor, creating what
was arguably the only aesthetically successful pairing of

buildings in the entire urban renewal undertaking. Two
decades later, the affinity between the two buildings
became even stronger. In 1998, Ecolab turned the Capital Centre Building into its corporate training center
and remodeled the plinth—originally a tall concrete arcade
finished in white stone aggregate—to match the black
granite frame at the base of the Osborn Building.[101]

The Capital Centre Building in effect marked the end
of the Capital Centre project, although the HRA did
not officially close its books on downtown renewal until
March 1974. At that time, one last building was still
under construction in a nearly empty block in the middle of the Capital Centre district. The builders of the
new twenty-six-story **American National Bank Building**
promised a "contemporary classic," but the completed
structure was merely a bland tower of glass, articulated
by fluted and finned precast concrete piers. For a few
years, it could boast of being the second tallest building
in the city. In its way, though, the American National
Bank Building was a fitting anticlimax to the downtown
urban renewal program, which had repeatedly promised
so much in the way of architectural design and had regularly delivered so little.[102]

While reconstruction of the urban center vacillated
between a hare's expectations and a tortoise's reality,
Modernism crept by degrees into monumental architecture elsewhere in the city. In the 1950s, high-rise apartment buildings had become one of the country's most
broadly accepted vehicles of the new architecture. St. Paul

met the trend with considerable resistance, for the city had been a bastion of single-family homes from its earliest years. Even with the decline in home building in the late 1950s and 1960s, privately financed apartment construction remained by and large a two- or three-story affair, with only the slightest of nods to Modernist design.[103]

A single outstanding exception paved the way to the apartment towers that would eventually line the interstate freeway and the northern edge of downtown in years to come. Overlooking the Mississippi River just north of the Ford Parkway Bridge, **740 River Drive Apartments** introduced the luxury, high-rise apartment concept to the Twin Cities (Figure 4.43). Its designer was Yale-trained Minneapolis architect Benjamin Gingold, its métier the clean-lined spare geometry of the International style. Completed in 1961, the twenty-one-story concrete tower was "the tallest apartment building in the upper Midwest," and with 164 units, it was also

the region's largest. With an optimism that flew in the face of St. Paul realities, Gingold affirmed that "today's sophisticate is not a hermit; he prefers being near the centers of civic and cultural activity. High-rise luxury apartments appeal to many for this reason."[104]

From an aesthetic standpoint, Gingold's achievement in luxury multiple housing was not to be surpassed during the next few decades, although Kellogg Square was intended to fill much the same need. Ironically, many of the more successful high-rise apartments of the 1970s arose from an unexpected and much humbler quarter: the HRA-sponsored, low-rent housing program that had been subjected to such vilification in the 1950s. A particularly fine building, the **Central Apartments,** appeared just north of the new freeway in 1964 (Figure 4.44). Designed by Brooks Cavin, the Central Apartments placed a hexagonal footprint into a parklike setting. In granting the project its Honor Award for Design Excellence, the Public Housing Administration commended the

FIGURE 4.43.
740 River Drive Apartments.
Rendering by architect Benjamin Gingold.
At the time of its completion, this was
the highest and largest apartment building
in the upper Midwest. From *Northwest
Architect*, 1959. Courtesy of the
Minnesota Historical Society.

FIGURE 4.44.
Central Apartments,
554 West Central Avenue.
This project demonstrated that
low-rent apartment buildings
could also be elegantly designed.
Photograph by John Lee Banks;
courtesy of the Minnesota
Historical Society.

FIGURE 4.45.
O'Shaughnessy Auditorium,
College of St. Catherine.
The monumental hexagonal
form features a beetling
concrete frieze.

FIGURE 4.46.
Concordia College Student
Union. The projecting wings
of the brick octagon connect
it to the landscape as well
as to other buildings.

"refreshing handling" of the balconies, which were alternately projected and recessed.[105]

Polygonal plans were not reserved for high-rises alone. In the late 1960s and early 1970s, they became de rigueur for new college campus buildings in the city, particularly for structures conceived as gathering places. For the College of St. Catherine, Hammel, Green, and Abrahamson in 1968–70 designed a monumental hexagonal structure to house **O'Shaughnessy Auditorium** (Figure 4.45). Thin vertical slabs rose up from the base, over which beetled a giant, folding frieze. In 1969, Cerny and Associates created a much quieter glass-walled hexagon for the **Weyerhaeuser Memorial Chapel** on the Macalester College campus. The **Concordia College Student Union,** designed by Twin Cities architects Frederick Bentz and Milo Thompson in the early 1970s, punctuated an octagonal volume with deep cuts and projecting shed roofs (Figure 4.46). All three collegiate projects displayed a refreshing liberty from the severe rectilinear restraints that dominated Capital Centre's program.

As Capital Centre started and stopped and started again, there grew a certain uneasiness about its promised benefits that had nothing to do with its fitful progress. Local architects and planners had urged the necessity of downtown urban renewal because the central business district was "drab" and "old." But for many people in St. Paul, the downtown throng of brick and stone buildings was familiar and reassuring in a way that the new high-rise boxes were not. As often happened in the capital city, events in Minneapolis helped throw issues into relief in St. Paul. Minneapolis had preceded St. Paul into the downtown urban renewal arena by several years. Although its plans for refurbishing its business district had helped goad St. Paul into similar action, its headlong commitment to Modernism also served as a cautionary tale. In the late 1950s, the Minneapolis HRA unyieldingly pursued the destruction of one of the Midwest's architectural gems, the 1890 Metropolitan Building. Although the structure's craggy Richardsonian Romanesque exterior was not especially remarkable, its interior light court was so exquisitely detailed and proportioned that even confirmed Modernists such as Ralph Rapson joined the "Save the Metropolitan" campaign. For the Minneapolis HRA, however, the Metropolitan Building simply stood in the way of progress. As the agency's chairman Charles Horn flatly explained, "Real estate research consultants advised the authority that retention of the building would be detrimental to the marketability of the land in the Gateway Center for the uses proposed."[106]

The Metropolitan Building went down in 1962, but not before it had brought together a loose coalition of people from throughout the Twin Cities who were interested in preserving the region's architectural heritage. Among those who listened and learned at "Save the Met" gatherings was Georgia Ray DeCoster, a member of the St. Paul City Planning Board. DeCoster's involvement with city planning was something of an accident. Although she had majored in art history at Wellesley College in the late 1940s, she had only a glancing acquaintance with American architecture and municipal design when she found herself a housewife on Summit Avenue in the 1950s. Her studies in these areas did not truly begin until she joined the League of Women Voters and agreed to sit in on City Planning Board meetings as part of an educational project. Her attendance was so regular and her interest so keen that the board invited her to become a full-fledged member. In 1961, *Northwest Architect* noticed DeCoster's presence when it announced that "on the urging of many citizens" the St. Paul City Planning Board had recently established a historic sites committee under her chairmanship. Said DeCoster, "It is our hope to prevent the complete demolition of the flavor of old St. Paul, at the same time working within the framework of over-all planning."[107]

Securing a financial grant from the local Hill Family Foundation, DeCoster initiated a survey of St. Paul's older architecture, which led to the identification of eighty-five buildings worthy of preservation for their aesthetic merit or historical associations. Published in 1964 as *Historic*

St. Paul Buildings, the survey's findings encouraged Capital Centre planners to spare several architectural landmarks within the renewal area, such as the Pioneer Press Building (Fourth and Robert Streets) and the Endicott Building (123 East Fourth Street and 350 Robert Street), and to place others outside the project boundaries altogether, such as the McColl Building (366–68 Jackson Street), the First National Bank (332 Minnesota Street), and the Germania Bank (6 West Fifth Street). Brooks Cavin later credited DeCoster's "timely work" for the fact that "there were no vital [historic] buildings knocked out by Capital Centre, nothing comparable to the loss of the Metropolitan Building in the Minneapolis Gateway Project."[108]

Most Capital Centre backers, however, charted the project's progress by the demolition, not the preservation, of older buildings. The same article that quoted Cavin on the importance of historic preservation exulted in the destruction of the city's historic fabric:

> Saint Paul has surrendered to life. The city has given up the tranquilizers of nostalgia and apology. . . . The city retains a love of its colorful past but has ceased to live in it. Saint Paul is living and building NOW and looking toward the future. "Loserism" is dead. You can measure this new living pulse in a number of ways: Count the old buildings tumbling down and the new ones going up, tally the flow of investment and renewal dollars into the city; study the plans shaping things to come.[109]

DeCoster understood that such attitudes placed the city's entire architectural heritage at risk. In 1965, she struck out against the "cataclysmic American form" of urban renewal in a thoughtful and well-researched article for *Ramsey County History,* the quarterly of the Ramsey County Historical Society. "American cities," she wrote, "are threatened by a steady dilution of historic character and architectural personality. . . . Today, almost everybody agrees that landmarks must be preserved but it is not generally recognized that many of the more ordinary older structures have a useful role to play in revitalized urban centers." According to DeCoster, the failure of architects and planners to develop viable methods of recycling older buildings would ultimately seal the fate of landmark properties themselves. DeCoster singled out seven threatened downtown St. Paul buildings "designed by leading architects and constructed with the finest materials and workmanship available." The threat to four of them—the Pioneer Press and Endicott Buildings, the McColl Building, and the St. Paul Building—was not immediate, for the Capital Centre plan had spared them. But their demise was simply a matter of time "if prevailing attitudes continue." Three others were in acute danger: the **Guardian Building** (razed, Minnesota and Fourth Streets) and the New York Life Insurance Company Building (razed, Minnesota and East Sixth Streets) stood at the heart of Capital Centre, while the U.S. Courthouse and Post Office on Rice Park would soon become vacant when its government tenants moved to the new Federal Building on Robert Street. "It is unlikely that architectural qualifications alone could save these threatened buildings," wrote DeCoster. "Of more importance to their combined fate is the gathering of evidence that they could be economically useful in a revitalized downtown St. Paul."[110]

DeCoster's fears for the Guardian Building and the New York Life Insurance Building were well founded; both soon went the way of the wrecking ball. But the magnificent Romanesque Revival U.S. Courthouse and Post Office defied the odds and became the city's first major example of adaptive reuse. The building owed its salvation to the determined efforts of historic preservationists on the local, state, and national levels.

As part of the country's growing environmental awareness, Congress in 1966 passed the Historic Preservation Act, which established the National Register of Historic Places and granted a measure of protection for properties listed thereon. Specifically, the act enjoined federal agencies and federally financed undertakings from harming listed properties without first establishing that such action was unavoidable for the public good. The legislation also created the federal Advisory Council on Historic Preservation to mediate disputes. In 1969, the Minnesota Historical Society took charge of nominating the U.S. Courthouse and Post Office to the National Register, making it the state's first structure to be so designated. This action frustrated an attempt by the building's federal steward, the General Services Administration, to convey the property to a demolition-minded developer in exchange for a parking lot required by the new Federal Building. The last-minute reprieve gave local preservationists time to develop a viable plan for transforming the landmark into a municipal cultural center. It took additional federal legislation to effect the property's transfer to city ownership, but by 1973, Brooks Cavin was at work on an initial restoration plan. Before the end of the decade, the old U.S. Courthouse and Post Office assumed its new identity as the refurbished "Landmark Center," managed by the nonprofit Minnesota Landmarks.[111]

Beyond the downtown area, other preservation-related activities began making headlines. The migration of middle-class home owners back to the Summit Hill area led to the formation in 1967 of the Summit Hill Association to represent collective interests. In that same year, Old Town Restorations was set up as a nonprofit neighborhood corporation for buying, restoring, and reselling homes in danger of demolition. In 1969, municipal government installed a Model Cities program in the freeway-disrupted Summit-University area north of Summit Hill. This program combined clearance of deteriorated structures with an extensive restoration initiative. In varying degrees, all these activities led to the displacement of low-income residents by more affluent newcomers—a process that came to be known as "gentrification." Not unlike the developers who had once doomed older buildings as a matter of simple economics, preservationists tended to shrug off the social costs of gentrification as an unavoidable consequence of the marketplace. As David Lanegran, who sat on the board of directors of Old Town Restorations, explained:

Neighborhood conservation cannot be expected to provide housing for low income households because whenever it promotes investment by either middle class professionals or blue collar workers, land values and rents are increased. This process cannot both increase inner-city tax bases and provide cheap housing. People who expect it to do so are quite simply missing the mark.

For Lanegran, the remedy to gentrification-related displacement lay not in devising strategies to retain an area's original residents but rather in figuring out "how best to build new affordable and humane housing for low-income households in locations accessible to sources of employment." As was true during the public housing debates of the 1950s, the most realistic and humane solution happened to place the financially less fortunate in an area other than one's own.[112]

Although advocates of urban renewal, historic preservation, and neighborhood stability continued to wrangle, they could achieve consensus, as was demonstrated during the 1970s by events in Irvine Park, a residential neighborhood located just west of downtown. The process, however, was not without turbulence. Laid out in 1849, the area around the park had been a fashionable place to live through most of the nineteenth century. Its slow but steady deterioration during the twentieth century culminated in 1971, when the neighborhood planning entity, the West Seventh Street Association, laid out a proposal that called for the HRA to level and redevelop about four and one-half blocks, an action that would destroy much of the community's historic housing. At a public meeting, neighborhood residents turned out in force to voice their dissent. "This means I'll have to leave and I'm interested in staying," said one resident. "You're going to chase the old neighborhood out and put in a new neighborhood," said another. Although some home owners were clearly interested in the anticipated buyout from the HRA, the majority of the area's residents were opposed to the urban renewal scheme, and they resoundingly voted it down. In the aftermath, neighborhood activists took control of the West Seventh Street Association.[113]

The HRA, however, remained interested in eliminating a blighted district so close to the downtown. Although area residents seem to have been mostly concerned about saving their homes, historic preservationists saw the HRA's intentions as a threat to the city's best collection of mid-nineteenth-century residential architecture. In addition to several Greek Revival dwellings, the Irvine Park area also contained the home of the state's first governor, the Alexander Ramsey House (265 South Exchange Street), an 1872 Italian Villa owned and maintained by the Minnesota Historical Society as a historic site. In the summer of 1973, the historical society sent Washington a National Register Nomination for an **Irvine Park Historic District**, which enumerated the area's architectural and historical resources (Map 4.3). Shortly afterwards, Washington informed the St. Paul HRA that federal urban renewal funds for Irvine Park

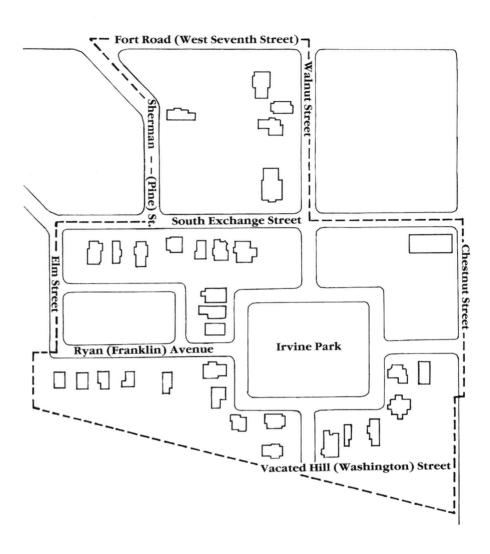

MAP 4.3.
Irvine Park Historic District, the first local heritage preservation district in St. Paul.

would be frozen until the agency worked out a redevelopment plan compatible with the new National Register district, as required by the Historic Preservation Act of 1966.[114]

In the fall of 1973, the HRA invited representatives from the Minnesota Historical Society, the Ramsey County Historical Society, the city planning department, and the neighborhood planning group to form a "Special Redevelopment Committee" that would establish "a system of historical and environmental monitoring," including the review of all development proposals. Since this experiment in urban renewal had no precedent anywhere in the nation, it is perhaps not surprising that it did not run smoothly. For more than a year, the participants fought over matters of jurisdiction, and public meetings sometimes degenerated into shouting matches. But by the spring of 1975, the HRA had a plan that

seemed to satisfy all concerned. The HRA achieved its goal of building new housing units, the state historical society succeeded in preserving the area's historic character, and the local community secured a redevelopment scheme that emphasized home ownership and encouraged home remodeling.

Perhaps most important, the final plan established a permanent oversight committee to monitor all future construction activities within the Irvine Park Historic District to ensure architectural compatibility. Staffed by the Historic Resources Committee of the Minnesota Society of the American Institute of Architects, the Irvine Park Review Committee presided over the restoration of the area's homes, the construction of in-fill housing, and the relocation of historic houses from other sites to the West Seventh Street neighborhood. Its success in working with builders and home owners helped pave the way for the establishment in 1976 of a citywide Historic Preservation Commission with full powers of building permit review over designated historic sites.[115]

The successes of historic preservation in the early 1970s were in part the incidental product of a serious economic situation. Long-term financing for real estate ventures was simply not available, and the public was loathe to support bond issues. Without financial backing, developers were unable to exert much pressure on historic neighborhoods. What was good for preservation, however, was disastrous for some architectural offices, particularly the large firms that had led the way in Capital Centre. By 1975, Lundgren's office had shrunk from eighty architects to fewer than ten, and Grover Dimond Associates, once 85 strong, was out of business altogether. In Minneapolis, Robert Cerny had enough major projects on hand during the first years of tight money to enter 1973 with 125 architects, but in 1975 even his force had shrunk to less than half.

In the meantime, downtown languished incomplete. Twelve new office buildings had risen in the urban renewal district, and the city could boast of two and one-half miles of enclosed skyways connecting old and new buildings at the second-story level. But multiple gap sites remained. No one spoke of the hole in the doughnut anymore; the current locution was "superhole" to describe the two gap sites that occupied entire city blocks. Worse than this mark of incompleteness was the plight of the downtown merchant. According to the local press, the number of stores downtown plunged from more than

400 in 1963 to 160 in 1975. By the mid-1970s, civic embarrassment over the bare Capital Centre lots paled before the one problem that had been at the top of every prospective city plan's agenda for three decades—the disappearance of shopping.[116]

A chamber of commerce study in 1973 concluded that the new skyway system was not reinvigorating downtown St. Paul in the manner anticipated by Capital Centre planners. The second-level pedestrian routes simply "were not people places like Nicollet Mall" in Minneapolis. Indeed, it was gradually becoming clear that the skyways were actually diminishing the downtown's image of vitality by removing people from the streets. To figure out how to get shoppers back on the streets, the chamber of commerce set up a committee of business leaders with former MIC director Robert Van Hoef as head. Van Hoef promptly hired consultants who had worked on the Nicollet Mall to plan an attenuated version for Seventh Street in downtown St. Paul. With plans in hand, the committee secured the interest, but ultimately not the commitment, of two developers. The dream of creating a magnet for downtown shopping would have to be deferred until the arrival of more favorable economic conditions and a more supportive political climate.[117]

In 1976, the political and financial pictures brightened simultaneously. Spring municipal elections ushered in a mayor who brought with him an enormous fund of entrepreneurial energy and economic optimism. George Latimer also had the good fortune to serve under a city

FIGURE 4.47.
Town Square, 445 Minnesota Street. Completed in 1980, this was the most ambitious mix of retail and office space in the city. Courtesy of the Minnesota Historical Society.

charter that seemed tailor-made to his personality and perspective. Rewritten in 1972, it made the mayor the focal point of the city's planning and development efforts. A city planner in 1980 called the new system "one-stop shopping for anyone wanting to do business in the city," a great improvement over the former system in which developers had to deal with myriad agencies individually before throwing themselves at the unpredictable mercies of the city council. Latimer took downtown renewal as his personal mission and regarded the positioning of a uniquely appealing retail space in the superhole near the middle of Capital Centre as one of his primary tasks.[118]

Latimer's skill at convincing businessmen to invest in downtown St. Paul became legendary. As investment money began to free up, Oxford Properties, a Canadian developer, supported an ambitious plan for a mixed-use complex that promised to fill the worst of the superholes (bounded by Sixth and Seventh Streets and Cedar and Minnesota Streets), as well as the block immediately

to the north. This project, named **Town Square**, would conjoin asymmetrical office towers, a three-level retail galleria, and a hotel built by another developer (Figure 4.47). Perched on top of the shopping court was the most compelling—and the costliest—piece of the design, a four-level, glass-enclosed garden replete with cascading waterfall (Figure 4.48). Based on a similar concept executed by the project architects Skidmore, Owings, and Merrill for a retail-office complex in Calgary, Alberta, the indoor garden was expected to be "very significant, if not spectacular, to the overall impact made on the shopper."[119]

After Town Square was completed in 1980, critics were quick to chastise its repetitive window openings and dreary expanses of concrete, as well as its unabashedly inward look. Yet these aspects were, in their way, appropriate contextual responses by the architects to an urban fabric that had not been receptive to the slightest show of outward ostentation. In the end, Town Square did indeed present the city with a truly unusual indoor attraction. Nevertheless, it failed to provide the inviting

FIGURE 4.48.
Interior of Town Square,
ca. 1980. The indoor waterfall
is the centerpiece of a
glass-covered garden atop the
retail wing. Photograph by
Jerome R. Stransky.

public commons that would have justified both its name and its placement at the nexus of the downtown's office and retail sectors. As a succession of landings, walkways, and small spaces, the garden court was indeed a place that welcomed private wanderings and sittings, but it was not a space that encouraged familiarity among strangers, let alone public assembly.

However effectively it might have been realized, Town Square's promise of an inviting enclosed village was probably inappropriate for St. Paul, a city that was still struggling to accept multiple-housing units. A vision substantially more suited to the physical and cultural fabric of the city emerged from another Latimer initiative, this time for a public and private partnership in what by then was known as "Lowertown," the city's warehouse district on the eastern edge of downtown. The catalyst was a $10-million grant from the local McKnight Foundation in 1978. This seed money, with watering from additional public and private investment, was expected to bear fruit as a $200-million redevelopment project.[120]

As a condition of the foundation grant, a private, nonprofit corporation was established to administer the project. The resulting Lowertown Redevelopment Corporation (LRC) immediately became a major force in the revitalization of the downtown area east of the commercial core. According to Weiming Lu, its executive director since 1979, the corporation performed three quite distinct functions from the outset. As a design center it

generated ideas for renewal and new construction, as a development bank it offered gap financing in the form of loans and loan guarantees, and as a marketing office it sought developers and investors for all aspects of the "urban village" it oversaw.[121]

In the early years of the warehouse redevelopment program, Lowertown's empty streets and low tenancy rates discouraged prospective investors, but by the early 1980s aggressive marketing and the cooperation of city agencies brought the hoped-for mix of retail business, rental and for-sale housing, artistic activity, and light industry. Of the many restoration projects supported by the LRC, the crown jewel was **Park Square Court,** the old Noyes Brothers and Cutler Building (400 Sibley Street), which had experienced its first renovation by St. Paul businessman Norman B. Mears in the early 1970s.[122]

In the 1980s, the LRC also struck out in a new direction that posed significant risks for both the aesthetic makeup and the financial health of the warehouse district. With the enthusiastic support of Mayor Latimer and city development officials, an ambitious new mixed-use, high-rise complex was touted for the block bordering the west side of Lowertown's only public space, Mears Park. Named **Galtier Plaza** after Father Lucien Galtier, the Catholic missionary priest who gave St. Paul its name, the proposed entertainment, retail, and residential development was considered as crucial to downtown rehabilitation as the Town Square project (Figures 4.49 and 4.50).

FIGURE 4.49.
Galtier Plaza, Sibley Street
between Fifth and Sixth Streets.
This project has been credited
with "breaking the modernist
stranglehold on downtown."

FIGURE 4.50.
Galtier Plaza at the
pedestrian level: a sequence of
brick wall, glass and steel,
and an 1880s facade.

Difficulties in sustaining financing for Galtier Plaza halted construction repeatedly, leading to a succession of "grand openings" and a sense of anticlimax when all the interiors were finally completed in 1989. In the interim, the building failed to live up to expectations, suffering at times from a commercial occupancy rate below 40 percent. In addition, its architecture drew mixed reviews. Designed by the local firm of Miller, Hanson, Westerbeck, and Bell, it was credited with "breaking the modernist stranglehold on downtown." Its varied materials and window treatments, multiple relationships to the historic fabric around it, and bright colors were a welcome relief from the profusion of drab rectangular solids that had come to dominate the central city. But at the same time, its use of salvaged historical facades for part of its Mears Park frontage spoke more to false nostalgia than meaningful historic preservation. Nevertheless, Galtier Plaza was outwardly flamboyant in a way that no other postwar downtown building had been. Its succession of tower-top gables introduced the tongue-in-cheek historicist detailing generally known as Post-Modernism, while its glass-walled apex, bursting surprisingly free from the otherwise traditional brick carapace, seemed to wink and say, "I'm really a very Modern building beneath it all."[123]

While Galtier Plaza was bringing high theater to apartment design, a much quieter building at the other end of the central business district had brought a profound sense of humanity to theater design. Rice Park had long been a center of cultural activity, sponsored by the public library on the south, and the Minnesota Club, the Elks Club, and the Amherst H. Wilder Charity Foundation on the west. The restoration of the Landmark Center on the north had continued this tradition, and it ultimately spurred the replacement of several small office structures on the west with a single building of great beauty and taste.

On its completion in 1984, the **Ordway Music Center** (since renamed the Ordway Center for the Performing Arts) drew the accolades of architects and the general public alike (Figure 4.51). Brooks Cavin praised it for "the masterful way in which the architect Ben Thompson has modulated the forms and surfaces of the exterior [and] produced a lively, human-scaled architecture which is entirely appropriate for its Rice Park setting." Fronting the park, the building's low main facade—an elegant, undulating band of cubiform glass-and-copper crystals—made a stage of the theatergoer's intermission area, while the actual theater space behind rose unobtrusively behind a gently faceted brick wall.[124]

With the erection of the Ordway Center and the simultaneous restoration of the St. Paul Hotel on the east, Rice Park captured nearly a hundred years of community cultural life and emerged as a near-perfect blend of modern and historical sympathies. Significantly, each successive change to the surrounding streetscape proceeded without a general plan for the park as a whole, yet met with broad public approval and resulted in architecture of considerable merit. Public and private sectors found their own niche, and restorations, compatible reuses, and new construction all merged in a common public legacy.

FIGURE 4.51. Ordway Music Center, now Ordway Center for the Performing Arts, Fifth and Washington Streets. An elegant crystal in the magnificent necklace of buildings around Rice Park.

CHAPTER 5
Melding the Past with the Future

1985 – 2000

As St. Paul approached the close of the twentieth century, the dynamic between preservation issues and the city's growing architectural needs became increasingly complex. Architectural Modernism rediscovered its ties to the past, and in the guise sometimes labeled "Post-Modernism" made a point of echoing ornamental devices and even architectural forms of the past. In the meantime, city planners and officials began to look beyond the signature office towers of Capital Centre and its aftermath to multiple-use developments that would pay equal attention to historic buildings and modern needs.

Preservation activity also widened its focus to embrace new construction within historic districts. In many cases, the gravest threat to the integrity of historic districts is posed not by alterations to the historic building stock itself but by the introduction of pretenders to the fraternity of historic buildings, the neo-Victorians, neo–Prairie Schoolers, and neo-Revivalists. The largest of these tower over their neighborhoods, leaving once-lordly mansions to cower in their shadow. A blurring of the line between modern and traditional, progressive and protectionist, has created a breed of developers who claim to be devotees of history and a breed of preservationists who advocate buildings that are transparently modern to distinguish them from the historic fabric of their setting.

For the past two decades, the buzzword in all of these various transformations of the tension between new development and heritage protection has been "context." From a historical point of view, the concept of context has both a chronological and a physical axis. Buildings arise within periods characterized by specific styles, senses of scale and proportion, and material usages. Understanding and evaluating them as exemplars of their time are one key to evaluating their significance and guiding their rehabilitation. That is one kind of context.

But city neighborhoods grow up over many decades, developing their character from an accretion of successive building types, styles, and materials. Understanding the evolving physical and aesthetic parameters of those environments and how new construction might either operate within them or extend them provides a second sort of context. Nobody in recent times has put it better than AIA vice president J. Monroe Hewlett in 1930:

One reason for the fantastic and absurd designs seen in present day types of buildings arises from a desire to outdo or overshadow the adjoining building. Such practices defeat their own purposes, for they are a form of architectural discourtesy. The value of the building is enhanced, not by startling design, but by the harmonic relations to other buildings in the vicinity.[1]

The first of these contexts is informed by a sense of stewardship, of watchful protection of a valued heritage;

the second by recognition of the values resident in the built environment around any new construction site. In the world at the dawn of the twenty-first century, this second kind of context calls the planner, architect, builder, and preservation advocate into a dynamic partnership with the past that will impact both what is kept and what is created.

All such partnerships are by their very nature a work in progress. But the struggle to engage modern design with its geographical and historical setting has produced a number of remarkable buildings in the closing decades of the twentieth century. All are markedly distinct from the downtown high-rises of the decade following the Capital Centre project. These were the last monumental buildings in the city designed with the presumption that Modernism would ultimately triumph over rather than partner with historic building stock. This presumption diminished the importance of defining a new building's place in the existing urban fabric or even making it responsive in some way to its immediate neighbors. For the most part, the products of Capital Centre could have arisen in any part of any American city's commercial sector, including the outlying stretches along major suburban arteries. The most admired building of that era continues to be its most outstanding exception: the Ordway. Its human scaling and polymorphic composition both respond to its setting on the park and pay friendly regard to the more insistent monumentality of its historic neighbors.

Surveying all of the significant architectural projects in the city over the past twenty years is beyond the scope of this closing essay. We shall pick out ten of them simply by way of illustration of the diverse forms of contextual engagement. The principle of selection throughout is not the architectural merits of the project per se, which judgment awaits a future generation, but the distinctiveness of its response to its geographical and historical setting.

The first Modernist high-rise in St. Paul to display specific and emphatic relationships to its historic surroundings was the 450,000-square-foot **St. Paul Companies Headquarters Building**, constructed in 1987–91 (Figure 5.1). Situated on a large pentagonal block at the western edge of downtown, its various facades address three of the buildings that have figured prominently in early chapters of this history: Landmark Center, the Hamm Building, and Assumption Church. A fourth historic property, Mickey's Diner, nestles into one corner.

From the outset, the design strategy of architects Kohn Pedersen Fox revolved around the complex programming of the building, leading them toward a work described by design partner William Pedersen as "almost discrete pieces, each with a specific urban role." This would "enable a large corporation to reveal its diverse programmatic constituency." The most conspicuous of these "discrete pieces" are an eleven-story circular pavilion enclosing an entry, arts gallery, and offices; a nine-story office block; and a seventeen-story office tower. Other clearly defined areas of the building house an extensive cafeteria, a day-care facility, and a health club.

There is a century-old but still vital local precedent for this way of tying programmatic complexity to an

FIGURE 5.1.
U.S. Courthouse and Post Office
(now Landmark Center) and St. Paul
Companies Headquarters Building,
viewed from Fifth Street and
St. Peter Street. A companionship
of the old and new.

assembly of diverse formal elements: the great brewery complexes of the late-nineteenth century. The Grain Belt Brewery in Minneapolis and the Schmidt Brewery in St. Paul were both designed so that each phase of the brewing and bottling operation would have its own architectural persona. The result in each case was a broken building mass that presented the appearance of a city within a city. Diverse though they are, breaking out individual components of that building mass would be as destructive to the additive nature of the composition as would stripping off one of the monumental components of the St. Paul Companies Building.[2]

Using a diversity of building components, apart from their functional significance, allowed Kohn Pedersen Fox to engage the building in simultaneous dialogue with its quite different neighbors. According to design associate Richard del Monte, "The grouping of forms does not intend to mimic its surroundings, but instead tries to give concrete form to the forces at work on this site." The rounded entry pavilion softens the rapprochement with the north tower of Landmark Center; the midrise office tower to the north steps the tower down to the scale of St. Peter Street office buildings; the stepping of

the rear elevation brings the design down to the parking lots and vacant land on the west side of downtown. Only one piece could be accused of something like mimicry: a utility tower in the form of an extended trapezoid that burlesques the twin spires of Assumption Church across Seventh Street.[3]

The cycle of demolitions in the 1960s and 1970s and the maze of automotive arteries that weave through the western edge of St. Paul's downtown have stripped that edge of its definition. To make matters worse, the St. Paul Companies Headquarters Building shows its back and a parking lot to the west, forcing the edge to retreat to the east. In 1999 the **Lawson Software Building** (Figure 5.2) sealed off the retreat at St. Peter Street. Since construction, the clearing of a small parcel of land separating the site from Landmark Center and Rice Park has enhanced its role as a gateway to the downtown, as well as lending the building a strongly frontal presence at the corner of Rice Park.

BWBR Architects conceived their design for Lawson Software to be "a weaving of twenty-first-century technology within the historic context of St. Paul" that would "respect and reinforce the existing neighborhood character."

FIGURE 5.2.
Lawson Software Building,
380 St. Peter Street. This building
defines the western edge of the
central business district.

"Weaving" was the operative term. Rather than addressing the complexities around it with an equally complex formal composition, the design borrows bits and pieces of its environing streetscapes to attach onto a single building mass. A cast-stone arcade at the ground floor, facings of warm-hued brick, and a vertical division of the surface into less monumental components by vertical glass bands are all intended to integrate the building into its neighborhood. On the other hand, the upper floors, which rise considerably above the neighboring buildings, are faced largely in glass. This area of the building, in which aluminum is the most conspicuous component, is intended to reflect the cutting-edge, high-tech business identity of the firm and symbolize its "forward vision."[4]

The park facade of Lawson Software contains three other features of interest for their kinship with environing architecture. Circling the base of the building is a plinth of dark red granite specifically related to the historic midrise buildings around it. A flat aluminum plate descending down each pier from the cornice reiterates in simplified fashion the ornate drip moldings of the Lowry Building. Crowning the building is a monitor that echoes at a greater height and scale the one atop the St. Paul Hotel built almost a century earlier. It is hard to say how these features will look to critics of the future: respectful

responses to environing streetscapes, or mechanical iterations of a lost art.

Almost identical in volume to the St. Paul Companies Building, Lawson Software surpasses it in pedestrian friendliness by achieving some degree of human scale on all sides of the building. The Wabasha Street side may be the most successful at this effort, for the arcade dispenses with monumental components and deep recesses, creating a sense of rhythmic continuity that does indeed "weave" the building to a walk down Wabasha. Sharply defined neo-Deco grilles in front of the ramp openings at Wabasha and Sixth Streets also relate the building to one of its most striking companions, the 1930 Northern States Power Company building (now an Ecolab annex) across the corner to the southeast.

The **Science Museum of Minnesota,** completed the same year as Lawson Software, helps to define another edge of the city, one that historically has been both the most promising and the most neglected: its frontage on the Mississippi River (Figure 5.3). On the city side, Ellerbe Becket concentrated most of their design energies on an out-scaled, formal entry. But as the building faces the river, the design breaks into a stepped sequence of brick boxes cascading down to the floodplain. The 390,000 square feet of the building are distributed through

FIGURE 5.3.
Science Museum of Minnesota,
120 West Kellogg Boulevard.
Green space is beginning to
bridge the Mississippi River and
downtown St. Paul.

a large array of variously dispersed and connected rectangular solids, which helps to abate the windowless box requirement of the modern, conservation-driven museum.

The building has been subjected to some local criticism for what architecture critic Larry Millett calls its "serious pizzazz deficiency" on the street side. However, the riverfront, rather than the stream of automobiles that confronts the entry elevation, is arguably the most critical context for the building's design. Many of the rooftops of the building segments contain pedestrian terraces, each providing a sweeping view of the Mississippi. A sixteen-acre site with ten acres of it devoted to parkland also helps to bridge the building to future riverfront developments that may have quite a different character. "While many museums are interior-focused, the new Science Museum is engaged with its surroundings," said Ellerbe Becket principal David Loehr. "This project is a significant first step in advancing new riverfront development in the city of St. Paul."[5]

Apart from its purely visual relationship to the river, the museum is the first building project in the city to provide pedestrians with a public walkway to the water's edge. A triangular glass-enclosed staircase spirals down to the river side of the main lobby. Linked public walkways also lead to historic Irvine Park and the East Seventh Street commercial district. These connections express the overall commitment of the design team to providing a receptacle for the museum's mission and activities rather than "thinking about making an architectural monument." According to senior project designer Andy Cers, "Success for us was to design a structure that first supports [the museum's] activities, and second makes the visitor's experience of these activities more potent and exciting through the architecture."[6]

In the downtown core there have been multiple opportunities for rebuilding on derelict or underutilized properties. The challenge in these cases is to create a lively yet companionable associate for a nest of buildings that mix historic architecture with the products of the Capital Centre project. This was the challenge taken up by the designers of the 401 Building at Sixth and Robert Streets (Figure 5.4). "We wanted it to be a good neighbor to the structures around it in downtown St. Paul," said Julio Fesser, director of facility planning for the owners of the building, Minnesota Life. Rather than focusing on the features specific to its immediate urban neighborhood, the Architectural Alliance looked for ways to connect to the broad character of the site's larger environment, in particular the "tradition of rich and colorful midrise buildings in downtown St. Paul." Red granite facings complement the brick of the historic commercial buildings around it, while gray stone facings unite

FIGURE 5.4.
401 Building,
400 North Robert Street.
A Modernist gesture toward
the complexities of historic
urban streetscapes.

it to the Bedford stone facings of historic buildings and the Minnesota Life headquarters erected twenty-four years earlier across the street.[7]

At 635,000 square feet, the 401 Building is considerably larger than either the St. Paul Companies or the Lawson Software buildings. At the same time, it presents a less monumental aspect, largely because of the complex way its footprint and contours are handled. It blends comfortably with the streetscape without resorting to either the complex geometries of the St. Paul Companies Building or the historical resonances of Lawson Software. This is achieved through a succession of volumes of different height, fenestration, and scaling. Historically, this kind of streetscape generally arises over a period of time, the accidental creation of multiple

building programs. In effect, the 401 Building creates in a single process the image of an accretive streetscape.

The **Minnesota Children's Museum** developed within an environmental context that was at first glance anything but an inspiration (Figure 5.5). Located on Seventh Street at the northern edge of the historic theater district, its immediate predecessors were a derelict movie theater, a seedy residence hotel, and a hodgepodge of commercial buildings stripped of their historic fronts by a widening of Seventh Street. The edge of the property wrapping around Wabasha Street butted up against a post–World War I multiple-use building housing the St. Francis Hotel and a sequence of street-level stores. On the St. Peter Street side were four old commercial slivers, the two nearest slated for demolition. Across Seventh Street

FIGURE 5.5.
Minnesota Children's Museum,
10 West Seventh Street. This
structure provides a splash of
light in the shadow of the
World Trade Center.

was the former Wabasha Hotel, a truncated shell of its towered nineteenth-century splendor.

Though in the words of one critic "hardly the neighborhood to host a giant civic playground," the site was in fact ideal for a museum looking to create an image of playfulness and vitality in the midst of a gritty urban environment. "Our urban location is part of our persona," said museum director Ann L. Bitter. Lead architects were Vincent James of James/Snow Architects and Thomas DeAngelo of the Architectural Alliance. Rather than succumb to the "black box" strategy of museum design, the architects chose to open up the building's contents to street view. Three stories of open lobbies connected by a tree-house-like staircase face onto West Seventh Street. As James explained it, "Our metaphor for the museum's design was an open toy box, its contents spilling over."[8]

The museum opened in September 1995 with 65,000 square feet of gallery and program space. Polychromatic treatment of the various building segments and a playfully projecting, glass-walled corner bay give the building a unique persona in the city. At the same time, the building earns its stripes as a responsible citizen by matching the height and echoing some of the building materials of the historic building to which it is connected. No building in the city demonstrates so delightfully that contextual sensitivity need not be a tedious affair.

Within the city's historic residential neighborhoods, the most carefully considered in-fills and replacements of the past twenty years run the gamut of contextual responsiveness, from slavish adaptations of historic styles to Modernist statements that press the limits of historic district guidelines. For developers, architects, and the Heritage Preservation Commission, that has meant a constant reopening of questions regarding appropriate materials, scaling, massing, and detailing.

Even on so sacrosanct a street as Summit Avenue itself, property owners range from those avid to invest whatever it takes to make their house what it once was to those who are intent on soaking in the ambience of a historic neighborhood without having to put up with the inconveniences of an old house. The city is also witnessing a surge of "carriage house" building on rear lots, gobbling up green space, shutting off the long visual prospects from street to street, and gradually creating a wall of new homes with old-looking faces on the alleys.

A large part of Dayton's Bluff was added to the city's stock of historic districts in 1992, just as Metropolitan State University was considering rebuilding on the gateway St. John's Hospital site. Creation of the district and a significant influx of public and private investment have spurred widespread rehabilitation of houses and business blocks. Like parts of Summit Avenue in the 1970s,

many of them had been so long and so thoroughly covered over that their restoration has had the effect of creating new buildings and even new neighborhoods, regardless of whether new design or material elements were introduced.

Much of the city's most characteristic historic fabric, particularly in the colorful period between the world wars, remains little studied and unacknowledged by any branch of public policy, or indeed by the general public itself. New construction in areas dense with this as yet undervalued part of the city's historic fabric presents challenges as well as dangers. Where context is unknown or unwritten, the most heritage-conscious property owners and their builders pursue a re-creation of history in their own manner.

A case in point is the King's Maplewood development highlighted in chapter 3. A growing number of historic houses are being replaced by larger, modern buildings that echo historical themes. Most of them are responsibly designed, the best of them equivalent or superior in architectural values to what they have replaced. How are these to be regarded?

One such rebuild arose at **136 South Mississippi River Boulevard** just after the dawn of the new millennium (Figures 5.6 and 5.7). It is particularly interesting because it clearly displays the conceptual problems faced by architects and home builders across the city who attempt

new construction in a historic style. Kenneth Worthen placed one of his larger period-revival homes there in 1925. Its three thousand square feet and $15,000 price tag were equivalent in size and price to houses of that era on Summit Avenue. The current owners originally sought to remodel and expand the original house. But Mississippi River Boulevard south of Shadow Falls Park presents particular difficulties for expansion or rehabilitation because of the uneven quality of the subsoil, coursed by underground streams and mixed with topsoil dumped from several generations of Summit Avenue development. In addition, an earlier unsympathetic rear addition was difficult to integrate into the design of the historic house.[9]

Sharratt Design & Company developed a plan that responded to a generalized historical context defined by the area of the river boulevard within the King's Maplewood development. In general outlook, the approach to context was much the same as that of the 401 Building downtown. But the new house, nearly twice as large as Worthen's design, also incorporated numerous self-consciously "historical" features, such as massive turned columns, segmental arches, and wrought-iron balconies.

Similar incorporations of historic elements, or outright attempts to build in a historic style, have also begun to populate the Summit Avenue historic districts. In some cases, the new building reaches for a style predating that

FIGURE 5.7.
Scott and Ann Billeadeau House, 136 South Mississippi River Boulevard, 2004. Sympathetic neighbor or mimicking intruder?

of the house it is replacing, further blurring the line between appropriate and inappropriate modifications. This is the kind of issue that historic district guidelines in their current form fail to address. Like the Lawson Software use of historic ornamental devices, residential historicisms can be regarded as a respectful response to an environmental context—or bogus quotations of the past in a post-Modernist script.

Rebuilds of large-scale buildings in St. Paul's older residential neighborhoods have taken a more straightforwardly Modernist approach to neighborhood context. Among the most conspicuous and widespread of these is a new generation of playground buildings that offer a full range of recreational and community services. Linwood and Highland Park were the first of these neighborhood megacenters, and Dayton's Bluff was the last. All were built between 1991 and 1999, with price tags ranging from $2 million to $3.4 million.

Perhaps because of its location at the edge of Crocus Hill, the **Linwood Community Recreation Center** responds the most specifically and dramatically to its setting (Figure 5.8). Only the third floor rises above St. Clair Avenue, and this is topped by a cupola meant to complement "the Victorian style of the neighborhood." The dramatic fall of the grade away from the street presented an opportunity for response to quite a different

context, the natural environment of the sunken playground. The designers took full advantage both in the interior plan and in the fitting of the building into the site. Broad glazing on all three floors addresses the playgrounds and its environs to the south, and a long projecting wing spills down to playground height via a sequence of stepped, planted terraces. As with all of the new community recreation centers, the design was produced by a team on the staff of St. Paul Parks and Recreation.[10]

In the city's first planned park, the **Como Park Conservatory Addition** presented St. Paul with a daunting challenge: to significantly enlarge one of the most revered buildings in the city without violating its clarity and integrity as an independent structure. Within the park setting, the only architectural point of reference was the glass house itself, now known as the Marjorie McNeely Conservatory. Under intermittent restoration since 1984, private and public investment in the 1915 conservatory restoration alone exceeded $12 million, roughly twenty times the original cost of the structure.

The new addition, designed by HGA Architects, springs from the rear of the conservatory as it steps back behind the central palm house, providing large lawns and preventing interference with the lines of the original structure (Figure 5.9). Like the rebuilt conservatory, the

FIGURE 5.8.
Linwood Community Recreation Center,
860 St. Clair Avenue. This building
continues St. Paul's tradition of thoughtfully
designed, signature park buildings.

new greenhouses and a Tropical Encounters room are wrapped in white steel, glass, and anodized aluminum frames. According to design principal Kara Hill, the strongest uniting visual feature is a white steel band that travels at a height of sixteen inches from the original conservatory throughout the new construction. This metal band collects all the storm water from the building and transfers it to the pools and retaining tanks that provide water for both interior and exterior gardens. Rather than

replicate the curvilinear structure of the original, the new greenhouse roofs rise at a steep angle, then cascade down to an orchid house. In addition to the orchid house, the greenhouses incorporate a fern room, a bonsai room, and a children's activity zone.[11]

The last two recent buildings we shall consider were designed and built in happy oblivion of their surviving historic context. In each case, that context had been so shattered by tear-outs, modern construction, and/or

FIGURE 5.9. Addition to Como Park Conservatory, Como Park. This rendering from Hammel, Green, and Abrahamson captures the linkage of old and new.

FIGURE 5.10.

Crossroads Elementary School,
543 Front Avenue. The school
contributes a sunny new face to
a neighborhood in need of cheer.

changing property uses that sensitivity to anything more than the possibilities of the site itself was out of the question. The contextual question then narrows to the universal challenge that a distressed historic setting offers to an environmentally responsive architecture: how is the building to address its site in a way that renews and reinforces its lost contextual framework?

In St. Paul's North End, a spur of the Great Northern Railway once served a clearly demarcated, blockwide industrial site bounded by Kent Street, Front Avenue, Mackubin Street, and Cook Avenue. To the west was a mixed commercial and residential section of Dale Street; on all other sides was an erratic mix of residential and small-scale commercial and industrial buildings. The lower part of the concentrated industrial site was never one of the glories of the city. But after years of underutilization and dereliction, the city seized on it as an opportunity both to refocus and to reinvigorate a scattered community by creating an overtly Modernist school at its midst. Designed by the Cunningham Group, **Crossroads Elementary School** opened for the 1999–2000 school year (Figure 5.10).

Vibrant, near-Day-Glo colors, pastels, and natural brick surfaces combine to create both a playful mood and a sense that the building is its own environment. Like the Children's Museum downtown, it pointedly sheds a new kind of light on long-neglected historic building stock around it. The diverse forms of the various building components also reflect the layout and programming of the school. Responsive to district curriculum initiatives, the school combines pre-K–6 Montessori and K–6 science programs. Again like a children's museum, the two curriculum programs interface at a central "inquiry zone," which doubles as a hands-on project area and a display space. The facility also includes conjoined spaces for Early Childhood Family Education, Early Childhood Special Education, and Discovery Club, three programs for which the school district wished to develop an integrated method of delivery.[12]

An equal challenge arose in quite a different geographical context on the West Side. For a brief period in the early 1890s, an elevated section of land overlooking the Mississippi developed into an enclave for wealthy St. Paul citizens wishing to escape the hurly-burly of Summit Avenue. The land on and around Prospect Boulevard mushroomed in value and began to sprout with costly mansions. But like the efforts to create upscale developments on other elevated parts of the city, the initiative never really took hold. The spaces between the mansions filled in with small lots of ordinary housing, and the mansions themselves became divided into apartments and fell into disrepair.

Prospect Boulevard retains its splendid vistas today, with an opportunity much like that of the abandoned North End industrial property: to create anew in an area that history appears to have abandoned. In 2000, the **Peter and Julie Eigenfeld House** rose to the challenge (Figure 5.11). Its site on Mount Hope Drive has unexcelled panoramic views of the river and the city, but it occupies a small plot, and the owners had a limited budget. The one piece of historic neighborhood character that survived was its great diversity of housing stock in size, style, and period. A conspicuously modern house could simply expand on this diversity. Peter Eigenfeld characterized it as "an anti-suburban move." Said Julie Eigenfeld, "We want to show people you can get creative without a ton of money."[13]

Project architect Gar Hargens produced what he termed a "vertical viewing box," taking maximum advantage of the location and the small footprint dictated by the lot. Low-maintenance materials like blue corrugated steel siding and industrial louvers add a colorful, high-tech flair to what is at base a minimalist design. On the bluff side, a balcony wraps around the back of the three-story, three-bedroom house. On the front, a bright yellow spiral stairway winds up from the master suite to a rooftop deck, creating a virtual fourth floor.

St. Paul retains vast, underutilized stretches of Mississippi River overlook, as it does many abandoned railroad and industrial sites. These open the way for an architecture of opportunity and surprise at the fringes of historic areas. Like new construction in the historic districts themselves, development in fresh environments can best pay homage to the historic city in a spirit of companionship rather than fawning imitation.

At the opening of a new millennium, St. Paul is still in its infancy, barely past its 150th birthday. Yet each generation of its planners, builders, and property owners has had to make decisions within a national culture that historically has presumed the artifacts of prior generations already to be in their dotage. We tend to appreciate the buildings of our forebears in much the same way as we do a keepsake from an attic trunk, as nostalgia pieces, relics of history, rather than part and parcel of a human community's ongoing life.

Two generations of preservation activity have done little to alter the mind-set that presumes the inevitability of replacement. A core element of that mind-set is the perception that survivals from the past are more a matter of accident than of intent—which may be statistically true—and that there is nothing wrong with that. "Every now and then," wrote local reporter Roy Dunlap in 1949, "Old Man Time misses a sweep with his scythe and some portion of the past escapes obscurity." Even while being appreciated, the rows of mansions on Summit Avenue are often regarded as "picturesque reminders of the grandeur" of St. Paul's Victorian years. That they have an evolving, ongoing role to play, that they speak of the living city itself, has not yet fully dawned on public consciousness.[14]

The larger view of architectural preservation as a guardian and nurturer of a city's life and identity will always prove a hard sell in a culture whose view of its history so often consists of heroic episodes and larger-than-life personalities. Buildings have a quiet, unobtrusive way about them. But they also span history in a way that no single human life can. The growth of St. Paul's architectural legacy mirrors the expanding history and consciousness of its people. Studying, appreciating, and preserving older buildings on their own terms—that is, the values and visual language of the period that gave birth to them—does not simply take us back in time. It makes us stand on time's shoulders, with a wider view and understanding of our own place.

NOTES

1. ST. PAUL'S FOUNDING YEARS, 1840–1875

1. The quoted passage is from *Minnesota Pioneer*, April 28, 1849. This section on the early development of St. Paul is indebted to Paul Donald Hesterman, "Interests, Values, and Public Policy for an Urban River: A History of Development along the Mississippi River in Saint Paul, Minnesota" (Ph.D. diss., University of Minnesota, 1985), 2 vols.; see especially vol. 1, 82–97.

2. Johann Georg Kohl, "A German Traveler in Minnesota Territory," *Minnesota History* 49 (Fall 1984): 129–30. On the establishment of Fort Snelling, see William Watts Folwell, *A History of Minnesota* (St. Paul: Minnesota Historical Society, 1956), 1:92–93, 134–39.

3. The quotation is from an informal census report prepared, under Plympton's direction, by Lieutenant E. K. Smith in the fall of 1837; see Folwell, *A History of Minnesota*, 1:217–18, n12.

4. As quoted in J. Fletcher Williams, *A History of the City of Saint Paul to 1875* (St. Paul: Minnesota Historical Society, 1875; reprint, 1983), 79.

5. Folwell, *A History of Minnesota*, 1:221–23; Williams, *A History of the City of Saint Paul*, 99–100.

6. Williams, *A History of the City of Saint Paul*, 65, 85.

7. As quoted in Williams, *A History of the City of Saint Paul*, 111. Parrant staked out a new claim a few miles downriver along the east bank in a swampy area known as "Grand Marais." In time, his presence also baptized this locale as "Pig's Eye." With poetic justice, perhaps, it eventually became the site of a waste treatment plant.

8. Hesterman, "Interests, Values, and Public Policy for an Urban River," 1:84; Henry S. Fairchild, "Sketches of the Early History of Real Estate in St. Paul," *Collections of the Minnesota Historical Society* 10 (1905): 417–19; Henry A. Castle, *History of St. Paul and Vicinity* (Chicago and New York: Lewis Publishing Company, 1912), 84–85; Williams, *A History of the City of Saint Paul*, 143. In 1876, Fletcher Williams remembered the chapel being taken apart log by log "about 1856," the parts being marked for an intended later reassembly on a different site; Williams, *A History of the City of Saint Paul*, 113. An original daguerreotype of the derelict chapel in its final setting reposes in the Catholic Historical Society, St. Paul Seminary. Several copies dated "ca. 1855" are in the Minnesota Historical Society collections.

9. As quoted in Ambrose McNulty, "The Chapel of St. Paul, and the Beginnings of the Catholic Church in Minnesota," *Collections of the Minnesota Historical Society* 10 (1905): 238. In traditional corner-notched log buildings, wooden pins were used only for special purposes, such as securing planks against the logs at window and door openings; see Warren E. Roberts, "The Tools Used in Building Log Houses in Indiana," in *Common Places: Readings in American Vernacular Architecture*, ed. Dell Upton and John Michael Vlach (Athens: University of Georgia Press, 1986), 199. For an excellent overview of the methods and geography of French and American log construction, see Fred B. Kniffen and Henry Glassie, "Building in Wood in the Eastern United States: A 'Time-Place Perspective,'" in *Common Places*, ed. Upton and Vlach, 159–81.

10. August L. Larpenteur, "Recollections of the City and People of St. Paul, 1843–1898," *Collections of the Minnesota Historical Society* 9 (1901): 378; Williams, *A History of the City of Saint Paul*, 99–100, 165, 170–71. Brunson was assisted in his survey by his brother Benjamin W., who became a resident of St. Paul and subsequently platted several other sections in his own right. When we refer to "Brunson's plat," however, we mean only the first survey of the town site. A copy of the plat is in the Ramsey County Recorder's Office, Ramsey County Courthouse, St. Paul.

11. As quoted in Frank C. Bliss, *St. Paul, Its Past and Present* (St. Paul: F. C. Bliss Publishing Company, 1888), 91–92.

12. Prominent topographical features are shown in George C. Nichols, *A Map of the City of Saint Paul, Capital of Minnesota* (New York: Miller and Boyle's Lith., 1851); see also George C. Herrold, "The Story of Planning St. Paul from the Beginnings to 1953," 1958, 5–7, Herrold Papers, Minnesota Historical Society.

13. *Weekly Pioneer and Democrat*, February 21, 1856. On the rivalry between Upper Town and Lower Town, see Fairchild, "Sketches of the Early History of Real Estate in St. Paul," 434–36.

14. In the early 1850s, two villages sprang up at the Falls of St. Anthony: Minneapolis on the west bank and St. Anthony on the east bank. In 1873, Minneapolis annexed its neighbor.

15. As quoted in Bliss, *St. Paul, Its Past and Present,* 92.

16. "St. Paul," *Northwest Magazine* 4 (April 1886): 2; "St. Paul as a Capital City," *Northwest Magazine* 6 (March 1888): 2; "St. Paul," *The Northwest* 2 (June 1884): 1; "A Practical Guide to the Twin Cities," *Fortune* 13 (April 1936): 118.

17. Both quotations, as well as the construction statistic, are from *Minnesota Pioneer* of 1849; see, respectively, the issues of April 28, May 19, and May 26. On steamboat arrivals, see *Minnesota Chronicle and Register,* January 26, 1850.

18. On balloon framing in early St. Paul, see *Minnesota Pioneer,* May 26, 1849. For the development of the technique, see Paul E. Sprague, "The Chicago Balloon Frame," in *The Technology of Historic American Buildings: Studies of the Materials, Craft Processes, and the Mechanization of Building Construction* (Washington, DC: Foundation for Preservation Technology, 1883), 35–61. The population statistic is from Williams, *A History of the City of Saint Paul,* 228.

19. *Daily Minnesotan,* June 2, 1857; *Pioneer and Democrat,* September 30, 1856; *Map of the City of Saint Paul* (St. Paul: Goodrich and Somers, [1857]).

20. Kohl, "A German Traveler in Minnesota Territory," 130–31.

21. Williams, *A History of the City of Saint Paul,* 380–81. An official territorial census, completed in the fall of 1857 in preparation for statehood, placed the population of St. Paul at 9,973 residents.

22. *Stillwater Gazette,* February 2, 1876; Williams, *A History of the City of Saint Paul,* 440–54. Although the Mississippi River has an overall north-south orientation, it flows through downtown St. Paul in an east-west direction. St. Paulites have always ignored this fact when referring to the south shore of their city. By traditional usage, it is called "the West Side."

23. Patricia A. Murphy and Susan W. Granger, "Historic Sites Survey of Saint Paul and Ramsey County, 1980–1983," prepared for Ramsey County Historical Society and St. Paul Heritage Preservation Commission, 1983, 344–45. Subsequent research has added a few other pre-1875 buildings to the list; see Paul Clifford Larson, "Dayton's Bluff Historic Site Survey, Final Report," prepared for St. Paul Department of Planning and the Heritage Preservation Commission, 1989, 43. St. Paul officially began keeping statistics on new construction in the fall of 1883, when the city instituted a system of building permits. The identification of buildings constructed prior to that date is often a difficult affair, requiring intensive research in deed records, maps, and city directories, supplemented by physical investigation of surviving building fabric. The research problem is compounded by the fact that early buildings were occasionally moved from their original site and frequently remodeled beyond recognition. Additional investigation by historians and architects will undoubtedly identify additional survivors from the pre-1875 period, but there is little question that the vast majority of the city's earliest buildings have disappeared.

24. *St. Paul Daily Pioneer,* July 22, 1874.

25. On the establishment of the first brickyard and steam-powered sawmills, see Thomas M. Newson, *Pen Pictures of St. Paul and Biographical Sketches of the Old Settlers* (St. Paul: Published by the author, 1886), 111; *Minnesota Pioneer,* July 14, 1849; October 3, November 21, 1850. On the scarcity and high price of building supplies and labor, see *Minnesota Pioneer,* July 4, September 26, 1850; *Minnesota Democrat,* May 26, 1852; May 28, 1853; *Minnesotan,* October 23, 1853; *Weekly Pioneer and Democrat,* August 11, 1859. The exorbitant interest rates are noted in Folwell, *A History of Minnesota,* 1:363.

26. The quotation is from Alexius Hoffman, "Frogtown," 1936, 8–9, Hoffman Papers, Minnesota Historical Society. Tom Grace was a partner in the early St. Paul contracting firm of Day and Grace; Richard Ireland was a professional carpenter. Both men received a brief mention for their work on several buildings for the Catholic Church in Lower Town in the *Daily Pioneer and Democrat,* September 6, 1859. The informal census was published in the *Pioneer and Democrat,* December 4, 1858.

27. Unless otherwise noted, historical information on St. Paul buildings is derived from individual research files on these structures in the possession of the St. Paul Heritage Preservation Commission. For additional information on the Dahl House, see "Historic Preservation Feasibility Study [of] the William Dahl House," prepared for the City of St. Paul by Miller-Dunwiddie Architects Inc., 1977, in Reference Library, Minnesota Historical Society. During its long tenure with the Dahl family, the Dahl House received a stucco veneer, two rear additions, and a slightly higher basement made necessary in the 1880s by a change in road

grade at its original Thirteenth Street site. After the building's relocation to 508 Jefferson Avenue, these accretions were peeled away, leaving the simple rectangular form originally built by William and Catherine Dahl.

28. The standard work on the Greek Revival is still Talbot Hamlin, *Greek Revival Architecture in America* (New York: Oxford University Press, 1944; reprint, New York: Dover Publications, 1964). An excellent introduction to the topic is provided by William H. Pierson Jr., *American Buildings and Their Architects*, vol. 1, *The Colonial and Neoclassical Styles* (Garden City, NY: Anchor Books, 1976), 205–15, 395–460. For a look at other Minnesota examples of the style, see Roger Kennedy, *Minnesota Houses* (Minneapolis: Dillon Press, 1968), 31–33, 84–109.

29. Information on the Adams House was provided by its present owner, historian Jim Sazevich, who has compiled an extensive research file on the property. Adams purchased the lot for his residence in 1854, and when he sold it a year later, the warranty deed noted that "a small brick house" was included in the transaction; see Avery Ward Adams to John Lee Rorison, May 5, 1855, Deed Book K, in Ramsey County Recorder's Office, St. Paul.

30. The story of the Parker House and its immediate neighborhood is told in *A Brief History of the Irvine Park District* (St. Paul: Historic Irvine Park Association, 1986), 10–13, 42–43.

31. On Rondo's dwellings, see Williams, *A History of the City of Saint Paul*, 104, 127; Newson, *Pen Pictures of St. Paul*, 21. On Oakes, see Kennedy, *Minnesota Houses*, 17–18; Jean Anne Vincent, "Saint Paul Architecture: 1848–1906" (master's thesis, University of Minnesota, 1944), n.p. For an illustration of the Oakes House with its two-story verandas, see *Map of the City of Saint Paul* (Goodrich and Somers, 1857).

32. For a historical sketch of the Simpson-Wood House and its owners, see *A Brief History of the Irvine Park District*, 22–23.

33. For an admirable overview of the Federal style, see Pierson, *American Buildings and Their Architects*, 215–39.

34. On the American public's sympathy for Greek themes during and after the Greek War of Independence, see James Marston Fitch, *American Building: The Historical Forces That Shaped It* (Boston: Houghton Mifflin Company, 1966), 77–86. The ubiquity of Greek Revival statehouses and courthouses is discussed, respectively, in Henry-Russell Hitchcock and William Seale, *Temples of Democracy* (New York and London: Harcourt Brace Jovanovich, 1976), 65–120; and Paul Kenneth Goeldner, "Temples of Justice: Nineteenth-Century County Courthouses in the Midwest and Texas" (Ph.D. diss., Columbia University, 1970), 127–51.

35. The descriptions of the capitol's dome are from *Pioneer and Democrat*, August 21, 1856; *Daily Press*, August 28, 1873.

36. The census results, with alphabetical index, are published in *Minnesota Territorial Census, 1850*, ed. Patricia C. Harpole and Mary D. Nagle (St. Paul: Minnesota Historical Society, 1972).

37. The quotation concerning the copying of buildings is from *Pioneer and Democrat*, March 6, 1861. It was a common practice throughout the country. As one New York architect of the 1830s noted: "Some proprietors built without having any regular plan. When they wanted a house built, they looked about for one already finished, which they thought suitable for their purpose; and then bargained with a builder to erect for them such another, or one with such alterations upon the model as they might point out"; *Autobiography of James Gallier, Architect* (Paris: E. Briere, 1864), as quoted in Hamlin, *Greek Revival Architecture in America*, 140.

38. This discussion of the planning and construction of the First Minnesota Capitol is based on the unpublished records of the Board of Commissioners of Public Buildings, 1851–53, State Archives, Minnesota Historical Society; see also William B. Dean, "A History of the Capitol Buildings of Minnesota," *Collections of the Minnesota Historical Society* 12 (1908): 1–8. Prentiss mentions his years of experience in a letter to the Board of Commissioners, dated June 24, 1851. Daniels jointly submitted his plan for the capitol with Jacob Fisher, who is not listed in the 1850 census; the design was "in the Doric Style, Plain but admired by the Architect." None of the plans survives.

39. Daniels held the courthouse contract with John Freeman, another carpenter. Construction commenced in July 1851 and was completed about a year later; see *Minnesota Democrat*, July 15, 1851; *Minnesota Pioneer*, August 26, 1852. Reflecting his combination of roles, Daniels is described as both a "contractor" (*St. Anthony Weekly Express*, July 27, 1852) and an "architect" (*Minnesota Democrat*, October 28, 1851). On David Day, see Williams, *A History of the City of Saint Paul*, 242; Newson, *Pen Pictures of St. Paul*, 109–11. The only other known example of Day's design work is a mortuary chapel (since demolished) in Oakland Cemetery in St. Paul. According to Newson, it was "beautiful . . . , built of Minnesota stone and on an entirely original plan, different from anything in existence" (110). Day's brother, James, was a stonecutter and a partner in the contracting firm of Day and Grace (see Newson, *Pen Pictures of St. Paul*, 730).

40. Alan Lathrop, "Augustus F. Knight, Architect, 1831–1914," *Northwest Architect* (November/December 1974): 274–75. For an early biographical sketch of Radcliffe, see Edward D. Neill and Fletcher Williams, *History of Ramsey County and St. Paul* (Minneapolis: North Star Publishing Co., 1881).

41. Architectural historian Dell Upton offers a good introduction to the field of vernacular architecture in the following two

articles: "Ordinary Buildings: A Bibliographical Essay on American Vernacular Architecture," *American Studies* 19 (Winter 1981): 55–75; "The Power of Things: Recent Studies in American Vernacular Architecture," *American Quarterly* 35, no. 3 (1983): 262–79. See also Thomas Hubka, "Just Folks Designing: Vernacular Designers and the Generation of Form," in *Common Places*, ed. Upton and Vlach, 426–32.

42. See Richard W. E. Perrin, *Historic Wisconsin Buildings: A Survey in Pioneer Architecture 1835–1870* (Milwaukee: Milwaukee Public Museum, 1981), 85–89, 92–96, 103–8; Charles van Ravenswaay, *The Arts and Architecture of German Settlements in Missouri: A Survey of a Vanishing Culture* (Columbia: University of Missouri Press, 1977), chapter 8, "Stone Construction." Among Minnesota's German-immigrant stone buildings, the 1860s Stoppel Farmhouse near Rochester, now owned and maintained as a historic site by the Olmsted County Historical Society, offers a particularly close parallel to the Spangenberg Farmhouse; the building is pictured in *An Illustrated Historical Atlas of the State of Minnesota* (Chicago: A. T. Andreas, 1874), 121.

43. Weber was a cooper, Waldman a grain merchant, and Schilliger (who occasionally used the first name "Charles") a Swiss-German stonemason. In the past, the Schilliger House has been called the Joseph Brings House, after an owner who occupied the dwelling in the early 1860s. Research by historian Jim Sazevich, however, has established that Schilliger built the house in 1859; for this identification, see St. Paul Common Council, Proceedings, August 30, 1859, State Archives, Minnesota Historical Society. On the "Germanic" character of the West Seventh Street neighborhood, see Donald Empson, *Portrait of a Neighborhood* (St. Paul: Empson, 1980), 5–7; Hildegard Binder Johnson, "The Germans," in *They Chose Minnesota*, ed. June Drenning Holmquist (St. Paul: Minnesota Historical Society, 1981), 169.

44. On the German classical revival, see Henry-Russell Hitchcock, *Architecture: Nineteenth and Twentieth Centuries* (New York: Penguin Books, 1971), 43–54.

45. As quoted in Margaret Mussgang, "The Germans in St. Paul" (master's thesis, University of Minnesota, 1932), 40, n1.

46. *St. Paul Pioneer*, October 18, 1874.

47. The founding of Assumption Parish is discussed in James Michael Reardon, *The Catholic Church in the Diocese of St. Paul* (St. Paul: North Central Publishing Company, 1952), 99–100. On Bavaria, the Benedictine Order, and Assumption Church, see Colman J. Barry, *Worship and Work* (St. Paul: North Central Publishing Company), 5–24, 55. The newspaper quotation on the overcrowded conditions is from *A History of the Assumption Parish, St. Paul, Minn.* (St. Paul: Wanderer Printing Co., 1931), 18.

48. *A History of the Assumption Parish*, 18–19. For a sketch of Riedel's career, which mentions his Minnesota church commission, see Hans Vollmer, ed., *Allgemeines Lexikon der Bildenden Kunstler* (Leipzig: E. A. Seemann, 1934), 28:316.

49. Eberhard Drueke, "Friedrich von Gartner," trans. Beverley R. Placzek, *Macmillan Encyclopedia of Architects*, ed. Adolf K. Placzek (New York: The Free Press, 1982), 2:169–70.

50. On the origins and characteristics of the Romanesque Revival, see Carroll L. V. Meeks, "Romanesque before Richardson in the United States," *Art Bulletin* 35 (March 1953): 17–33; Marcus Whiffen, *American Architecture since 1780* (Cambridge: Massachusetts Institute of Technology, 1981), 61–67. The construction history of the St. Paul Custom House (officially characterized as being of "Norman architecture") is chronicled in *Report of the Secretary of the Treasury*, 192, H. Doc. 2, 40th Cong., 3rd sess., 1868; *Report of the Secretary of the Treasury*, 677, H. Doc. 2, 43rd Cong., 1st sess., 1873. The building's granite came from newly discovered quarries near St. Cloud, Minnesota.

51. *St. Paul Sunday Pioneer*, October 18, 1874. In the same vein, see *St. Paul Daily Dispatch*, October 15, 1874: "The building . . . is an exact counterpart of a famous church at Munich, Bavaria." This is echoed by Vincent, "Saint Paul Architecture" (n.p.) and Frederick Koeper, *Historic St. Paul Buildings* (St. Paul: St. Paul City Planning Board, 1962), 92.

52. *St. Paul Daily Dispatch*, October 19, 1874.

53. *St. Paul Daily Press*, April 25, 1872. On Boyington's career, see Harold M. Mayer and Richard C. Wade, *Chicago: Growth of a Metropolis* (Chicago: University of Chicago Press, 1974), 98; Henry F. Withey and Elsie Rathburn Withey, *Biographical Dictionary of American Architects (Deceased)* (Los Angeles: New Age Publishing Company, 1956), 71.

54. See William H. Pierson Jr., *American Buildings and Their Architects*, vol. 2, *Technology and the Picturesque* (Garden City, NY: Doubleday and Company, 1978), 271–431.

55. For a historical sketch of the Knox House, see *A Brief History of the Irvine Park District*, 20.

56. On the development of the ecclesiastical Gothic Revival in England, see Basil F. L. Clarke, *Church Builders of the Nineteenth Century* (New York: Augustus M. Kelley, 1969). The authoritative work on the movement's early years in America is Phoebe B. Stanton, *The Gothic Revival and American Church Architecture* (Baltimore: Johns Hopkins Press, 1968); also see Pierson, *American Buildings and Their Architects*, vol. 2, 159–269, 432–55. The construction of Christ Episcopal Church in St. Paul is discussed in Mrs. Gilfillan, "Sketch of Christ Church," 1907, in Protestant Episcopal Church, Diocese of Minnesota, Papers, Minnesota Historical

Society; George C. Tanner, "Early Episcopal Churches and Missions in Minnesota," *Collections of the Minnesota Historical Society* 10 (1905), 216–17. According to Gilfillan, "A builder, Mr. Cazone, submitted a plan for a building twenty by fifty feet, with tower and chancel, which could be built for eleven hundred dollars. This plan was accepted, and Mr. Cazone authorized to purchase material, and take charge of the construction of the edifice" (2).

57. The original drawing is reproduced in *A Church in Lowertown: The First Baptist Church of St. Paul* (St. Paul: Mason Publishing Company, 1975).

58. *St. Paul Daily Dispatch,* May 15, 1875.

59. *First Baptist Church, 100 Years of Christian Service, 1849–1949* (St. Paul, privately printed, 1949), 16–17; *A Church in Lowertown,* 44, 48.

60. The Thompson House is briefly described in *St. Paul Pioneer and Democrat,* November 25, 1860. On the development of the Italian Villa style, see Whiffen, *American Architecture since 1780,* 69–72.

61. An illustration of Sibley's residence appears in *An Illustrated Historical Atlas of the State of Minnesota,* 37. The Drake House, designed by master builder Monroe Sheire, is noted in *St. Paul Press,* November 2, 1865.

62. *St. Paul Pioneer,* December 9, 1863.

63. Burbank's career and house are discussed in Robert Orr Baker, "James C. Burbank, the Man Who Used Coach and Boat," *Ramsey County History* 9 (Fall 1972): 9–16; Christina H. Jacobsen, "The Burbank-Livingston-Griggs House: Historic Treasure on Summit Avenue," *Minnesota History* 42 (Spring 1970): 23–34.

64. Withey and Withey, *Biographical Dictionary of American Architects,* 648.

65. The mansard roof first attracted international attention with its appearance on the expanded Palace of the Louvre in Paris during the 1850s. The form reached a zenith of popularity in the United States in the decade following the Civil War; see Whiffen, *American Architecture since 1780,* 103–8. On the construction of the St. Paul Fire and Marine Company Building, see Kevin Galvin, "The Necessities of Life—Available Early on the Frontier," *Ramsey County History* 10 (Fall 1973): 9, 12.

66. Ramsey's place in Minnesota history is assayed by Marx Swanholm, *Alexander Ramsey and the Politics of Survival* (St. Paul: Minnesota Historical Society, 1977). For Yoerg's role in the St. Paul brewing industry, see Gary J. Breuggemann, "Beer Capital of the State—St. Paul's Historic Family Breweries," *Ramsey County History* 16, no. 2: 3–15.

67. Williams, *A History of the City of Saint Paul,* 3. The "Squirrel Problem" is noted in *100 Years in the Pioneer Press* (St. Paul: St. Paul Pioneer Press, 1949), 25.

2. ST. PAUL COMES OF AGE, 1875–1920

1. J. Fletcher Williams, *A History of the City of Saint Paul to 1875* (St. Paul: Minnesota Historical Society, 1875; reprint, 1983), 445, 447.

2. For statistics on St. Paul's burgeoning population in the early 1880s, see the remarks of Mayor C. D. O'Brien and the other city officials in *Proceedings of the St. Paul Common Council,* June 5, 1883, 73–75 (unpublished, Minnesota Historical Society). St. Paul's territorial growth is mapped and described in Calvin F. Schmid, *Social Saga of Two Cities* (Minneapolis: Bureau of Social Research, Minneapolis Council of Social Agencies, 1937), chart 38, 338. On the city's wholesale trade, see Mildred L. Hartsough, *The Twin Cities as a Metropolitan Market: A Regional Study of the Economic Development of Minneapolis and St. Paul* (Minneapolis: University of Minnesota, 1925), 126–27. The boast about St. Paul's future originated with a remark of Western Telegraph president William H. Seward, which was first reported in *St. Paul Daily Dispatch,* October 7, 1876.

3. Henry Castle, *History of St. Paul and Vicinity* (Chicago: Lewis Publishing Company, 1912), 1:266; Conde Hamlin, "St. Paul," *New England Magazine* 11 (July 1890): 546.

4. A map of St. Paul's population density in 1875 is found in Schmid, *Social Saga of Two Cities,* chart 28. For the best general treatment of the city's residential expansion and initial suburbanization during the 1880s, see the various neighborhood sketches in Patricia A. Murphy and Susan W. Granger, "Historic Sites Survey of Saint Paul and Ramsey County: A Final Report" (unpublished, 1983).

5. A second group of quasi-architects emerged in the 1880s, civil engineers who offered simple plans in connection with their laying out of plats. Louis Cuisimer, for example, advertised "beauty, solidity, and economy," with "cottages a specialty." Polk's *St. Paul Directory,* 1880–81, 644.

6. Many of the buildings shown in Figure 2.2. are likely to be mid-1860s designs by Augustus Knight or Monroe Sheire, as they closely resemble descriptions of stores by them farther up the street. See "The City: Building Statistics" in the *St. Paul Press,* November 2, 1865.

7. All of the buildings on the first two blocks of the northwest side (on the right in Figure 2.3) from Jackson Street to Wacouta Street were designed by E. P. Bassford. His work on the blocks began with the Centennial Block of 1876 at the north corner of Jackson and continued downtown (toward the foreground of Figure 2.3) until 1886.

8. The buildings in the foreground of Figure 2.4 were built between 1884 and 1889. The first four are the Scandinavian-American Bank, the first DeCoster Block, the Mayall Block, and the second DeCoster Block.

9. The designer of the Shipman-Greve House is hardly the mystery that several modern publications make it appear, for L. S. Buffington's name is cited under a colored lithograph of the house published in *American Architect* (April 4, 1896). That the Queen Anne style was liberating was a fairly common view, even among its harshest critics. See, for example, Thomas E. Tallmadge, *The Story of Architecture in America* (New York: W. W. Norton and Co., 1927), chapter 6, passim.

10. In architecture, the principal figures were A. W. N. Pugin and John Ruskin, who helped to turn national attention to Gothic building practices as paradigmatic expressions of their principles; and William Nesfield and R. Norman Shaw, who devised the updated late-medieval/early-Renaissance domestic style that acquired the chronologically challenged label of "Queen Anne."

11. Under Greve's ownership, Buffington added the latticework porch, one of the few exterior local expressions of the "Chinoiserie" (so named because of its supposed association with Chinese decoration) that played so important a role in the aesthetic movement.

12. For a critical survey of how the celebrated Richardson's influence swept into the Midwest and the role played by such architects as Bassford, see Paul Clifford Larson, "H. H. Richardson Goes West: The Rise and Fall of an Eastern Star," in *The Spirit of H. H. Richardson on the Midland Prairies* (Ames: Iowa State University Press, 1988).

13. *Northwest Magazine* 2 (June 1884).

14. C. C. Andrews, ed., *History of St. Paul, Minn.* (Syracuse, NY: D. Mason and Co., 1890), 143. On Rundlett's career, see "The Organization of the City Engineer's Office at St. Paul, Minn.," *Engineering Record* 23 (December 6, 1890): 7; Robert M. Frame III, "Historic Bridge Project Report" (unpublished, State Historic Preservation Office, Minnesota Historical Society, 1985), 94–95.

15. The importance of the Seventh Street Improvement project to Dayton's Bluff is noted in Josiah B. Chaney, "Early Bridges and Changes of the Land and Water Surface in the City of St. Paul," *Collections of the Minnesota Historical Society,* vol. 12 (St. Paul: Minnesota Historical Society, 1908), 135–36, 141–42. The project itself is discussed in detail in W[illiam] A[lbert] Truesdell, "The Seventh Street Improvement Arches," *Association of Engineering Societies Journal* 5 (July 1886): 317–24; "The Arches of the Seventh Street Improvement," *Engineering News and American Contract Journal* 14 (October 17, 1885): 245; Jeffrey A. Hess, National Register Nomination for the Seventh Street Improvement Arches (unpublished, State Historic Preservation Office, Minnesota Historical Society, 1988).

16. "The Arches of the Seventh Street Improvement," 245; Truesdell, "The Seventh Street Improvement Arches," 318. Biographical information is derived from Truesdell's obituary in *Association of Engineering Societies Journal* 28 (June 1909): 369–71.

17. A brief historical discussion of the helicoidal method is found in Edward Dobson, *Rudimentary Treatise on Masonry and Stone Cutting* (London: John Weale, 1859), 28–32. American "disgust" with the method is noted in John L. Culley, "Treatise on the Theory of the Construction of Helicoidal Oblique Arches," *Van Nostrand's Engineering Magazine* 208 (April 1886): 265.

18. Truesdell's obituary, *Association of Engineering Societies Journal* 28 (June 1909): 370.

19. For a good discussion of Munster's European background and career in St. Paul, see Kenneth Bjork, *Saga in Steel and Concrete: Norwegian Engineers in America* (Northfield, Minn.: Norwegian-American Historical Association, 1947), 140–41, 145–46; see also Munster's obituary in *Norwegian-American Technical Journal* 2 (July 1929): 5.13. For the Colorado Street bridge, see "Colorado Street (St. Paul) Skew Arch Bridge," *Engineering and Building Record* 20 (November 23, 1889): 365; and Jeffrey A. Hess, National Register Nomination for the Colorado Street Bridge (unpublished, State Historic Preservation Office, Minnesota Historical Society, 1988).

20. Unlike Knight and Sheire, Radcliffe remained a highly visible force in St. Paul architecture into the 1880s, though it is doubtful how much of the actual design work of his office engaged his attention in his later years. He retired to California in 1887 and died seven years thereafter with only a scant notice in *Architect, Builder, and Decorator,* May 1894.

21. See Muriel Christianson's master's thesis on Buffington (University of Minnesota, 1941), condensed in *Art Bulletin* (March 1944). The competition for the Minnesota Building at the 1876 Centennial Exposition in Philadelphia provided a fair indication of the local state of the profession in the 1870s. In spite of a $200 prize and obvious collateral benefits, there were only six entrants: Radcliffe, Knight and associates, Sheire, Bassford, Buffington, and Minneapolitans Long and Haglin. The competition became moot when the state legislature failed to fund the building in time for the exposition. See letters of 1875–76 in John Fletcher Williams Papers, Minnesota Historical Society, and *St. Paul Dispatch,* December 20, 1875, and January 7, 1876.

22. The local publication was Andrew Morrison, *The Industries of St. Paul* (St. Louis: J. M. Elsner, 1886), 114. Edward Payson Bassford (1837–1912) apprenticed with Radcliffe between 1869 and 1872. William H. Castner (fl. 1884–1893) was an apprentice under Radcliffe from 1882 to 1883 before joining Knight in a brief

partnership. Didrich A. Omeyer (1851–1907) was with Radcliffe only one year, 1883. Gilbert and Johnston also apprenticed with Radcliffe after dropping out of high school in the late 1870s. Radcliffe's finest personnel gift to the state was probably Winona's Charles G. Maybury, who was Radcliffe's major contractor during his four years in that city (1862–65) and took over Radcliffe's architectural practice on the latter's return to St. Paul.

23. For Bassford's Maine roots, see Gregory K. Clancey, "Asher P. Bassford," in *A Biographical Dictionary of Architects in Maine*, vol. 2, n. 3, 1985. For detailed accounts of his St. Paul life and career, see a commemorative article, "E. P. Bassford," *The Western Architect*, September 1903, 16; his obituary, "Death Summons E. P. Bassford," *St. Paul Pioneer Press*, July 20, 1912, 4; and Alan Lathrop, "Edward Payson Bassford, Architect (1837–1912)," *Architecture Minnesota*, January-February 1977, 37–41.

24. *St. Paul Dispatch Souvenir*, 1892, 72.

25. For information concerning Gauger's life and career, see his obituary in the *St. Paul Dispatch*, February 18, 1929; and the entry in Henry F. Withey and Elsie R. Withey, *Biographical Dictionary of American Architects (Deceased)* (Los Angeles: New Age Pub. Co., 1956), 230.

26. For sketches of Wirth's career and major commissions in St. Paul, see Morrison, *The Industries of St. Paul*, 94; and *The Northwest*, March 1885, 18. For a thoroughly documented account of a grand tour typical of the architectural profession around 1880, see Paul Clifford Larson, *Cass Gilbert Abroad: The Young Architect's European Tour* (Afton, MN: Afton Historical Society Press, 2003).

27. Illustrations of the National German-American Bank occur in nearly all of the city directories and subscription publications of the period. Good images produced by eminent local photographers Truman Ingersoll and Charles Gibson are in the Minnesota Historical Society library.

28. The source of information for Stevens's arrival is the city directories. He first appeared in 1880 as an apprentice with his father, John H. Stevens, but was on his own the following year. The arrivals of Wirth, Johnston, and Gilbert were well documented in a number of biographical sketches published while the architects were still in practice. The offices of these four architects immediately replaced Radcliffe and Bassford as the major local training centers for young draftsmen.

The most reliable source of information on Ellis's background and St. Paul–Minneapolis career continues to be Eileen Manning, "The Architectural Designs of Harvey Ellis" (master's thesis, unpublished, University of Minnesota, 1953). Much has been discovered since that time, but it has often been interlaced with imaginative attributions and absolute fictions, beginning soon after his

death with a heavy dose of mythologizing by his younger contemporaries W. G. Purcell and Frank Chouteau Brown. The St. Paul chronology is at least clear from city directories and published drawings. In early 1886, Ellis was a draftsman for Mould and McNicol. By the fall of that year he had joined J. Walter Stevens, and during the next fall (1887) he left for Minneapolis and L. S. Buffington.

29. The quotation is from *St. Paul and Minneapolis Pioneer Press*, December 25, 1887, 11. The erratic building history of Noyes Brothers and Cutler's new warehouse can be tracked in the foregoing and *St. Paul and Minneapolis Pioneer Press*, January 1, 1890 (sketch and notice of permit); *Inland Architect and News Record*, November 1892 (building start for addition); *Inland Architect and News Record*, June 1895 (building start for second addition); and the 1908 building permit for the easternmost bays. The extent of Ellis's involvement in the final design is far from certain, as the earliest extant illustrations of the building are newspaper engravings from 1889, which may or may not conform to the designs referred to in 1887.

30. Some of McLaughlin's work for Stevens, the renderings of the Mayall and northernmost DeCoster and Clark Blocks and the State Normal School at Moorhead, were published in the *American Architect* on February 25 and June 2, 1888. The engravings are clearly signed by McLaughlin, but just as clearly are in Ellis's style, illustrating the difficulty of attributing architectural designs to single draftsmen within any architect's office of the period. The southernmost DeCoster and Clark Block was designed before either had arrived in Stevens's office; see note 28. The pen-and-ink rendering of the Germania Building, dated 1888, was published in *American Architect and Building News*, March 26, 1892. It is tempting to trace its designer's use of a projecting, classically inspired cornice to, say, the work of Richardson's successors, Shepley, Rutan, and Coolidge, but the Germania Building design was coterminous with SRC's similar experiments. It is possible that Ellis was involved in the design—he produced a similar hybrid for LeRoy Buffington in the University of Minnesota's Nicholson Hall—but the commission arrived in Stevens's office after Ellis had left, and the published rendering is too hard-edged and evenly worked to be either his or McLaughlin's.

31. For pictures of and references to many of Stevens's houses, see Ernest R. Sandeen, *St. Paul's Historic Summit Avenue* (Minneapolis: University of Minnesota Press, 2004).

32. *Inland Architect and Builder*, December 1885. The Architectural Association of Minnesota, formed in 1882, was the first statewide architectural association west of Illinois. Wirth's European tenement tour was reported in *St. Paul and Minneapolis Pioneer Press*, January 28, 1883.

33. Minneapolis architect Harry W. Jones cited the building slowdown on the East Coast as a major factor in his decision to prolong his Minneapolis honeymoon into a career there. See Marion D. Shutter and J. S. McLain, eds., *Progressive Men of Minnesota* (Minneapolis: Minneapolis Journal, 1897), 120. Trade journals of the period are filled with references to the remarkable building market in the Twin Cities. See, for example, *Carpentry and Building,* May 1884: "St. Paul and Minneapolis, Minn. . . . are veritable cities, growing with almost unparalleled rapidity. The building business in both of them is very active, and seems likely to continue so for some time to come. . . . A few towns [farther west] have fitful spells of building, but in general there is comparatively little to be done." In the middle states, St. Louis and Kansas City were also cited for a relatively high level of building activity.

34. The architects known to be born in Germany were (in order of their arrival in St. Paul) Otto Buechner, Emil Ulrici, Albert Zschocke, George Reis, Emil Strassburger, Mauritz Weiser, and Herman Kretz; the English were H. Sackville Treherne, Walter Ife, and Louis Lockwood; the Norwegians were Didrich Omeyer, Martin P. Thori, and Henry Orth; the Swede was Silas Jacobsen; and the Canadians were William Kingsley, John McCarthy, and H. R. P. Hamilton.

35. The most complete published list of Willcox's projects occurs in his promotional and, for its day, quite informative brochure, *Hints to Those Who Propose to Build* (St. Paul: privately printed, 1884). Many of his most important commissions survive in nearby Stillwater as well as Chicago. Earlier buildings such as the Nebraska State House and a number of New York City churches were replaced many years ago.

36. Willcox, *Hints to Those Who Propose to Build,* 4–5. Willcox distinguished between "so-called Queen Anne" and true Queen Anne. Several of his local contemporaries, such as Minneapolis architects Harry Jones and W. C. Whitney, shied away from the term (and the style as they understood it) altogether.

37. Willcox's chapter on "Residences" contains one of the most sustained arguments of this sort; Willcox, *Hints to Those Who Propose to Build,* 3–6.

38. St. Paul was a relatively long stopover in Willcox's career. By the time he retired at the turn of the century, he had added Seattle, Los Angeles, and San Francisco to his list of venues.

39. For a portfolio of Gilbert's drawings and letters from his first architectural tour of Europe, see Larson, *Cass Gilbert Abroad.* Gilbert initially intended to take Johnston with him, but Johnston waited until his practice had gotten under way in 1884.

40. The characterization of Johnston first occurred in *Illustrated St. Paul: A Souvenir of the St. Paul Dispatch* (St. Paul: Dispatch, 1892), 71. The thumbnail sketches of several architects provided in this booster publication are unusual for singling out some architects for artistic gift, others for administrative skill. Johnston is the only one to be accorded high praise on both counts. Several anecdotes revealing Gilbert's artistic side were recorded in a laudatory article by Walter Tittle, "The Creator of the Woolworth Tower," *The World's Work,* tear sheets numbered 96–102 in St. Paul Public Library, St. Paul Architects file. After Gilbert showed him a number of his watercolor sketches, Tittle concluded that "success as a painter could have been his if he had not chosen architecture instead." For a detailed assessment of Johnston's work and a more complete account of his relationship with Gilbert, see Paul Clifford Larson, *Minnesota Architect: The Life and Work of Clarence H. Johnston* (Afton, MN.: Afton Historical Society Press, 1998).

41. The Merriam House burned to the ground in 1895. Several photographs taken shortly after construction are in the Minnesota Historical Society photo collection. The Griggs and Foster Houses were featured in a widely read pictorial monograph on modern suburban homes, George W. Sheldon's *Artistic Country Seats* (New York: Appleton and Co., 1886–87). The modern edition by Arnold Lewis, *American Country Houses of the Gilded Age* (New York: Dover, 1982), unfortunately replaces Sheldon's unabashedly enthusiastic but still valuable descriptions with modern analyses based largely on photographic observation. Many of the dates of construction assigned by Lewis are also erroneous.

42. The first systematic study of Gilbert's Minnesota work was the master's thesis of Patricia A. Murphy, "The Early Career of Cass Gilbert: 1878 to 1895" (unpublished, University of Virginia, 1979). Her work has been expanded and brought up to date in Geoffrey Blodgett, *Cass Gilbert: The Early Years* (St. Paul: Minnesota Historical Society Press, 2001), and by considerable research by Paul Clifford Larson for a pending publication. For a sampling of the trove of drawings Gilbert brought home from his 1880 European grand tour, see Larson, *Cass Gilbert Abroad.*

43. Much of the information regarding specific St. Paul buildings is drawn from original permits, now archived by Ramsey County Historical Society. The unusual note on the Bethlehem Church permit is not in Gilbert's hand; it was probably inscribed by the contractor.

44. The seminal McKim, Mead and White designs were the Henry A. C. Taylor and William Edgar Houses at Newport Beach completed in 1886. Gilbert adapted the frame Taylor House to an urban lot, while W. C. Whitney did the same in Minneapolis for the brick Edgar House. Both were designed as the McKim, Mead and White houses were being built. See Paul Clifford Larson,

National Register Nomination for the William H. Hinkle–William J. Murphy House (unpublished, State Historic Preservation Office, Minnesota Historical Society, 1984).

45. Many articles, some of near-monograph length, were published on the State Capitol on its completion in 1905. The most important from the standpoint of design documentation and analysis are Kenyon Cox, "The New State Capitol of Minnesota," *Architectural Record* 18 (August 1905): 94–113; and the entire issue of *The Western Architect* 4 (October 1905). The prizewinners after Gilbert were George R. Mann of St. Louis; Traphagen and Fitzpatrick of Duluth, associated with E. P. Bassford; W. B. Dunnell of Minneapolis; and Harry W. Jones of Minneapolis. All but Gilbert's design were inspired by later and much more complex building forms than Gilbert's Renaissance palazzo, from Jones's studied use of English baroque to Dunnell's and Fitzpatrick's unrestrained World's Fair baroque.

46. This sketchy background is all that is known of Stem prior to his immigration to St. Paul. See *Little Sketches of Big Folks* (St. Paul: R. L. Polk and Co., 1907), 377; and *Inland Architect and News Record* 3 (June 1884): 71–72.

47. *The Building Budget* 2 (January 1886). See "Reed and Stem Led Midwest Boom," *St. Paul Sunday Pioneer Press* [1947], in architects file at St. Paul Public Library.

48. The firm claimed to have produced over 650 buildings before the Panic of 1893 hit; *City of Superior Directory*, 1891–92, 55. It was commonplace for directory listings to play loose with spellings, but in Omeyer's case, R. L. Polk & Co. outdid themselves: Didrick, Diderick, and Diedrich all got into print before the obituary notice in 1907 finally got it right. For Thori, see his obituary, "An Old Resident Dies," *St. Paul Pioneer Press*, February 9, 1905. An excellent summary of the firm's work up to their last two years, along with photographs of a number of their out-state buildings, is given in a subscription book to which they were obviously heavy contributors, *The Book of Minnesota* (St. Paul: Pioneer Press Co., 1903), 103 and passim. See also "Omeyer & Thori, Architects," *Minnesota's Resources and Industries: St. Paul* (St. Paul: Railway Publishing Co., 1904), 30.

49. A brief summary of Ulrici's local accomplishments can be found in Morrison, *The Industries of St. Paul,* 98. His arrival from St. Louis was noted in the *St. Paul Globe*, March 18, 1883, but his work was all but ignored by the local press in the ensuing years.

50. A synopsis of Strassburger's work prior to 1887 can be found in E. E. Barton, *City of St. Paul* (St. Paul: privately published, 1888), 155. Some of the West Side's most distinctive early building stock, such as the Rau-Strong House at 2 West George Street (1884–86), carry his earmarks but no documented connection to his office.

West Side development in general was given little coverage in the local press. Strassburger was unique among the city's architects in remaining through the Panic of 1893 and its aftermath, then moving on (to Crookston, Minnesota) when recovery began in 1901. The only other architect to settle on the West Side was John Fischer (fl. 1884–1912), whose background is unknown, although like Strassburger he was patronized primarily by clients with German names.

51. The only published account of Zschocke's life and work, and the source of the quote on his two years of apprenticeship, occurred in *Illustrated St. Paul*, 41. A modern freeway now isolates the Giesen House from its Dayton's Bluff neighborhood. The Minnesota Historical Society retains an early photograph that exemplifies the difficulty of seeing the house all at once because of its elevation and surrounding foliage. Other important remaining work of Zschocke is well documented in the files of the 1982–83 Historic Sites Survey of Saint Paul and Ramsey County; original forms and photographs are at the Ramsey County Historical Society.

52. The best of many biographical sketches of Kretz is in Castle, *History of St. Paul and Vicinity,* 829–30.

53. For a broad historical analysis of the style within the context of America's first distinctive native architecture, see Vincent Scully, *The Shingle Style and the Stick Style* (New Haven: Yale University Press, 1971).

54. City directories and architectural periodical notices and illustrations provide the only available information on Castner's career. He did all his own renderings for publication. In 1891, he left St. Paul to join Frank Hyde in Dubuque, Iowa.

55. For information on Joy, see Morrison, *The Industries of St. Paul,* 81; *Illustrated St. Paul,* 71; and *Northwest Magazine* 6 (February 1888): 38–39. The latter also supplies detailed information on the prospective Burlington Heights development. See also *Northwest Architect and Improvement Record,* June 1888. In 1887 Joy and his then-partner, F. W. Fitzpatrick, began to pick up Ellis's drawing and designing mannerisms in their published renderings, a mark of Ellis's instant influence on the local architectural community.

56. In a turn of events not at all unusual in such affairs, W. H. Castner actually won the competition for the Minnesota Club in 1883, but by the time construction actually began in 1885, the commission was in Mould's hands. The elaborate ornamental scheme of the Merriam House, its stylistic unity, and its creation during just those months that Ellis worked for Mould are all the evidence we have of Ellis's involvement in the design. Early photographs of the house abounded in local subscription publications, and famed

illustrator Harry Fenn did a wonderfully romantic drawing for an article by Montgomery Schuyler, "Glimpses of Western Architecture: St. Paul and Minneapolis," *Harper's Monthly Magazine* 83 (October 1891).

The dating of signed drawings for other commissions suggests that Ellis and McNicol traded places in late 1886, Ellis leaving Mould for Stevens, and McNicol leaving Stevens to join Mould. See also Eileen Manning, "The Architectural Designs of Harvey Ellis"; and Roger Kennedy, "Long Dark Corridors: Harvey Ellis," *Prairie School Review* 5 (1958): 5–18. Like many others, Kennedy attributes several buildings to Ellis on stylistic evidence alone, a dangerous game in an era when ideas wandered as freely as draftsmen. His remark on the published "Ellis-like sketch" of the Merriam House, for example, is trivialized by the appearance of popular magazine artist Harry Fenn's distinctive monogram in one corner of the engraving. See Schuyler, "Glimpses of Western Architecture," reprinted in Montgomery Schuyler, *American Architecture and Other Writings,* ed. by William H. Jordy and Ralph Coe (Cambridge, MA: Belknap Press, 1961), 323.

57. Coxhead was listed as a regular member of the Chicago Architectural Sketch Club in the *Inland Architect and News Record* 10 (December 1887) and 12 (December 1888). This periodical also followed his career quite closely, commenting, on his departure from St. Paul for Buffalo in 1892, that he was to supply the quality and W. W. Carlin the quantity for their new partnership; *Inland Architect and News Record* 19 (February 1892): 15. Brief sketches of Coxhead's life and career are contained in Barton, *City of St. Paul;* and *Illustrated St. Paul,* 73. A more complete account is in Nancy Mingus, "John Hopper Coxhead: The Client Connections" (unpublished master's thesis, University of Virginia, 2001).

58. For a brief account of Treherne's accomplishments in the city, see Morrison, *The Industries of St. Paul,* 93; for Millard, see *Illustrated St. Paul,* 72. Apart from the few buildings captured in the 1982–83 Historic Sites Survey, the only other sources of information regarding the prolific St. Paul output of each are building permits and notices published in the trade press and local newspapers, particularly the Sunday building reviews in the *St. Paul and Minneapolis Pioneer Press.* The loss of national census records for 1890 makes something as simple as establishing birth and death dates extraordinarily difficult for many of St. Paul's architects during its great building boom; most of them arrived in the city after 1880 and were gone by 1900.

59. The guiding hand for the design of the exterior was Chicagoan W. J. Edbrooke, the Supervising Architect of the Treasury during the early planning stages. The northern part of the building was designed later under the tenure of Gilbert's former partner, James Knox Taylor. A comparison of Edbrooke's uninspired cloning of Richardson's Trinity Church for the upper portion of the south tower with Taylor's urbane piece of Norman scholarship for the north makes a good argument for MIT training. For a full history of the building, see Eileen Michels, *A Landmark Reclaimed* (St. Paul: privately printed for Minnesota Landmarks, 1977), 17–43.

60. Russell Sturgis, *How to Judge Architecture* (New York: Baker and Taylor Co., 1903), 210–11. Gilbert was encouraged to refrain from entering the competition by William Mead; he kept an oar in by becoming local supervising architect, a role he soon reprised for the initial stage of U.S. Courthouse and Post Office construction, beginning in 1892.

61. Schuyler, *American Architecture and Other Writings,* 313. Schuyler praised the design for having "no architecture that is not evolved directly from the requirements of the building."

62. Reed and Stem had gotten their feet wet in a series of elegant little railway stations for the Northern Pacific and New York Central Railways in the early 1890s. Curiously, the American press never picked these up, though many years later they were discussed as paradigms of American railroad architecture in the progressive German *Der Architect* 16 (1910): 89–96.

63. Kretz accumulated a large amount of real estate between 1888 and 1915, including many of the apartment buildings he designed during the depression and the monumental Kasota Building in Minneapolis.

64. For a good biographical sketch of Holyoke, see Henry Castle, *Minnesota, Its History and Biography* (Chicago: Lewis Publishing Co., 1915), 759.

65. The most accurate biographical sketch of Lockwood is in Albert Nelson Marquis, ed., *The Book of Minnesotans* (Chicago: A. N. Marquis and Co., 1907), 313. Many of Lockwood's houses were captured in the 1982–83 Historic Sites Survey.

66. The firm was established upon Thori's death in 1905, when the chief draftsmen bought the business from the remaining partner, Didrich Omeyer. It continued to use Thori's name until Alban and Fischer parted ways in 1908.

67. For a carefully researched account of Masqueray's training and career, see Alan Lathrop, "Emmanuel L. Masqueray, 1861–1917," *Minnesota History* 47 (Summer 1980): 42–56.

68. Masqueray interlaces his views on religious architecture, his design intentions regarding the Cathedral of St. Paul, and a general description of the building in *Western Architect,* October 1908, 43–44.

69. The brewing innovations with the largest impact on construction were pneumatic drying, which dispensed with the need

for extensive malt houses, and mechanical cooling, which brought the fermentation chambers out of caves and ice houses and into massive refrigerated buildings.

70. A writer for a trade journal thought the Schmidt plant was "in the feudal castle style," while praising it for its economical arrangement, efficient planning, and modern equipment; *The Western Brewer* 26 (July 1901): 274. See also the city designation study for the Schmidt Brewery by Paul Larson in the Heritage Preservation Commission files, City of St. Paul.

71. *St. Paul Pioneer Press,* September 10, 1910. Like many of the developers, Lane did everything he could to conceal the fact that the design of the houses he built on speculation did not originate in his own office. Architect Mark Fitzpatrick's name appears in neither the extensive promotional material about the Lane model house on Marshall Avenue nor on the building permit; it was found only by a survey of *Improvement Bulletin,* in which the building start appeared on January 1, 1910. On the site form for the Historic Sites Survey of St. Paul and Ramsey County, Patricia Murphy notes the resemblances between the Lane house and Greene and Greene's work in suburban Los Angeles.

72. One of Blood's tile-walled houses, the H. W. Smith Spec House at 2271 St. Clair Avenue, is one of the first flat-roofed houses in the city. Erected in 1917, its only known predecessor was the William Linley Alban house (see note 82).

73. The biographical material is from Castle, *Minnesota, Its History and Biography,* 928–29. Pedersen published several books with his plans. One that survives in local collections (Minneapolis Public Library) is *Beautiful Homes and Plans* (St. Paul: privately printed, 1919). Pedersen also designed a number of larger homes in the prevailing Tudor Revival and Colonial Revival fashions. The St. Paul and Ramsey County Historic Sites Survey uncovered many examples of his work, and once his plans have been studied, it is easy to spot them in numerous undocumented locations throughout the Summit-University and Macalester Groveland districts.

74. The Olaf Lee House, which is on the National Register of Historic Places, has a file both in the State Historic Preservation Office at the Minnesota Historical Society and in the Ramsey County Historical Society.

75. These relationships are explored on an architect-by-architect basis in Paul Clifford Larson, "The Prairie School in Its Midwestern Setting" and "The Prairie School House as Environmental Structure," in *Prairie School Architecture in Minnesota, Iowa, and Wisconsin* (St. Paul: Minnesota Museum of Art, 1982), 9–41.

76. The Beebe House is a telling instance of the many continuities between Wright's work and the progressive architecture of his contemporaries in England. The ground-floor corner windows superficially resemble Wright's work, for example, but their emphatic framing clearly indicates an intention to emphasize the corner rather than make it disappear à la Wright. Parker and Unwin were doing exactly the same thing in suburban London.

77. In this country, English Gothicism even became academically correct, largely because of the writings and influence of Ralph Adams Cram. St. Paul has one outstanding example of Gilbert in an English Gothic mode, St. Clement's Church, illustrated in *American Architect* 48 (June 8, 1895), 82.

78. Castle, *Minnesota, Its History and Biography,* 1083–84. For the reference to Chicago architects and anecdotal information regarding Hausler's work for the City of St. Paul, I am indebted to his son, Donald Hausler.

79. As none of the working drawings from Hausler's tenure as city architect (1913–1922) are initialed by their draftsmen, there is no way of confirming what hands were involved. An intensive scanning of city directories of the period reveals that no one listed himself as a draftsman for the city prior to 1916, and only two were so listed prior to 1918. Much of the city's early drafting corps was in fact made up of temporary employees, whom Hausler was at first authorized to hire outside of the mandates of the Civil Service Bureau. This opened the way to bringing in his associates on a piecework basis. According to his son, Donald Hausler, Charles Hausler often hired outside designers to assist on city projects. Comparison of Bentley's work in La Crosse and the joint Bentley and Hausler projects in St. Paul and La Crosse with the three Prairie School city projects noted leaves little doubt that Bentley got the call for them. Interview with Donald Hausler, September 1981.

80. The flap over the library and Gilbert's involvement in it is chronicled in several letters in the Cass Gilbert Collection at the Minnesota Historical Society and the Cass Gilbert letterpress books at the New-York Historical Society.

81. Hausler was induced into flexing his muscle early by a suit brought against him by the general contractor, claiming that Hausler was not fit to be the superintending architect. The city stood behind its employee, authorizing Hausler to stop construction until the contractor changed the type of backing brick he was using. *St. Paul Pioneer Press,* August 25, 1914.

82. The sole published biography of Alban, in *Little Sketches of Big Folks* (St. Paul: R. L. Polk, 1907), 8, states that he was a graduate of the "Chicago School of Architecture," which probably refers to Armor Institute rather than to the University of Chicago. His most original building was a one-story rectilinear house for himself at 966 Tuscarora Avenue, erected in 1908. He and Hausler also did an ecclesiastical design reminiscent of Sullivan's late work,

Knox Presbyterian Church (1913). Drawings from several of their projects survive in the Northwest Architectural Archives, University of Minnesota.

83. For La Crosse examples of the work of Bentley and Hausler, see H. Allen Brooks, *The Prairie School: Frank Lloyd Wright and His Midwest Contemporaries* (New York: W. W. Norton and Co., 1976), 263–64.

84. The other house attributable to Bentley and Hausler is the Frank B. Thompson House in Falcon Heights (ca. 1915). Initial permit information is lacking for all three houses, but the Seifert House blueprints survive with the architects' title block, and the interior detailing of the other two houses, including woodwork and stained glass, is distinctive of Bentley and Hausler's known work in La Crosse and St. Paul. The Seifert house is featured in H. F. Koeper, *Historic St. Paul Buildings: A Report of the Historic Sites Committee* (St. Paul: St. Paul City Planning Board, 1964); and David Gebhard and Tom Martinson, *A Guide to the Architecture of Minnesota* (Minneapolis: University of Minnesota Press, 1976).

85. No written documentation exists for any of the architects and draftsmen who assisted Hausler outside of the Civil Service draftsmen introduced in late 1914. However, the projects of 1915 are exceptional in Hausler's tenure in both the artistic quality of the drawings and the architectural merit of the designs, suggesting that outside talent was brought in to supplement the young draftsmen. Donald Hausler, the architect's son, remembers that "Bentley worked for my father" during the latter's tenure as city architect; interview with Donald Hausler, September 1981.

86. Several Prairie School practitioners held to this broad view of stylistic usage, most notably Richard Schmidt in Chicago; William Steele in Sioux City, Iowa; and Percy Dwight Bentley. These and many other regional architects looked to Wright's work for inspiration for only a few years and even then for select building types, ranging freely through other current styles for the rest.

3. FROM THE PICTURESQUE TO THE MODERNE, 1920–1940

1. This is part of an extended memo dated April 26, 1886, and written to no one in particular. Most of it is devoted to singling out the contributions of teachers and fellow architects to Gilbert's outlook and career; Cass Gilbert letters, Library of Congress.

2. Cass Gilbert, memo of April 26, 1886.

3. Among Prairie School followers, the immediate retreat into eclecticism was particularly true outside of Wright's own circle. Such far-flung architects as Charles Hausler and Percy Dwight

Bentley in St. Paul; Bray and Nystrom in Duluth, Minnesota; Claude and Starke in Madison, Wisconsin; Bohnard and Parsons in Cleveland, Ohio; Shephard and Belcher in Kansas City, Missouri; and Ernest Wood in Quincy, Illinois, had all but abandoned Wright's style by 1918. For a typical interpretation of the retreat from the Prairie School, see H. Allen Brooks, *The Prairie School: Frank Lloyd Wright and His Midwest Contemporaries* (Toronto: University of Toronto Press, 1972), passim.

4. A particularly lucid and well-documented local example of this relationship between war experience and house design is Rufus Rand's neo-Norman mansion on the other side of Minneapolis from St. Paul. See Paul Clifford Larson, "The French in Our Midst," *Architecture Minnesota* 15 (May/June 1989).

5. "French Style for an American Setting," *St. Paul Pioneer Press,* November 7, 1926.

6. The quotations are from an ASHSB plan for an "Ideal Six-Room English Cottage," *St. Paul Pioneer Press,* January 23, 1927.

7. Elwood's life and career are thoroughly documented in a typescript autobiography retained by Elwood's daughter, Valerie Card. An excerpt detailing his professional career was published in *Who's Who in the Central States* (Washington, DC: Mayflower Publishing Co., 1929). The Gordon Van Tine Millwork Company of Davenport, Iowa, published several of Elwood's designs (all unattributed) in ads for builders' magazines. Elwood also did standard and prefab designs for Thompson Lumber Yards in Minneapolis and American Farms Building Company in St. Paul.

8. The latter place name is particularly poignant because it was used to signify a design marking Elwood's return to private architectural work at the end of a difficult career. He built "Beyond Avalon" at 648 South Lexington for himself in 1949; it was indubitably the last pure Prairie School design to be constructed under the supervision of the original architect.

9. See, for example, James Early, *Romanticism and American Architecture* (New York: Barnes and Company, 1965). In the statement "Wright was unique among the major twentieth century architects in the extent of his debt to the picturesque tradition," Early summarily dismisses all of the architects consciously working in the picturesque tradition.

10. *St. Paul Pioneer Press,* July 18, 1926.

11. All dates given for buildings are for the year of completion. Unless otherwise indicated, the source of dates and architects is the initial building permit. The original occupant was determined by a combination of permit and city directory research. The Jefferson House design was published in the *St. Paul Pioneer Press,* May 17, 1925. In this case, that is the only source of information about its architect.

12. Surprisingly for so important a house and so publicity-conscious an architect, no notice of its planning or erection reached the local papers.

13. For a sketch of Lundie's life and contributions to Minnesota architecture, see the exhibition catalog, "Encounter with Artists Number Nine: Edwin Hugh Lundie," Minnesota Museum of Art, St. Paul, 1972, especially the essay by Eileen Michels. Most of what Michels says about Lundie in particular, for example, his mastery of proportion and detail and his knowledge of building materials, can be said of historical revival architects generally, at least in the city of St. Paul. The most complete published survey of Lundie's work is Dale Mulfinger, *The Architecture of Edwin Lundie* (St. Paul: Minnesota Historical Society Press, 1995).

14. While the Shadow Falls house was being built, Lewis lived in a much simpler pseudo-English house in the division just to the north, Desnoyer Park. Also designed by Lewis, this house was an experimental effort to fuse the English Cottage manner to an all-concrete base, along the lines of Atterbury's work on the East Coast.

15. A monograph on Worthen's St. Paul career is in process. Attaching an architect's name to buildings after September 1924 is a laborious task, as building permits after that date do not provide the name of the architect. Birth and death dates for Worthen have been graciously provided by his son Frederick A. ("Dusty") Worthen, with the ship's architect story coming from another son, Kenneth Worthen Jr.

16. An illustration of the Mussell House appeared for some time in a local newspaper ad for Flax-li-num, a form of rigid insulation introduced in 1910. The ad shows that a tuck-under double garage was original to the design. See, for example, the *St. Paul Pioneer Press*, May 17, 1925. The site form for the house in the St. Paul and Ramsey County Historic Sites Survey quite properly notes the design's affinities with the turn-of-the-century work of Englishman C. F. A. Voysey.

17. Other examples of Worthen's mature English style are the Hugh Beals House at 74 Otis Avenue, the J. H. Wilkinson House at 682 Goodrich Avenue, and the lavish remodeling of the Guthrie House at 444 Laurel Avenue. All of these date from 1924.

18. Axelrod's design was prominently featured in the *St. Paul Pioneer Press*, June 28, 1925. Construction began in January.

19. This was the second house Shapira built on Woodlawn Avenue. His earlier house was in Kenneth Worthen's English manner. Blueprints dated April 1932 are the source of the attribution to Liebenberg and Kaplan. This and the information about the interior of the tower come from a telephone conversation with the owner, Tom Minter, on July 19, 1990. Liebenberg and Kaplan's most prominent works in St. Paul are the Jewish Educational Center at Holly Avenue and Grotto Street and the William Harris House at 2029 Summit Avenue.

20. *Building Age,* March 1928, 97.

21. These are illustrated in the *St. Paul Pioneer Press*, June 26, 1932.

22. Frederick M. Mann's own house plans, ranging from English cottage to Renaissance palazzo, won a number of prizes; many of them were erected in Minneapolis. No house of his design is known to have been erected in St. Paul. The contest made front-page news in the *Highland Park Herald,* May 23, 1926.

23. *St. Paul Pioneer Press,* April 6, 1930. The house was built by A. N. Thome, who purchased plans for spec houses from Lundie as well as Ingemann.

24. The 1930 directory lists Worthen's home address as 54 North Mississippi River Boulevard and his business address as 37 Otis Avenue. The house is featured in Larson, "The French in Our Midst."

25. By coincidence, the largest local example of the "Versailles type" was erected at 221 Mount Curve Boulevard, across the corner from Jemne's house. Built in 1926, it had the same contractor as the 1930 Better Homes Demo; this together with its detailing suggests that it had the same architect as well, William Ingemann.

26. The house and its "type" were first mentioned in the *St. Paul Pioneer Press,* November 6, 1927. A display ad and feature article on the house appeared in the *St. Paul Pioneer Press,* February 12, 1928.

27. The Lampland Lumber Company in particular published a number of "Spanish" designs in the local papers, many of them beautifully rendered by draftsman Grann Seitz. Even the ASHSB, which made a point of regionally sensitive design, frequently submitted house plans in the Spanish style for newspaper publication in St. Paul and Minneapolis.

28. "More about Jazz-Plastering," *Improvement Bulletin* 68 (October 16, 1926).

29. Both designs, and the Nicholas Brewer House in particular, show a degree of sophistication unmatched by Linden's other known work, suggesting that he had significant input from Brewer.

30. *St. Paul Pioneer Press,* September 11, 1932. There is some confusion regarding the address, as Nicholas Brewer was listed at 468, not 510, Glenham (the old name for Frontenac) in the City Directory and the newspaper article, but the original permit and Brewer's descriptions both refer to the building at 510. Brewer's son, Edward, assembled an equally quirky home at 387 Pelham Boulevard but in the English cottage vein. See Patricia Condon, "Edward Brewer, Illustrator and Painter," *Minnesota History* (Winter 1980): 14.

31. The von Nieda House could be inferentially attributed to Worthen by a reference in *Improvement Bulletin,* September 8, 1923, to a building start of an "English" house by Worthen at that approximate location. The date is consistent with the issuance of the building permit. Calling the house "English" is a stretch that illustrates the commitment of the building and real estate community to getting some kind of stylistic label on all of their products.

32. See the *St. Paul Pioneer Press,* April 12, 1925. All of the renderings appear to be in the same hand, though the one of the Bremer House is unsigned.

33. *St. Paul Pioneer Press,* May 18, 1930. Brenny did a large number of spec houses in Highland Park in the late 1920s and 1930s. The sophistication and complexity of many of them suggest the involvement of a trained architect, but a significant amount of research has failed to assign an architect's name to any of the projects he reported to the local press and the *Improvement Bulletin,* suggesting that he either did his designs himself or had an in-house designer.

34. A. Lawrence Kocher, "The American Country House," *Architectural Record,* November 1925.

35. Weyerhaeuser Corporation and Thome Corporation. Thome also used plans developed by William Ingemann and Kenneth Worthen, apparently through the same range of European and American-based styles that Lundie mined. The Thome name, usually under A(nna) N. Thome, appears on scores of building permits in the 1920s and 1930s; most of them are houses in Highland Park, Groveland, and King's Maplewood. Without the plans in hand or clear references in local newspapers or trade journals, it cannot safely be determined which of the architects was involved in any particular project.

36. A map plotting buildings erected between 1920 and 1925 was published in the *St. Paul Pioneer Press* on March 21, 1926. All of the major growth patterns of the late 1920s and the 1930s are anticipated in that map except for the explosion of housing and commercial construction in Highland Park.

37. The role of the Ford Plant and its ancillary projects in the history of St. Paul city planning and development deserves much more study and attention than it has gotten. I have relied for much of my information on the typescript of a lecture by Timothy Glines, "Development of the Twin Cities Ford Assembly Plant in St. Paul," delivered at the annual conference of the Society for Industrial Archeology in Minneapolis in April 1984.

38. A detailed statement on the Highland Park venture while it was still under way is given by city planning engineer George Herrold in *Improvement Bulletin,* October 1, 1927.

39. This quote, which has endless variations, appeared with an ASHSB plan in the *St. Paul Pioneer Press,* 1938, precise date unknown. The article on the plan continues, "When this house is built of good materials, real architecture results." See also the ad Moravec placed illustrating the house at 1680 Highland Parkway, in the *St. Paul Pioneer Press,* April 2, 1939, and several following Sundays.

40. The remodeling was featured as "The Home of the Month" in an article by Virginia Stafford for the regional sporting and style magazine *The Golfer and Sportsman,* May 1933, 31–33.

41. Michels, in "Encounter with Artists Number Nine."

42. Gebhard and Martinson identify it as a "central-hall Greek Revival house with Italianate detailing," whereas the Ramsey County Historic Sites Survey is content to call it an "Italianate style wood farmhouse." Both descriptions mistake the plan and the rectangular form of the 1929 remodeling for the original building. David Gebhard and Tom Martinson, *A Guide to the Architecture of Minnesota* (Minneapolis: University of Minnesota Press, 1977).

43. *St. Paul Pioneer Press,* June 8, 1930.

44. The Sunday *Pioneer Press* ran a full-page feature on the Princeton Avenue house every week from June 8 to October 5, 1930, then again from November 16 to December 21. Before-and-after views of the house were published on November 23, and finally, on the opening of the house to public view on December 7, the name of the architect was released in a brief interview. Remarked Lundie, "The home, with these restorative measures, may continue existence as a source of satisfaction to the occupants and of pleasure to the passerby." Nationally, homemakers' magazines led the way in popularizing modernization through stylistic upgrade, usually to some variant of Colonial Revival. Several of these designs were collected into a book edited by Harold Donaldson Eberle and Donald Greene Tarpley, *Remodelling and Adapting the Small House* (Philadelphia: J. B. Lippincott Co., 1933).

45. Beginning in 1910, several enormous speculative developments on Long Island were designed and built by period-revivalist Grosvenor Atterbury, all made with hollow-core concrete panels and all in the Jacobethan English style. These anticipated by several years the concrete houses of Wright and his followers. The original patent dates to 1908, two years after Wright's famous "Fireproof House for $5000," which was designed but never executed in poured concrete.

46. All of the St. Paul houses of "formless concrete" (i.e., block) construction so far discovered were speculative investments of local financier Truman Gardner. Who designed Gardner's houses has not been determined. The fact that draftsman-architect Harry

Firminger lived in one of them suggests that he may have been a designer for Gardner's company.

47. *St. Paul Pioneer Press,* May 19, 1935. This article on the house was accompanied by an excellent rendering of the design. The only other Steel Construction Products Company house that has been so far identified is the L. van Bergen House at 2177 Fairmount Avenue.

48. Heime and Lund were probably the company architects, with St. Paulite MacLeith acting as local supervisor. Porcelain steel panels returned to Twin Cities residential building with the Lustron houses of the post–World War II period. Most of the Minnesota examples were built in South Minneapolis. See Gebhard and Martinson, *A Guide to the Architecture of Minnesota,* 72.

49. The progress of construction was closely and enthusiastically monitored by the *St. Paul Pioneer Press.* For articles describing the house, see May 19 and September 29, 1935. The initial building permit reads "metal outside, wood inside."

50. Articles on the house were published in the *St. Paul Pioneer Press,* September 29, October 13, and October 27, 1935.

51. Weekly Sunday ads in the *St. Paul Pioneer Press* first focused on the novelty of the design ("Excitingly new! Excitingly different! A modern miracle of streamlined BEAUTY!") but quickly shifted to its suitability as a home ("Everyone's talking about the practical liveability"). See consecutive Sundays in October and November 1937.

52. For a lengthier discussion of the differences between "modernistic" and "modern," see Ada Louise Huxtable, *The Tall Building Artistically Considered* (New York: Pantheon Books, 1982), 39–45.

53. The "Home for $7,550" was part of a joint advertisement with a building and loan association, a lumberyard, a realtor-developer, a department store, and numerous building supply companies. Jemne's ad first appeared in the *St. Paul Pioneer Press,* June 2, 1935. Other architects working a modern vein, such as Ellerbe and Company and Kenneth Fullerton, also contributed their designs to the ad campaign. Telephone interview with Marjorie Edwards, June 18, 1990. The Edwardses, who have occupied the house since 1967, were longtime friends of Jemne and frequently heard him express his thoughts about the design of the house.

54. This information on Firminger's career is derived from the St. Paul City Directories, a scattering of drawings in trade periodicals and in the Charles A. Hausler collection at the Northwest Architectural Archives, and an interview with Margaret Marrinen in January 2005. As of this writing, most of Firminger's architectural records and drawings remain in private collections.

55. Between 1924 and 1929, the increase was from 34.3 percent to 62.3 percent. These figures are from the *Minneapolis Journal,* November 10, 1929.

56. Large illustrated ads for the Realty Service Company Apartments appeared for several weeks in local newspapers. The source of the adjectives quoted is a display ad headed "Own Your Own Apartment" in the *St. Paul Pioneer Press,* August 9, 1925.

57. "Terra Cotta: A Recent Example of Its Use in Building," *Common Clay* 2, no. 6 (June 1921): vi. *Common Clay* was a publication of the American Terra Cotta and Ceramic Company based in Chicago.

58. See Ramsey County Historic Sites Survey Form for 908 West University Avenue. Much of the information about Brioschi was apparently drawn from the unpublished Minnesota Historical Society Minnesota Biographies Project.

59. The Chapel of Our Lady of Victory was prominently featured in the *Western Architect,* June 1925.

60. For discussion of the St. Luke's and St. Catherine's designs in connection with other local bits of creative medieval archaeology, see Philip Larson, *World Architecture in Minnesota* (St. Paul: Minnesota Landmarks, 1979), 12–19.

61. For a contemporary description, see the feature in the *St. Paul Pioneer Press,* June 11, 1939. The source of the attribution to Hausler is the *Improvement Bulletin,* June 12, 1926.

62. The cost of the Red Wing Stoneware Company building was $21,000, an unusually large sum for a one-story commercial building of the period. See "$25,000 Midway Building Begun," *St. Paul Pioneer Press,* May 11, 1930; and obituary of Kenneth Fullerton, *St. Paul Dispatch,* January 22, 1960.

63. *St. Paul Pioneer Press,* August 9, 1925.

64. The so-called Dutch Mill service stations, attributed to local architect Myrtus Wright, were located at Third and Robert Streets, Dayton Avenue and Dale Street, Grand and Snelling Avenues, and Snelling and Edmund Avenues. All were demolished in the mid-1960s.

65. For a nationwide, cross-sectional review of this building type, see Richard Longstreth, *Main Street* (Washington, DC: Preservation Press, 1987), 68–75.

66. The Studebaker showroom, intended for new cars, was featured in the *St. Paul Pioneer Press,* February 2, 1930, along with a simpler used-car showroom up the street. The term *Zigzag Moderne* was first applied to Minnesota's early Art Deco buildings by David Gebhard. For examples and extended definitions, see Gebhard and Martinson, *A Guide to the Architecture of Minnesota,* 419.

67. The Frigidaire and Borchert-Ingersoll buildings are part of the recently created University-Raymond Historic District. The designation nomination form, which contains additional descriptive contextual information about the buildings, is in the St. Paul Heritage Preservation Office. The *St. Paul Pioneer Press,* January 19,

1930, published an early picture of the Borchert-Ingersoll building in a feature on recently sold and completed buildings.

68. "Guide to the Industrial Archeology of the Twin Cities," 116, an unpublished catalog of manufacturing and engineering structures prepared for the 1983 Annual Meetings of the Society of Industrial Archeology.

69. The paper reported a possible plan to expand the course to a full eighteen holes in 1925. For a linecut of the complex and a description of its 1925 addition, see the *St. Paul Pioneer Press,* September 20, 1925.

70. The rendering was credited to Wigington when first published in the *St. Paul Pioneer Press,* July 24, 1927, but City Architect Frank X. Tewes was given credit for "direct charge of the design," creating an ambiguity that was resolved when the city Board of Water Commissioners gave Wigington a posthumous tribute in 1977. Wigington's initials fill the box for "Architect in Charge" in the working drawings, now at the Northwest Architectural Archives.

71. "Guide to the Industrial Archeology of the Twin Cities," 28.

72. *St. Paul Pioneer Press,* August 1, 1925.

73. The quotation comes from an unpublished article on Jemne in the St. Paul Collection of St. Paul Public Library. Haupt's rendering was first published in local newspapers, then picked up by Cornelia Hallam Miller, "Regardez Les Femmes!" *Amateur Golfer and Sportsman,* November 1931, 22.

74. Miller, "Regardez Les Femmes!" 23. The building was also featured in *Architecture,* May 1932; *American Architect,* June 1932; and in a Parisian review of modern architecture in the United States in *La Revue Moderne,* August 1932.

75. Miller's article provides excellent illustrated descriptions of several of the Women's Club interiors shortly after completion; Miller, "Regardez Les Femmes!" 23–25. The ASID (D for Decorators) was established in 1931, with the Minnesota chapter forming in the spring of 1932. In 1935, it shortened its name to the SID, then in 1975 merged with the National Society of Interior Designers to form the ASID (D for Designers) of today.

76. The altered shell of the cosmetics factory held on at 2218 University Avenue until ca. 1988, when it was razed for a shopping strip. Some of the restaurant designs are listed in the only local publication on Wittkamp, Beverly Vavoulis's brief article, "Werner Wittkamp: Setting the Stage for the Gracious Life in St. Paul," *Architecture Minnesota,* June 1980, 22–23.

77. Attribution of the design to Hausler comes from an interview with his son, Donald Hausler, who at the time (September 1981) held several of the renderings from his father's office. These have since been donated to the Northwest Architectural Archives.

78. For a complete account of the political processes surrounding both the building of the new courthouse and the disposing of the old site, see Dane Smith, "The City Hall-County Courthouse and Its First Fifty Years," *Ramsey County History* 17, no. 1 (1981): 3–16.

79. Interestingly, Milles's first designs for the monument were of a piece with the limpid, romantic style in vogue in Sweden since the turn of the century. The aggressive geometries of the final design were unique in his work, before or since.

80. A sketch of the proposed high-rise was published in the *St. Paul Pioneer Press,* September 22, 1929. Saarinen's Chicago Tribune design received wide circulation and universal accolades, though it came in second in the competition.

81. For a more complete account of the place of the First National Bank design in the rising skylines of the Twin Cities, see Paul Clifford Larson, "Tall Tales: The Twin Cities' First Towers," *Architecture Minnesota,* March 1989.

82. Gebhard and Martinson, *A Guide to the Architecture of Minnesota,* devised the term *PWA Moderne.* It leads to many anachronisms, such as its use for buildings designed outside of or even prior to PWA sponsorship. For a fuller account of Wigington's contributions to city architecture, see David Vassar Taylor and Paul Clifford Larson, *Cap Wigington: An Architectural Legacy in Ice and Stone* (St. Paul: Minnesota Historical Society Press, 2001).

83. See the *St. Paul Pioneer Press,* May 16 and May 30, 1926.

84. The working drawings for the Ace Café prototype survive in the archives of Ellerbe Becket in Minneapolis. No other instances of the Ace Café design have been discovered.

85. *St. Paul Pioneer Press,* August 22, 1937.

4. PLANNING THE MODERN CITY, 1940–1985

1. Max Shulman, *The Zebra Derby* (Garden City, NY: Doubleday and Company, 1946), 20, 22.

2. The Wilder survey was reported in the *American City* 18 (May 1918): 406. Its most immediate result was a strong housing ordinance, although it may also have stimulated interest in formulating a citywide plan; see Gary Phelps, "Aronovici's Campaign to Clean Up St. Paul," *Ramsey County History* 15, no. 1 (1980): 11–17.

3. For a review of the City Planning Board's proposals for street-widening, see *Engineering News-Record* 87 (November 3, 1921): 735. The Third Street widening plan was reported in the *St. Paul Dispatch,* June 5, 1929. A favorable feature on its completion appeared in *Collier's,* January 10, 1931, 54. See also "Kellogg

Boulevard: The Story of Old Third Street," *Ramsey County History* (Fall 1969): 14–15.

4. The evolution of Gilbert's Capitol approach plans is discussed in Gary Phelps, *History of the Minnesota State Capitol Area* (St. Paul: Capitol Area Architectural and Planning Board, 1983).

5. *Plan of Saint Paul* (St. Paul: City Planning Board, 1922).

6. George Herrold, "Capitol Approaches," n.d., Herrold Papers, Minnesota Historical Society.

7. "The Twin Cities: An Examination of Minneapolis and an Autopsy on St. Paul," *Fortune Magazine* 13 (April 1936): 118–19.

8. The housing statistics are from George H. Herrold, *The St. Paul Housing Situation: An Analysis of the Real Property Inventory Made for the Citizens' Housing Committee, St. Paul, Minnesota* (Minnesota Emergency Relief Administration Project, 1934), 5–6, 29. Herrold discusses the grant in "The Story of Planning St. Paul," George Herrold Papers, Minnesota Historical Society, 92. On the St. Paul Apartment House Owners' Association and Minnesota's rejection of the federal low-income housing program, see *Housing Yearbook 1938*, ed. Coleman Woodbury (Chicago: National Association of Housing Officials, n.d.), 76–77; *Housing Yearbook 1941*, ed. Coleman Woodbury and Edmond H. Hoben (Chicago: National Association of Housing Officials, n.d.), 108; *Housing Yearbook 1943*, ed. Hugh R. Pomeroy and Edmond H. Hoben (Chicago: National Association of Housing Officials, n.d.), 17. The PWA did select Minneapolis for a pilot housing project, which was to remain in federal ownership because of the legislature's failure to support a program for the state as a whole; see Jeffrey A. Hess, "Sumner Field Homes: Public Housing in Minnesota before World War II," *Hennepin History* 52 (Winter 1993): 4–17.

9. "Highland Village," *St. Paul Pioneer Press*, October 15, 1939; "$4 Million Deal Is Transacted," *Minneapolis Tribune*, October 28, 1939; *Housing Directory 1946–1947* (Chicago: National Association of Housing Officials, 1946), 157; C. W. Short and R. Stanley-Brown, *Public Buildings* (Washington, DC: Government Printing Office, 1939), 660.

10. George H. Herrold reported in detail on the formation of the United Civic Council in "St. Paul Forms United Civic Council," *Minnesota Municipalities* (September 1942), abridged in "Joint Study of City Problems by Civic Group," *American City* 57 (November 1942): 71.

11. "An Improvement Program for Downtown St. Paul," *Engineering News-Record* 131 (July 29, 1943); see also newspaper articles dated February 5, 8, 1944, in John J. McDonough Papers, scrapbook vol. 3, Minnesota Historical Society.

12. The first major historical assessment of Loewy's career was the exhibition "Raymond Loewy, Pioneer of American Industrial Design," organized by the International Design Center in Berlin, Germany, in 1990. The exhibition sponsored an excellent series of essays compiled in *Raymond Loewy*, ed. Angela Schonberger (Munich: Prestel-Verlag, 1990).

13. Snaith joined Raymond Loewy Associates in 1936, became a partner in 1945 and the company's president in 1961; for biographical details, see the obituary of William T. Snaith in *Interiors* 133 (April 1974): 40; *Industrial Design* 21 (April 1974): 10. The goals of the planning study are briefly sketched in Raymond Loewy Associates, "Proposal for Development of the St. Paul City Plan," February 21, 1944, Minnesota Historical Society.

14. Loewy's plan was never publicly printed, and apparently no copy has survived. Our discussion is based on Herrold's detailed description in "The Story of Planning St. Paul," 160–65, and on a fourteen-part series in the local press written by reporter Franklin Page. The newspaper coverage, containing extensive quotations from the original study, began on March 25, 1945, in the morning *St. Paul Pioneer Press* with a piece titled "Loop Face Lifting Program Outlined," and then continued with the following articles in the afternoon *St. Paul Dispatch:* "Loop Business Can Be Materially Increased," March 26; "New Roads Would Bring Trade to City," March 27; "8 Plans Suggested to Improve Streets," March 28; "Two Traffic Bottlenecks Scheduled for Elimination Here," March 29; "City's Short Blocks Called Traffic Dam," March 30; "Rim of Garages Is Urged for Loop," April 1; "New Bus Depot and Rail Plaza to 'Re-Vitalize' Loop Area Urged," April 2; "Kellogg Blvd. Hailed as Site for Modern Housing Units," April 3; "More St. Paul Hotel Facilities Urged," April 4; " 'Face Lifting' for Stores Urged," April 5; "Amusement Area Recommended Here," April 6; "Loop Revitalization Cost 'Far Below Gain,' " April 7.

15. Raymond Loewy, *Never Leave Well Enough Alone* (New York: Simon and Schuster, 1951), 77, 213–15. The quotation is from Raymond Loewy Associates, "Proposal," n.p.

16. Loewy, *Never Leave Well Enough Alone*, 219.

17. Ibid.

18. Herrold, "The Story of Planning St. Paul," 165. In 1953, Murphy expanded the facade treatment; see "Glamour of New Orleans Brought to St. Paul Loop," *St. Paul Dispatch*, March 24, 1948; "Beauty of New Shop Dazzles Crowd," *Pioneer Press*, April 22, 1953.

19. "Davidson Architectural Porcelain Enamel," *Northwest Architect*, 16 (May-June 1952): 36.

20. "Remodeling Will Make Golden Rule Ultra-Modernistic," *St. Paul Pioneer Press*, August 27, 1950.

21. The Emporium first considered a face-lift in 1945. The store's vice president at that time, Russell Ratigan, had served as

chairman of the committee sponsoring Loewy's planning study, and it is therefore not surprising that Loewy was retained for the remodeling job. Loewy's original concept for the Emporium called for a glass and granite entrance arcade and "an entire new front" of unknown design for the main Robert Street facade. The final design for the makeover, completed in 1959, was credited to Ellerbe and Company of St. Paul. Loewy probably exerted a continuing influence, since he designed a restaurant space for the store during the exterior remodeling. When the Emporium building was rehabilitated for office space in the 1980s, almost all of the aluminum siding was replaced by blue reflective glass. See "Million-Dollar Remodeling Will Be Launched Feb. 1 at Emporium," *St. Paul Dispatch,* December 2, 1945; "A New Plastic Exterior" and "Emporium Exterior to Be Improved," *Dispatch,* September 26, 1957; "Emporium Unveils Million Dollar New Look" and "Loewy-Designed Rose Tree Room Makes Eating Fun," *St. Paul Pioneer Press,* August 30, 1959; "New Face," *Minneapolis Star,* September 14, 1959.

22. See Loewy, *Never Leave Well Enough Alone,* 202–3; Angela Schonberger, "Inside, Outside: Loewy's Interiors and Architecture," in *Raymond Loewy,* 105–6.

23. "Emporium Exterior to Be Improved," *St. Paul Dispatch,* September 26, 1957.

24. For a brief history of Ellerbe and Company, see *The Ellerbe Tradition,* ed. Bonnie Richter (Minneapolis: Ellerbe, Inc., 1980). On the company's postwar growth, see "50-Year Old Ellerbe Firm Looks to Future," *Northwest Architect* 22 (March-April 1958): 35, 39; "Twin Cities Firms among 'Biggest,'" *Northwest Architect* 26 (July-August 1962): 91.

25. For Ellerbe's remarks on Modern aesthetics, see "A Company's Experience Guides Architect in Functional Design," *Northwest Architect* 9 (March-April 1955): 16–18; "50-Year-Old Ellerbe Firm Looks to Future," 39. The comment concerning stone's symbolic virtues was made in regard to another stone box, the Minnesota Mutual Life Insurance Company Building (345 Cedar Street), erected in the downtown district in 1955; see "A Minnesota Insurance Company Builds with Fine Minnesota Materials," *Northwest Architect* 18 (May-June 1954): 26.

26. "Jury Reports on Design Competition," *Northwest Architect* 10, no. 4 (1946): 10–12.

27. W. Brooks Cavin Jr., interview by Jeffrey A. Hess, April 3, 1991.

28. On the construction of the Veterans' Service Building, see Jo Blatti, "The Minnesota State Capitol Complex, the 1940s to the 1980s," prepared for the Governor's Office, 1987, 26–35.

29. The rejection of Mendelsohn's more dynamic concept of the exterior may have been as much a result of skyrocketing costs occasioned by the onset of the Korean War as it was a matter of the congregation's conservative tastes; W. Gunther Plaut, *Mount Zion: The First Hundred Years* (St. Paul: North Central Publishing Co., 1980), 3–6, 109–10; Bruno Levi, *Erich Mendelsohn* (New York: Rizzoli, 1985), 191; "Mount Zion Temple: A Dramatic Place of Worship," *Northwest Architect* 19 (July-August 1955): 22–23.

30. On Mann and the early architectural program at the University of Minnesota, see James Gray, *The University of Minnesota 1851–1951* (Minneapolis: University of Minnesota Press, 1951), 326–27; "Mann, U of Minnesota Architecture School Founder, Dies in California," *Northwest Architect* 23 (November-December 1959): 35; Bernard Jacob, "As It Were," *Sala Libre,* 4–16, manuscript draft. For a helpful discussion of the Beaux-Arts tradition and its tremendous impact on American architectural education, see Turpin C. Bannister, ed., *The Architect at Mid-Century* (New York: Reinhold Publishing Corporation, 1954), 1:96–103.

31. S. C. Lind, "The Institute of Technology—Its Organization and Objectives," *Bulletin of the Minnesota Federation of Architectural and Engineering Societies* 23 (January 1938): 4; Roy Jones, "A Brief Account of the Early Years of the School of Architecture, University of Minnesota," *Northwest Architect* 25 (March-April 1961): 22; Jacob, "As It Were," 12.

32. Roy Childs Jones, letter to L. D. Coffman, June 27, 1938; Jones to S. C. Lind, August 20, 1938, in Papers of the Institute of Technology, Box 13, University of Minnesota Archives.

33. Cerny described his activities during his four years away from Minnesota in a letter to Roy Childs Jones, dated April 21, 1936, in Papers of the Institute of Technology, Box 13, University of Minnesota Archives. Commenting on Cerny's role as an employer, architect Frederick Bentz, himself a Cerny alumnus, wrote in 1976: "A casual review of the last Minnesota Society of Architects roster pinpoints his influence on the profession. I found 52 principals in firms who owe some or the greater part of their training to experience in his office. More than one firm in five listed in the roster has one or more principals who are 'Cerny graduates'"; Frederick Bentz, "Robert Cerny Master Architect," *Architecture Minnesota* 1 (July-August 1975): 53–54; see also "Robert Cerny Dies," *Minneapolis Star,* February 1, 1985.

34. Bentz, "Robert Cerny Master Architect," 52.

35. Students pursuing a bachelor of architecture degree, normally a five-year program, were required to submit a final thesis; see Roy Jones, "Architecture," *Bulletin of the Minnesota Federation of Architectural and Engineering Societies* 23 (January 1938): 18. The discussion of the changing nature of student work is based upon an examination of surviving theses filed in Walter Library, University of Minnesota. The earliest identified example of an

International style design is found in Janet Bollum, "Project for an Apartment Nursery," undergraduate architecture thesis, 1939.

36. Bentz, "Robert Cerny Master Architect," 52.

37. Louis Lundgren, interview by Jeffrey A. Hess, March 28, 1991. St. Luke's School is described in "Designed for Children," *Northwest Architect* 15 (September-October 1951): 18, 20. In 1972, Haarstick and Lundgren parted company, forming Haarstick Associates, Inc., and Lundgren Associates, Inc. On the growth and eventual dissolution of their partnership, see "Haarstick-Lundgren Expands," *Northwest Architect* 17 (March-April 1953): 16; "Haarstick, Lundgren and Associates Inc.," *Northwest Architect* 21 (September-October 1957): 21–30; "D.S. Haarstick Founds New Architect Firm," *St. Paul Pioneer Press,* April 4, 1972.

38. Richard F. Hammel, "St. Paul Pushes New Construction and Rehabilitation Program," *Northwest Architect* 16 (November-December 1952): 4–5, 19–20.

39. For statistics on postwar residential construction, see "Building Trends in Saint Paul, 1940–1966," unpublished report prepared by St. Paul City Planning Board, November 1967, in St. Paul Collection, St. Paul Public Library. Hammel's hiring by the St. Paul Board of Education is discussed in Bette Jones Hammel, *From Bauhaus to Bowties* (Minneapolis: Hammel, Green and Abrahamson, 1989), 5–6.

40. For Hammel's design guidelines, see "Program for Addition to Chelsea Heights School," 1951, 8–10, in Louis Lundgren Collection, Northwest Architectural Archives, University of Minnesota. Hammel presented his general philosophy of school design, illumination, and construction in "St. Paul Pushes New Construction and Rehabilitation Program," 4–5, 19–21; "Manufactured Light versus Daylight for Schoolrooms," *Northwest Architect* 19 (July-August 1955): 34–35, 37, 39, 66–69, 71, 75; see also Hammel, *From Bauhaus to Bowties,* 5, 8.

41. On the formation of the Hammel-Green partnership, see Hammel, *From Bauhaus to Bowties,* 6–9. For Green's concerns about brickwork in the Chelsea Heights School project, see Robert E. Howe, "Memorandum," November 7, 1951; Curtis H. Green, "Memorandum," April 25, 1951; Green to Hammel, April 25, 1951, in Lundgren Collection, Northwest Architectural Archives.

42. Bruce Abrahamson, interview by Jeffrey A. Hess, April 23, 1991; see also Hammel, *From Bauhaus to Bowties,* 9–10.

43. For Abrahamson's original intentions concerning the house, see "Residence for Bruce A. Abrahamson," *Northwest Architect* 23 (September-October 1959): 29. He acknowledged the design's uneconomical aspects in Abrahamson, interview. Located at 7205 Shannon Drive in Edina, Minnesota, the building has been enlarged since its completion in 1956. Other young architects, especially in California, also experimented with the residential steel frame in the 1950s, with results similar to those of Abrahamson; see Esther McCoy, *Modern California Houses: Case Study Houses, 1945–1962* (New York: Reinhold Publishing, 1962), 70–71.

44. "Grant Store Will Erect Big Building," *St. Paul Dispatch,* March 15, 1954; "New 2 Million-Dollar Grant Store Opens Thursday," *Dispatch,* November 9, 1955. Located at the intersection of Seventh and Cedar Streets, the building was later demolished to make way for the Town Square project.

45. For an excellent discussion of Mies's designs, see Franz Schulze, *Mies van der Rohe: A Critical Biography* (Chicago and London: University of Chicago Press, 1985), 224–27, 241–44.

46. Abrahamson, interview; Hammel, *From Bauhaus to Bowties,* 13–14.

47. For a brief description of the Group Health building, see "Health Insurance and Outpatient Clinic," *Architectural Record* (March 1958). The building has been so extensively remodeled that it no longer resembles its original design.

48. Just as a corrugated piece of cardboard has greater strength and rigidity than a flat piece of the same section, so folded-plate concrete roofs are capable of larger clear spans than flat slabs. According to the noted historian of building technology, Carl W. Condit, "folded plates as covers for an entire enclosure did not appear in the United States until about 1950"; *American Building* (Chicago: University of Chicago Press, 1982), 279.

49. Foster Dunwiddie, interview by Jeffrey A. Hess, August 8, 16, 1991; "The Story behind Midwest Federal's Progress and Leadership" (Minneapolis: Midwest Federal, 1968).

50. Gwendolyn Wright, *Building the Dream* (Cambridge, MA: MIT Press, 1983), 251. "In Discussion-Rich Sessions Minnesota Society Elects E. R. Cone President," *Northwest Architect* 15 (May-June 1951): 8.

51. Donald and Elizabeth Lampland, interview by Jeffrey A. Hess, June 22, 1991. Authorized in the spring of 1945, the Edgcumbe Road project was originally intended as housing for war-plant workers, but the war ended before construction was completed; see "Houses Will Be for War Plant Workers," *St. Paul Dispatch,* April 1, 1945; "St. Paulites Spending $1,500,000 on New Homes," *St. Paul Dispatch,* August 10, 1945. The Lamplands' transition from Cape Cod bungalow in the late 1940s to ranch house rambler in the early 1950s was part of a general stylistic shift in the Twin Cities; see Rebecca Lou Smith, *Postwar Housing in National and Local Perspective* (Minneapolis: Center for Urban and Regional Affairs, University of Minnesota, 1978), 23–25. The distrust of Modern design as an investment was apparently shared by many architects as well.

52. John Normile, "One Story—But Three Bedrooms," *Better Homes and Gardens* 26 (November 1947): 46; see also Thomas Hine, "The Search for the Postwar House," *Blueprints for Modern Living: History and Legacy of the Case Study Houses* (Cambridge, MA: MIT Press, 1989), 180. For descriptions of the Lampland House, see "Home of 2004 [Lower St. Dennis Road] Embodies New Building Techniques with Extensive Savings in Cost," *Mississippi Valley Lumberman* 84 (November 14, 1952): 7, 10; "Lumberman's Residence Spotlights Latest Building Procedures," *Northwest Architect* 17 (January-February 1953): 10, 13.

53. "Norman C. Nagle, Architect," *Everyday Art Quarterly* 22 (Spring 1952): 4. Trained in architecture and planning at the University of Michigan and Cranbrook Academy, Nagle became an assistant professor of architecture at the University of Minnesota in 1948. He remained a part-time faculty member while employed at the Walker, resuming full-time teaching in 1958; see "Norman C. Nagle," *Notes and Comments from the Walker Art Center* (May 1952), n.p.; "Services Set Friday for Norman C. Nagle," *Minneapolis Star,* January 19, 1965.

54. "On a Minnesota Hillside: A Mezzanine House," *House and Home* 1 (April 1952): 94–95.

55. Bonnie Richter, "Elizabeth Close Minnesota's Premiere Woman Architect," *Architecture Minnesota* 4 (March-April 1978): 27–29; Linda Mack, "Close Associates," *Architecture Minnesota* 9 (January-February 1983): 42–47; David Smith, "Pioneer Architect Elizabeth Close Still Opening Doors to New Design," *St. Paul Dispatch,* April 13, 1983.

56. For background on the university's "faculty ghetto," see Rollin C. Chapin, "University Grove—A Restricted Homesite Development for Faculty Members," *Bulletin of the Minnesota Federation of Architectural and Engineering Societies* 15 (July 1930): 13; Bruce N. Wright, "St. Paul's University Grove: A Designed Community," *Architecture Minnesota* (May-June 1979).

57. Marlin Bree, "Sod House," *Minneapolis Tribune Picture Magazine,* August 4, 1968, 4–5, 10.

58. The Close quote is in Richter, "Elizabeth Close Minnesota's Premiere Woman Architect," 29.

59. Rapson's quote is from "AIA First Honor Award—1955: American Embassy Stockholm, Sweden," *Northwest Architect* 19 (May-June 1955): 39. The quote about Rapson is from Frederick Koeper, "A Master of Modernism," *Architecture Minnesota* 10 (August 1984): 43. The discussion of Rapson's background draws on Ralph Rapson, interview by Jeffrey A. Hess, April 5, 1991; Koeper, "A Master of Modernism," 38–43.

60. Rapson made the comment on University Grove during an interview by Hess, April 4, 1991. His quote concerning design and environment is from "'U' Architect Designs 'Doughnut' House for Inexpensive Living," *Minneapolis Sunday Tribune,* September 16, 1956. Rapson also believed that the environment should be exploited when the site warranted it. He was, for example, quite critical of the University of Minnesota for failing to take advantage of the Mississippi River in its design of the West Bank campus: "Although the original [Cass] Gilbert plan did recognize the river, the university has chosen to turn its back on that view and thus ignore a fabulous setting"; see "Rapson Looks Askance at University of Minnesota Campus," *Northwest Architect* 24 (May-June 1960).

61. For a sampler of Rapson designs, see "Ralph Rapson AIA," *Northwest Architect* 24 (January-February 1960): 18–29. To keep the cost of the Shepherd House below the university's ceiling of $27,500, Rapson covered the side elevations with white-painted Masonite, which did not hold up well in the Minnesota climate. When Shepherd eventually replaced the Masonite with redwood siding, Rapson urged him to paint it white, as in the original color scheme. Shepherd declined and instead gave the redwood a coat of stain, introducing a false "woodsy" note into the design; William G. Shepherd, interview by Jeffrey A. Hess, May 30, 1991; "View, Too," *Minneapolis Tribune,* October 5, 1958.

62. City Planning Board of St. Paul, *Preliminary Land Use Plan* (St. Paul: City Planning Board of St. Paul, 1959), 201; Don Boxmeyer, "Building of Homes Down Again," *St. Paul Dispatch,* March 24, 1971; "Home-Building Pace Heads Back Upward," *St. Paul Pioneer Press,* April 2, 1972.

63. Carl G. Langland, "Last of Housing Units for Vets Soon to Close," *St. Paul Dispatch,* May 30, 1956; "History of Public Housing and Urban Renewal in St. Paul," 1–2; n.d., Microfilm Roll 1, St. Paul HRA Papers, Minnesota Historical Society.

64. The quotation is attributed to State Representative Eugene J. McCarthy in "Low-Renters Not Socialistic Plan," *St. Paul Dispatch,* November 2, 1951. See also "McDonough Homes, St. Paul's First Low-Rent Housing Units, Dedicated," *St. Paul Pioneer Press,* September 18, 1951; "Roosevelt Homes Open," *St. Paul Pioneer Press,* November 1, 1951.

65. "History of Public Housing and Urban Renewal in St. Paul," 5–12.

66. The Mt. Airy site was first considered by the HRA in 1951 but rejected because of the cost of developing its uneven terrain. Changing architects required the HRA to fire their attorney and former chairman, William B. Randall. Construction was unusually slow, taking from 1955 to 1959. The 446-unit complex featured a ten-story apartment building intended primarily for the elderly, as well as about ninety two-story apartment buildings and row

houses. See "Home Outlook Indefinite," *St. Paul Pioneer Press,* March 6, 1952; "HRA Hires New Architect," *St. Paul Pioneer Press,* September 25, 1954; "Butler Wins OK to Design Mt. Airy Job," *St. Paul Pioneer Press,* February 12, 1955.

67. Davidson's criticisms were first publicly aired in a downtown planning workshop that included the city's mayor, the directors of the St. Paul and Minneapolis HRAs, and a number of St. Paul businessmen; see "Redevelopment Plans Get Sharp Criticism," *St. Paul Pioneer Press,* May 27, 1957.

68. Philip Troy's remarks are quoted in "Redevelopment Plans Get Sharp Criticism." For the HRA's original plans for the Capitol area, see Fred W. Fisher, "St. Paul Plans to Revitalize Its Capitol Area through Redevelopment," *American City* 67 (October 1952), 106–7; "St. Paul—'Capitol Approach' to Redevelopment," *Journal of Housing* 9 (October 1952): 342–44. On the agency's trials and tribulations, see Alan A. Altshuler, *The City Planning Process* (Ithaca, NY: Cornell University Press, 1965), 75–76; Alan A. Altshuler, *A Report on Politics in St. Paul, Minnesota* (Cambridge, MA: Edward C. Banfield Joint Center for Urban Studies of the Massachusetts Institute of Technology and Harvard University, 1959), part 6, 8–9; Judith A. Martin and Anthony Goddard, *Past Choices/Present Landscapes: The Impact of Urban Renewal on the Twin Cities* (Minneapolis: Center for Urban and Regional Affairs, 1989), 26–30.

69. George H. Herrold, "Disruption, Long Chaos Seen in Proposed Twin Cities Freeway," *Northwest Architect* 20 (September-October 1956): 47; "Veteran Planner Retires after 40 Years' Service to St. Paul," *American City* 68 (April 1953): 96. For an excellent discussion of Herrold and the planning of Interstate 94 in St. Paul, see Altshuler, *The City Planning Process,* 17–83.

70. Altshuler, *The City Planning Process,* 54–56, 88–93, 131.

71. City Planning Board of St. Paul, *A Report on Central Business District, St. Paul, Minnesota* (St. Paul, 1958), 1, 3.

72. Ibid., 6, 9, 16–17.

73. Ibid., 68–69. On the report's hostile reception, see Altshuler, *The City Planning Process,* 131.

74. "Downtown, Inc., Picks 18 Directors," *St. Paul Dispatch,* June 6, 1955. The quotation is from an interview with Nason in Virginia Brainard Kunz, *St. Paul: A Modern Renaissance* (Northridge, CA: Windsor Publications, 1986), 17–18.

75. "Plan for St. Paul Loop Modernization Speeds Up," *St. Paul Pioneer Press,* April 15, 1956.

76. "Architects Offer 'Dream' Plan for Loop," *St. Paul Pioneer Press,* July 8, 1956; "St. Paul Gets Plan for Shopping Mall," *Minneapolis Tribune,* July 8, 1956; "Minneapolis and St. Paul Architects Develop Plans for Improving Cities' Loops' Attractions," *Northwest Architect* 20 (July-August 1956): 22–27.

77. For Gruen's philosophy of shopping, see Victor Gruen and Larry Smith, *Shopping Towns USA* (New York: Reinhold Publishing Corporation, 1960), 146–47. He discusses Southdale in Victor Gruen, *Centers for the Urban Environment* (New York: Van Nostrand Reinhold Company, 1973), 33–39.

78. Victor Gruen Associates, *A Greater Fort Worth Tomorrow* (Greater Fort Worth Planning Committee, 1956); see also "Typical Downtown Transformed," *Architectural Forum* 104 (May 1956): 146–55. On the remarkable influence of Gruen's Fort Worth plan, see "Upgrading Downtown," *Architectural Record* 137 (June 1965): 176. On the hiring of Gruen, see Gordon Richmond, "Plan Drawn to Make Loop Traffic Free Shopper Center," *St. Paul Pioneer Press,* December 8, 1957.

79. "Loop Advised to Go Modern," *St. Paul Pioneer Press,* August 5, 1958; "Group Back City Council on Freeway," *St. Paul Dispatch,* February 18, 1959; "City to Get Blueprint of Improvement Plan," *St. Paul Pioneer Press,* October 9, 1960; Carl G. Langland, "City to Plan Own Loop Improving," *St. Paul Pioneer Press,* December 10, 1961.

80. "A Downtown Store with Indoor Parking," *Architectural Record* (June 1964): 171.

81. Nason's remark is quoted by Mary Davis in *Architecture Minnesota* 1 (July-August 1975): 48. On Minneapolis's urban renewal effort, see Martin and Goddard, *Past Choices/Present Landscapes,* 60–69.

82. For an excellent discussion of the traditional roles of labor and business in St. Paul politics, see Altshuler, *A Report on Politics in St. Paul,* part 2, 1–13; part 4, 1–11.

83. "7 Named to Develop Loop Plans," *St. Paul Dispatch,* September 10, 1962; "MIC Was Brainchild of Mayor Vavoulis," *St. Paul Pioneer Press,* August 19, 1962; "Saint Paul Today," *Northwest Architect* 32 (January-February 1968): 36.

84. Carl G. Langland, "City to Plan Own Loop Improving," *St. Paul Pioneer Press,* December 10, 1961; Herbert C. Wieland, "Planning St. Paul's Central Business District," *Northwest Architect* 26 (November-December 1962): 26–27.

85. For descriptions of the Capital Centre project in its original form, see the following articles in the *St. Paul Dispatch* of August 16, 1962: "Master Plan for Downtown Given to Council," "Loop Rebuilding Proposed," "Convenient, Attractive Downtown Is Goal," "Here's Block-by-Block Description," "Council Asked to OK Request for Federal Funds." The MIC also put out a lavishly illustrated promotional brochure: *Capital Centre: A Project for the Central Business District of Downtown Saint Paul* (St. Paul: Metropolitan Improvement Committee, [1962]). On the plan's origins, see the following pieces in *Northwest Architect:* Robert

Van Hoef, "Capital Centre," 26 (November-December 1962): 17–25; "Saint Paul Today," 32 (January-February 1968): 27–59.

86. On the planning board's work, see Herbert C. Wieland, "Planning St. Paul's Central Business District," *Northwest Architect* 26 (November-December 1962): 27–29, 51.

87. Langland, "City to Plan Own Loop Improving"; Bentz, "Robert Cerny Master Architect," 53.

88. For Dimond's quote, see "Convenient, Attractive Downtown Is Goal," *St. Paul Dispatch,* August 16, 1962.

89. Lundgren's quote is in "Convenient, Attractive Downtown Is Goal." For the second comment, see "St. Paul's Goal—A Downtown without Weather," *St. Paul Pioneer Press,* September 12, 1965. On the skyway system in general, see "St. Paul to Relieve Pedestrians," *Engineering News-Record* (April 13, 1967): 37; "Sidewalks in the Sky," *Northwest Architect* 36 (January-February 1972): 28–31.

90. "Crowd Cheers Loop Rebuilding as Details Told," *St. Paul Dispatch,* August 16, 1962.

91. "Wabasha Court Project Starts," *St. Paul Dispatch,* April 1, 1964; "Wabasha Court," *Northwest Architect* 29 (September-October 1965): 28. The enclosure of the pedestrian court in the late 1970s diminished the building's precise jewel-box quality; see "Wabasha Court," *C[itizens] L[eague] News* 27 (January 20, 1978): 3.

92. Abrahamson, interview.

93. Paul Presbrey, "Contract Awarded for 'Superblock' in Downtown St. Paul," *Minneapolis Tribune,* February 4, 1965; *Progressive Architecture* 46 (August 1965): 53; Sam Newlund, "St. Paul Starting 12-Block Project," *New York Times,* March 7, 1965.

94. For Osborn's remarks, see the following stories in the *St. Paul Dispatch* of October 26, 1965: Don Larson, "23-Story Structure Due in Capital Centre"; Kathryn Boardman, "Detergent Firm Headquarters to Be Model of Cleanliness." On the Lever House, see "Shiny New Sight: Soap Maker's Washable Building Is World's Glassiest," *Life* 32 (June 2, 1952): 44–46.

95. Pamphlet on Osborn Building in Minnesota Historical Society.

96. The Osborn Building is described in "The Osborn Building," *Northwest Architect* 32 (November-December 1968): 24–39; "Clean, Clean," *Progressive Architecture* 49 (July 1968): 51.

97. "New Structure Graces Skyline" and Alan LeWin, "New Building Will Become Part of Superblock Skywalk System," both in *St. Paul Pioneer Press,* July 13, 1969.

98. Herbert C. Wieland, "Planning St. Paul's Central Business District," *Northwest Architect* 26 (November-December 1962): 31.

99. Financing was made possible by a limited partnership that included the architectural team known as Convention Center Architects and Engineers, Inc. See "32-Floor Apartment Project in Loop OKd," *St. Paul Dispatch,* December 1, 1965; Eleanor Ostman, "Kellogg Square: New Luxury in Downtown Area," *St. Paul Pioneer Press,* April 16, 1972; Don W. Larson, "Downtown Experiment Succeeding," *St. Paul Pioneer Press,* April 22, 1973.

100. Don W. Larson, "St. Paul Loop Takes on Different Look," *St. Paul Pioneer Press,* January 22, 1966; Glenn F. Ickler, "Buildings Keep Rising Despite Tight Money," *St. Paul Pioneer Press,* January 22, 1967.

101. Virgil W. Smith, "Loop's Future Seems Bright," *St. Paul Pioneer Press,* January 24, 1971; "Capital Centre Addition Begun," *St. Paul Pioneer Press,* May 18, 1971; David Gebhard and Tom Martinson, *A Guide to the Architecture of Minnesota* (Minneapolis: University of Minnesota Press, 1977), 85.

102. "Building a Contemporary Classic," *St. Paul Pioneer Press,* April 13, 1975; "HRA to End Downtown Renewal," *St. Paul Pioneer Press,* March 29, 1974.

103. On home ownership, see Altshuler, *A Report on Politics in St. Paul,* part 1.

104. Gingold's remark is from "New St. Paul High Rise Apartment Has Special Construction Features," *Northwest Architect* 26 (July-August 1962): 102–3. See also "High-Rise Apartment in St. Paul Will View Valley," *Northwest Architect* 23 (November-December 1959): 55; Ralph Mason, "5-Million, 23-Story Apartment Building Planned on Riverfront," *Minneapolis Star,* September 22, 1959; Carl Hennemann, "New Apartments to Look Like UN," *St. Paul Dispatch,* September 22, 1959; "Fete Set for Plush Apartments," *St. Paul Dispatch,* March 2, 1961.

105. The Central Apartments are described in "Three Area Designs Win PHA Awards," *Northwest Architect* 28 (September-October 1964): 42–43.

106. As quoted in "To Be or Not to Be, That Is the Metropolitan Question," undated newspaper clipping attributed to *Minneapolis Tribune,* in Metropolitan Building File, Minneapolis History Collection, Minneapolis Public Library. On the movement to preserve the building, see "Save Metropolitan Committee Selected," *Minneapolis Star,* June 20, 1959.

107. As quoted in "St. Paul Planning Board Sets Up Historic Sites Unit," *Northwest Architect* 25 (May-June 1961): 35. DeCoster discussed her participation in St. Paul activities in an interview by Jeffrey A. Hess in August 1992.

108. As quoted in "Saint Paul Today," *Northwest Architect,* 58. DeCoster discussed the survey's origins in her foreword to H. F. Koeper, *Historic St. Paul Buildings* (St. Paul: St. Paul City Planning Board, 1964).

109. "Saint Paul Today," 28.

110. Georgia Ray DeCoster, "St. Paul's Stately Old Buildings—Going, Going, Almost Gone," *Ramsey County History* 2 (Spring 1965): 10–15.

111. "Old Courts Building Wins Historic Status," *St. Paul Dispatch*, March 25, 1969; Mary E. Osman, "A St. Paul Landmark Saved by a Bill," *AIA Journal* 61 (March 1974): 33–37; "A New Landmark Center for St. Paul," *Architectural Record* 164 (December 1978): 100–105.

112. David A. Lanegran, "Neighborhood Conservation in the Twin Cities," *Architecture Minnesota* (July-August 1978): 14–18.

113. The quotes are from "West Seventh Plans Unveiled," *St. Paul Pioneer Press*, September 3, 1971. See also Don Ahern, "Plan to Demolish Area Hit," *St. Paul Pioneer Press*, September 22, 1971; "Controversial Plan Defeated," *St. Paul Dispatch*, November 4, 1971; Gareth Hiebert, "Optimism Flavors Attitude of W. Seventh Residents," *St. Paul Sunday Pioneer Press*, April 7, 1974.

114. For city, state, and federal correspondence dealing with the creation of the Irvine Park Historic District and the resulting implications for the area's redevelopment, see Irvine Park File, St. Paul Heritage Preservation Commission.

115. Neighborhood support for the Irvine Park Review Committee was so strong that it remained in operation until 1982, well after the formation of the St. Paul Historic Preservation Commission, which had oversight of the other historic districts in the city.

116. Bernard Frieden and Lynne B. Sagalyn, *Downtown, Inc.: How America Rebuilds Cities* (Boston: MIT Press, 1989), 119–20.

117. Ibid., 120.

118. John Kostouros, "It's Onward and Upward for St. Paul," *Minneapolis Tribune*, December 2, 1978; "Latimer Sees Building Boom, Job Progress as Top Issues in 1978," *St. Paul Pioneer Press*, February 5, 1978.

119. As quoted in "Enclosed Waterfall Would Cascade at Unknown Cost," *St. Paul Pioneer Press*, June 22, 1978. See also "Town Square, St. Paul, Minnesota," *Architectural Record* 169 (March 1981): 120–22.

120. "10-Million McKnight Grant Spurs Project," *St. Paul Dispatch*, March 16, 1978.

121. Weiming Lu, *Public/Private Partnership: Building an Urban Village* (St. Paul: Lowertown Redevelopment Corporation, 1994). See also James B. McComb Associates, *Economic Impact of the Lowertown Redevelopment Program, 1979–1985* (St. Paul: Lowertown Redevelopment Corporation, 1985).

122. "Park Square Court Renovation Planned," *St. Paul Pioneer Press*, December 20, 1980.

123. Larry Millett, "City's Tallest Skyscraper Begins to Rise Today," *St. Paul Dispatch*, May 16, 1984; "Galtier Plaza an Architectural Jewel Ready to Breathe Life into Lowertown," *St. Paul Pioneer Press and Dispatch*, November 1, 1985; Wilma Randle, "Center May Be Retail Drawing Card," *St. Paul Pioneer Press and Dispatch*, August 9, 1987.

124. Brooks Cavin, "Ordway Theatre Blends High-Tech with Sophisticated Design," *Downtowner*, December 1984. See also Roy M. Close, "How Music Looks," *Architecture Minnesota* 11 (March-April 1985): 24–29; D. J. Tice, "A Theater in a Park on a River," *Twin Cities* (January 1985): 29–37; Grace Anderson, "Technique Made Visible," *Architectural Record* 173 (November 1985): 144–51.

5. MELDING THE PAST WITH THE FUTURE, 1985–2000

1. "Architect Raps Building Styles," *St. Paul Pioneer Press*, March 16, 1930.

2. The quotation from William Pedersen is from Warren James, ed., *Kohn Pedersen Fox: Architecture and Urbanism, 1986–1992* (New York: Rizzoli, 1993), 137. Robert Cioppa was the partner-in-charge of the project. For an analysis of the incremental architectural style of the Grain Belt Brewery, see the first draft of the National Register Nomination by Paul Clifford Larson, on file in the Historic Preservation Office, Minnesota Historical Society.

3. Richard del Monte, quoted in James, *Kohn Pedersen Fox*, 138.

4. Quotations in this paragraph are from an unpublished, undated BWBR flyer titled "Lawson Commons."

5. Larry Millett, "Building Block," *St. Paul Pioneer Press*, December 2, 1999; Ellerbe Becket press release, September 16, 1999.

6. Joel Hoekstra, "Science Project," *Architecture Minnesota* 26 (January-February 2000), 23.

7. Quotations are from a Minnesota Mutual Web site, www.minnesotamutual.com/news; and an Architectural Alliance Web site, www.archalliance.com/features.

8. Heidi Landecker, "Kid City," *Architecture*, November 1, 1996.

9. I am indebted to the building owners, Ann and Scott Billeadeau, for much of the background information on the building of their house. The Worthen design for the original house was published with other examples of his work in "New Houses Represent Unusual Designs in Home Building," *St. Paul Pioneer Press*, April 12, 1925.

10. Sean T. Kelly, "New Linwood Recreation Center to Open Doors in April," *St. Paul Pioneer Press,* December 11, 1991, SE 4; Ann Baker, "Linwood Recreation Center Is Most Elaborate," *St. Paul Pioneer Press,* April 29, 1992, SE 2.

11. For most of the information regarding the conservatory addition, I am indebted to design principal Kara Hill.

12. Much of the information regarding Crossroads Elementary School comes from *American School & University* 73 (November 1, 2000).

13. Debra O'Connor, "Home Sweet Homes," *St. Paul Pioneer Press,* May 4, 2002. Additional information for this thumbnail sketch of the Eigenfeld House comes from Lynn Underwood, "A Modern House Turns Heads in St. Paul Neighborhood," *Star Tribune,* October 3, 2002; and the Web site closearchitects.com/eigenfeld.

14. "Ancient Cabins Still Dot Valleys" and "Old Mansions Recall Victorian Gingerbread Grandeur," *St. Paul Pioneer Press,* April 24, 1949.

INDEX

Bassford, Edward Payson, 39, 48–49, 60, 66, 71; commercial buildings by, 51–52, 247 note 7, 248 notes 21, 22
Beals House, 255 note 17
Beatty House, 122, 123
Beaux-Arts: style of, 80, 82, 84, 88–90, 95, 97, 100, 104, 129, 142, 161, 189; training in, 80, 85, 101, 140, 152, 156, 184
Beebe House, 95, 253 note 76
Beman, Solon, 77, 96
Bennett, Edward H., 170
Bentley, Percy Dwight, 96, 253 note 77, 254 notes 3, 86; houses by, 98–99, 117–18, 254 note 84
Bentz, Frederick, 217
Berg, Charles K., 186
Bergstedt, Hirsch, Wahlberg, and Wold (architecture firm), 209
Bethlehem German Presbyterian Church, 62
Bethlehem Lutheran Church, 95, 96
Better Homes and Gardens (magazine), 193
Better Homes Committee of St. Paul, 113–14
Better Homes Week Demonstration House, 114, 115, 255 note 25
Billeadeau House, 237
Binswanger House, 107, 108
Bishop House, 53, 70
Bitter, Ann L., 235
Blair Flats, 71, 78
Blood, George W., 92
board-and-batten construction, 27–28
Borchert-Ingersoll Machinery Company, 148, 149, 257 note 67
Boston and Northwest Realty Company, 62–63
Boyington, William W., 26, 28, 32
Bremer House, 121, 122
Brenny, John S., 122, 256 note 33
Brewer, Nicholas, 119
Brewer House, 119, 120, 121, 255 notes 29, 30
breweries, 34, 88, 231, 252 note 69
brick construction, 14; steel and, 134–35
bridges, 45–47, 151. See also individual bridges

Brings House. See Schilliger House
Brioschi, Lawrence, 142
Brioschi-Minuti Studio and Shop, 142–43
Brooks House, xxiv, 123, 124
Brown, Frank Chouteau, 249 note 28
Brown and Bigelow Company, 150
Brunson, Benjamin W., 243 note 10
Brunson, Ira B., 4–6, 243 note 10
Brunson House, 16
Buetow, Carl, 158
Buffington, LeRoy S., 248 notes 9, 11, 21, 249 notes 28, 30; commercial buildings by, 47; houses by, 43
buildings, copying of, 245 note 37
bungalow courts, 111, 119–21
bungalows, 89–93, 95, 97, 101, 117
Burbank, James C., 32
Burbank-Livingston-Griggs House, 30–32, 128–29
Burlington Heights neighborhood, 39, 71–72
Butler, Emmett, 134
Butler House, 133
BWBR Architects, 231–32
Byers-Prestholdt Motor Company, 148, 149
Byrne, Barry, 181–82

Cape Cod style, 126, 127
Capital Centre Building, 214, 215
Capital Centre project, xxiv, 51, 54, 70, 206–14, 217–19, 223–24, 229–30
Capitol buildings. See Minnesota State Capitol Buildings
Capitol Mall, 169–70, 171, 174, 180–81
Carman Double House, 75
Carnegie, Andrew, 97
Carnegie libraries, 98
carpenters, xxiv, 17–18, 39
Carrere, John, 84
Castle, The. See Shapira House
Castner, William H., 71, 74, 78, 248 note 22, 251 note 56
Cathedral of St. Paul, 84–85, 86
Catholics, 23, 26. See also churches, Catholic
Cavin, W. Brooks, Jr., 180–81, 202–3, 206, 215, 219–20, 227

Cazone (Mr.), 247 note 56
Cemstone Products Company "House of Tomorrow," 136, 137
Centennial Block, 247 note 7
Centennial Exposition (1876), 248 note 21
central business district, 201–5, 212, 214, 218, 223, 227, 232. See also urban renewal
Central Apartments, 215, 216
Central Business District Authority, 173
Century of Progress Exposition, 133–36, 147, 155
Cerny, Robert G., 185, 188, 189, 193, 223, 260 note 33
Cerny and Associates (architecture firm), 206, 217
Cers, Andy, 233
Chapel of Our Lady of Victory, 143, 145
Chapel of St. Paul, xxiii, 3–4, 243 note 8
Chelsea Heights Elementary School, 158; addition to, 186, 187–88
Chicago School, 78, 99, 106, 152
Chicago World's Columbian Exposition of 1893, 80
Chinoiserie, 248 note 11
Christ Episcopal Church, 28, 246 note 56
Christianson, Theodore, 170
churches, 47; Catholic, 71, 85, 143–45, 182; German-American, 23–26; immigrant, 87–88; Protestant, 26–28, 80, 83, 95. See also individual churches
Church of St. Columba, 182
Church of St. Luke, 143, 144
Cinderella Cosmetics Factory, 155, 258 note 76
city architect, 95–97, 113, 151. See also Hausler, Charles A.; Wigington, Clarence W.
City Beautiful Movement, 169
City Hall Annex. See Lowry Medical Arts Building and Annex
city planning, xxiv, 126–27, 169–70, 172–76, 200–205, 229. See also urban renewal
Clark Block, 249 note 30
classicism, 80–84, 104, 123, 152, 163. See also neoclassicism
Classic Moderne style, 156–58, 160–63

religious buildings, 181. *See also* churches; synagogues

remodeling: of commercial buildings, 156, 160, 164–67, 175–76; period, 128–29, 131–32, 136. *See also* rebuilding

Renaissance Revival, 55, 63, 67, 75, 79, 80–82, 85, 99, 251 note 45. *See also* English Renaissance style; French Renaissance style; Italian Renaissance style

Rhinehardt, Christian, 20

Rice and Irvine's Addition, 6

Rice Park, xxiv, 97, 227, 231

Richardson, Henry Hobson, 44, 58–59, 62, 72

Richardsonian Romanesque style, 51, 55, 70, 72, 73, 75, 218

Riedel, Eduard, 24, 26

Ries, George, 87

Riley's Row, 58

riverfront, development of, 233

Riverview Branch Library, 97

Robertson, Rhodes, 134

Robert Street Bridge, 47, 151–52, 153

Romanesque Revival style, 60, 69, 186. *See also* Richardsonian Romanesque style

Romanesque style, 24, 48–49, 72, 143. *See also* French Romanesque style

Roman Renaissance style, 80

Rome, influences from, 101

Rondo, Joseph, 12

Rondo Avenue, 201, 208

Roosevelt Homes, 199

Root, John W., 57

Round Style, 24, 69

row houses, 60–61

rubble-masonry construction, 20

Rugg House, 66–67

Rundlett, Leonard W., 45

Ruskin, John, 248 note 10

Scandinavia, influences from, 88. *See also* Norwegian-Americans

Scandinavian-American Bank, 247 note 8

Scheffer Avenue Houses, 127

Schilliger, Charles, 246 note 43

Schilliger House, 20–22, 246 note 43

Schmid, Calvin, 38

Schmidt, Jacob, 88

Schmidt, Richard, 254 note 86

Schmidt Brewery, 88, 89, 231, 253 note 70

Schneider House, 67, 68

schools, 47, 158, 186–88

Schornstein Grocery and Saloon, 52

Schroeckenstein House, 118, 119

Schulke, W. E., 123

Schulke Garden House and Garage, 123, 125

Schuyler, Montgomery, 77

Science Museum of Minnesota, xxv, 72, 232–33

Scott House, 79

Sears, Roebuck and Company, 91, 200, 201

Second Empire style, 39, 103, 112

Second Ramsey County Courthouse (1885), 19

Seifert House, 99, 254 note 84

Seitz, Grann, 255 note 27

service stations, 117, 147, 257 note 64

740 River Drive Apartments, 215, 216

Seventh Street, widening of, 165, 234

Seventh Street Improvement of 1883–85, 45

Seventh Street Stone Arch Bridge, 45, 46

Shadow Falls Park neighborhood, 107–9, 114

Shadycrest, 104

Shapira, Albert, 255 note 19

Shapira House, 111, 113

Sharratt Design & Company (architecture firm), 236

Shaw, R. Norman, 248 note 10

Sheire, Monroe, 28, 32–34, 39, 247 note 6, 248 notes 20, 21

Sheire House, 32–34

shell treatment, 175, 177–78, 180. *See also* facades, alterations of

Shepherd House, 195–96, 197, 198, 262 note 61

Shepley, Rutan, and Coolidge (architecture firms), 249 note 30

Shiely House, 104, 105

Shingle style, 62, 67, 71–72, 103

Shipman-Greve House, 43, 44, 248 note 9

shop-front architecture, 142. *See also* storefronts

showrooms, automotive, 148, 149, 257 note 66

Shulman, Max, 169

Sibley, Henry S., 30

Simpson, James Hervey, 14

Simpson-Wood House, 14, 15

Sixth Street, 42, 45

Skelly Oil Company, 147

Skidmore, Owings, and Merrill (architecture firm), 188, 224

skyscrapers, 161. *See also* high-rise buildings

Skyway Building, 212

skyways, 176, 207–9, 223

Slifer and Abrahamson (architecture firm), 143

Slifer and Cone (architecture firm), 186

slums, 169, 171–72, 174; clearance of, 198, 199–200. *See also* tenements

small houses, 102–3, 109–11, 127, 135. *See also* pattern-book houses

Smith Avenue Bridge, 47

Smith Park. *See* Mears Park

Smithsonian Institution Building (Washington, D.C.), 24

Smith Spec House, 253 note 72

Snaith, William T., 173

Snelling Avenue, 127

Social Saga of Two Cities (Schmid), 38

Southdale Shopping Center, 203, 204

Spangenberg House, 20, 21, 246 note 42

Spanish style, 117–21, 123, 151, 255 note 27

Specialty Manufacturing Company, 166

speculation, real estate, 8–9, 37

Spink House, 126

St. Agnes Church, 85, 87

St. Anthony, Minnesota, 244 note 14

St. Anthony Park Branch Library, 97, 98

St. Anthony Park neighborhood, 39

St. Bernard's Catholic Church, 87, 88

St. Clement's Church, 253 note 77

St. Francis Hotel, 234

St. John's Hospital, 235

St. Luke's School, 186

St. Paul, Minneapolis and Manitoba Railroad, 38

University of Minnesota, 249 note 30; architecture training at, 184–86

University-Raymond Historic District, 166, 257 note 67

Upper Town, xxiii, 6, 8–9, 12

urban renewal, 77, 167, 198, 200–201, 206–14, 218–19, 221–25. *See also* redevelopment projects

U.S. Courthouse and Post Office, 75, 76, 100, 219–20, 231. *See also* Landmark Center

Van Bergen, John S., 104

van Bergen (L.) House, 257 note 47

Van Hoef, Robert, 205, 223

Vavoulis, George, 205

vernacular architecture, xxvi, 19–20, 49, 91; French, 112

Versailles style, 114, 115, 255 note 25

Veterans' Service Building, 180–81

Victor Gruen Associates (architecture firm), 204

Victorian styles, 42–43, 60, 80, 90–91, 100, 112, 237

Victoria Theater, 165

Viennese Secession, 88

von Nieda House, 121, 256 note 31

Wabasha Court, 209

Wabasha Hotel, 234

Wabasha Street Bridge, 47

Waldman, Anton, 246 note 43

Waldman House, 20, 22

Wallingford, Charles A., 66

Walsh Building, 49, 50

Walter Butler Construction Company, 172, 199

Ware, William, 60

warehouses, 38, 48–49, 82, 225

Warrendale, 39

Warrendale Improvement Company, 52

Weber, Martin, 246 note 43

Weber House, 20, 23

Wee Haven, 104, 105

Weikert House, 72, 73

Welch House, 81

Wells, William, 63

Western Association of Architects, 56

West Publishing Company, 177

West Seventh Street, xxvi

West Seventh Street Association, 221

West Seventh Street neighborhood, 20, 222

West Side neighborhood, xxvi, 239–40, 244 notes 22, 23, 251 note 50

West St. Paul, 9, 38

Weyerhaeuser Corporation, 256 note 35

Weyerhaeuser Memorial Chapel, 217

Wheelock, Otis Leonard, 32

Whitehead, Kenneth J., 192

White Pine Series of Architectural Monographs, 102

Whitney, W. C., 250 notes 38, 44

wholesale trade, 37

Wieland, Herbert C., 201, 205–6

Wigington, Clarence W., 151, 158, 163, 258 note 70

Wigington Pavilion. *See* Harriet Island Pavilion

Wilkinson House, 255 note 17

Willcox, William H., 56–57, 70, 78, 250 notes 36, 38; houses by, 58–60

William M. Linden Company (architecture firm), 119, 255 note 29

Williams, J. Fletcher, 35, 37

Willwerscheid Mortuary, 155, 156

Wilson, John L., 111

winter-built houses, 116–17

Wirth, George, 53, 56, 78, 249 note 28; apartment buildings by, 70; commercial buildings by, 69

Wittkamp, Werner, 155

Wold, Clark D., 210–11

Women's City Club, 137, 154–55

Wood, Charles, 14

wood-frame construction, 10, 74, 132

Woodland Park, 72

World War I, aftermath of, 102–4, 106, 113, 117

World War II, aftermath of, 169, 186–87, 192, 193

Worthen, Kenneth B., 109–10, 125, 146, 255 note 24, 256 notes 31, 35; commercial buildings by, 139–40; houses by, 121, 123, 236, 255 note 17

Worthen House, 110, 114, 116

Wright, Frank Lloyd, 101–2, 178, 182, 194, 253 note 76, 254 note 9, 256 note 45. *See also* Prairie School style

Wright, Gwendolyn, 192

Wright, Myrtus, 118, 156, 157, 257 note 64

W. T. Grant Company Department Store, 189

Wunderlich House, 99

Yoerg, Anthony, 34, 39

Yoerg Brewing Company, 34

Yoerg House, 34, 35

Young-Lightner Double House, 65

Zigzag Moderne style, 136–40, 148, 156, 160, 257 note 66

Zschocke, Albert, 69–71, 78

In 1977, **Jeffrey A. Hess** founded one of the country's first historical consulting practices, later Hess, Roise, and Company, in the Twin Cities. During the next twenty-five years, he served as principal investigator or consulting historian on more than one hundred studies of the built environment in twenty states. His previous publications deal with the history of American art, architecture, and engineering.

Paul Clifford Larson is an architectural historian and historic building consultant. He has written twelve books on regional historical topics, including *Minnesota Architect: The Life and Work of Clarence A. Johnston* and *The Spirit of H. H. Richardson on the Midland Prairies*.